Youth Baseball Coaching

by John T. Reed

2

ISBN: 0-939224-38-0
Library of Congress Catalog Card No. 99-074696
Manufactured in the United States of America
www.johntreed.com/coaching.html
johnreed@johntreed.com

OTHER MATERIAL BY JOHN T. REED

- Aggressive Tax Avoidance For Real Estate Investors, 16th edition
- Coaching Youth Flag Football
- Coaching Youth Football, 2nd edition
- Coaching Youth Football Defense, 2nd edition
- Distressed Real Estate Times (Special Report or cassettes)
- Football Clock Management
- High Leverage Real Estate Financing (cassettes)
- How To Buy Real Estate For At Least 20% Below Market Value
- How To Buy Real Estate For At Least 20% Below Market Value, Volumes 1 and 2 (cassettes)
- How to Buy Residential Property (cassettes)
- How to Do a Delayed Exchange (Special Report or cassettes)
- How To Find Deals That Make Sense In Today's Market (cassettes)
- How To Increase The Value Of Real Estate
- How To Manage Residential Property For Maximum Cash Flow And Resale Value (book or cassettes)
- How To Use Leverage to Maximize Your Real Estate Investment Return
- Office Building Acquisition Handbook
- Real Estate Investment Strategy (selected newsletter articles)
- John T. Reed's Real Estate Investor's Monthly (newsletter)
- Residential Property Acquisition Handbook
- Single-Family Lease Options (Special Report or cassettes)

For more information, see the order forms elsewhere in this book, call 925-820-7262, visit www.johntreed.com/coaching.html, fax 925-820-1259, or email johnreed@johntreed.com.

About the author

John T. Reed has coached 15 baseball teams from tee ball to semi-pro. During most of his youth baseball coaching years, he was also playing adult baseball or semi-pro baseball. Every team he coached had one of his three sons as a player.

He is a member of the American Baseball Coaches Association, the California Coaches Association, The National Federation of Interscholastic Coaches Association, the American Football Coaches Association, The Football Writers Association of American, and the Professional Football Researchers Association. Reed is a West Point graduate and a Harvard MBA.

Thanks to…

"Mr. Baseball" (Dick Steiner) my college and army roommate and the "Unofficial Magician" of the Baltimore Orioles…Norm Osborn, who let me help coach my oldest son's tee-ball team…Oscar Miller, who taught me hitting mechanics…Fellow coaches Jim Bradfield, Bruce Burrows, Len Swec, Mark Friedman, Ray Hilsinger…Parents who helped, especially the parents of my 1993 tee-ball Dodgers: John Callahan, Dave Greiner, Jerry Hokanson, Rich and Marie Imes, Paul Lopez, Kurt Sinz, and Nick Vergis…my adult and semi-pro baseball teammates…Former pros who gave advice: Rob Andrews, Duane Anderson, and Dan Meyer…Pro outfield instructor Sam Suplizio…Cardinals manager and neighbor Tony LaRussa…authors Pete Palmer and Cliff Petrak.

Contents

1 Overview

98% of youth baseball coaches are **incompetent**. I am not exaggerating to get your attention. I mean 98% **precisely**.

How do I define "incompetent?" A competent coach is one who **causes his team to play better** than they would if he or she were not their coach. An incompetent coach is one who either has **no measurable effect** on his team's play or, worse, has a **negative** effect.

To identify the competent coaches among your coaching acquaintances, fill in the blanks in the following statement:

> Year in and year out, (*coach's name*)'s teams are always good at (*some aspect of baseball*).

Chuck Moore

When I asked myself this question about the coaches I have known in the various leagues in which I have played and coached, I could only come up with one name (other than myself): **Chuck Moore** (all amateur youth coach names in this book are changed). His teams always used to be good at **baserunning**. They may, and probably did, have another couple of things they were good at, but baserunning is the only one that I recognized from casual observation.

I asked one of my coaching colleagues who had also coached many years in my area to fill in the blanks. I gave him no hint as to how I would answer. He thought for a few seconds and said, "Chuck Moore, baserunning."

I can recall two other coaches who had stuff they could execute year in and year out. The player coach of my Men's Senior Baseball League team was big on the squeeze.

In 1998, a 10-12-year-old AAA team we played executed the pitcher-cover-first play nicely. I do not know the name of the coach, but it was clear they had worked on it. They are the only youth coaches I can recall in my whole life who could get their teams to do anything well year in and year out.

'Motivation?!'

When I was giving a football-coaching clinic in Orlando, I posed the fill-in-the-blanks baseball question to one of my fellow speakers there. He named a guy in his local Little League. "What skill are his teams always good at?" I asked. "Motivation," was his answer.

"MOTIVATION!" I said, "I'm not talking about subjective, touchy-feely, psychobabble like motivation. I'm talking about stuff I can verify in the league's score books—stuff like bunting or strikeouts or base stealing." He was unable to come up with a single name of a coach he had ever known in his life whose teams were good at some skill year in and year out.

Year in and year out

Note the phrase "year in and year out." Anyone who coaches for more than one year will have seasons in which his pitching is good or his hitting is good or whatever. That's the luck of the draw. Good hitters hit well no matter who their coach is this year. Good pitchers pitch well no matter who their coach is this year. The test of coaching competence is what he accomplishes **year in and year out** because only multi-year consistency with different players proves coaching competence.

Incompetent league champion coaches?

The typical league has six to eight teams. That means the league champion team comprises 12.5% to 16.7% of the league. If I say that only 2% of the coaches are competent, it suggests that I am claiming that even **most of the coaches whose teams won the league championship are incompetent**.

Correct. They are.

In the land of the blind, the one-eyed man is king. By the same token, in the league of the incompetent, the coach lucky enough to draw the best pitchers wins the championship. Furthermore, it is even quite possible for a league, which has among its managers one of the rare competent coaches, to see a coach **other** than that competent coach win the league championship.

Not a very coachable sport

How could that happen? I also write football-coaching books. In football, which is a highly coachable sport, a bad coach can lose every game even if he has great talent. And, in football, a great coach can win, even if he has mediocre talent.

The most successful modern NFL coach (100 or more games) is George Seifert, with a win-loss percentage of .755 (when he left the 49ers). The most successful modern Major League Baseball manager (ten or more years) was Earl Weaver, who had a win-loss percentage of only .583.

It's hard for a good coach to produce wins in baseball. Baseball is not a very coachable sport. It has some highly coachable aspects and some somewhat coachable aspects, but it is not a very coachable sport in general.

For the most part, baseball wins stem from **player talent** and, to a lesser extent, **luck**. The phrase, "That's the way the ball bounces" is probably shortened from, "That's the way the baseball bounces." Baseball also has the saying, "You win some. You lose some. And some get rained out," reflecting the fatalistic acceptance of losses that is necessary to maintain your sanity as a baseball player or coach.

One to four wins a year

I think I am an excellent baseball coach, but I feel that my coaching only increases our number of wins by one to four games per season. If I coached another five years and busted my butt to improve, I suspect I could only move it up to two to five games per season, but no more.

In his book, *The Complete Idiot's Guide to Baseball*, Hall of Famer Johnny Bench says, "I think a manager can make a difference in about seven or eight games a year…" There are 162 games in a Major League season so Bench thinks the manager can make a difference in $7/162 = 4\%$ to $8/162 = 5\%$ of the games. In his book, *Billy Ball*, Billy Martin says, "It has been said that a good manager can win anywhere from eight to twelve games a year for his team." Twelve games would be 7.4%.

Competent **youth** coaches make a difference in a **higher** percentage of games because the vast majority of their opponents are incompetent, unlike in the Major Leagues. Also, the typical youth player is more affected by coaching, good or bad, than the typical pro.

If your goal is to win your league's championship, you don't understand the game. You should strive for maximum success on every play. If you do that, and you are the best coach in your league, you may **eventually** win a league championship, but it will only be because you **combined** excellent coaching, with good **luck** and good **talent**.

Little victories

I strive for **little victories**. In one game in 1997, my eleven-year old team smoothly pulled off a pitcher-cover-first put-out, which we had practiced. It was one of my proudest moments of the season. I do not even remember whether we won the game.

In 1998, one of my proudest accomplishments, the only one that inspired me to rise and speak at the post-season party (I was an assistant coach), was a rather slow runner who became the best delayed-steal guy in the league. He had paid close attention to the instruction I gave the team on the delayed steal and became expert at it. Faster players should have done it even better, but his extra determination and intelligence that made him the best in spite of his lack of speed.

I also try to coach the team so that if a former Major Leaguer were watching one of our games, he would think, "That coach knows what he's doing." Maybe he notices that all my players go to the right place on a defensive play. Or that my batters are very disciplined. Or that my runners use perfect sliding technique.

I do not know that that ever happened, or would if such a person came, but that's what I shoot for rather than team victories, which are really not within the coach's control.

A perennial champion is suspect

Any youth baseball coach or organization that wins championships year in and year out is probably cheating—either in the draft or in the size of the pool the team draws from or one or more of the players are over the league's maximum age.

Taiwan used to win the Little League World Series almost every year. Then someone discovered misbehavior regarding the ages of players and the area from which the team was drawn. Result: Taiwan stopped sending a team to the Little League World Series.

'Home of Champions'

My local Little League, the San Ramon Valley Little League, bills itself as "the Home of Champions." Indeed, they won the Little League national championship in 1978 and 1991 and the Senior Little League national championship in 1990. An impressive number of other lesser championships are celebrated on the wall of the majors field press box. (I never had the slightest thing to do with any post-season San Ramon Valley Little League team.)

The Little Team That Could

Jeff Burroughs wrote a book called *The Little Team that Could*. It was about the 1992 and 1993 Long Beach, CA Little League teams. He coached those teams and his son Sean was pictured on a national news magazine over the caption "The best Little Leaguer in America." Jeff Burroughs, himself, was an American League MVP one year.

They won the 1992 Little League World Series by rule after it was learned that the original champion Philippines team had cheated. And they won the 1993 Little League World Series on the field. Burroughs devotes considerable space in his book to denouncing my local San Ramon Valley Little League, a team which he had to beat both years to advance to Williamsport.

E pluribus vici

San Ramon Valley Little League received a letter dated 3/8/90 from Little League's Western Regional Director Carlton Magee requesting that SRVLL correct its "ratio imbalance of minor to major players." Little League Baseball, Incorporated wanted a maximum of 300 to 400 players in the league. It also said that there were supposed to be just **two** minor-league teams for every major-league team.

San Ramon Valley had a **thousand players**, one eight-team majors league, and **eight** times that many minors teams. That meant that San Ramon Valley's **one** all-star team consisted of the best players from what was supposed to be **three** separate all-star teams.

The year after it won the national championship in 1991, San Ramon Valley Little League was forced to break into two leagues. The spin-off was the Tassajara Little League in the *nouveau riche* Blackhawk area. Existing major-league players from Blackhawk were permitted to remain with their San Ramon Valley Little League majors team, which was the situation in 1992 and 1993 when Burroughs was fighting San Ramon Valley for the U.S. Western Championship.

The "Home of Champions" has not won so many national championships since they were forced to split into two leagues.

Not year-in-and-year-out winning

Earlier, I said competence was shown by year-in-and-year-out superior performance in one or more aspects of baseball. Winning championships is definitely **not** one of the aspects of baseball to which I was referring.

Youth baseball rules are designed to produce **parity** as far as player talent is concerned. Since baseball victories are determined mainly by talent, and only to a lesser extent by luck and coaching, consistent year-in-and-year-out youth baseball championships are suggestive not of extraordinary coaching competence, but of violations of the rules designed to create parity.

A two-year run like Long Beach had should not, by itself, raise suspicion. In two consecutive years, many of the players on the particular all-star team remain the same. The rules that are designed to create parity cannot stop a particular team from having a talent bonanza in one year group.

But if a particular youth baseball **league** wins more than its share of championships over a period of years with totally different personnel, they are probably violating rules regarding league size, number of majors teams, residency within league boundaries, player age, or some other rule designed to maintain parity between leagues.

For example, I know nothing about Toms River, NJ except that they got to the Little League World Series tournament three times over a period of years. Knowing what I do about youth baseball, I find that suspicious on its face.

My competences

Applying the fill-in-the-blank question to myself, I claim my teams were good, year in and year out at the following:

- baserunning
- baserunning defense
- safety-consciousness
- one-throw double plays
- rules knowledge
- the pitcher-cover-first play
- knowing where to go when the ball was not hit to them
- waiting for a good pitch to hit
- putting the tag on the ground
- sportsmanship
- optimizing position assignments, pitching rotation, and batting order

Notice some of the things I do **not** claim expertise in:

- pitching in general
- hitting in general
- fielding in general

But note also that neither I nor my local colleagues nor my Orlando colleague were able to think of any coaches whose teams were good at those skills year in and year out either.

Safety and sportsmanship?

You may think safety consciousness and sportsmanship are touch-feely, like motivation. Nope. I'll discuss them in detail later in the book, but few would doubt that I am one of the most safety-conscious youth coaches in the world. It has to do with specifics like equipment, pitch counts, and so forth.

Sportsmanship just means my teams—players, coaches, parents—did not talk trash to the opponents. On a few occasions, the steady stream of trash talk from the other side momentarily inspired my players or parents to respond in kind, but I ended that in a matter of seconds. Those who attended our games probably never noticed, but our players and parents could confirm that I discussed sportsmanship at the parent meetings and quickly ended any deviations during the season.

Important, but hard to coach

Are pitching, hitting and fielding important? You bet. So how come I was focused on baserunning, pitcher-cover-first and so forth? I didn't always. For years, I tried to coach pitching, hitting, and fielding mechanics. But when I stepped back and looked at our numbers in those areas, I concluded that not only were we not better, we seemed to be **worse** as a result of my efforts.

By emphasizing those areas in practice, I made my players **self-conscious** when they were performing those skills in games. That caused a **deterioration** in their performance, not an improvement.

Getting better in pitching, hitting, or fielding is extremely difficult, but doable. However, the effort required far exceeds the practice time available to a youth baseball coach and/or the time the vast majority of youth-baseball players are willing to spend.

10,000 swings

One of my hitting mentors is Oscar Miller. He is the inventor of the SwingRite™ batting tee. That's a reddish-brown plastic device with 48 holes in it so that one or two batting tees can be placed at various spots. It has a home plate painted on it. It folds up like a suitcase. If you go to a college or a professional baseball game early, you will probably see the players using a SwingRite™ for pre-game batting practice.

Oscar says it takes 10,000 swings the **new** way to change a player's batting mechanics. That's because a hitter's swing must be **instinctive**. As Yogi Berra said, "You can't think and hit at the same time." (Young people think of Yogi as a joke. He was a Hall of Fame player with 358 home runs and a lifetime .285 average who played in fourteen World Series and was the only catcher to ever have an error-free season.)

You cannot change your instincts except with an enormous number of repetitions in which you swing the new way. You must swing the new way so many times that your body forgets how to swing the old way, and your body has a **long** memory.

Ted Williams, one of the greatest hitters in history, used to hit until his hands bled. Your kids won't.

Pitching and fielding are similar. Read about the great ones like Tom Seaver and Ozzie Smith and you are astounded at their incredible work ethics. You can **tell** your players about that kind of work ethic and the results it achieved, you can **encourage** them to follow the example of Ted Williams, Tom Seaver, or Ozzie Smith, but it ain't gonna happen in your youth-baseball practices. The kid in question has to do that stuff on his own, outside of team practice.

Are YOU incompetent?

Having read my 98% are incompetent statement, you may be wondering if I am accusing **you** of being incompetent. The fact that you are reading this book, or any book about baseball coaching, reveals that you are an **above-average** coach. The vast majority of youth-baseball coaches have never read a book on baseball coaching and never will. They have extremely high opinions of their baseball coaching knowledge, even though their baseball experience is meager and their study of the game is nil. About 99.9% of **those** guys are incompetent.

The incidence of incompetence among readers of this book is probably only about 75%.

So my answer to your question, "Are you saying that I am incompetent?" is, "Probably." That's the **bad** news. The **good** news is that you will be in the competent category by the time you finish reading.

The nature of expertise

This is a how-to book. If a how-to book author writes a how-to book competently, the readers who apply its teachings will have more success. A how-to book ought to say that if you do X, Y will happen, and be correct about that.

For example, cook books say that if you raise the temperature of water to 212 degrees Fahrenheit at sea level, it will boil. And they are right.

Baseball how-to books say, or imply, that if you teach batting mechanics to your players, their batting averages will improve. The problem with that is that they are **wrong**. In fact, if you teach batting mechanics to your players, their performance at the plate will almost certainly **decline** as a result.

So what I am striving for in this book is water-boils-at-212 kind of advice. That is, I want to tell you to do something so that if you follow my advice, you will see a measurable, positive result in your team's performance. If I can achieve that, I will be one of the few who ever did in the youth baseball realm.

World champs, but unopinionated

The most **un**opinionated guy I ever met in baseball was Tony LaRussa, current manager of the St. Louis Cardinals. He is my neighbor. Not close. We are in the same homeowners association. His house is close enough that my kids trick-or-treated there.

But he is near enough that I have run into him a couple of times around town. Once, we were both filling up at the local Shell station. I don't like to bother celebrities when I encounter them. But on that particular occasion, I happened to be wearing a Baltimore Orioles uniform. He was, at the time, the manager of the Oakland Athletics, so I faced him in my uniform and did a kind of TaDa! pose to kid him.

He followed me into the station where I was buying some candy and asked about the uniform. It was the uniform of the semi-pro team on which I played at the time and I was wearing it because my son and I had just gone to a father-son night at school where everyone was supposed to wear baseball stuff.

He was friendly and unaffected. I ended up exchanging brief correspondence with Tony about my theories on left-handed hitting. (You'll read them later in the book.) Tony said he agreed with everything I advocated, although he liked switch hitting more than I.

I also heard him speak at the American Baseball Coaches Association convention the year the A's won the earthquake World Series. He began his speech by talking about how many games they had **lost** that year and explaining that, although they had won the Series in four straight, he hardly had all the answers about how to manage or coach baseball. LaRussa says, "Baseball is the all-time humbler." I wish that any of my players' parents or opposing managers were half so humble about **their** baseball knowledge.

Truth about youth baseball coaches

Virtually all youth baseball coaches can **talk** a great game. They can hold forth for hours about the correct mechanics of the swing or of a pitcher's motion. Some, by virtue of some youthful success as a player and by virtue of the self-confidence with which they speak, convince many around them, "Boy, he really knows his stuff!"

Show me the score book. If his teams do not hit better or pitch better or field better, as evidenced by actual score-book stats, his coaching is just talk.

I am even leery of former pros. I have seen a number of youth baseball managers bring out some former pro to coach his youth players. Those guys look fabulous when they demonstrate a correct pitching motion or swing. Every word they speak is correct. But I see little or no effect in the team's score books afterwards.

Not enough

It is not enough to have an impressive resume. It is not enough to put on a great demonstration. It is not enough to speak many learned and absolutely correct words on the subject. All that matters when it comes to coaching competence is whether there is a discernible improvement in the team's score books.

In other words, your better-trained pitchers ought to have fewer walks per batter faced, more outs per batter faced, fewer hit batsmen, something, compared to the pitchers on the other teams in the league. Your better-trained hitters ought to get more walks, more hits, and more extra-base hits compared to other teams. In fact, I have never seen or heard of a youth coach whose pitchers or hitters were better in **any** category, year after year, let alone more than one category.

Plenty of knowledge, but not enough time

Am I saying these former pro players are incompetent? They certainly are not incompetent at **playing** the sport. Nor are they incompetent at **coaching** the sport, **if they are given sufficient time**. But the notion that a brief guest appearance or even series of guest appearances at a youth baseball team's practices can make a score-book difference in the team's performance of skills like hitting or pitching is incorrect.

Most likely, the former pro player himself would agree with me. They come not so much because they think it will make a difference as to accommodate a request from a friend. Youth baseball coaches are generally starstruck and awestruck in the presence of former big-time players and they assume that any coaching from such accomplished, talented, inspirational men can be nothing but good.

But the overriding fact is that the amount of time it takes to improve a pitcher's or hitter's performance through coaching is probably a hundred times what any youth coach or his friends can hope to spend. So the attempt is likely to be ineffective or even harmful as the kids struggle to change their mechanics to match the fuzzy memory of the big-time pitcher or hitter who came through last week.

The scientific method

We all learned the scientific method in junior high school. It says that when you are tying to figure something out, you go through five steps:

1. State the problem
2. Read all existing research on the subject
3. Form a hypothesis (theory) about the solution
4. Test your hypothesis with objective experiments
5. Draw a conclusion as to whether your hypothesis was correct

My *Funk & Wagnalls Encyclopedia* article on the scientific method says, "Objectivity indicates the attempt to observe things as they are, without falsifying observations to accord with some preconceived world view."

Well put. The vast majority of youth baseball coaches have many preconceived views about how to coach. As a consequence, they see positive results from their coaching—regardless of the fact that the results are not there in the score books.

Funk & Wagnalls goes on to say that the results of the experiments must be **reproducible**. That is, if I say in this book that doing such-and-such in practice will result in your team executing the pitcher-cover-first play, it must be that if you follow my advice, your team does, in fact, execute at least two or three successful pitcher-cover-first plays during the season in question.

I have read well over a hundred baseball books and attended dozens of baseball clinics and studied dozens of baseball training videos. I have implemented many, many things that they told me to do. In the vast majority of cases, they did not have any beneficial effect on my team. They were not reproducible. In fact, they were probably just half-baked theories that the writer or speaker never actually tested with a youth team.

Hypothesis, yes; test, no

The main problem with the vast majority of youth baseball coaches, and to a lesser extent, with other baseball-coaching-book writers, is that they are pretty good at steps one (state problem) and three (form hypothesis) of the scientific method, but they do little of step two and virtually none of step four. That is, they do not research and they do not experiment.

To put it another way, they hypothesize, for example, that teaching batting mechanics will make their players better hitters. But they never check the score books to see if their hitters do, indeed, hit better than those on other teams. They take the attitude that, "I **believe** it is so, and we all know that I am a smart guy and a great coach, therefore it **is** so."

In 1990, I did that. Then I checked the score books to see how much better we were hitting than the teams of my less enlightened opposing coaches. We were getting five hits per game LESS than my opponents! That was the year I took a zillion hitting clinics then came back and taught all that stuff to my players. It was also the **last** year I taught all that stuff to my players!

I will cover hitting, pitching, and fielding

Make no mistake. I will cover hitting, pitching, and fielding in this book. I tried a number of things over the years. Many did not work. Some did. I will tell about both. That will save you from going down the same dead ends I went down. And it will prevent you from wasting time reinventing "wheels" that I already invented.

Over the years, I **did** learn some ways to make my team's hitting, pitching, and fielding as good as it can be. I believe I discovered ways to increase my team's on-base average above the norm. And we were better at fielding in some regards like the pitcher-cover first play and some other aspects of defense.

The main point I am trying to make is that the vast majority of youth-baseball coaches are spending almost all their time trying to change the hitting, pitching, and fielding mechanics of their players. That is a waste of time at best, and has a negative effect at worst.

"First, do no harm"

When you become a doctor, you take the Hippocratic Oath. According to one version of it, its beginning words are, "First, do no harm." They should also be the first words of the youth baseball coach's oath.

I started this book by saying that 98% of youth baseball coaches are incompetent. By that I mean that their coaching has no beneficial effect on their teams. In fact, the situation is far **worse** than that. I suspect that about 75% to 80% of them actually **hurt** their teams.

How do they do that? One way is they **criticize** their players, thereby making them self conscious, more afraid of failure, and less self-confident. That's bad in any endeavor, but it is especially bad in baseball, which is largely a mental sport. Old-time outfielder Jim Wohlford said, "Baseball is ninety percent mental half the time." (Yogi didn't have **all** the funny lines.)

They also hurt their teams by giving too many live signs—too many bunts, too many take-the-next-pitch signs. They hurt their teams by prohibiting players from advancing to the next base on their own initiative. They hurt their teams by wasting practice time. I could go on, and I will later in the book.

Duct tape

If I had the power, I would take one simple step that would significantly improve the quality of youth baseball played all across the country **overnight**. I would order that all coaches and parents have their mouths taped shut with duct tape at the beginning of each game. The tape would not come off until the final out.

Currently, the background noise at youth baseball games consists of dozens of comments like, "Oh, Sean, C'mon! You pulled your head again!" or "I need strikes, Scott!" Maybe you've even heard the favorite line of the authors of the book *The Mental Game of Baseball*: "C'mon @#$%^&*, RELAX!!!"

Under my duct-tape plan, all those negative comments would be reduced to a bunch of adults saying nothing but "Mmmmm! Mmmmm!" and applauding when their kids do well. The Northern Ohio Girls Soccer League held a "Silent Sunday" during which parents were prohibited from cheering or jeering. Board Member Carl Pavlovich said, "The kids had a ball."

Disowning the player

A great many of the critical comments leveled at players in youth baseball games are **not** intended to **help** the player in question. Rather the person making the comment, coach or father, is publicly **disowning** what the player just did. In other words, he is announcing to the crowd, "The screw-up you just saw was not MY fault! It was totally the fault of the dumb kid. **I** taught him better than that."

Not only is the coach or father **not** worried about the kid's well-being at that time, he is totally consumed with mitigating his own possible embarrassment at being the coach or father of the kid in question, EVEN THOUGH IT MEANS DEEPENING THE KID'S EXCRUCIATING MORTIFICATION! This is quite outrageous when you think about it, but go to a youth baseball game and see if that is not exactly what's happening.

Shut up

Basically, one of the big messages I have in this book is, "Shut up!" That's a message for both coaches and fathers. Your players will strike out, walk batters, and make errors. If you have to disown the player publicly every time that happens because of your own insecurities, you should stay away from the games. Just coach practices and appoint another adult to be the game-day manager.

He could announce to all the adults present before the game, "I am not related to any of these players, nor did I ever coach any of them." In other words, publicly disown the entire team before the game. That way he will not feel the need to disown them individually as they commit errors during the game.

In my later years as a coach, I tried to get out of the dugout and go sit in the stands during the game. That helps me shut up. It also helps me shut the parents up.

Sometimes you have to talk

Silence can be overdone. In 1992, I remember standing in the first-base coach's box when one of my players chased a chin-high pitch. I said not a word and moved not a muscle. I didn't even want my body language to suggest any criticism of what the kid just did.

But he stepped out of the batter's box and looked at me indicating with **his** body language that he wanted some kind of response from me about what just happened. So I asked, "Do you know what you did wrong?"

He nodded and held his hand palm down at his chin indicating the pitch was too high to swing at. "You got it," I said. "Now forget about it and focus on the next pitch."

'Good take!'

I don't know that I handled that correctly. But clearly the player wanted some sort of feedback from me, perhaps he only wanted assurance that I was not mad at him. I make an extremely big deal about waiting for the right pitch in practice. But I also know that **games** are absolutely **not** the place to criticize pitch selection.

If you attend one of my games, you will often hear me say, "Good take." Many times, my batter will deliberately take (not swing at) a first or second strike because it was a pitcher's pitch, not a hitter's pitch. (I'll explain that in the batting chapter.) Frequently, the opposing parents will explode with delight, cheering my batter's failure to swing at a called strike. Often, the opposing manager will add some disparaging remark like a sneering, "He's just looking for a walk."

In that case, I wait for the psychological warfare waged against my eleven-year old player by the middle-aged parents and coaches on the opposing side to die down. Then I say in a calm, firm voice, "Good take." Sometimes I add a comment like, "Pitcher's pitch," or "That was at the bottom of the strike zone. It would have been a weak grounder if you had swung."

The opposing parents apparently thought my comments were nullifying their psychological warfare, because they often complained to the umpire about them. They couldn't get the ump to make me stop saying "Good take," but they would get him to force me stand somewhere else when I said it or some similar harassment.

Deliberate incompetence

Why are 98% of youth baseball coaches incompe-

tent? In most cases, it's probably the obvious reason. They greatly underestimate the difficulty of coaching the sport of baseball in the very short span of a youth season and no one ever taught them how to do it correctly.

But there are a surprising number of coaching who coach in an incompetent manner **deliberately**. I'm not the only coach who figured out how to achieve results in my local leagues. I already mentioned Chuck Moore and some other people. And there are no doubt others who have figured out some of what I will tell you in this book, plus many things that I have not yet figured out.

Double steal is 'showing up' opponent

The president of the whole San Ramon Valley Little League once tried to persuade me to stop using baserunning tactics like the double steal. He knew I was playing semi-pro at the time and phrased the argument in a way he thought would strike a semi-pro chord. He said something to the effect that our double-steal plays were "showing up" opposing coaches. He then asked if it was not true that when you "show up" an opponent in semi-pro, the opposing pitcher throws at your head next time you come up.

The phrase "showing up" generally refers to batters, catchers, or pitchers engaging in some theatrical body language which strongly criticizes a ball or strike call by a home-plate umpire. If a semi-pro batter did some sort of taunting celebration directed at the opponent, like college and pro football players commonly do nowadays, I suspect the opposing pitcher might subsequently throw at you. But baseball players do not do such things, probably **because** of the bean-ball threat.

However, I have never heard of the execution of a double-steal play being considered "showing up" an opponent. Coaching that play well requires competence. So does defending it. Inability to defend it is **in**competence.

I think what the league president was saying was that my competence in coaching the double steal was revealing the **in**competence of our opponents in defending the double steal, and that since the incompetent guys had me outnumbered, I ought to stop engaging in that particular form of coaching competence.

'I stopped, so should you'

Chuck Moore was once part of a three-man panel that interviewed me for a AAA manager position. During the interview, I made the comment that baserunning was one of the most coachable aspects of baseball. Moore nodded agreement.

But then he said something to the effect that, like me, he once emphasized baserunning. However, he discovered that other people in the league, especially opposing coaches, hated it. So he stopped.

I told him that he was in large part the example I had followed when I focused on baserunning. He urged me to follow his **more recent** example of backing off emphasis on baserunning.

I **declined** to follow that part of his example. I also did not get the AAA manager job. Moore, it should be noted, was at the time, a majors manager, one of only eight such positions in the 170-coach San Ramon Valley Little League.

In other words, Moore was one heck of a baserunning coach until he saw it was hurting him politically in the league, then he deliberately stopped coaching his players to be such excellent base runners, at least in some respects. His political career advanced. His base runners did not.

I am sure many other youth-baseball coaches also concluded that being one of the 2% competent coaches would not make you as popular as being one of the 98% incompetent ones.

At the opening-day ceremonies for the San Ramon Valley Little League, they recite the Little League Pledge. It ends with the words "I will always do my best." That makes it especially outrageous that so many Little League coaches deliberately give less than their best coaching efforts to those same players.

This book is about coaching your team to play as well as they can. It will benefit **all** coaches, including those who "pull their punches" because of ulterior motives, but it will benefit most those who **lack** ulterior motives.

If your youth-baseball-coaching career plans focus on coaching your league's post-season all-star team or attaining the league presidency or some other political post, I suggest another book: *The Prince* by Niccolo Machiavelli.

'The kids had fun and that's all that matters'

"Oh, well. The kids had fun and that's all that matters." Know what that line is?

It's the "mating call" of the youth coach who just lost a game or who just concluded a losing season.

Matter of fact, the only people I have ever heard say those words were youth baseball coaches whose kids were most definitely **not** having fun. To those guys, "fun" is an infinitely elastic word that grown-ups can apply to any situation in which children participate.

Kids are resilient. Even in an 0-16 season, the kids will find opportunities to smile and laugh. But there can be no doubt that the amount of fun kids derive out of a youth baseball season is proportional to the individual and team success they have.

Making outs or errors is most definitely not fun. Losing games is definitely not fun.

As I said earlier in the book, baseball is not that coachable a sport. But baserunning is its most coachable aspect. If you learn about base running and emphasize it in practice and games, your kids will have extraordinary success. In the process of having that success, they will have more fun than if you had not been their coach.

2 The nature of youth baseball

In order to coach youth baseball, you must understand its true nature. I wrote four football coaching books, but none of them has a chapter on understanding the true nature of that sport. I could write books on basketball, soccer, volleyball, and a bunch of other sports without such a chapter. But baseball is different.

Almost all other sports are played on a rectangular field. The object is to move a ball or puck to a goal at one end. In comparison, baseball is downright weird. It's almost as if they should have another word than "sport" for it. It resembles the kids' game of tag. It's like golf in some respects. In some ways it is more like a board game than a sport.

Failure rate

One of the most important characteristics of baseball is its high failure rate. You often hear people say, "Even a .300 hitter fails 70% of the time." The fact that people **say** that suggests they **do** understand the true nature of baseball. But it's one thing to say it in the abstract. It's quite another to be so philosophical when the person who struck out is your son or one of the other players on your team.

Earlier, I noted that the most successful modern manager is Earl Weaver, but his win-loss percentage is just .583. The guy barely had a winning record!

Who is the best pitcher ever? Tom Seaver got the highest percentage of votes for the Hall of Fame. His career win-loss percentage was just .603.

How about Hall of Fame legend Nolan Ryan? Would you believe .519?

Get used to it. Accept it. Baseball is diabolically designed to subject its players and coaches to a very high failure rate. If you cannot accept that as normal, you will be a very unhappy coach.

When I was player-manager of a semi-pro team, I had a catcher who threw a major tantrum every time he struck out or made an error. He'd scream, "I hate this game!" as he left the batter's box after every single strike out.

He was really an excellent athlete, but he made himself too tight and nullified his athletic ability with his tantrums. Furthermore, I thought he was making the rest of us tight, too. At season's end, I replaced him.

If you focused a video camera on the face of a youth-baseball manager throughout a typical game, you would see an occasional smile, but mostly frowns, grimmaces, rolling eyes, and so forth, as his team committed the usual number of errors, strikeouts, and walks.

You should not be getting upset at **normal** performance. Find out what is normal in your league regarding errors, strikeouts, and walks. Then, if your team does **worse** than that, you can feel a little sorry for yourself. But it is ridiculous for youth baseball coaches to be wallowing in self pity or anger when their team is performing at a **normal** level for their age and skill level, or even better than normal, but not as good as the pros do on TV.

TV baseball versus youth baseball

TV baseball, that is Major League Baseball, sets the standard. Almost all of the unhappiness youth baseball coaches feel about the performance of their team stems from comparing them to professional major leaguers.

You're going to tell me you are well aware they are not pros. So why do you **act** the way you do when the strike out or commit an error? You **say** you understand, but actions speak louder than words and your actions say you cannot bear even normal errors by your kids.

'The way it's supposed to be'

Adults involved with youth baseball tend to regard professional games as the way it's supposed to be. Much of the unhappiness in youth baseball stems from the game not **looking** like the major-league model. They don't walk six guys in a row on TV. TV players don't throw the ball over the first baseman's head. (OK, other than Steve Sax.) TV outfielders don't let routine fly balls hit the ground.

There is a certain mix of things in the pros. For example, in 1987 in the American League, the league batting average was .265 and the league fielding percentage was .980. There were about two strikeouts for every walk. There were about 65,000 at bats (hits or outs) and 7,812 walks, suggesting a ratio of about one walk for every ten batters.

But at your local youth-baseball game, there is usually **more** than one walk per every ten batters. That makes people mad. They start ragging on the umps to call a larger strike zone than the rule book says and they rag on the batters to swing more.

Coach pitch or machine pitch

The real problem is the pitchers suck compared to pros, especially below age eleven and especially in the minors. The American Academy of Pediatrics says (www.aap.org/policy/00161.html),

> Compared with older players, children less than ten years of age often have less coordination, slower reaction times, a reduced ability to pitch accurately, and a greater fear of being struck by the ball. Some developmentally appropriate rule modifications are therefore advisable for this age group, including the use of an adult pitcher, a pitching machine, or a batting tee.

The solution is better pitchers or pitching machines. I coached in one league, the Orinda Valley Pony League, where, when the ratio of walks got too high, we cut back on the number of kid-pitched innings and increased the number of innings pitched by coaches or machines.

Every team had at least one good pitcher. But only one team had three. So the second-string pitchers on every team but one were walking in runs by the bushel. Originally, we were supposed to have four kid-pitched innings (two-inning limit per pitcher) and two machine-pitched.

We simply went to a format in which a kid pitched the first two innings of each game and a machine pitched the next four. If the machine did not work, the offensive team supplied an adult pitcher to pitch to their own hitters.

It was like two different games. There was relatively little hitting when the kids pitched; a great deal of hitting when the machine or coach did. One of the strategies became to put your weak fielders in the game during the kid-pitched innings.

In Rookie Ball, a baseball program for eight- to ten-year olds, they use machine pitching because they know from experience that kids that age have inadequate control. A study was done by Dr. William T. Weinberg of the University of Louisville regarding whether it is better to use pitching machines or kid pitchers at the 7-10-year old level.

The answer is pitching machines are better. Players in the machine leagues swung at 71% of pitches versus 32% in the kid-pitched leagues. Machine-league kids attempted and caught twice as many balls and made 60% more throws per minute of activity than kid-pitched leagues. When the machine-pitched league teams faced the kid-pitched teams in post-season tournaments, the machine-pitched kids won 14 out of 16 games and out-scored the kid-pitched opponents by more than two-to-one. The tournament games were kid-pitched. Kids from the machine-pitched leagues made fewer errors, got more assists, and converted a substantially higher number of batted balls into outs.

'Let's cheat and chase bad pitches'

But in the San Ramon Valley Little League, the so-

lution to nine and ten-year old pitchers who had normal control for their age, i.e., lousy, was to have the umpires cheat in favor of the pitchers and to have the batters chase bad pitches.

Basically, the SRVLL adults involved were outraged that the walkfest games did not look like TV games, so they ordered the umps and batters to become as incompetent as the normal, but struggling, pitchers. Teaching good baseball took a back seat to keeping up appearances. Every SRVLL minors game starts with the managers telling the umpire to call a huge strike zone.

In keeping with the admonition to "First do no harm," I do **not** teach batters to swing at bad pitches. I agree that it is no fun if the game turns into a walkfest, but the solution is **not** bigger-than-rule-book strike zones or telling batters to chase pitches that are not in the strike zone. To do so is another example of the deliberate coaching incompetence I mentioned earlier.

I recommend that a new rule be adopted for the 12-and-under level. The coach of the team that is on defense, may, at any time, ask that the pitching duties be taken over by a coach from the opposing team or a machine, if available. There would then be a five-pitch limit per batter. No walks or hit batsmen. The ump would continue to call strikes only. Three strikes or five pitches and you're out.

That would eliminate those embarrassing walk-a-thons when the team that is on defense cannot find a pitcher who can throw strikes and the pitcher of the moment suffers a nervous breakdown and goes into a "death spiral" where the previous walk begets another walk which begets another walk and so forth.

Throwing and fielding errors

Youth-baseball players make more throwing and fielding errors than pros. You knew that. But why do so many youth coaches who know that still behave as if they do not.

Fielding percentages in the pros range from the 1.000 achieved by several outfielders each season to .930 for a weak third baseman. Fielding percentages in tee ball are about .100 to .200. You can interpolate the fielding percentages in between tee ball and the pros if you keep in mind that they rise exponentially. That is, higher levels like professional minor leagues, college, and high school tend to be up around the .900 area.

If you know anything about statistics, you know that the probability of two events occurring is derived by multiplying their individual probabilities together. For example, the probability of Oakland's short stop Mike Bordick catching a grounder and throwing it successfully to first baseman Mark McGwire in 1996 was .979 (Bordick's fielding percentage that year) x .990 (McGwire's fielding percentage) = .969.

Even in the pros, the probability of **two** guys handling the ball successfully is less than the probability of **one** handling it successfully. Now apply that to a

14

couple of youth-baseball players with fielding percentages of .500 each. .500 x .500 = .250.

When you have such low fielding percentages as you do in youth baseball, you must **avoid** ball handling. Even in the pros, they try to limit a pickle (run down of a runner caught between bases) to one throw.

The typical youth-baseball pickle involves three or four throws and would go longer were it not for an error. When you apply the math to four throws you get the following probability of defensive success in that pickle. .500 x .500 x .500 x .500 = .063. Yet youth-baseball coaches practice that play. They practice pickles involving three, four, five, and six throws, even though the probability of success approaches zero.

Youth-baseball coaches must try to eliminate all unnecessary throws far more than higher level coaches because of the much higher fielding and throwing error rates in youth baseball.

Field conditions

If the pros came and played on your youth baseball field, their fielding percentages would drop. That is, they would make more errors. Matter of fact, they would probably **refuse** to play on your field for fear on injury and loss of their multimillion dollar salaries.

Why? Because your field stinks. The surfaces are uneven and poorly maintained. There are rocks and stones and clumps of grass or weeds. There are numerous dangerous obstructions around the field.

So many of the errors your players make are due to their lack of skill compared to pros. But a great many are due to the lousy condition of your fields compared to pro fields. Cut the kids some slack.

Field perimeter

Youth baseball field perimeters are different, too. College and pro fields generally have much more playable foul territory than youth fields, especially behind home plate. That means that the typical baseball play book, which is based on pro fields, is **wrong** for youth baseball.

For example, in the pros, the pitcher will often get directly behind the catcher on an extra base hit with a runner on base. But in youth baseball, the distance from the plate to the backstop is so short that there is no room there for the pitcher to back up. Instead, he backs up by playing the carom off the backstop if the ball gets past the catcher. The tight backstop also sometimes turns a passed ball into an out at second if the passed ball courtesy bounces off the backstop right back to the catcher.

Pro fields all have outfield fences. I played most of my playing career on fields with**out** outfield fences. In 1994, I hit a ball a mile into left field on Father's Day at the Sycamore Valley Field in Danville, CA. With 48-year old legs, I only got a double out of it. Left field

there turns into an unused (at the time) soccer field, then it becomes the right field of another baseball field. The lack of an outfield fence changes how and where you play the outfield.

In the pros, the **batter's background** for seeing the pitch is generally a blank green area. In youth baseball, not only are the balls not replaced as often as Major League balls, but the background that the batter sees behind the pitcher is often slightly-used-baseball-colored houses. Even the pros would have lower batting averages against such backgrounds.

Lousy equipment

Another reason youth players make more errors than pros is lousy equipment. If you forced major leaguers to play with the actual gloves your kids wear, they would revolt. And if you actually got them to play with those gloves, they would commit many more errors.

I was a catcher in 1957. My glove was the manager's fast-pitch softball catcher's mitt. It had no hinge. It was an adult's mitt. It was like wearing an upholstered pie plate. To catch the ball, I had to stop it with my mitt then quickly bring my bare hand around to trap the ball between the mitt and my hand, a feat I rarely accomplished.

In one game, my manager borrowed the opposing catcher's mitt for me. It was a kid's mitt with a hinge. The first pitch was low and outside. I am right-handed. I backhanded it with one hand. My teammates cheered. They had never seen me catch a pitch like that.

Nowadays, the catchers will all have kids' catchers mitts with hinges, but they are still not good enough. I mentioned earlier that our local Little League spun off the Tassajara Little League in 1991. I scouted a Tassajara opponent that season, and noted that their catchers could not catch routine pitches. Why? As a brand new league, they had all brand new catcher's mitts. I told my base runners to be more aggressive than normal against Tassajara's catchers.

A new catcher's mitt is about as useful as a crocheted prophylactic. It is too stiff. The same is true of a great many gloves worn by youth players. Their parents take them to a sporting goods store. They buy a brand new, stiff glove, sometimes made of plastic rather than leather. And the ball won't stay in it. On a number of occasions, I have noticed one of my players dropping almost every ball thrown or hit to him. I borrow his glove and I can't catch anything with it either.

Pros generally use the right size bat. But youth players almost always use a bat that is much too heavy.

Youth catchers' protective equipment is ill fitting requiring frequent game stoppages to reattach shin guards. Because it fits poorly, it restricts the catcher's movements.

Youth batting helmets are shared and ill-fitting. Pros have their own individual helmets.

Real Major League balls

Youth baseballs are cheaply made. Once, I bought real Major League baseballs for one of my Little League team's games. My reason was they are slightly safer than Little League balls because they are wound with wool yarn instead of nylon. Little League balls are actually **harder** than Major League balls. I figured that if they were slightly safer they might save a life and that would be worth the extra cost.

But I quickly yanked them out of the game after just two or three batters. I was afraid someone was going to get killed. The Major League balls came off the bats like rockets. If you doubt the lively-ball theories, put some real Major League balls into your next game, but don't leave them in for very long.

In other words, much of the difference in performance between pros and your youth teams stem from better field conditions and better equipment. Even the pros would not play at a normal pro level if they were forced to play on your youth fields with the same equipment that your players have.

Luck

Baseball is a **game of chance** to a large extent. In football, championships are decided by one game, like the Super Bowl. Almost all fans accept the result as a legitimate indication of who is the best.

But in pro baseball, championships are decided by a **series**. Why? Because people know that winning one baseball game proves little. I even wonder about the series. In 1998, 1989, and 1990, my local Oakland A's went to the World Series. They were favorites every time, but they only won in 1989. To this day I question whether the Dodgers were the best team in 1988 or the Reds in 1990.

When I batted in adult and semi-pro hardball, I tried to take the attitude that I was a bystander thinking, "I wonder how Reed's going to do at the plate today?" A common saying in baseball is "Don't try to **make** it happen. **Let** it happen."

In baseball and everything else, you will drive yourself crazy if you worry about things outside of your control. And in baseball, almost everything is outside of your control. You have to take what happens in stride and not beat yourself or your team up about every little misfortune.

Dr. Jekyll and Mr. Hyde

Baseball turns everyone into Dr. Jekyll (he can play) and Mr. Hyde (who sucks) over time.

Who is Mark McGwire? Is he the guy who hit 70 home runs in 1998? Or is he the guy who slumped so badly in 1991 that the kids at the Alamo School were yelling, "McGwire, you suck!" into his nearby back yard.

Baseball has a thing known as a slump. Joe Montana never had a slump. Wayne Gretsky never had a slump. But baseball players have slumps. Inexplicably, star hitters cannot hit for extended periods. No one knows why the slump started or why it ended. In youth baseball, where the season is so short, a hitter can slump for the whole season then be back to normal the next.

Pitchers and catchers talk about whether a pitcher "has his stuff working today." Some days a pitcher has his curveball; others, he doesn't. What's that about? No one knows.

All experienced youth coaches have had the experience of their best pitcher or best hitter or whole team having a lousy day.

In 1992, we smashed our first two playoff opponents so badly the games were both over by the fourth inning. One opposing manager threw in the towel voluntarily to avoid further embarrassment. The other was forced to concede defeat because we were up by 21 runs (25 to 4), there were only two innings left, and the league had a ten-batters-per-inning-maximum rule.

Then we faced the team we had beaten the most during the regular season. Furthermore, they got into trouble for using an ineligible player and were forced to replay a playoff game just before their game with us. In other words, they would play two games in one day one day after playing another game.

Sixth-string pitcher

By the time our game started, they were tired from having just played a full game and they were forced to start their sixth-string pitcher because they had used up the first five in the previous two games. We had all our pitchers available because we had not played in several days.

Their sixth-string pitcher threw a complete-game victory against us. They went on to the championship game where they lost to the team we had blown away in four innings by 25-4.

Were we robbed? Nah. That's baseball. If you cannot accept the fact that your players' Dr. Jekyll will show up for one game, and their Mr. Hyde for another, find another sport.

'Que sera, sera.'

Patti Paige had a hit with the song "*Que sera, sera*," Spanish for "Whatever will be, will be." That is a mandatory philosophy for baseball players and coaches. I often told my players about it, then used the phrase, "Que sera, sera," in games to remind them when bad stuff happened.

A kid comes up with two outs and two men on in a tie ball game. He grounds out and storms back to the dugout mad.

"Hey, Will. *Que sera, sera*. This is baseball. Stuff happens. Nothing you can do about it. They got nine guys out there. Sometimes one of them happens to be where you hit the ball. All you can do is get the bat on the ball and hope for the best. Forget about it now and focus on your fielding."

Center of attention

In most sports, you are often part of a mob—invisible. In baseball, you almost never are.

In basketball, foul shots are lonely. You stand at the foul line all alone. All eyes are on you. Many an otherwise great basketball player stunk at foul shots.

In football, all eyes are on the place kicker. And they sometimes miss "chip shots."

In baseball, everything is a foul shot. Everything is a place kick.

You stand alone on the pitcher's mound. One of my better pitchers in 1991 refused to pitch anymore. Why? He could not stand being the center of attention. He was good at baseball otherwise. He had also played on my football team and was excellent at that. He was actually quite good at pitching, but he just could not stand it psychologically.

You also stand alone in the batter's box. All eyes are on you. You are trying to do something which is so hard that the best pros fail most of the time.

'Out there on an island'

In football, color men sometimes express sympathy for the cornerback who has man coverage on a top receiver. "He's out there on an island all alone," they say. In baseball, **everyone's** on an island **all the time**.

Germans have a saying: "Geteilte Freude is doppelte Freude." It means "Joy that is shared is doubled." True enough. That's why it's more fun to get a hit or throw a great pitch or make a great catch in front of a crowd of parents and peers.

However, the crowd is a double-edged sword. The pain of a failure is similarly multiplied by the number of people in front of whom you fail.

As a coach, you cannot remove the crowd. Therefore, you cannot remove the enormous pain your players feel when they fail in front of the crowd. But you darned well can refrain from making it worse. And you can console the player by helping him put it in perspective and reassuring him of your continued confidence in him.

Psychological warfare

Baseball has an extremely unfortunate tradition: taunting the opposition. When I was a Little League catcher in the fifties, my coach taught me to harass the opposing batters constantly. And I did. I was the Don Rickles of the catchers box—a non-stop motor-mouth spouting every distraction and insult from "Suwing batter!" to "Is that your nose or are you eating a banana?"

That is unsportsmanlike. It is prohibited by Little League and other youth baseball rules. Little League Rule 4.06 (2) says,

No manager, coach, or player, shall at any time, whether from the bench or playing field or elsewhere— (2) use language which will in any manner refer to or reflect upon opposing players, manager, coach, an umpire or spectators;

Unfortunately, in my experience, those rules are never enforced. You should abide by them nonetheless.

Spectators should applaud and/or cheer their own team's success. They should also recognize exceptional play by a member of the other team. And it is polite to applaud a player from either team who leaves the field because of an injury.

Spectators should NOT celebrate the failure of a child on the opposing team. In the San Ramon Valley Little League, this was routine practice. I attended a **San Ramon** Little League game, not San Ramon **Valley**, with my son and we were laughing at the contrast. (The San Ramon **Valley** Little League is in north Danville and Alamo; The San Ramon Little League is in the town of San Ramon, which is the next town south of Danville. To make it even more confusing, there is also a Danville Little League in Danville.)

My sons also played a couple of seasons in the Orinda Valley Pony League and the parents there were generally exemplary in their treatment of children on opposing teams.

The worst parents I ever saw were from the Tassajara Little League, the Blackhawk spinoff of the San Ramon Valley Little League. They invariably waged blatant, cruel, psychological warfare against the children of the opposing teams. I'm talking about things like laughing theatrically when a child on an opposing team made an error or struck out.

I hope your local league is at the good end of the spectrum or that you will speak out to try to move it there. But until that happens, you must realize that heckling and taunting are an ugly part of youth baseball and they are part of what your players have to deal with.

If you ask the typical 12-year old boy what the worst moment of his life thus far has been, he will often tell you about the time he struck out or walked in the winning run or made an error at a youth baseball game. Keep that awful pressure and potential for embarrassment in mind in both your dealings with your own players and if you are inspired to comment about a child on an opposing team during a game.

Too much time to think

Most sports are chaotic. Action is continuous or, as in the case of football, all hell breaks loose periodically. Not baseball. Almost every act in baseball is preceded by time to think about what is about to transpire. The authors of the book *The Mental Game of Baseball* end their Introduction with this quote from the 1940 book *Father and Son.*

> *When he didn't have time, a few seconds in which to think, it was different. That was why he was better in football and basketball than he was in baseball. In baseball, when you batted, there those few seconds and fractions of a second between pitches when your mind undid you. In football and basketball, you didn't have time to think as you did in baseball. That made the difference.*

Any experienced baseball coach or player has seen instances where a ball was sharply hit to the pitcher or other fielder. He caught it so early that he had plenty of time to throw to first. But you could see that during that extra time, something popped in his mind, and he would make a ridiculously inaccurate throw—the same throw he had made accurately dozens of times when he had to hurry.

One of my Padres teammates in the San Francisco Men's Senior Baseball League was a decent baseball player—when he was all alone. He could fungo the ball a mile. But he tightened up when playing in front of other people and played poorly. However, I remember once when he was surprised and not quite ready for a pitch. He reacted instinctively and poleaxed a screaming line drive, easily the best hit any of us had ever seen from him. It had been the only time we ever saw him play where he did not have time to think about it beforehand.

Some Major Leaguers deliberately seem unready at the plate. The pitcher starts his windup, but the batter seems to still be in his relaxed mode. Sometimes they point the bat head at the pitcher for what seems like too long as the pitcher is in his windup. I suspect they are trying to artificially create the situation I described regarding my teammate. They are trying to reduce the amount of time they have to think. I suggested that to my players once. One did it in the next game and hit a triple.

Your players' baseball careers

Many youth baseball coaches justify how seriously they coach and what they spend time on as helping their players get ready for possible professional careers. Gimme a break.

There are 30 Major League teams. Each has about 20 players who start or pitch regularly. That's 600 players at any given time. Baseball has long been played throughout the western hemisphere. Lately, it has become an Olympic sport and the Major Leagues now have players from the eastern hemisphere, including Japan, Korea, and Australia. Maybe five million boys play baseball around the world.

That means $600/5,000,000 = .00012$ make it to start or pitch regularly on a Major League team. To coach one future Major Leaguer as a youth coach, you would have to coach $1/.00012 = 8,333$ kids. Since there are about 13 kids per team, you would need to coach for $8,333/13 = 641$ seasons to coach one Major Leaguer on average.

Bottom line, it is almost certain that you are **not** coaching any future Major Leaguers. Some youth baseball coaches **are** obviously coaching future Major Leaguers. Those kids will almost certainly be extreme standouts. They often will be moved up to higher age levels than they would normally play in. They should get special, quality coaching, but that level of coaching comes from former pros and coaches who get paid to coach like those in high schools and colleges.

My bottom line is that if you are so fortunate to have a future Major Leaguer, refer him to a top-notch coach for individual instruction outside of your team practices. This book is definitely NOT about the training of future Major Leaguers.

Future high school players?

Are you coaching future high school players? There are 300 to 400 players in the typical youth baseball league and there are about 18 players on the typical high school varsity. A high-school varsity baseball team is generally composed of players from three classes. Three classes of youth baseball players would be about half the league or about 175 players. That's a ratio of $18/175 = .1$. That means that the typical 13-player youth baseball team has among its members $.1 \times 13 = 1.3$ future high school varsity players.

If your league has different levels based on skill, the higher levels probably have two or three future high school varsity players per team and the lower level teams have none or one.

So the answer to the question, "Am I coaching a future high school varsity player?" is, "Probably." But so what? To tailor your coaching to just one of your players would be the tail wagging the dog. Even your league's post-season all-star team is composed primarily of kids who will be **cut** from the high school varsity.

Maybe one future high school player

Remember, the high school varsity has only about 18 players taken from the sophomore, junior, and senior classes. Your all-star team also has about 18 kids, but they are probably from just **one** class. Only about half that many will make it to the high school varsity and because of growth spurts, late bloomers and such, some of the high-school varsity players will be kids who did not make the youth all-star team.

'Retired' by age twelve

The nature of a youth baseball team is that it is composed almost entirely of kids who are rapidly nearing the end of their careers, which will be entirely in youth baseball. The number of youth baseball players drops dramatically as their age level goes up. According to the 7/12/99 *Time* magazine cover story, only about 27% of those who ever play youth sports still play as 13-year olds, let alone play for their high school. What are you really preparing your players for? Most likely, careers that will end when they are eleven or twelve.

My oldest son played until he was seventeen. (He normally would have played Big League at age 18, but he was recruited to play for the Columbia University football team and spent his pre-freshman summer complying with the instructions in Columbia's 3/4-inch thick summer-workout program.) My middle son played one year of tee ball and retired at age six. And my youngest son quit after his eleven-year-old year. So my three-son family average youth baseball career ended at an average age of $17 + 6 + 11 = 34/3 = 11.33$ years of age.

Do not coach like you are a junior member of the New York Yankee's organization or even of your local high school coaching staff. If you think you have a kid with potential to play at higher levels, recommend to his parents that they send him to baseball camps and/or get him private instruction. Do **not** tailor your practices to that kid or to the notion that you have thirteen such kids.

Huge differences between age levels

I am distinguishing between youth and high school and pro baseball in this chapter. But that sort of implies that youth baseball itself is all the same. It most definitely is not.

At the **tee-ball** level, they do not keep score, a policy with which I agree. But nevertheless, most coaches at that level try to teach far too much. Those kids need to play catch a lot. They need to be taught basic rules like run through first base after you hit the ball. And they need to be taught what to do on defense whether the ball is hit to them or to a teammate.

Unfortunately for the tee-ball players, the tee-ball coaches are often rookie coaches who have their oldest child on the team. They try to teach batting mechanics, throwing mechanics, double plays, and all that. Even teaching tee-ballers to tag up is tough. The best way to teach hitting and throwing mechanics at the tee-ball level is by silent example.

Once you get to the **nine-year old level**, you are dealing with kids who have some capacity to absorb the finer and more advanced points of the game. But again, you only have so much practice time and their ability to absorb information is limited. So is their interest.

Eleven-and twelve-year olds are the most fun to coach. They are smart. Their bodies are fairly well coordinated. They are experienced. And, except for a small percentage of the twelve-year olds, they generally do not question what the coach tells them.

Dr. Bobby Brown, the former President of the American League said, "...11 and 12 year olds usually have better lateral movement..."

Teenagers

I used to wonder why the San Ramon Valley Little League seemed to peak at the 12-year old level. The seniors (13 and up) portion of the league seemed to be almost an afterthought. I assumed coaching seniors would be the best job of all because they can take a lead, play on 90-foot diamonds, and all that.

Then my oldest boy turned 13 and I became manager of his team. I resigned after three practices—or tried to. Too many of the kids misbehaved at practice. The league wouldn't let me resign because they said it was extremely difficult to get people to coach the 13-year olds.

So we had a meeting where I told the parents and players I would only come back under certain circumstances. One was I had to have at least one other adult present to help supervise the boys (and to be a witness—a couple of these kids were hard core). Another thing I said was that I would henceforth have a hair trigger regarding discipline. I ended up throwing one boy off the originally twelve-man team and asking another to request a transfer to another team, which he did.

About 10% to 20% of the 13-year olds were discipline problems. Once the worst left the remaining kids behaved. About 90% of them were relatively uncoachable. They would say things like, "Hey coach, I've been playing baseball since I was five. I know what I'm doing. OK?"

Six guys showed up

They had such lousy attendance records at practices that I had to stop holding them. And they had lousy attendance records at games. That 13-year old league adopted a special rule that the team that was batting had to supply fielders to the defense if they had fewer than nine players. We played one game with just six—and won. We played another game with seven players and won in spite of a rogue umpire who awarded us two automatic outs every time our phantom eighth batter was due up.

The following year, they eliminated the 13-year old league and folded it into the 14-15 league. I coached subsequent years at higher teenage levels. It was never as bad as the 13-year-old only league, but we always had problems with attendance and coachability at the teenage levels.

Few problems in high school

By the way, I coached high-school **football** at the

freshman, junior varsity, and varsity levels, and we had virtually none of the problems we had with teenage **baseball** players. The reason seemed to be that our football players were highly motivated to start on the high-school teams, we had far more on the roster than we could put on the field (50 versus 11), and the vast majority had never played football before so they were not yet know-it-alls.

The same is true of the high school baseball teams I am familiar with. At the teenage level, it is important from the coach's perspective to either have lots of players, say 18 or more, or a highly motivated smaller group.

You should be very wary of taking a job coaching teenage baseball players if the number of players on the team is 15 or fewer and it is not a prestigious team like a high school freshman team or an all-star team or an American Legion team.

Practice time

Another thing that makes youth baseball different from higher levels, and which is not fully appreciated by the adults involved, is the amount of practice time. In our local Little League, we have tryouts in late January and early February. (I live in California.) In 1991, for example, we drafted teams on February seventh. We held our parent meeting on 2/18/91.

Our league said we could practice in small groups during February, but discouraged us from using the fields which were still wet from winter rains. We generally practiced on asphalt parking lots in February and started three-day-a-week practices in March. Our first game was April 8.

During the season, we had two games and one practice per week. So we practiced about 16 times in the pre-season and about eleven times during the season. Our practices were an hour and a half so that's 27 practices x 1.5 hours = 40.5 hours total.

In contrast, high school teams practice five or six days a week in the pre-season and have fewer games per week during the season. College teams do off-season workouts and their players participate in off-season leagues. Pros have batting cages in their basement, weight rooms in their house and devote their entire lives to baseball.

So the frustration and anger adults involved in youth baseball feel when their players fall far short of higher level performance is absurd. If you limited high school, college, or pro players to 40.5 hours of practice per year, they would play a lot more like your youth team.

Lighten up and revise downward your expectations of what you can accomplish as a coach during your season. I am going to tell you how to make the most of your 40 hours. Just keep in mind that it's **only** 40 hours.

Birth dates

Youth baseball is the only level at which birth dates matter. But, boy do they matter!

I believe that having a "good" birth date or a "bad" birth date in relation to youth baseball rules can have a **lifelong** effect, good or bad, on a player. Coaches and parents should do more to point out the importance of birth dates to kids so they can keep their performance relative to their "peers" in proper perspective. I sometimes provide my parents and players with a list of the ages **in months** of all the players on our team.

The cutoff in Little League and many other youth baseball leagues is August 1. Your age on July 31st is your official age for deciding which age level you play at. The ideal youth baseball birth date in those leagues is August 1. The worst possible birth date is July 31.

Accident of birth

Our local youth-football programs also used August 1. I know one kid who was an excellent athlete, but who also had a super birth date for the August-1-cutoff leagues. As you would expect, with his birth date, which enabled him to play with kids in the grade below him, he was quite the star in both baseball and football. He became extremely cocky and he was in for a rude awakening in high school when he had to play with kids in the same **grade** as opposed to his "league age."

By the same token, some kids with lousy birth dates often lose self-confidence because they perform so poorly compared to their teammates and players on opposing teams. Sports and academics are about the only ways kids have to compare themselves to peers, so they tend to draw overly broad conclusions from their sports successes or failures.

'League age'

My oldest son Dan and I have lousy youth baseball birth dates. I'm July fifth. He's June 26th. Neither of us was ever our "league age" until the season was over. In other words, when we were "league age" 12, we were actually eleven on the last day of the season. We never got to play a day of Little League as actual 12-year olds.

When I was ten ("league age" eleven) I made the majors and started at catcher, but batted ninth. When I was eleven ("league age" twelve), I batted third and made the county all-star team. When I was twelve, I came out to the first day of Little League looking forward to having a great year with my classmates, and I was stunned to learn I was too old.

Swimming star

In youth **swimming**, my son Dan's birth date was great. Their cutoff was June 15. Result: he was one of the oldest kids in the league and broke all sorts of pool, team, and league records, sometimes by three seconds or more. New records are usually only fractions of a second better than the previous record. He still holds his team record in breast stroke after ten years. His record time is five seconds better than the next best time and better than the record for the next **older** age group.

In 1995, we got an unexpected taste of what Dan's youth baseball career would have been like if he had a better birth date. He went to a high school twenty miles from our home on an interdistrict transfer. (I coached football there at the time and it is the best academic high school in the region.) We decided to try a pony league in the community where Dan went to high school.

We told them Dan's birth date and provided a birth certificate. For some reason we never understood, they put him on a team where his actual age, 14, was right, but his "league age," 15, was too old (by 35 days). There were also several other boys in the same situation age-wise, including at least one who was older than Dan.

He was by far the dominant player in the league. He hit eight inside-the-park home runs compared to zero for the rest of the league combined. He was so dominant on the mound that they generally would not let him pitch.

A kid once tried to tag up and score from third on a fly to Dan in shallow right-center field. He threw him out by a mile with a throw that never hit the ground. When he got on first, we would bet in the dugout whether it would take him one, two, or three pitches to score—assuming the batter never put the ball in play. It usually took him one or two because there would often be passed balls or throwing errors.

Afraid to catch his throws

When he threw a pick off to third once as catcher, the kid who caught it suffered a hand injury just from making a clean catch and had to leave the game. (He caught it in the **palm** of his glove. He should have caught it in the **web**.) A subsequent accurate catcher pick-off throw to third went into left field because the third baseman was afraid to catch it. In general, Dan looked like a man playing with boys all season.

We only learned Dan was too old when we asked why he did not make the all-star team. "They check birth certificates." "So?" "Technically, Dan doesn't make the cutoff for this league." "Say what!?"

32% older!

The younger the age level, the more birth dates matter. On my 1993 tee-ball team, the oldest kid was 91 months old and the youngest was 69 months old. That's a 32% difference—the equivalent of a 14-year old playing on a 21-year old team!

Parents in areas with more than one league should look at birth dates when selecting which league to sign their kid up for and pick the league where he has the best birth date. Coaches should take a hard look at birth dates when drafting their team. All adults involved with youth baseball should strive to keep the players aware of the misleading nature of relative performance between players with the same "league ages," but very different actual ages in months.

Lifetime effect

I said the erroneous conclusions kids draw from doing well or not doing well when competing with "peers" who are really different ages can affect them for a **lifetime**. Let me tell you where I got that idea.

I am a West Point graduate. You can enter West Point at age 17 to 22. I entered at age 17. Some of my classmates had already graduated from college when they entered West Point! Others had attended one to three years of college. Still others had been in the army for one to four years. A year or two after my class entered in 1964, there were even 22-year old decorated Vietnam-veteran army officers entering West Point alongside 17-year-old kids fresh out of high school.

As you would expect, the older cadets excelled in all areas of competition including academics, athletics, social areas, and making cadet rank. But unlike youth baseball players, all concerned recognized the advantages the older cadets had. Or so we thought.

Generals

But as the years passed after graduation, it became apparent that the advantage these guys had was lasting a **lifetime**. For example, the highest ranking general in my class earned three stars. He started his military career inauspiciously by flunking out of the West Point class two years ahead of me then got readmitted in my class!

The guy who led General Swartzkopf's "end-run Hail Mary" tank charge in Desert Storm was Bill Nash, a classmate of mine who had an extraordinarily successful military career after entering West Point as a former enlisted man. When my class got early promotions to major, lieutenant colonel, and colonel, the guys who had entered West Point several years after leaving high school were disproportionately represented on the early promotion lists.

My theory is that those older cadets, who I suspect were ordinary in high school, got a great self-confidence boost from being big men on campus during four years at West Point, and they continued to benefit from that boost for decades.

Psyche up

In general, psyched-up athletes play better. In football, basketball, soccer, and other sports, you often see players putting all their hands together and executing a simultaneous pre-game cheer like "Win!" It helps. I did it in football.

Once, we faced the defending league champion in a football playoff. They seemed to go out of their way to avoid any psyche-up activities. I felt we beat them 6-0 because we made a point of doing a psyche-up cheer at the beginning of the second half. They did not do any such thing. They came out flat. We scored within a minute or two of the start of the second half, then the game settled back into the stalemate it had been all throughout the first half.

Give 100%?

So, should you do that in baseball like I have seen many youth coaches do? Nope. Baseball is different. Football coaches constantly ask their players for "100%." (Football coaches who were PE majors ask for "110%!") Shouldn't baseball players give 100%? No. They most certainly should **not**.

H.A. Dorfman and Karl Kuehl wrote the book *The Mental Game of Baseball*. Dorfman has a masters in psychology and was, at the time of the book, a full-time performance-enhancement instructor for the Oakland Athletics. Kuehl was the A's Director of Player Development and has spent his whole adult life in baseball.

They took an informal poll of Major Leaguers asking what percent of maximum effort a baseball player should exert in a game. The consensus was **85%**. What they are saying is that if a pitcher or fielder throws as hard as he can, he will lose too much accuracy. If a batter swings as hard as he can, he will be less likely to hit the sweet spot of the ball with the sweet spot of the bat.

Orel Hershiser says he only throws his fastball at maximum velocity about five times a game. The rest of the time, he throws it about 85% of maximum.

Overmanaging

It's not just players who can try too hard in baseball. Managers can, too. Billy Martin said Gene Mauch was "…the classic case of a guy who overmanages. He tries to be so brilliant. He takes the game away from his players. His problem is that he often tries to show how much he knows… He takes himself out of more games than any manager I ever managed against."

I thought some of the 1999 Little League World Series Tournament managers were overmanaging in some respects. For example, there was **always** a cut man, and the outfielder **always** hit the cut man, including on some plays where the cut man saved the runner's butt by delaying an accurately-thrown ball from getting to the base in question.

A more common form of overmanaging I often see is base coaches putting on too many plays that they have not practiced enough, too many take signs, and not enough steal signs. Coaches seem to think the players cannot make good decisions. My experience is that

they usually can, and that trying to control runners too much makes them hesitant to take advantage of split-second opportunities.

Undermanaging

You cannot just lay back and thereby win Manager of the Year either. Many base runners must be pushed hard to steal. They are too afraid of making an out. Many batters stick with the full swing too much against tough pitchers or with two strikes.

The squeeze is a great play and must be coordinated by someone. Your job is to get the players to play to the best of their abilities. If a particular boy is playing up to his abilities in some aspect of the game, or saying something would do no good, shut up and leave him alone regarding that aspect. On the other hand, if he is **not** playing up to his ability, like being too scared to steal, you must lean on him. Managing is like being a parent: you have to know when to push and when to lay off. There is no easy answer like always doing one or the other.

Even keel

Another phrase that came up in the book over and over was the need for baseball players to be on an "even keel" throughout the game. Screaming "Rockies!" or whatever before a game or inning works against both the 85% and the "even keel" goals. Youth baseball coaches who engage in that sort of rah-rah stuff reveal their lack of understanding of the nature of baseball.

In his book *Billy Ball*, Billy Martin complains about George Steinbrenner. Steinbrenner was a football player at Williams College. He sometimes wanted to give a psyche-up speech to the Yankees. Martin told Steinbrenner,

George, I'm trying to key everything down and you're trying to key everything up. I'm trying to make them relaxed and you're trying to stir them up. They don't need your motivation. This is not football.

Baseball players must be loose and relaxed. But they must be ultra alert and they must be hair-trigger ready to act. I highly recommend *The Mental Game of Baseball* to all baseball coaches.

Amnesia

It is said in football that cornerbacks need short memories to be successful. That is, they are going to get beat very publicly for touchdowns on occasion. They cannot be effective unless they can forget those failures and focus on the next play.

Earlier, I said football cornerbacks are often described as "being all alone on an island." I further said that baseball players are always on an island. Accordingly, to be successful in baseball, you must be able to forget the last pitch, regardless of whether what happened was good or bad for you, and focus completely on the next pitch.

For example, if your shortstop muffed a grounder on the last pitch, he is likely to still be thinking about that when the next pitch is thrown. If so, he is more likely to muff another or make a bad throw.

Muff drill

I sometimes do drills where I tell the player to **deliberately** muff each ball so he can practice recovering from the error immediately as well as on the next pitch. For example, I might give the instruction, "Muff and get one." Then I throw a grounder to the shortstop. He deliberately lets it hit the back of his glove. Then he smoothly picks it up and guns it to first. No panic, just a judicious amount of urgency.

I want my players to think of errors, strikeouts, and walks as **normal** parts of the game, not some big deal failures on their part.

Baseball is very, very difficult

When my oldest son first started playing baseball, I could not believe all the dumb and clumsy mistakes he made. Then I did something that few youth baseball parents or coaches do, I joined an adult hardball team. And I couldn't believe all the dumb and clumsy mistakes that **I** made.

I was much less critical about the play of my son and my other players after that. Every youth coach should have that experience.

The pre-season coaches hardball game

I wish we had a tradition in youth baseball that every practice season started with a hardball game on a local high school, college, or pro field between two teams made up of the local youth baseball coaches. Every player and parent in the league should be invited to watch. Every coach would be required to play. In the typical league, you would have to have two or three games to accommodate all the coaches.

There is no doubt that almost all the coaches involved would be greatly embarrassed by their performances. Thereafter, their players and parents would have a far more accurate idea of the expertise of their coach. And the coaches would no doubt be infinitely less critical of their child players than they typically are now.

My fallback suggestion is that the coaches be required to hit against pitching machines, again, in front of their team's players and parents. They could also pitch from a mound at a life-size picture of a strike zone and batter with points awarded or subtracted for what you hit. A radar gun could be used to measure velocity, which would be publicly announced after each pitch. Let the coaches also take the field while some-

one hits them infield and outfield practice. (Actually, I think the average youth baseball coach would do pretty well at fielding, but not as well as they would like their players to believe.)

Probably not a single youth league in the world will take up any of those suggestions. The coaches know darned well they would play lousy. And they would actually play worse than they fear.

But I still think you have a responsibility as a coach, to your players, to refresh your recollection as to exactly how difficult the game of baseball is. There are now adult hardball and semi-pro leagues all over the country. Join one for at least one season. It will give you an appropriate amount of humility and an appropriate amount of empathy for your players.

Whole spectrum of athletic ability

High school and higher level baseball teams are the equivalent of youth all-star teams. Actually, they are **better** than youth all-star teams because they choose from a much larger pool of prospects.

In youth baseball on the other hand, you have a wide spectrum of athletic ability including players who have very little athletic ability and, below the twelve-year old level, you have players whose lack of athletic ability is exceeded only by their lack of interest in baseball.

You are their coach, too. For the sake of the team, you need to find a defensive spot where they will do the least harm. That is typically in the outfield.

At the same time, you have an obligation to the kid to give him the best chance to succeed. That means you train him. Indeed, you will probably spend **more** time training him than you will you average player because he **needs** more time. Most importantly, you must specialize him at one position.

Specialize at one position

Many players do not like being specialized at an outfield position. Some fathers get quite angry about it. The father of one of my 1997 players angrily ordered me to let his right fielder son play infield. I had tried the kid out for infield once and said I would try him again in practice. I pointed out that the father practicing with the kid might make the difference.

Ultimately, I kept the kid in the outfield. The kid seemed to accept it and like the position as the season went on. But the father never got over the embarrassment of his son being a right fielder. They were the only family missing from the post-season party.

'Hey! I'm a right fielder'

By the way, **my** position is right field. I take pride in it. In the Major Leagues, many great players have played that position. It requires the strongest arm in the outfield (because the right fielder often throws to third, but the left fielder never throws to first).

Those of us who are experienced at right-field play it better than newcomers because there are certain nuances, like the ball hooking toward foul territory or the need to take charge on balls hit in the right-center gap if both you and the center fielder are right handed (you are running to your throwing-arm side).

But mainly, I just regard it as a position like any other. I do not happen to have the athletic ability to be an infielder. Most people don't. The rest of us need to play outfield.

'No small parts, only small actors'

I acted in the play "Cheaper by the Dozen" with my youngest son in 1998. I played Doc Burton. I commented that it was only a "small part" once at rehearsal. The director said, "There are no small parts, only small actors."

Thus it is with right field. While it may be quiet on average, once or twice in most games, it becomes the most important place in the world to the players on that team.

Also, like a part in a play, it can be what you make of it. I was an extremely aggressive backer upper in the outfield. My attitude was that I am only a right fielder if the ball is hit to right field. Otherwise, I'm leaving to go where the action is.

Once, while playing **left field** in a semi-pro game, I saved a run by covering **home plate**! The catcher had gone down to back up third (which was incorrect on his part) and the pitcher just remained on the mound (also incorrect). I prevented a number of other runners from advancing by backing up first and second bases from right field.

Zen

Baseball is a Zen-like activity. What is Zen? I am **not** glad you asked. It's hard to define. But since I brought it up, I guess I have to try. My *Webster's New Universal Unabridged Dictionary* says Zen is:

An anti-rational Buddhist sect...it differs from other Buddhist sects in seeking enlightenment through introspection and intuition rather than in...scripture.

Note the words "anti-rational," "introspection," and "intuition." Most of our lives are spent in the world of the rational. But baseball is not of that world.

My *Funk & Wagnalls Encyclopedia* has an article on Zen which says in part,

Zen is the peculiarly Chinese way of accomplishing the Buddhist goal of seeing the world just as it is, that is, with a mind that has no grasping thoughts or feelings. This attitude is called 'no-mind.'

Sounds like Yogi Berra's statement that "You can't think and hit at the same time." I didn't know he was a Buddhist.

When Dizzy Dean heard the opposing Tigers were having meeting before the 1934 World Series, he said, "If them guys are thinking, they're as good as licked now." Dean's Cardinals won the Series.

Funk & Wagnalls continues,

Unlike other forms of Buddhism, Zen holds that such freedom cannot be attained by gradual practice but must come through direct and immediate insight.

Hey, that happened to me when I was eleven! I had a Zen experience which transformed me in a flash into a much better hitter. As a ten-year old, I batted ninth and had far more than my share of strikeouts. The following year, in my first at bat, it was the same old thing. I went to the plate overwhelmed with fear that I would strike out and embarrass myself yet again. It was a self-fulfilling fear. I struck out.

'Who cares?'

But when I approached the plate for my second at bat, I had my Zen insight. I told myself, "Aw, to heck with this misery. Yeah, you're probably going to strike out, but who cares? Everyone here has seen you strike out dozens of times before. Another one won't make any difference. But at least stop tormenting yourself about it. Just accept the inevitable, go take your hacks, then sit down."

But I did not sit down. Thus relaxed, I hit a single—into shallow right center. I can still see it like it was yesterday. It was not yesterday. It was April of 1958.

I kept that Zen insight for the rest of the season. I moved from ninth to third in the batting order. I hit safely in every single game. My batting average was probably over .400. And I made the county all-star team on the strength of my hitting and in spite of my fielding.

One other thing: the opposing pitcher that day turned out to be unusually good. He threw a one-hitter.

I went from being the worst hitter on the team to being the best hitter on the team—not because of practice or coaching or gradual improvement. Rather it happened in the space of about twenty seconds because I figured out that I had to stop worrying about striking out.

More *Funk & Wagnalls* on the subject of Zen:

"...its point of view is connected with action rather than theory and with direct vision of nature rather than interpretation...suffering [like when you strikeout] is the result of grasping desire, for it holds that the mind and feelings frustrate their own proper functioning when they cling deliberately to the world of experience."

In other words, if you want to get a hit, stop trying to grasp control of the effort with your conscious mind, just see the ball and let your body react naturally to it.

The "inner game" of baseball

Professional tennis instructor W. Timothy Gallwey wrote a book called *The Inner Game of Tennis*. I recommend that you read it to become a better baseball coach. Here are some of its relevant thoughts.

To succeed, you need "…relaxed concentration …self-confidence…The secret to winning…lies in not trying too hard. Use the subconscious mind more than the deliberate 'self-conscious' mind. This process doesn't have to be learned; we already know it. All that is needed is to **un**learn those habits which interfere with it and then to just let it happen." [emphasis in original]

"I began saying less and noticing more. Errors that I saw, but didn't mention were correcting themselves…verbal instruction to a conscientious student seemed to **decrease** the probability of the…correction occurring." [emphasis in original]

"…images are better than words, showing better than telling, too much instruction worse than none, and that conscious trying often produces negative results."

"Trust thyself. Trusting your body…means letting your body hit the ball. The key word is **let**." [emphasis in original]

Gallwey refers several times to Zen. He recommends the book *Zen in the Art of Archery* by D.T. Suzuki.

'Swami Ralph'

The actual word "Zen" is probably not a good one to use with parents and players. One of my fellow youth football coaches once pushed us real hard to use yoga during our stretching period. Forever after, we called him "Swami Ralph." The players thought even it was his name. They called him "Coach Swami." If I used the word "Zen" with my baseball players, I would probably now be known as "Samurai Jack."

'Use the Force'

Instead, I recommend you use the most widely known expression of Zen in modern American popular culture: "The Force" from the four *Star Wars* movies. As in, "May The Force be with you."

As you'll recall, in the original *Star Wars* movie, Obi-Wan Kenobi teaches Luke Skywalker, "The Force is what gives the Jedi its power." Later, when Luke is practicing, he swings a light saber, which he holds in

two hands like a baseball bat, at a floating ball about the size of a softball.

"Remember a Jedi can feel the force flowing through him."

Luke asks, "You mean it controls your actions?"

"Partially, but it also obeys your commands.
"I suggest you try it again, Luke. This time let go your conscious self and act on instinct."

In the climactic battle scene, Luke is trying to put two torpedoes down a heat-ventilating shaft. He turns off the targeting computer and relies on "The Force," hearing the voice of Obi-Wan Kenobi as he makes his final approach.

"Luke, trust your feelings. Use The Force, Luke. Let go, Luke. Luke, trust me."

Coach Obi-Wan Kenobi

This is an excellent model for a youth baseball coach to follow, as well as a concept that is already familiar to your kids.

A **baseball player needs to trust something other than his conscious brain** to succeed at hitting pitching, fielding, or throwing. He can trust his hands, like a Houston Astros player once told me. Or he can trust external things like The Force or prayer ("Please, God, let me get a hit.").

Baseball players are generally regarded as the most superstitious in all of sports. I do **not** think coaches should **encourage** superstition. I only point it out to prove further my case that to succeed at baseball, you must **let it happen** as opposed to trying to **make it happen**.

How NOT to coach

There is another movie which has a model of exactly how **not** to coach a youth baseball player. What's worse, is that the scene is intended to show the perfect coach and it is a pivotal scene in the movie. I am talking about Wilfred Brimley in *Cocoon*. In that movie, Brimley is coaching his grandson on hitting. He tells him,

Hitting a baseball is the hardest thing in sports. You have a round bat and a round ball and you have to hit it squarely.

Now what exactly is the point of that statement? It sure as heck is not to build confidence. Can you imagine Obi-Wan Kenobi whispering to Luke as he zooms toward the heat-ventilating shaft.

Luke, getting a torpedo to go down the shaft is the hardest thing is space warfare. You're traveling 3,000 miles an hour at a two-meter-wide shaft while being shot at by Darth Vader from behind, and you have to do this with the pressure that civilization as we know it will end if you fail.

Later in *Cocoon*, Brimley and his wife turn down a chance to go another planet where they can live forever. He prefers to hang around his grandson so he can give him more great baseball-playing advice. I can hear him now.

Pitching is the second hardest thing in sports. You have to throw a round ball with an area of 6.44 square inches 60 feet 6 inches through a rectangular strike zone with an area of 400 square inches guarded by a guy with a bat that has an area of 50 inches.

A couple more bits of baseball wisdom like that and the grandson will ask if he can switch to swimming.

Subconscious activity

Baseball requires that players perform amazing feats of hand-eye coordination like hitting a moving ball with a relatively thin bat or catching a bouncing ball and hitting a distant target with it in a fraction of a second. We don't know how humans can do such things at all. But they can. However, players and coaches must understand that those things happen at a **subconscious** level. Trying to consciously control the bat will cause you to whiff. Thinking too much about a throw will put it in the seats.

The word "trust" comes up a lot when pro players are talking about their sport. Once, while on a business trip to the Dallas area, I visited a batting cage there. I was taking turns at one cage with a guy who was using a wood bat with adhesive tape around the sweet spot. That usually signifies a pro, but I did not recognize him. He was crushing screaming line drives back through the hole in the net where the pitching machine was.

When we both went to the counter to buy more tokens, I commented, "This doesn't look like your first day here." "I'm with the Astros," was his reply. I asked if I could watch him so I could learn how to hit better. He said, "Come on in. I'll give you a lesson."

One thing he said over and over was, "You have to trust your hands." This was a variation of the theme, "Don't **make** it happen. **Let** it happen." It also is reminiscent of Obi-Wan Kenobi's, "Trust your feelings. Trust me."

Baseball is boring

Baseball is boring. Now some readers may think, "If you have that attitude, you shouldn't be writing a book about it."

It's not an attitude. It's a fact. I am only about the millionth writer to comment on baseball's boredom.

I am also well aware of the nuances of baseball. If you are not, I recommend you read two books: George Will's *Men at Work* and Tim McCarver's *Baseball for Brain Surgeons*.

But this is not a book about the nuances of professional baseball. It's a **youth** coaching book. Your youth players do not know that a shortstop moves over to the left a little when the pitcher gets ahead of a right-handed hitter and the catcher calls for a fast ball. And you don't have time to teach them.

The reason you need to keep in mind that baseball is boring is that you do not want to bore your players. This is especially a problem at the tee-ball level. Tee-ball players sit down and start playing with the grass. Tee-ball infielders look up at the sky while the batter is swinging.

Keep the game moving

What can you do about it? Keep the game moving. Don't let batters do a bunch of screwing around like golfers slowly moving their club head up against the ball repeatedly. This is really a problem at **all** levels. I often had to admonish my pitchers in semi-pro that they needed to speed up the pace because they were putting the fielders to sleep.

During a youth-baseball game, all eyes tend to be on the batter. He is **never** bored even though he is knocking nonexistent dirt off his cleats or taking his umpteenth practice swing.

But don't look at him. Look at the **fielders**, especially the outfielders, to see if they look bored. When they do, tell the batter or pitcher to speed up the pace.

20 seconds per pitch

There is actually a 20-seconds-per-pitch time limit in Little League rules, but I have never seen it enforced. (Rule 8.04 When the bases are unoccupied, the pitcher shall deliver the ball to the batter within 20 seconds after the pitcher receives the ball. Each time the pitcher delays the game by violating this rule, the umpire shall call "Ball.") Umpires should be supplied with a stop watch or simpler 20-second timer so they can enforce this rule.

There is also a delay rule pertaining to the batter. Rule 6.02(c) says, "If the batter refuses to take position in the batter's box during a time at bat, the umpire shall order the pitcher to pitch, and shall call 'strike' on each such pitch. " There is no 20-second rule *per se* for the batter, but given that there is for the pitcher, it seems as though that ought to indicate to the ump when he orders the pitcher to pitch.

In the Babe Ruth Bambino Rookie Division, they use pitching machines "…to speed the games along." Smart move.

3 Tryout and draft

New players only

The only players who should be required to participate in tryouts are **newcomers** to the league or community and players **coming up from levels at which no score books were kept**. For players returning from levels at which score books were kept, their previous year's stats should be compiled and distributed.

Unfortunately, I suspect there in not a snowball's chance in Havana of that happening, so you have to sit in a lawn chair at your local tryout, in cold weather, all day, for a weekend or two, to watch rusty players get three chances to catch a grounder and throw to first, three chances to catch a fly and throw home, and ten chances to hit against an unfamiliar pitching machine. At my local league, those who want to be pitchers and catchers also perform in a bull-pen setting.

The information you gather at these tryouts pales in comparison to the information you could gather looking at last year's score books. But some kids are not in last year's score books and you may not be allowed to look at last year's score books, so you have to waste a couple weekends at the league tryout.

My suggested tryout

The only single-event tryout I think makes sense is a 60- to 90-foot sprint against a stop watch.

Would I like to know how fast the players can **throw**? Yes. But we cannot test it in a pre-season tryout because you have to get your arm in shape and a maximum effort throw is never advisable for safety reasons. You should never hold a distance-throwing competition in baseball for the same reason you should not hold competitions to see who can stay under water the longest. There is too much danger of injury.

Would I like to know who can hit? You bet. But I have no interest in knowing who can hit against a pitching machine, unless the league in question will use the same pitching machine at the same speed in our games.

Learning to hit a machine

It takes a long time to learn to hit against a pitching machine that is throwing at competition speeds. But the skill of learning how to hit a particular machine is a total waste as far as game performance is concerned. (There goes my batting-cage endorsement contract.)

We used to have a Grand Slam Batting cage in Pleasanton, CA. Its fastest cage was extremely hard to hit. It was throwing in the 80's, but it was much harder to hit than other 80's machines I had faced at other locations. At first, I had so much trouble with it I said, "Forget it." Hardly anyone else could hit it either. I watched many a man try.

Then one day, the place was mobbed. All the other cages were booked. I figured I might as well try the fastest machine again. In particular, I decided it would be a good time to work on my bunt. Somehow, doing ten bunts enabled me to figure out the machine. I hit against it thereafter every time I went there.

My adult baseball team came there a couple times. They were astounded at my ability to hit it well, and embarrassed by their great difficulty hitting it at all. One teammate predicted I was going to hit .400 that season. I did not. I had an ordinary year and hit less well than my teammates who could not hit the Pleasanton Grand Slam 80-mile-an-hour machine. So much for success at hitting a machine.

However, if you hold a tryout against human pitchers, you have the problem of the humans getting tired or deliberately throwing easy pitches to a friend or different batters facing different pitchers and so forth.

In the early nineties, I decided to upgrade the quality of the semi-pro team of which I was player manager. My tryout consisted simply of four baseball games. Each game was nine innings. Each had a paid home-plate umpire. I reserved the varsity baseball field at California High School for the purpose. I publicized the tryout and when each person called, I asked him what position he wanted to play and insisted he select one position. I also signed up five pitchers for each team.

It was really great fun for everyone. I kept a score book for each game and picked my team based on performance in those games. I also took into account previous play at the professional or college level. (The result was a great team in terms of baseball ability. But their chemistry was lousy and the team later dissolved. If I had it to do over, I would hold a similar tryout only for two or three positions per year. The other positions would be occupied by my strong good chemistry guys. Then, if we got a bad-attitude case, we could dump him without losing the whole team.)

I think local youth-baseball tryouts should do the same. Just play a full-length game with real umpires and score books. Coaches would get to attend the game and examine the score book.

That still does not give you a completely accurate reading because some people have **bad** days and some people have **good** days during the tryout, but it about as good as you can do for measuring newcomers to the league.

Past score books

I once discussed using past score books with another coach. He said they were worthless because the mothers who kept them were all screwed up on errors. I think he was probably right about scoring of errors. But there are many other items in the score books which are useful, but not subjective, like:

- walks
- strikeouts
- hit batsmen
- reaching base whether by error or hit
- put-outs
- assists
- over-the-fence home runs

Even the subjective stuff can still be useful. Stolen bases may be passed balls or clean steals. Clean steals are more of an accomplishment, but advancing on a passed ball is not automatic. Errors are probably not totally reliable, but it is still useful to see who was charged with errors.

Where do you get score books?

If you coached in the league last season, you should still have your score books. Other coaches should still have theirs. Frequently, the players you need to judge were in a lower league last year so they did not appear in your games or score books. Your league may keep score books, although they may not permit coaches to see them for this purpose. Some local newspapers may publish detailed box scores of games. You can probably look up last year's games at the library or newspaper office.

My point is to get them by whatever legal means available to you. Trying to go on tryout information only borders on silly.

Blind versus own-team drafts

There are two ways to run a draft: blind and own-team. In a blind draft, the coaches in the league all put their heads together and come up with **teams that are equal in ability**. They are highly motivated to achieve as much equality as possible because they **do not know when they are creating the teams which team they will be coaching**. Coaches are assigned to teams by blind drawing out of a hat after the teams have been created. In an own-team draft, coaches know when they are drafting that these are the players they will have on their team.

Own-team drafts are typical. They are the only kind I have ever participated in. They are also **unethical** in my opinion. No youth sports league should **ever** allow own-team drafts. National league rules-making bodies should ban them. The owners of the youth fields should ban them. State legislatures should ban them. Parents and players should demand the end of them.

Own-team drafts serve only one purpose: they enable **some** adult coaches to draft a superior team by outsmarting opposing coaches at evaluation and drafting strategy or, often, by cheating. That goes against the stated purpose and policy of every youth sports league. **Player** enjoyment and development is maximized by teams being as **equal** in talent as possible.

It is unfair to the children for one or two teams to have disproportionate talent compared to the other teams in the league. It may be fair to the **adults** because the draft rules were the same for all coaches. But youth sports are not supposed to be for the adults.

Most of the youth-baseball championships on this planet are determined on draft night. Knowledgeable local observers may not be able to pinpoint it down to **one** team, but they can probably name **two** teams, one of which will win the championship and the other will come in second or third. This is an outrage. Every kid ought to be on a team that has an equal chance to win.

Coach's child

It is standard for the coach's son to be on the coach's team. Most youth coaches would quit if they could not coach their own son.

How do you do that in a blind draft? In 1998, I coached in a youth flag football league where every coach had to rate every other coach's kid. Those ratings were then used to assign the coaches' sons to a particular round of that own-team draft.

In theory, this should not work because the coaches have incentive to rate opposing coaches' kids as first-round draft picks. But in the event, it seemed to work OK. My youngest son, who is not very interested in athletics, was rated a fifth-round draft pick.

I suspect the best system would be to agree on a quality rating for every player in the draft including each coach's son. The non-coaches' sons are distributed equally leaving each team with one player vacancy. Then equal teams are distributed by blind drawing to each coach.

Then the coaches' sons are added to the teams they drew. If any coaches have unusually strong or weak sons, the league will need to trade one good player from the team with the strong coach's son to the team with the weak coach's son. This should be a mere mathematical exercise based on the original quality ratings.

Pre-draft coaching duos and trios

One of the most popular ways to cheat in the draft is for two fathers of two excellent players to pair off as a manager-and-coach team before the draft. Sometimes there are even **three** fathers of excellent players band-

28

There should only be one manager for each team. Those managers must **not** be allowed to pair up with a coach before the draft. To allow that is to allow them to circumvent the draft. Since there are only 13 players on the typical team, two players represents a full 2 / 13 = 15% of the team. Three players would be 3/13 = 23% of the team. One is 7.7%.

It is obviously wrong to have a league in which some teams get 92.3% of their players in a blind draft, some get 85%, and some get 77%. Almost certainly in such a league, one of the 77% teams will win the championship.

At the above-mentioned flag-football league, they initially announced that no father pairs would be allowed. But on draft night, they allowed several, in spite of the strenuous protests of the other coaches who had not allied themselves with the father of an excellent player. One team had no first- or second-round draft picks because both coaches' sons were excellent players. There were only eleven players on each team in that league (nine-man football) so two players represented 2/11 = 18% of the team.

My records of that league do not indicate which team had an assistant who was the father of their second-round draft choice. There were four teams where the head coach was father of the first-round draft pick.

One of the teams where the head coach was father of the first-round pick beat my team by three points. Another father-first-round combo beat my team by one point in the "Rose Bowl" when my first-round draft pick stayed home sick. We upset another father-first-round team 24-7 in the playoffs. The other father-first-round team lost to us in a close pre-season game, but ended up playing in the "Super Bowl," the top game in our league. So you can see the competitive power of getting top players through the coach's-son back door.

Team size

In our flag-football league, every team had eleven players. They deliberately picked a total number of teams to make it work out that way. But in baseball drafts in which I have participated, there were always two different sizes of teams.

Which size team is best involves two issues:

• average ability
• danger of forfeit

If **ability** were the only criteria, you would want to have a **smaller** team. That's because the last-round draft picks are almost certainly weaker than your average player so by choosing them, you weaken your team.

I made that mistake in 1990. At the end of the draft, we were told we could have one more player. The experienced coaches passed. I took a kid. He was weak, as you would expect of a leftover player, and made us a weaker team.

On the other hand, if league rules say you forfeit when you have fewer than nine players, you may not want to risk cutting it too close on number of players on your team. This is especially a problem at the age-13-and-older levels. Teenaged players usually have lousy attendance records.

Siblings

Most leagues have rules that permit parents of siblings to have them on the same team. In 1990, I felt we stole a march on our opposing coaches by handling a sibling situation better than anyone else. One brother was relatively strong. The other, younger brother was relatively weak. I had previously coached the older brother in football.

If you picked one, you had to pick the other. The older brother alone would have been about a third-round pick; the younger brother, about a ninth round pick.

Like all the other coaches, we passed on the older brother when his normal round came up. But then all the other coaches simply forgot about the brothers. In fact, so did I, through the tenth round. Then I realized I could not only get a ninth-round pick, the younger brother, for the price of an eleventh-round pick, I was also getting a third-round pick for the price of a twelfth-round pick!

I used my eleventh-round pick for the older brother and was immediately informed that I had to take the younger brother as well. "I know" I smiled. I was lucky I didn't lose them. In fact, when you have a brother pair of unequal ability, you should draft them at a level or two above the weaker brother's natural draft round. In this case, I should have drafted the older brother in the eighth round. That would be a bargain for him and I would then have to use my ninth-round pick for the younger brother, which would be fine.

In fact, I should have taken the younger brother with my **last** pick, not the next one after I picked the older brother.

Unknown players

Here's another mistake I made, although I did not realize it until too late. In the typical draft, there are unknown players. You might hear an announcement like, "I have two players to add to your list. Sean Smith and Jeff Brown. Sean just moved to the area and missed the tryout. Jeff has lived here, but has not previously played baseball and was sick the day of the tryout."

The coaches then clamor for information about the kids. Generally, other than height, weight, and age, none is forthcoming.

We had a totally unknown kid in our 1998 flag-football draft. I should have drafted him in one of the last three rounds. Why? If you know nothing about him, chances are he is **average**. Since you know the kids in the last several rounds of the draft are below average, you probably will be better off picking the unknown kid.

The unknown kid may be good, bad, or average. The chances of his being the worst kid in the league are about one in 150, whereas the chances of the known kid you have rated as the worst in the league actually being the worst in the league are about 149 in 150. Yet in my experience, all the coaches treat the **unknown** kid as if he were the **worst** kid in the league. Take the unknown kids when you get past the middle rounds of the draft.

Different-age quotas

You may be required to take a minimum number of players of a certain age. In 1990, in the San Ramon Valley Little League, I was a nine-ten minors coach. That age group overlapped with the majors which included ages ten-twelve and the farm league which was for eight- and nine-year olds.

The majors got first pick. But they only took about two ten-year olds per team. Nine-ten minors coaches were forced to take **all** the remaining **ten**-year olds, but got first crack at the **nine**-year olds. You were only allowed to have two nine-year olds on each nine-ten minors team. Nine-year olds who were not picked by the nine-ten minors coaches stayed in farm.

This meant that the average nine-year old in nine-ten minors was a better athlete relative to his peers than the average ten-year old in that league. The previous year, my son was drafted into nine-ten minors as an eight-year old ("league age" nine). He ended up with the second-highest batting average on that team, behind the coach's ten-year-old son. Slightly behind him in batting average was the only other nine-year old on the team and the son of a former Major League pro player. (Note, I think batting average is a dumb stat. But I was not a named coach on that team. The coaches who were in charge of that team published batting averages.)

Because of the very different average abilities of the nine- and ten-year olds in nine-ten minors, many coaches thought you should have a different drafting strategy for each age.

There were 145 ten-year olds left after the majors draft and we had 14 teams in nine-ten minors. That meant five nine-ten minors teams would have eleven ten-year olds and nine would have ten ten-year olds.

The total number of players on each team was to be 13 to the total number of kids in the league would be 13 x 14 = 182 meaning 182 -145 = 37 nine-year olds were allowed. That meant nine teams would have three nine-year olds and five would have two.

I guess the basic theory as to why you would have different drafting strategies for each age was that you did not want to end up as one of the teams with eleven ten-year olds and two nine-year olds. But it seems to me that it depends on the particular kids. I ignored the ages of the kids and just took the best kid available at the time my turn came up.

My first and second round picks were ten-year olds. By league rule, the coaches' sons were third- and fourth-round picks. My fifth- and sixth-round picks were nine-year olds. The rest were ten-year olds.

Coaches' sons shenanigans

The policy of automatically making the coaches' sons third- and fourth-round draft picks creates an opportunity for shenanigans. Under that system, it would be smart for a manager to recruit the father of a first-round draft pick for his coach. In fact, he could try to recruit the father of the top-rated kid in the whole draft. That, if successful, would enable him to circumvent the draft completely regarding its best prospect and to get that first-round player for the price of a fourth-round draft pick. If both coaches' sons on a team were first-round picks, joining together would, in effect, give that team **three** first-round picks.

That's another reason why league officials should ban the formation of pre-draft coaching pairs. League officials should respond to requests for pre-draft coaching pairs with something like, "Mr. Manager, if you are so hot to coach with Joe, use your first-round draft pick to choose his son."

I have also seen some managers try to get even a **third** coach's son player by selling the boy's father on the idea. Then they bring the father to the draft night and as soon as his son gets picked by the "wrong" manager, the father protests saying his son has his heart set on playing on so-and-so's team because he is friends with one of the coaches' sons already assigned to that team. (In fact, the star player probably has a friend on **every** team in the league.)

To their credit, the managers against whom that trick was tried rejected it out of hand making the son of the protesting father their first-round pick regardless of the protest. But I suspect that many youth coaches around the country fall for it.

In 1990, my team whose drafting I described above, made it to the semi-finals of the league championship tournament.

Ways coaches cheat the draft

There are many ways coaches cheat in the draft. Every draft I have ever seen involved either rules that give some teams unfair advantage, like the coaches'-sons-are-the-third-and-fourth-draft-pick rule, or they have good rules, but the guy in charge of the draft waives the rules for his cronies.

In a fair draft:

• all coaches have complete knowledge of each player
• all players are available to be drafted except the head coaches' sons

• the head coach must give up a draft pick that corresponds to his son's baseball skills to get his son

To cheat, coaches try to conceal information about good players from their fellow coaches by persuading them to skip the tryout or to sign up late. They also try to increase the number of coaches' sons that are exempt from the draft. Finally, they try to pay less than true value to get the coaches' sons on the team by using late round or middle round picks to get coaches' sons who would normally go in the early rounds.

Considering all the patting each other on the back about working "for the kids" that goes on at opening-day ceremonies and post-season awards banquets, all this cheating is a hypocrisy-a-thon. I complained about a lot of things, especially safety, in my league, but I said little or nothing about draft cheating. I figured I'd just draft my team from what was left after the cheaters got done arranging their various alliances and that we would do reasonably well and enjoy our season. And that's exactly what happened.

I wish somebody would reform the draft for the kids' sake, but the draft is primarily about winning the league championship, which is not that meaningful in youth baseball. If the championship were decided by a series of series like in Major League baseball, and there was enough time to rest your pitchers, it would be meaningful. But in youth baseball, the playoffs are generally single-game elimination tournaments with multiple games squeezed into just a few days, thereby preventing you from using your normal pitchers. It is also common for some players to leave town on family vacations during the playoffs.

As a general rule, the coaches that win local youth-baseball league championships did so because they cheated in the draft, had a bit of good luck, lost no one to summer vacations, and had better fourth- and fifth-string pitchers than their opponents.

What are you looking for in the draft?

What you are looking for in the draft depends on the level at which you coach and the particular rules for that level.

In the San Ramon Valley Little League, tee-ball players were assigned by neighborhood to facilitate car pools. Also, I was told when I was a tee-ball manager that my son could pick as many of his friends as he wanted. I agreed with both of those policies. We kept no score in tee ball, so who cares?

Actually, the answer in our case was that the administrator of the tee-ball league cared. He made himself a manager of one of the teams (usually the administrator of the league is a manager in **another** league) and he gave himself an **all-seven-year old team**. The rest of his had six- **and** seven-year olds. His explanation as to why he gave himself the only all-seven-year old team

was that he had "coached the kids last year and wanted to keep the team together." That, of course, was bull, not to mention illegal. Only majors teams are allowed to do that. He only coached about **half** of the kids the previous year. The rest had moved up to the next level. He replaced the previous year's seven-year olds with all new seven-year olds.

Although score was not kept, his team slaughtered all the other teams. And he went on to prominence in the "Home of Champions" organization.

At the eight-nine-year old level in our league, it was coach-pitched and no stealing was allowed. With that age and those rules, you need good **first basemen** and good hitters. Secondly, you need good fielders.

At the nine-ten-year old level, it's kid pitched and stealing is allowed. With those ages and rules, the most important player are the **catchers**. Second most important are the **pitchers**. Then come the hitters and fielders in that order.

The same is true of the eleven-twelve level.

At the **teenage** level, the most important thing is probably to avoid the attitude cases and attendance problems. Once you get to baseball issues, pitchers are more important than catchers at the teenage level. That's because stealing is done more against the pitcher than the catcher when the runner can take a pre-pitch lead. Also, the teenage pitchers can stay in the game longer.

One of the reasons pitchers are less important than catchers in the sub-teenage levels is that if you limit your pitchers to a safe pitch count, you have to remove them after two or three innings no matter how well they are doing. I said earlier that we were knocked out of the playoffs in 1992 by a sixth-string pitcher who threw a complete-game victory against us. I never allowed a pitcher of that age to pitch more than three innings.

At the teenage level, however, you can leave a pitcher in longer because their arms are stronger and there is less safety hazard to a four-to six inning pitching stint.

I am known as a baserunning coach, so you might think I would look for **speed**. I was not permitted to because our league generally did not test for speed. Plus, I have found that baserunning depends more on smarts and guts than speed. All things being equal, the faster player will have the most success at baserunning. But all things are **not** equal and the fastest player almost **never** is the best base runner.

In his book, *Off Base Confessions of a Thief*, the best pro base runner of all time, Rickey Henderson said:

> I don't claim to be the fastest runner in baseball. I don't think I've ever been the fastest. There have been other fast runners, such as Barry Bonds and Willie McGee. But guys like that are afraid to get thrown out.

My son used to get extremely angry at his faster

teammates who refused to try to steal when we needed them to.

Should you draft good base runners? Yeah, sure. But you probably will not be able to identify more than a handful. Most coaches not only do not emphasize base-running, they **prohibit** it by telling runners not to go unless they give the sign. Then they are reluctant to give the sign. The typical coach was a chicken base runner when he played and now he's a chicken base-running coach. Many also won't give the sign because they fear doing so too often will make them unpopular in their local youth baseball league.

Unfortunately for your efforts to identify good base runners to draft, almost every other coach essentially **forbids** aggressive baserunning, so it's very hard to tell what baserunning talent might exist in your league.

Also, good base runners are almost useless unless they can get on base, so you need a **combination** batter-base runner, not just a base runner.

Computer print out

After you evaluate the talent in your draft, you need to rank them. At my first draft, I expected that I would be the only one there with a computer print out. To my surprise, I was the only one there with an **8 1/2 x 11-inch** computer print out. Everyone else had a **14 x 11-inch** computer print out.

You should put each player's data into a spread sheet or database program. You need to put their scores on various skills in various columns. Then you need to weight each skill according to its importance at the level in question and come up with a composite score.

At the **professional** level, they treat pitchers and position players as two totally separate kinds of player. They also treat catchers differently from outfielders and first basemen and they treat the second baseman, shortstop, and third baseman differently from other position players.

But at the **youth** level, the best pitchers or catchers or first basemen are generally the best at everything else, too. So you can draft just for those skills and you will probably come out OK. You cannot have too many good pitchers, especially in the playoffs.

Just pick the next one on the list

One of my pet peeves about draft night is how long it takes. If every coach did it like I do we would be out of there in twenty minutes. Instead, it always takes several hours.

Just rank the darned kids then pick the highest-ranking one available when it's your turn. There is nothing to discuss and nothing to think about.

At our 1990 draft, there was a three-minute time limit on each pick. I could have met a three-**second** limit, except for not hearing who had previously been taken in some cases. All the thinking and discussing should be done **before** you generated your computer ranking and it should be incorporated into that ranking. The night of the draft, you just cross off those who have been taken and pick the highest-ranking un-crossed-off kid on your print out when it's your turn. In fact, if you could trust the people in charge and had the computer expertise, the best way to conduct the draft would be to turn in your ranking and let the computer conduct the draft. The computer would assign the draft order by random numbers, then assign the highest-ranking unclaimed player to your team every time it was your turn.

The national headquarters of the various youth baseball leagues could provide this service by Internet. They would have both the expertise and integrity required. Plus they could enforce nationwide rules about no more than one coach-son pair per team, players who missed the tryout could be assigned randomly, and so forth.

The entire draft would take about two seconds, at which time the computer would print out or display team rosters. As a check on cheating, it should also print out or display on a Web page every coach's entire-draft ranking so any suspicious coach could follow the draft on paper to see if the rankings were all followed correctly.

I suspect that I have overlooked some methods of cheating in youth baseball drafts. I would appreciate it if readers who know of any I have missed would contact me and tell me about them. I will post them at my Web site and incorporate them into future editions of this book.

4 Practice organization

The key question for a coach is on what should he spend his precious practice time. Some things, like **safety** and **rules**, are required. For everything else, the time should be spent on that which most helps the team play better.

There are two factors:

- **importance** of the skill in question
- **coachability** of the skill in question

Is hitting important? You bet. Should you therefore spend almost half your time on it? Nope. I tried that. It did not work. Why not? Hitting is not very coachable. It's important, but that does not mean that time spent practicing it will pay dividends in your games.

Delayed steals, on the other hand, are highly coachable. You can spend ten minutes on them in one practice and your players will execute successful delayed steals starting with the very next game. Is delayed stealing very important? Sadly, no. But it offers a combination of importance and coachability which is sufficient that it makes sense for you to spend ten minutes of your total 40 hours on the delayed steal.

Your kids will clearly be better off. They will benefit from having learned a specific new thing. They will enjoy the success of applying that lesson in games. And your team may win a game or two because of your delayed-steal skills.

Infield-fly-rule play

I once taught my players a play that takes advantage of the opponent's lack of understanding of the infield-fly rule. Was it coachable? Yep. One ten minute-session and they have it.

Was it important? Absolutely **not**. I taught that play for two or three years. We **never** got to use it. **Never**. If you **never** use it, it is not important enough to be in your practice schedule.

(I must add that my hitting-mechanics mentor, Oscar Miller, told me he once won a Little League cham-

pionship with that play. He said the opposing coach was so mad he challenged Oscar to a fight after the game.)

(The play is that you call for a pop then deliberately let it drop untouched to the ground. It will probably have a spin that makes it kick toward the sideline so my players were taught to get between the foul line and the ball. After it hits the ground, we would field it and throw to the base in front of the lead runner. Since there is no force, each runner needs to be **tagged**.

The batter is already out on the infield-fly rule. But the runners typically do not **know** the infield-fly rule, so they take off like mad men when they see the ball hit the ground.

They are allowed to advance on an infield-fly. It's **not** a **dead** ball as many think. But they are liable to be put out if they try to advance. They are also liable to be put out if they do not tag up on a caught infield fly. If you do this play correctly, you should get an easy double or triple play. That's why they **have** the infield fly rule—to eliminate the runners' need to tag up and advance if the ball is not caught in the air.)

Standardized, but idiotic

Practice organization in youth baseball is downright idiotic. What's worse, it's standardized. Normally, only the idiots would have idiotic practices. But in youth baseball, almost everyone has the same practice and the one they chose as their model was the idiotic one.

'Hit infield'

After playing catch to warm up, almost everybody starts by hitting infield. First they "get one," then they "get two." Infield is ended with some ritual involving each infielder charging a bunt and throwing to first or third. Then they hit the ball to the outfielders and give each one an opportunity catch a couple of fly balls, a grounder, and to throw to second, third, and home.

Batting practice

Phase two of the standard baseball practice is batting practice. Each player takes a turn at the plate hitting slow pitches thrown by a coach or low-level pitcher while everyone else stands around out in the field in groups of two or three chatting.

Productive?

Is this the most productive use of a youth baseball team's practice time? You gotta be kidding.

Don't hit infield, throw it

First, off, you should not **hit** infield, You should **throw** it. There are two problems with hitting infield. 1. It's hard to be accurate. 2. It's hard to impart the correct speed.

If you **hit** infield, time will be wasted when the ball

does not go where you want it to. Sometimes coaches miss the ball entirely. Sometimes they pop it up. Sometimes they hit to too far to one side. In the course of the typical session of hitting infield, the coach who is doing the hitting will frequently misfire, thereby wasting five to twenty seconds per misfire.

Other times, the coach hits the ball accurately, but softer or harder that he intended. That either wastes a repetition or endangers the child.

I stopped hitting infield and started throwing it for two reasons. 1. I read in a coaching book that it was more efficient to throw it rather than hit it. 2. I hit the ball too hard by accident once. The intended target expected it, but not that fast. It hit him in the chest injuring him slightly. Remember a ball hitting a child in the chest can kill him.

With most of what I advocate in this book, I was the only coach in the San Ramon Valley Little League who did it that way. But there was at least one other coach in our league who **threw** infield rather than hit it, and he did not get the idea from me.

Showing off

I believe youth baseball coaches hit infield rather than throw it partly because they don't know any better and partly because they like showing off their athletic prowess. Of course, it doesn't hurt that any spastic can hit fungoes with a little practice.

'What about the spin?'

Coaches who hit infield and outfield, and who want to continue doing so, will protest that the ball behaves differently when it is **hit** than when it is **thrown** and the players need to practice fielding **hit** balls more than they need to practice fielding thrown balls.

Actually, that is really a question for a physics professor or an engineer. Fortunately, for anyone who really wants the true answer to such questions, a physics professor and two engineers have written baseball books. One is called *Keep Your Eye on the Ball* by engineers Robert Watts and Terry Bahill. The other is *The Physics of Baseball* by Yale physics Professor Robert K. Adair.

RPM's and angles

Watts and Bahill say that a Major League fastball has a spin rate of about 1600 revolutions per minute and a curveball has about 1900 rpm. A bat hitting the ball more than about .3 inches above or below the center of the ball raises the spin rate up to as much as 7900 rpm.

But, of course, the farther above or below center the hit is, the greater the angle at which the ball leaves the bat either up or down. When a coach hits infield, he generally hits just a little bit below a line-drive trajectory. That changes the rpm of the ball relatively little.

Fungoed ball is a poor knuckleball

However, when you hit infield, the ball you hit is essentially a **knuckleball** with almost no spin. You just toss it up like a tennis serve. Furthermore, because it is so close, easy to see, and easy to hit, the fungoed ball is hit dead on. That imparts little spin.

The ball leaving the bat of a coach who is hitting infield has very little spin on it. But the ball hit by a batter in a game has 2000 to 8000 rpm because of the spin imparted by the pitcher and the spin imparted by the batter hitting it a little bit high or low.

In other words, the spin on a **thrown** ball is more like a game-batted ball than the spin on a **fungoed** ball is like a game-batted ball.

Major League manager Gene Mauch refused to hit fungoes to his infielders because he said they did not spin the same as a batted ball.

Ground imparts its own spin

Once the ball hits the ground, the contact is **always** off center. In other words, the effect of the ball hitting the ground is similar to the effect of the bat hitting the very bottom of a pitch. Except in the case of a relatively slow moving ball with extraordinary spin on it, a baseball will come out of its first contact with the ground with strong topspin on it.

In the normal case, how it came **in**to the ground spinwise matters little once it has been hit dead on the bottom by planet earth. Once the ball has hit the ground, it matters little whether it came from a bat or from a throw. In other words, there is no need to **hit** infield. Throwing gives a quite adequate spin to the ball and is better because of the greater control it gives the coach regarding location and velocity.

That's probably more than you wanted to know about ball spin, but it is the main objection I hear to throwing infield, and my position is controversial, so I had to give you the whole nine yards.

Timeline of a typical youth baseball practice

Here, down to the second, is the way things go during the "hit infield" phase of a typical youth baseball practice.

1:00:00 "Get one" to third baseman
1:00:05 Coach swings and misses ball
1:00:10 "Get one" to third baseman
1:00:15 Third baseman catches grounder and throws to first
1:00:20 First baseman muffs short hop, ball bounces into adjacent soccer field
1:01:00 "Again" to third baseman
1:01:05 Third baseman catches ball and throws to first

1:01:10 First baseman catches ball throws to catcher standing near coach

1:01:15 Catcher muffs short hop, ball goes around back stop where assistant coach picks it up and throws to catcher

1:01:25 "Get one" to shortstop is accidental line drive caught in the air

1:01:30 "Throw it home"

1:10:35 Short stop throws the ball home

1:01:40 "Again" to shortstop

1:01:45 Shortstop muffs grounder, makes lazy throw to first after retrieving it

1:01:55 First baseman throws home

1:02:00 "Again" to shortstop

1:02:05 Inaccurate hit to third baseman

1:02:10 Third baseman lets unexpected ball go through legs to left field

1:02:20 Left fielder throws ball to third

1:02:30 Third baseman catches ball and throws home

1:02:35 Catcher catches ball and tosses to coach

1:02:40 "Get one" to shortstop

1:02:45 Short stop catches ball and throws to first

1:02:50 First baseman catches throw and throws home

1:02:55 Catcher has hands full of ball and is unable to catch throw, throw rattles around backstop to first-base dugout area

1:03:05 Player on bench retrieves ball and throws to catcher

You get the idea. Thus far, three minutes of infield have transpired. During that time, the third baseman has had three chances to field a ground ball and two chances to throw to first. The shortstop has had two chances to field a ground ball and one chance to field a line drive and two chances to throw to first.

Just throw it against a wall

This is a colossal waste of time. Major League baseball has a training video tape where they recommend a drill in which the first player in a line of players throws the ball against a wall and runs to the back of the line. The next player fields the grounder coming off the wall, throws it at the wall, and runs to the back of the line. And so on.

This creates about one chance to field and throw every three seconds. In a minute, there would have been twenty throws and catches per line. If you did it for just ten minutes with five-man lines, there would be a total of 200 throws and catches—40 for each player.

The Major League video features a high school coach who says he uses this drill and has had excellent results.

Back up

When you hit or throw a grounder to a player, it often gets through. If there is no wall or backup player,

retrieving the ball wastes enormous amounts of time. In football drills, we often make the receiver **hand** the ball to the coach for the next repetition because if he **tosses** it, many will end up on the ground which slows down the drill. In baseball practice, you need to have a similar concern about balls that get past a fielder.

You can solve the problem best by having a wall behind the fielder. In other words, it may be better to do your infield practice where the fielder has his back to a wall than on the actual field. The second-best solution is to station another fielder behind the first fielder, but that is less efficient.

Practicing the throw to first

If you feel you need to practice the throw to first, you will have to use the actual field, or pace off an artificial one where you have a wall backstop. Again, you need to back up the throw to first with a fence or wall or screen or additional player or much time will be wasted chasing balls that get by the first baseman.

Even the throw-the-ball-against-the-wall drill needs provisions for back up. Sometimes, the players do not throw straight ahead, but throw at an angle and the ball bounces off to the side. The best place to do the ball-against-the-wall drill would be in a four-sided area like a squash court. The more walls the better for preventing wasting time chasing balls that bounce far away.

Bucket of balls

If you wanted to really give an infielder a good workout, you would take a bucket of balls and an empty bucket out to a field. Station an infielder and his backup at the position and a first baseman and his back up at first. The coach takes the bucket of balls and the first baseman takes the empty bucket.

The coach throws a grounder to, say, the shortstop. He catches it and throws to first. The first baseman catches the ball and drops it in the empty bucket behind him. If the ball thrown by the coach gets by the shortstop, his backup prevents it from going far. Same is true at first.

The coach throws one ball after another waiting only until the two fielders are ready. He varies his throws to the left and right of the shortstop. He throws straight at him, line drives, pop-ups, dribblers, hard shots, everything. He especially focuses on the player's weakness, for example, a back-hand catch.

Rotate

When the coach's bucket is empty, the first baseman takes the full bucket to the coach and brings the empty bucket back to first where he now becomes the backup first baseman. The shortstop and back-up shortstop trade places.

Using the bucket-of-balls format, you can give the two fielders about one rep every six seconds. The number of balls in the bucket should be the number at which the fielder starts to get fatigued. For added accuracy and speed, the coach can move closer to the fielder. He need not stay at home plate.

I am not so much trying to get you to do the ball-against-the-wall or bucket-of-balls drill as I am trying to get you think about such issues as the number of repetitions per minute and the need to avoid time-wasting problems like retrieving errant balls.

I like the bucket-of-balls drill better as a friend-or-relative outside-of-practice drill or as a position-clinic drill rather than as a drill to be done during team practice.

Five or ten minutes per drill max

You must limit the duration of drills to five or ten minutes maximum. If you spend longer on one drill, the kids will get bored and start to misbehave.

Batting practice

Batting practice generally means a coach takes the mound and throws pitches to a batter. There may or may not be a catcher. (If I ever did batting practice, I would have a catcher and he would alternate throwing to second and third after every caught pitch.)

Fielders who are not on deck man their positions. In the outfield, they tend to stand around in groups of two or three chatting.

The tempo is somnolent. Outfielders loaf after balls. Infielders let the difficult ones go by without a try. People joke around.

The pitches are **slow**, thereby screwing up the batters' timing *vis a vis* game-speed pitches.

Pitchers' pitches and balls

The pitches are also not often in the strike zone. Pitch selection is the most important thing you can do to help your players hit better, but the typical youth baseball coach gets impatient with his hitters in batting practice and starts whining about them waiting for a good pitch. "C'mon! We haven't got all day!"

So the batter, if he had the extremely desirable habit of waiting for a good pitch, now abandons that habit and gets, instead, into the habit of swinging at garbage, because that is mostly what he sees in batting practice. Batting practice, therefore, generally violates the "First, do no harm" rule.

I won't do another timeline for the usual batting practice. Having seen what I did in the hit-infield timeline and having been to a zillion batting practices like I just described, you know the how little gets accomplished in batting practice. Batting practice is an extremely inefficient exercise where your players practice swinging at slow, poorly-located pitches and loafing in the field. Mostly they stand around doing nothing.

I never do batting practice

I never do batting practice. Never all season. How do my teams hit? I haven't looked at batting averages since the 1991 season when I discovered my emphasis on batting mechanics was hurting my team. I focus on on-base percentage and Bill James Runs Created.

Eyeballing it, I suspect that our batting averages were average for the league or a little bit above average. We generally had the highest on-base percentage and highest number of walks, so our batting-average-calculation numbers would have the fewest at bats and outs per plate appearances in the league.

During the 1992 season, the very experienced administrator of our league watched one of our playoff games and said about my team, "I have never seen so many line drives hit by one team in one game." We never had batting practice that season.

Warm-up

Throwing arms need to be warmed up. But rather than just let kids pair up and play catch, you should have a thought-out routine. Here's a suggestion.

20 feet apart	3 throws
30	3
50	3
60	3
75	3
100	3

Of course, at the tee-ball level, this would be too much distance between players. Above that level, you should be able to do this with a minimum of errors. On average, each round trip of the ball ought to take about ten seconds. Having one side against a fence and coaches backing up the other side will save retrieving time. The whole warm-up should take two and a half minutes.

Conditioning

Don't do conditioning. I have never seen it matter in a youth baseball game. At the teenage level, pitchers and catchers need to be in decent shape to perform their jobs for extended periods, but you probably should not use team practice time for that. They have to condition on their own or you should proctor a separate conditioning period when the rest of the team is not present.

Conditioning is one of those things middle-age men impose on children, not because the children need it, but because the middle-age men need it. Of course, the middle-age men are not doing the conditioning. So the whole rationale for conditioning youth baseball players is bizarre.

This is a self-published book. One of the advantages of a self-published book is that I say what I believe. If I had a major publisher, they would have a committee of "experts" review the book and they would take out the part where I say forget about conditioning, because it's not politically correct.

On **hot days**, keep the kids in the shade and see that they get plenty of water. That's not conditioning, but if you fail to do it, they will appear to be tired in the game. They are not tired, they are dehydrated and feeling the early effects of heat stroke, which can kill.

Curriculum

You need a different curriculum for the various levels of baseball.

Tee ball. Tee ball players mainly need to learn the basic rules, like that you run to first after you hit the ball, and basic skills like throwing and catching. Give tee ballers practice:

1. catching grounders and flies
2. throwing
3. run through first
4. run to second and third
5. run through home
6. sliding
7. batting (preferably left-handed)
8. fielding assignment when ball not hit to you (cover a base or back up)
9. caught fly is out whether fair or foul
10. must tag up on fly
11. force out
12. tag out
13. run on anything with two outs
14. run out all hits

If you are a rookie tee-ball coach, this list probably seems too short to you. If you are an experienced tee-ball coach, you probably recognize that it is actually very ambitious.

By the end of the season, the typical tee-ball coach has **not** achieved numbers 3, 4, 6, 8, 10, or 13 and his players are shaky on the rest. If, however, you are competent and run efficient practices, you can achieve all thirteen items on this list.

8-9-year olds. At the 8- and 9-year old level, they start to keep score. Pitching is done by machine or coach. The players need to know the things listed on the above tee-ball curriculum, but they already know most of them. At the 8-9 year-old level, you should add:

15. pitcher-cover-first play
16. if bunting is allowed, how to bunt
17. if bunting is allowed, how to field a bunt
18. how to pick up a stopped ball
19. waiting for a good pitch to hit
20. rounding a base when running
21. one-throw double play (force or tag then throw to first)

22. one-throw double play (catch fly then throw to base of runner who did not tag up)
23. defender avoiding obstruction on extra-base hit
24. run-down (pickle) technique
25. often-misunderstood rules (I'll explain later)
26. double-steal play
27. delayed steal
28. steal second on a walk
29. pop-up and go to next base slide

Again, this is an ambitious list, but doable if you do not run inefficient practices where you hit infield and take batting practice. Note some of the things that are **not** mentioned:

- two-throw double plays
- pitching
- batting mechanics
- fielding mechanics

10-12-year olds. Ten-to-twelve-year olds are the best age group to coach. They are old enough to learn well and perform at a relatively high level, but not old enough to know "everything," like many teenagers. In most leagues, the 10-12 age group is also still running on 60-foot base paths and having to wait until the pitch gets to the plate to leave the base.

These guys already know much of the stuff on the tee-ball and farm lists. They need to learn new stuff and refine the stuff they already know. Plus you can teach them the following new things:

30. first-and-third-defense plays
31. take extra base on outfielder's throw to pitcher or wrong base
32. delayed-steal defense
33. defense against long secondary lead at third
34. runners-at-the-"other"-corners play
35. squeeze bunt
36. "day-o" play
37. catcher back up first when no runners
38. catcher block low pitches
39. defense against runner taking big secondary lead at second
40. pitcher-cover-home-on-passed-ball play
41. appeal half swing to base ump
42. appeal for not tagging on fly or not touching base
43. runners going on 2-out, 3-2-count, forced situation
44. runners going on 2-out, 2-strike, forced-situation swing
45. try to draw pick-off throw on secondary lead at all three bases
46. advance to next base on infielder's throw to first
47. score from third on infield ground ball
48. make sure you are out before leaving base after close play

49. base runners advance two bases on a single
50. relay technique
51. base-coaching signals
52. pitching from stretch
53. fastball grip
54. changeup
55. outfield technique for different situations

Again, notice what is **not** in this list—things like batting mechanics, pitching mechanics, hitting the cut man, the two-throw double play. That stuff is either too advanced or too time-consuming for a youth-baseball season.

All-star teams have more time

Note that I am talking about a **regular** youth baseball team. All-star teams practice more often like high school teams. With more practices, you could probably accomplish a little on mechanics of batting, pitching, and fielding. But in the standard youth baseball format, three practices a week in pre-season and one practice a week during the season, you must not waste time and screw kids up messing with their mechanics.

13-15 year olds. This level is marked by significant rules changes like 90-foot base paths, ability to take a pre-pitch lead, and occasional enforcement of the balk rule.

It is also an age where absenteeism and back talk becomes a problem if your team has fewer than 18 kids and is not prestigious.

'Background check'

Here is the additional curriculum for the 13-15 age group:

56. balk rule
57. how to take a primary lead at each base in different situations
58. how to dive back to base
59. pitcher pick-off and fake pick-off moves
60. how to hold a runner on base
61. how to take a secondary lead
62. cut off throw from outfield
63. two-strike hitting
64. how to draw a balk while on base
65. take advantage of pitcher who uses full-windup with runners on base
66. batter help runner at first regarding pick-off move by left-handed pitcher
67. steal home on the pitch
68. home-plate base coaching by on-deck batter
69. dropped-third-strike offense and defense
70. outfield throw two bases ahead of lead runner on base hit
71. curveball

16-18 year olds. I would not add anything new for this age level. Rather I would just work on execution. Again, I would be concerned about absenteeism, but back talk is less of a problem at this age level because the attitude cases have generally dropped out of baseball by this age. Sixteen- to eighteen-year olds are more interested in playing the game than in tormenting adults.

The above curriculum lists are not meant to be comprehensive. But they are almost complete. Most coaches would want to add a thing or two and subtract a thing or two depending upon what they emphasize. But it is important that you recognize what is possible at each level.

The typical coach spends far too much time hitting infield, taking batting practice, and criticizing his players' mechanics. As a result, his practices are almost totally a waste of time as measured by how much new stuff the kids learn about baseball and as measured by the score books.

For example, if you teach your players the pitcher-cover-first play, your team will probably be the only one in your league whose score books contain the notation "3-1" several times during the season. (First baseman threw the ball to the pitcher for the out.)

But if you spend all your practice time on hitting infield and batting, without taking time to run this particular play, your fielders will just look stupid when the ball is hit to the first baseman and he is too far away from the base to beat the batter to it. The same is true of all the other unusual things on my curriculum list.

Talk is not enough

Most coaches will say they taught most of the things on my list. But if you video taped all their practices and games you would almost certainly find that their way of coaching most of the skills was simply to say, "Hey, pitcher, you should have covered first on that play," after the play was over.

That does not get the job done. Most skills require explanation, demonstration, and at least a few repetitions by the players. There is hardly anything that they will get just from your verbal statement of it. That, in turn, means you cannot waste most of your practice hitting infield and batting.

Position clinics

As I explain in the parent-meeting chapter, I run a half-hour position clinic after each one-and-a-half-hour practice. These were quite popular with the players and many of the parents. Some players would attend every single one.

I will give you the detailed curriculum for each position clinic in the chapter for each position. My main point here is that position clinics, not team practice, are the time to teach the fine points of playing each position. After a particular position clinic has been held, you can use team practice to yell out reminders of technique that was taught in that position clinic when you see a position player make a mental error.

Former Major Leaguer Rob Andrews runs kids baseball camps. He did something similar to my position clinics. He held what he called "pre-practice" and "post-practice." These were *ad hoc* sessions to correct individual problems he saw. He would hand the kids he wanted to come early a slip of paper for their parents to tell them to bring their kid early or pick him up later. I prefer my post-practice-position-clinic approach, although I might use the pre-practice idea on an *ad hoc* basis to fix problems that cropped up.

Initial evaluation

Over the course of a youth season, you move from emphasis on evaluation to emphasis on execution. But there is no point on emphasizing defensive execution until you figure out who goes where.

Job one, therefore, is to evaluate your players. I do the following on the first day of practice:

- eye test (20/20 and dominance)
- running speed test (first base to second)
- infielding audition
- third baseman (catch grounder, throw to first)
- shortstop (same)
- second baseman (same)
- first baseman (catch throws to first)
- catcher (block low pitches, throw to second)
- practice game (keep score book)

Intrasquad game

The practice game is an intrasquad game with three teams of four players each. Players who are not batting or running bases, remain in the field. If the batting team has so many runners that you can not fill all field positions, coaches play those positions.

Score-book data from the practice game, along with tryout and infield audition data, start to tell you who plays what position on defense. Batting and base running performance start to tell you what your batting order should be. Pitching success start to tell you what your pitching rotation should be.

I also like to schedule a couple or three practice games with **other teams** during the pre-season to test my various pitching candidates and to collect further data on all other aspects of the team.

I make assignments of positions after the infielding audition, but I tell the players that they are not set in stone. As the season goes on, I typically discover that I have made a mistake or three and change the appropriate position assignments.

It is important to make the position assignments as early as possible so the players can begin learning their position. Some players tell me they have always played such and such position or that they want to "try out" for a certain position. I am mildly interested in their previous positions. But I make my own judgment.

For example, it may be that they belonged at catcher on their last team because of who else was on that team, or not on that team, but they do **not** belong at catcher on **this** team because I have more catching talent. Or it may be that they have always played shortstop in spite of lack of talent because their father was a coach, which nonsense will come to a screeching halt on my team.

To the players who want to "try out" for a certain position, I say, "Everybody on this team tries out for **every** position. If you prefer a position other than the one to which you are assigned, I recommend that you take the position clinic for that position and do extra practice to get better at that position with your dad or brother or friend at home. But after a couple of weeks, I want you to focus on becoming the best you can be at your **assigned** position and try to make any switch to the other in the off-season."

'One-step'

When my oldest son was at the tee-ball level, he and I invented what I think is the quintessential tee-ball drill. We call it "one-step." He and I would get our gloves and a ball and stand about five feet apart and play easy catch. Whenever he **caught** the ball, he would move one step **away** from me. That would make the next catch slightly more difficult.

If he **missed** the ball, he would move one-step **closer** to me. The object was to see how far away he could get.

To teach him to catch grounders, I would just roll the ball to him on our concrete driveway at first. Later I would toss him bouncers.

Silent teaching

I strongly recommend that you refrain from giving the kids **verbal** instruction. For example, most coaches tell fielders to put their glove on the ground. Is that correct? Yeah, it's correct, but kids learn better without words.

One silent approach is the monkey-see-monkey-do method. The grown-up playing catch with the kid should model the technique he wants. For example, throw each other grounders. The adult concentrates on using correct technique. If the child uses improper technique, the adult can gently suggest from time to time that the child "Do it like I do."

Another good silent technique is to **force** the child to do it right by the way you set up the drill. For example, if you want the child to put his glove all the way on the ground to field a grounder, do the drill on smooth pavement and **roll** each ball to him. In that case, the child will figure out for himself, always the best way to learn, that he must put his glove on the ground. You can roll him so many balls that putting the glove on the ground becomes instinctive.

Some kids like to hold their glove up, then flip it down with a flourish just before the ball arrives. Invariably, they are often late and the ball goes between their legs. To stop that, roll the ball **faster** and station the kid where there is no backstop.

After each ball goes between his legs, he has to run after it. Soon he will figure out that he better get the glove down faster or he is going to be running his butt off. Again, you have taught correct technique without saying a word and without trying to make him translate verbal instructions in his conscious mind every time a ground ball comes toward him.

If you want him to hold a bat so the door-knocking knuckles of both hands are lined up (the correct grip), don't **tell** him that. Just go to a hardware store and buy an **axe handle**. Stop at a sporting goods or toy store and buy a **poly ball** (light-weight, hollow plastic ball with round holes in it) or whiffle ball.

Then conduct a soft-toss hitting drill (you lob balls in front of the player and he hits them into a fence) using the axe handle instead of a bat. The oval shape of the axe handle will force the child's hands into the right alignment without your having to say a word. The thinness of the bat head will force the child to concentrate like a standard training device called a Thunderstick, a one-inch diameter steel bat used to force batters to hit the ball in its sweet spot (middle). I wish bats with such oval-shaped handles were legal in youth baseball for the first three or four years of play.

Hit a basketball off a tee

Another neat silent coaching trick is to have kids hit basketballs, volleyballs, or soccer balls off a tee. Make the needed tee by putting an upside-down toilet plunger in a regular batting-tee stem. Without a word from you, the kids will use perfect batting mechanics. Their heads will be down. Their hands will be close to their bodies—the "tight, compact swing" you hear TV color men rave about . They'll pivot their upper body perfectly—all without a single word from a coach. Why?

Their brain recognizes that they must do all those things because of the **mass** of the ball being hit. When you use a regular baseball, their brain figures they can hit it any old way, which is correct, but not optimal. By having them hit a large ball, you force them to do it right. By the way, kids **love** this drill.

It may be that you could actually effect an improvement in batting mechanics with this drill during the brief course of a youth baseball season if you did it enough times.

Its great virtue is that it does **not** cause the problem that causes me to stay away from teaching batting mechanics the regular way: verbal correction and instruction.

With the basketball-off-a-tee drill, you are not saying a **word**. You are not saying or implying that his swing is "wrong" or screwed up or flawed in any way. You are not loading his brain with a ten-step hitting instruction that will mess up his mind in the batter's box in a game. Just tee the ball up and let him hit. About the only verbal thing you might want to say would be, "Hit the baseball the same way you hit the basketball."

Another silent technique-correcter which is well known is to put a coin on the ground on the glove side of a pitcher's stride foot. After each pitch, the pitcher is to pick up the coin. This is to teach him to bend his back low in his follow through.

To teach young players where to put their feet when they bat or throw, I bring chalk to practice and draw an outline of their feet after I position them correctly. Then, when they throw or bat, I remind them from time to time, "Put your feet in the footprints."

To teach them to run **through** first and home, put a cone or some other marker beyond the base and tell the to keep running until they get to **that** marker, not just to the base.

Watch what you model

At one San Ramon Valley Little League clinic, they told us not to **short-arm** the ball when throwing with kids. The reason was they said the kids were coming up to the majors level short-arming the ball themselves. Grown-ups were just throwing with their forearms and or wrists to avoid throwing too hard. But the kids they were playing catch with assumed that was the way **everyone** was supposed to throw.

'Unh!'

I can give you a more extreme example of that. When I first started to play catch with my oldest son, I was 40. I had been jogging daily, but I had not played baseball in over twenty years.

I noticed my son was grunting every time he threw me the ball. I asked why he was doing that. He said, "Because that's what **you** do." I was straining to get my 40-year-old body back into baseball shape, resulting in my involuntary grunts. He thought grunts must be part of throwing.

'Good job, Daddy!'

When we were toilet training one of my sons, we praised him profusely whenever he used the toilet, just like the books told us too. After my wife and I had been doing this for several weeks, he and I went to a public rest room. I strode up to the urinal and used it for its intended purpose, at which time my son said loudly and proudly to the amusement of all present, "Good job, Daddy! Good job!"

He wasn't trying to be funny. He was only two and a half. He just figured from the way my wife and I had been behaving about **his** use of the toilet that part of general etiquette was to profusely compliment **anyone** whenever they used the toilet.

So you must keep in mind when teaching children that they may learn more things than you intended. In youth baseball, this means you must set a good technique example in everything you do.

Defensive play assignments

When the ball is hit, each of your nine or ten defenders should go somewhere. In most teams, not only youth but also semi-pro, only two or three players move. One of the things my teams do, but almost no others do, is cover their base or back-up assignment on every play. Even my tee-ball teams did this.

I teach this with a tennis ball and an half-size field. I make the pitcher's mound second base and put gloves or some such on the ground half way between home and first and home and third. The gloves become first and third bases. The area between the pitcher's mound and the regular bases becomes the outfield. I then stand at the plate and throw easy grounders or pops to the various players. Usually, we have one or more coaches or players who move in slow motion acting as base runners.

Shrinking the field in half makes the drill more efficient. This is a **mental** exercise. All I am trying to do is get the players to recognize their responsibility on each play and move to the correct spot. In a game, they will have to go a greater distance and hustle faster. By using a tennis ball and shrinking the field in half, each rep only takes a few seconds. I often do this on an asphalt parking lot.

If you do this drill on a full-size field, it will take far longer to get each repetition in, and the players will get tired and bored.

For example, I might start with no runners and flip a bouncing ball to the third baseman. When he catches it, I yell "Freeze!" All nine or ten players plus the base runners must then freeze in place. I then go through a checklist to make sure everyone is in the right place.

1. Is first base covered?
2. Is second base covered?
3. Is third base covered?
4. Is home covered? (At the higher levels, the catcher would run down to back up first when there were no other runners. This is too much of a strain on sub-10-year old catchers.)
5. Is the player who is fielding the hit backed up? Is his most likely throwing target backed up?
6. Is the subsequent most likely throwing target backed up?
7. Is the pitcher where he is supposed to be?
8. Is everybody at the place where they belong?

On that play, a grounder to third with no runners on, the defensive alignment after the hit would be:

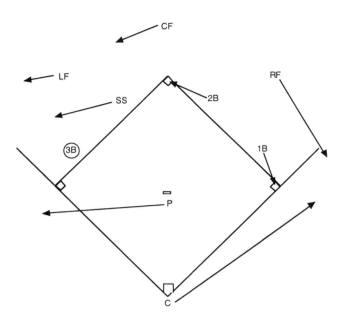

Here is a verbal description of where each player goes:

P	back up third base in case of subsequent throw
C	back up throw to first (10 or older only)
1B	cover first
2B	cover second
SS	back up 3B fielding hit
3B	field hit and throw to first
LF	Back up SS
CF	back up possible subsequent throw to second by player in the area of first
RF	back up 3B's throw to first

Backing up the play—catching the grounder and throwing the guy out at first—is fairly straightforward: you want both the hit and the throw backed up. But in this situation, that leaves two guys—the pitcher and center fielder—who cannot get in on the planned play. So they need to think, what if the best-laid plans go astray? In this case, that would mean the ball getting by the first baseman and the runner advancing beyond first base.

The center fielder cannot back up third or first—the original play—but he **can** back up a throw from the vicinity of first to **second**, and that's what he should do.

The pitcher cannot back up first or second bases in this situation, but he can back up **third**. When might that be needed. If the runner advances beyond second. That could happen if the throw really got away at first or if the throw to second also was not caught. So the pitcher must initially line up to back up a possible throw from the vicinity of first to third. For this drill, that would be where he should freeze. In an actual game, when it becomes apparent a throw from first to third won't happen, he should realign to back up a possible throw from the vicinity of second base to third.

In the situation described in the diagram, the typical youth baseball team (or even the typical semi-pro team) would cover first and second and the third baseman would field the hit, but everyone else would just stay where they started.

My teams will move to the positions shown because I have them do so in practice repeatedly, and because I do not rotate positions.

"Little League drill"

I dreamed this half-size field drill idea up myself. Years later I was amused to find it in John Witkin's book, *Maximizing Baseball Practice*. I do not think Witkin got it from me. It's just a case of great minds running in the same channels. Witkin was the head baseball coach at the University of Maine when he wrote the book.

Backing up

I was never a great fielder, but I am the best backer upper I ever saw. As you would expect, I emphasize backing up. It's something any kid can do regardless of ability. But there are a number of tricks to it.

You have to anticipate where to go and you have to stay back at least 15 feet behind the guy you are backing up. When I first teach backing up, my players all tend to back the guy up from eight to ten feet behind. That's too close. If the ball gets by the primary fielder, it will seem to explode up at the too-close backer up, like an unexpected short hop. When you are back 15 feet, you can see the ball coming and catch it.

The final thing about backing up is you usually have to really haul butt. For example, the right fielder is not in a good position to back up first an a throw from third. But if he breaks on the hit full speed to the area behind first, he can prevent a runner from advancing on a ball that gets past the first baseman.

My attitude was that I don't get many balls in the outfield so I will darned well **leave** the outfield every chance I get. As soon as the ball is hit somewhere other than my outfield area, we no longer need an outfielder. So I charge toward first or second (when I am playing right field) or back up the center fielder. That is the correct attitude and you should engender it in your outfielders.

Silent modeling

Once, at a public batting cage, I was waiting for a pro to finish using the cage I wanted to use. He had the telltale wooden bat with adhesive tape around the sweet spot. He also had the telltale habit of killing every pitch.

I was impressed by how he would flick the bat at pitches he did not like and foul them off. Then, to my amazement, without even thinking about it, I did that same flick, successfully, after I began hitting. I had learned it in the space of a minute or so just from watching him!

One year, the San Ramon Valley Little League held an all-day clinic taught by a couple of pro minor leaguers who used to be SRVLL players. They were both infielders. When they demonstrated infield technique, they were professionally smooth.

Later that day, my son and I were throwing grounders to each other. I found myself unconsciously imitating the pros I had seen earlier in the day. I would never be as good as they were. But just watching them briefly made me much better.

Demonstrate, don't explain

Professional tennis instructor W. Timothy Gallwey wrote a book called *The Inner Game of Tennis*. Gallwey discovered that his students learned better and faster if he just **demonstrated** the forehand, backhand, serve, and so forth. Previously, he gave the detailed **verbal** descriptions of the "correct" way to hit a forehand and so forth, just like the typical youth baseball coach.

So once again, I urge you to shut up and let the kids work it out for themselves. If you or another of your fellow coaches has a good swing or a good pitching motion or good fielding technique, show that to your players as often as possible so their unconscious brains can absorb it and mimic it.

If Little League coaches taught walking

We all have learned how to do complex things without any verbal instruction at all. We can speak our native language with no trace of an accent. We can walk. We can ride a bike.

We should all be grateful that youth baseball coaches do not teach walking. If they did, it would sound something like this.

Men, today we're going to learn to walk. Now walking is the hardest method of movement in nature. There are millions of animals—insects, mammals, lizards. They all walk on four or more legs. Humans are the only ones that walk upright on two legs.

In order to walk, you have to have your upper body going one way while your lower body is simultaneously going the other way. Timing is crucial. Your right hand much reach its forwardmost point at the exact same time as your left foot reaches the spot where your left heel hits the ground.

At the same moment, your right heel is at its rearmost point as is your left hand. Everybody got that?

Balance is also crucial. Your center of gravity must be between your legs and between your forwardmost body part and your rearmost body part. But, of course, in order to move forward, you must lean forward just a little so that your center of gravity is in front of where it was an instant ago. How far forward your center of gravity is depends on how fast you want to walk.

And we haven't even gotten into turns. In order to turn, you must pivot on the ball of the forward foot and lean your upper body slightly in the direction of the turn in order to get your center of gravity over your turnside foot. Again, the amount of the lean varies according to your speed.

The length of your step is about half your height. You swing your arms about nine inches to the front and six inches to the rear.

Imagine what the kids who were taught to walk by those instructions would look like. Actually, they would look like Little League batters who are trying to keep their head down while they "squash the bug" and stride six inches and pivot their hips and all that.

Pitching machine

A pitching machine would be a great asset in practice. I have rarely had one.

They can be used to give hitters confidence because they usually can be adjusted to throw the ball consistently right in the heart of the hitting zone, which is the main determinant of batting success. Although they can also give batters the bad habit of swinging at every pitch.

The safest pitching machine for hitting practice throws **poly balls**. They do not hurt when the hit although one in the eye at close range could probably cause an injury.

Outfielders need enormous amount of repetitions to get better. A pitching machine that could loft a fly or grounder accurately to the outfield would save much time. Hitting fungoes to outfielders is far less desirable because of their inaccuracy and wear and tear on the hands of the fungo hitter.

With right and left fielders, the fungoed ball engenders bad habits because fungoed balls travel in a straight line. Game balls hit to right and left field curve toward the sidelines. With a pitching machine, you can curve fly balls to the foul lines so right and left fielders can get used to playing the hook and slice.

Safe practice organization

You need to be careful when organizing practice that interaction between stations does not injure a player or coach. For example, If one group is throwing the ball and another is behind a target of the throws working on, say, sliding, a person at the sliding station might be hit by a ball that gets past a fielder. The injury could be worse than a normal hit-by-a-ball injury because the hittee would not be looking.

It is also crucial, if you allow kids to swing bats in practice, to make sure that no player or coach is walking near the bat swinger.

If you have ever been to a professional baseball game early, you have seen the standard pre-game practice. Batters take batting practice is a cage, fielders man their positions. Coaches hit fungoes to various fielders almost at the same time. Screens are set around the field to protect players and coaches from being hit by a ball that they do not see coming.

Pro pre-game practices are noteworthy for both their attention to safety and their attention to efficiency, although I would not recommend the pro format *per se*. It's still a little too inefficient for a youth baseball team, where you have far less talent and far less practice time. It's also a bit too dangerous in spite of the screens and such. Adult pros are safety conscious on practice field. But kids are far less so. So you have to keep them farther away from risks than the pros stay.

New stuff and every-practice stuff

My practices generally consist of two categories of segments: new stuff and old stuff.

For example, there will come a day when I introduce the delayed steal. I explain it verbally. I demonstrate it. Then I have each kid execute it while coaches or other players play the roles of the catcher and pitcher.

Because of the nature of the delayed steal—it's easy to learn—I probably will never do any delayed-steal practice the rest of the season.

Sliding is another matter. The first day, I explain it, demonstrate it, and have players do it (with their shoes off on cardboard). But sliding, although simple and within every player's grasp, regardless of talent, takes a lot of practice.

The natural inclination is to do it wrong. So I practice sliding every practice and every pre-game for almost the entire season. About two-thirds to three-quarters of the way through the season, they finally get it and do it correctly every time in games. But until then, at least some players keep fouling it up. (I do not make the "graduates" keep practicing it, only the guys who continue to do it wrong in games.)

Most coaches probably teach sliding. But hardly any players do it correctly. Mine all do because I know what my opposing coaches do not: it takes many, many reps to get kids to slide correctly.

Here are some other skills that take many, many reps to get right, and as such should be practiced daily and during pre-game whenever possible:

• Putting the tag on the ground
• Catcher throwing to second base
• Outfielder judging fly ball
• Catcher blocking low pitch

- Catching short hop
- Run through first base
- Tag up on a fly
- Base running with two outs
- Backing up throws
- Pickle
- Run on dropped third strike
- Pitcher-cover-first play (requires moderates reps)
- Bunting
- Taking a ball when bunting
- Waiting for a good pitch to hit (moderate reps)
- Pop-up slide and go to next base on error
- First-and-third defense
- Pitcher pick-off moves and throws
- Catcher pick-off moves and throws
- Bunt defense
- Pitcher cover home on passed ball
- Two-strike hitting
- Outfield throw to third from center or right or home from all three fields

When I teach new stuff, I generally teach the entire team at once. But when I teach every-day stuff, I like to use multiple stations if I have other coaches in whom I have confidence.

For example, I might run our daily sliding practice at one station while one assistant runs a two-out running drill and another helps a catcher practice throwing to second. Players would rotate between the sliding and baserunning stations. Catchers and middle infielders would rotate through the throw-to-second station and the other stations.

Pepper and around-the-horn

There are some common baseball drills which I like, but feel youth baseball players do not have time to learn them. Two prime example are pepper and around the horn.

Pepper is a great drill. Unfortunately, playing pepper requires its participants to learn a separate skill. Good baseball players cannot play pepper the first time they try. They have to **learn** to play pepper. In youth baseball, you have so little time to teach the sport, you do not have time to teach drills like pepper.

Around-the-horn is choreography. It wastes time. It looks pretty when it is done right, but I have seen a million youth baseball teams start an around-the-horn only to foul it up. That wastes even more time, plus it makes the player who makes the error feel even worse than he would had he made a normal game error because everybody regards the around-the-horn as a routine, easy exercise. It is not for youth players. Remember, the same probability equation applies.

You have a catcher, and each infielder throwing and/ or catching. That's .500 x .500 x .500 x .500 x .500 = .031. That is, you have a 3.1% chance of success at throwing the ball "around the horn." Granted, catching

a line-drive throw is easier than catching a grounder, but you still need four accurate throws. If you practice it, you will do it better. But such practice takes time away from practicing skills you **need**.

The around-the-horn is done as a celebration of an out when no one is on. Why risk turning your celebration and the momentum of that small success into a failure? Why risk snatching embarrassment from the jaws of victory? There is no benefit to the around-the-horn. It is simply a mindless tradition that is harmless at the high levels, but is often harmful at lower levels.

Inclement-weather practices

I never cancel practices on rainy days. I hold such practices under the roofs of the outdoor hallways of our local California public schools. You may not have such schools, but you probably have some sort of roofed area or gymnasium available to you. I cannot practice **everything** under a roof, but there is an extensive list of things I **can** practice. Here they are:

- Bunting
- Fielding a bunt
- Put the tag on the ground
- Warm-up catch
- Making low throws from the outfield
- Run through first
- Sliding (Need to pad hard surface under cardboard with mattress or some such)
- Pitch selection (batter deciding whether to swing using bat handle with no bat head and poly ball)
- Grounder fielding technique
- Catching ball in web rather than palm
- Pickle
- Pick up stopped ball
- Round a base when running
- One-throw double play (grounder)
- Rules clinic (no longer than five minutes)
- View training film (no more than five minutes at a time)
- Delayed steal
- Catcher blocking low pitch
- Make sure you are out before leaving base
- Relay technique
- Base-coaching signals
- Pitching from a stretch
- Fastball grip
- Changeup
- Different outfielder techniques for grounders
- Pre-pitch lead (teenage level)
- Dive back to base (need mattress or other padding)
- Run to first on dropped third strike
- Curve ball

Mindless drills

Coaches love drills. There are whole books of drills.

There seems to be a belief that if a baseball coach does a standard baseball drill, he is a good coach. I disagree. I think most baseball drills are either a total waste of time or they are so marginal in their benefit that they cannot be used in the extremely limited time available to a youth baseball coach.

Soft toss

I am a firm believer in the value of pre-game soft toss. When I bat in a batting cage, I always have trouble hitting the first few pitches. I generally have to bunt a few, then swing at a few to get my hand-eye coordination squared away.

If your players show up for a game and never see a single pitch until their game at bats, they are likely to do poorly on the first five to ten game pitches just like most people do on their first five to ten batting-cage pitches. So I do soft toss with poly balls for each player in pre-game.

I have little use for soft toss as a regular practice drill. Coaches love it because it takes very little space and it really looks like something is being accomplished. But it is a batting-mechanics drill and, as I said earlier in the book, you do not have time to mess with batting mechanics.

Soft toss would be fine as an **off-season** drill for a kid with a strong work ethic who wanted to work on his batting mechanics. But not in youth baseball team practice. Soft toss improves batting mechanics at a **glacial** pace—much too slow for a youth baseball season.

Hitting off a tee

The same is true for hitting off a tee. Mark McGwire once said 80% of his practice swings are off a tee. Same for me when I played. But unless your players are hitting basketballs, soccer balls, or volleyballs off the tee, which forces them to do correct batting mechanics on every rep, the tee is a waste of time because it is a drill where players must consciously convert verbal instruction into improved batting mechanics.

Batting cages

If you have a batting cage, I think you'd better be careful how you use it. I like it for practicing bunts, fake bunt and slash, waiting for a good pitch, blocking low pitches, or building confidence by teeing off on relatively slow pitches down the pipe. But I do not like using a batting cage for practicing batting mechanics. Again, you need 10,000 correct swings to change your batting mechanics. That takes far too long for youth-baseball team practice.

Holding team practice at commercial batting cages

Some of the managers I worked for occasionally held team practice at a commercial batting cage. So did my adult baseball manager.

Not a good idea. We had only one kid who kept working on his hitting. I saw absolutely no benefit in his subsequent game at bats. All the other kids kept running to the video games and midget basketball game at the corner of the complex. We had to drag them off to take their turn in the batting cage.

Logic tells you that the more game-speed baseballs you swing at, the better hitter you will become. In fact, I see no such effect. It appears to me that there is **no correlation** between time spent in a batting cage and game performance. I know it's not logical, but it is what I have experienced in my own hitting and that of my sons, as well as what I have observed with teams I have been involved with.

As I said earlier in the book, first you must learn the rhythm of the pitching machine. That takes a long time, but it is a totally useless skill when it comes to games.

Replicate game conditions

I am from the school of thought that says if you want to get better at something, practice exactly that thing. For example, if you want to get better at picking runners off first, you need a mound and a first base that is the proper distance and direction from the rubber, as well as a ball, a runner and first baseman. I do not think you get better at pick-offs by playing catch on one knee or by throwing while lying on your back or any other of the common throwing drills.

A great many baseball drills resemble game skills **distantly**, like playing catch while on one knee, but they are such distant relatives of the game skill in question that they must have extremely low priority. In youth baseball, with its mere 40.5 hours of practice time, extremely low priority means never.

I know the theory behind the one-knee drill and the lie-on-your-back drill. They isolate one part of the throwing motion so you can focus on it. Fine for pros or college players. But with just 40.5 total hours of practice, you do not have **time** to isolate different parts of the throw. You need to work on all of them at once. Sorry, but forty hours is forty hours.

In the context of a youth-baseball team, I would only use such drills on a kid who was in danger of injuring his arm because he throws sidearm or submarine style.

If it does not make your team better in the next two weeks, forget it

The first thing I said in this book is that competence is defined as getting your team to execute one or more baseball skills better—year in and year out. The test of whether you organized your practices correctly is did your team do something better because you were their coach.

The plain truth is that the vast majority of baseball coaches devote their practices to hitting infield, batting practice, and miscellaneous baseball drills that are of little or no benefit to the team. The average youth baseball team performs the same or worse than they would if they never had a single practice.

To state it as precisely as I can, I see no evidence that a group of children who take infield fifteen or twenty times in a season play better in the infield during games that season than a team, like mine for example, that **never** takes infield in practice. Taking infield is either a total waste of time or almost a total waste of time. If taking infield in practice fifteen or twenty times actually benefits a team, you would need a microscope to see the resulting improvement.

I see no evidence that a group of children who take batting practice fifteen or twenty times a season hit better than a team, like mine, that **never** takes batting practice.

Do what WORKS, not what has always been done

On the other hand, I **have** seen crystal clear evidence that if you spend ten minutes teaching your players how to do a delayed steal, they **will** play better **immediately** in games during that season, namely they will execute successful delayed steals, and they will play better in **future years** when they have moved onto the teams of other coaches, namely, they will **still** execute the delayed steals that you taught them.

The purpose of this book is to tell you how you can focus your practice time on those activities that combine both importance and coachability and therefore result **directly** in better play by your kids. To do that, you must **abandon the mindless, time-wasting rituals** of the standard youth-baseball-practice format. You must **only** do things that make your players better **now**. You must **avoid** all activities and comments that **harm** your players' performance.

Practice content changes over time

There are three general components to your practices:

- evaluation
- teaching new stuff
- drilling old stuff

As the season progresses, the amount you spend on each changes. The percentage of evaluation starts big, but declines to zero when you get to the playoffs. You spend more time on new stuff at the beginning of the season and more time mastering the old stuff at the end of the season. Here are rough breakdowns of first day, mid-season, and playoff practice schedules:

	1st day	mid-season	playoffs
Evaluation	50%	20%	0%
New skills	50%	50%	20%
Old skills	0%	30%	80%

This is not hard and fast, just a general concept. Also, This does not include arm warm-ups and jock checks which are required every day.

First-day practice schedule

Here is a suggested **first-day** practice schedule for a team above the tee-ball level:

	Station 1	Station 2	Station 3
5:00	Introduction		
5:02	Warm-up arms		
5:05	Sliding instruction		
5:10	Sliding practice	same	same
5:15	Eye tests	Speed test	
5:20	Auditions: 3B	1B	Catcher
5:30	Intrasquad practice game		
6:00	Four-seam fastball grip		
6:02	Catch ball in web, not palm, of glove		
6:04	Run through first base		
6:07	Run through 1B practice	same	
6:10	Batter's rest position before pitch		
6:12	Fielding technique for ground ball		
6:15	Practice fielding technique		
6:20	Safety		
6:30	End		

Normally, you would have a position clinic at 6:30. But you cannot have one the first day because you have not yet assigned any positions. Assign positions after practice that night and inform the players who need to attend the first position clinic before the next practice.

On a tee-ball team, you do fewer position evaluations because there is no throwing pitcher and the catcher has almost nothing to do. Speed is not important because there is no stealing. About all you need to figure out in tee ball is who are your fielding pitchers and who are your first basemen. Those two positions field a lot of balls. The left side of the infield should only be kids who can throw to first. Many tee-ballers' arms are not strong enough. Tee ballers who are better at fielding hot grounders, if any, should play infield. Your batting order in tee ball might as well be alphabetical one game and reverse alphabetical the next. The rest of the above first-day practice schedule will work for both tee ball and higher levels.

Mid-season practice schedule

Here is a mid-season practice schedule for an 11-12 team:

	Station 1	Station 2	Station 3
5:00	Warm-up arms		
5:03	Sliding	C-2B throw	run thru 1B
5:10	Double steal with runner at 3B and walk		
5:15	Fake-steal instruction		
5:20	Fake-steal practice from 1B	same @ 2B	
5:30	Pitcher cover home	Tag up on fly	

5:35	Half-size field defensive situations
5:45	IF: tag on ground OF-C: throw home
5:50	IF: 1-throw dp OF-C: throw home
5:55	2-out baserunning all bases
6:00	Intrasquad practice game
6:20	Go over pitch-selection chart from last game
6:30	Position clinic 1B foot placement
6:35	Stretch toward outfield, home, thrower
6:40	Sweep tag when pulled off base toward home
6:43	Jump straight up for catchable high throw
6:46	Go back on pop
6:50	Pitcher cover first play
7:00	End

At another first-baseman clinic you would cover other skills like covering a bunt, catching short hops, throwing to second, relaying throw from right to home, catcher pickoff, and so forth.

Kitchen timer

How do you remember to change to the next activity? I wear a kitchen countdown timer around my neck. At the beginning of each practice segment, I set the timer for the duration of the period. One of the timers I used is designed like a Soap on a Rope, only it's a timer on a rope.

You dial up the amount of time desired and it ticks down to zero, at which time a bell rings. Most kitchen countdown timers beep, but I cannot hear beeps because of a high-frequency hearing loss I suffered in the Army. On occasion, I have had to use beeping timers because I could not find the bell type. Although I cannot hear it, my players and assistant coaches can and they tell me, "Coach, your timer is going off."

Multiple stations

Note that I run two or three stations some of the time and one station other times. In the mid-season practice, the warm-up is just paired-off players all in one line so no one is hit by passed balls from another group.

At 5:03, we go to three stations: sliding, running through first base, and catchers throwing to second. All players rotate through the sliding and run-through-first-base stations; only catchers and middle infielders rotated also through the throw to second station.

Sliding and running through first are what I call brainwashing skills. That is, the kids will do them wrong unless you make them do it right so many times that they **forget** how to do it wrong. Throwing to second requires no brainwashing, but it takes many repetitions to get it right.

The 5:10 and 5:15 activities are one-station, whole-team activities. Some players will play the role of opposing defenses and will rotate back to the offense during the period. The 5:20 fake-steal practice is two stations, namely first and second bases. Half the team would be at each base taking turns.

5:30 is a two-station activity with the pitchers and catchers practicing covering home on a passed ball and the other players at the other three bases practicing reacting to a fly ball as base runners when fewer than two are out.

At 5:35 the entire team will take a half-size field and work on the drill described earlier where I throw a tennis ball to a fielder and everyone freezes when he catches it to see if all are at the right place. The coach should have a script or list of situations he wants to cover in the session in question.

At 5:45, the infielders practice putting the tag on the ground next to the base. Kids will do the "AT&T tag" ("Reach out and touch someone") if you do not brainwash them into putting the tag on the ground next to the base. My excellent sliders slide under our opponents' AT&T tags all season.

While the infielders are practicing tag on the ground, the outfielders are practicing throw to home, where the catcher puts the tag on the ground. Emphasis in this period is on throwing instantly home rather than looking around to see where to throw (assumes runner is at second when the ball was hit). Also emphasize throwing low line-drive trajectory. There is no "cut" man. The pitcher covers off-line throws.

At 5:50 the infielders switch to practicing one-throw double plays. That's where you field a grounder and step on a nearby bag then throw to first or you catch a fly and throw to the bag where a runner failed to tag up. Outfielders continue to practice throwing home because each of their repetitions takes much longer than a tag-on-the-ground repetition.

At 5:55, all players divide into three groups and go to first, second, or third base. The coach throws fly balls to an outfielder or coach playing outfield. The fielder deliberately lets each fly hit his glove then drops it. That is to teach the runners that they go when the outfielder touches the ball, not when he catches it. Otherwise, some runners are momentarily taken aback by a muff rather than a catch. ("What do I do now?") Runners at second and third leave when the ball touches the outfielder's glove (deep throw). Runners on first do what is often erroneously described as "going half way."

Intrasquad practice game

At 6:00, the whole team does a practice game. If twelve players are present, divide them into three equally-talented teams of four each. The batting team provides a fielder unless they have bases loaded. This is an evaluative exercise designed mainly to see who can pitch. Kids who have not been pitching regularly in real games should pitch in intrasquad games to show what they can do.

You also keep a score book on everyone else as further evaluation of their errors, hits, and so forth. A coach umpires calls balls and strikes. Whenever there is a screw up, stop the game and redo the play that was just screwed up.

If only one player screwed up, have just that player do it over correctly. For example, if the pitcher stayed on the mound on a base hit to left, he should be made to run to the foul territory behind third base several times in response to the coach standing at the plate and throwing a base hit to the left fielder. I call this an instant-replay practice. Any screw-up will be done over correctly. Do it right or do it over.

Pitch-selection chart

We keep track of where every pitch is thrown in every game. At the subsequent practice, each player gets a photocopy of the pitch location chart from the last game or two. I sit the kids down in a circle or in the bleachers and I go over every at bat every player had pointing out the quality of the pitches he received, the quality of his decision making, and the consequences of good or bad decision making. After a couple of weeks of this, the kids become believers that waiting for a good pitch is one of the main keys to hitting.

First-baseman position clinic

At 6:30, practice is over for the team. The first basemen and anyone wishing to learn how to play first base then stay for another half hour.

In this session, I start with foot placement. Your throwing-side foot goes on the base. A common mistake is to put your toes on the ground and your heel on the base. That's a no-no because when you stretch, your heel comes up off the bag. You have to put your toes on the bag before you stretch.

At first, I have the first baseman get ready and I stand between first and the mound and just point left of him, right of him, or straight at him. He is then to stretch accordingly with no ball being thrown. At 6:35, we do the same, only this time with a live ball. The back-up first baseman backs up the coach's throws to the first baseman. Then they rotate.

Sweep tag

At 6:40, I deliberately throw far enough toward home that the first baseman cannot catch the ball and keep his foot on the bag. He is to step off the bag, catch the ball, then sweep the glove back toward the base to tag the runner.

In 1997, my first baseman made the all-star team. In the all-star game, he had a runner at first. The batter hit a line drive. The first baseman caught it then instinctively did a sweep behind him like I had taught him in my position clinic. Double play. I believe it was the final play of the game. I do not remember whether they won or lost, but those are the kinds of little successes that give me my greatest satisfaction as a coach.

High throw

Infielders tend to panic whenever the throw from a fielder forces them to take their foot off the bag. The throw that is a little too high for a first baseman to catch without leaving the ground is a classic example of that. I stand close to the first baseman and deliberately throw the ball directly over his head so he can catch it with a little jump, but not if he stays on the ground. The idea is to teach him that it's no big deal. You jump up a little and catch the ball then come back down on the base.

This is easy. It only takes a few reps to convince the kids and get them to stop panicking in this situation. But if you never teach this and give your players a few repetitions of it, they will panic for the rest of their lives. This is another thing that gives me satisfaction when I see one of my players do it right in a game, but it is so subtle and my kids make it look so easy that no one else at the field notices that my players are almost the only ones in the league who can do this.

Going back on a pop

Another thing that unnecessarily causes players to panic is a ball that causes them to have to go back. My aforementioned all-star first baseman panicked once on a little pop hit behind first base.

At the next pre-game, I took a ball and threw a little lob over his head so he had to trot back and catch it at a jog. I just kept doing that with the two of us moving farther and farther into the outfield with each throw. After we were near the outfield fence and he had done this a half dozen times, he had figured out that there was no reason to panic and that this was an easy catch.

I do not recall that he had another chance to do it in a game that season. But if he had, he would have made it look so easy that no one would have realized that most kids cannot execute that play.

Pitcher-cover-first play

I do the pitcher-cover-first play in every pre-game warm-up. So I generally do not use regular practice time for it after initially introducing the play and how to do it. But a first-base or pitcher position clinic is an occasion for working on this play.

In the 1998 season, I was coaching a AAA (minors) team. A **majors** team manager had a mid-season vacancy and came to sit in our dugout to watch our game and look for a player to draft.

During the game, we executed a pitcher-cover-first play just as smooth as could be. I commented to our manager that we were probably the only team in the AAA league who could do that, but no one even noticed. The majors manager chimed in that no one in the majors could do it either. I was surprised to hear that.

What my practice schedule is NOT

Now think about what my practice schedule is NOT.

It is NOT the usual practice schedule, which looks like this.

5:00   Warm-up throws
5:10   Hit infield and outfield
5:50   Batting practice
6:30   End

The usual youth baseball practice schedule is a waste of time at best, and harmful to the players at worst. In **my** practices, the kids really learn something. They are almost never bored. And the particular stuff they learn almost always pays a direct dividend in one or more subsequent games.

We got most of the same things done

Did we warm up our arms like the usual practice? Yep. We just got it done in three minutes instead of screwing around with it for ten.

Did we practice infield technique? You bet. We got the tag on the ground, practiced one-throw double plays, we practiced the catcher throwing to second base, we practiced the pitcher covering home on a passed ball, we practiced defensive situations (which is what "get one" is about also). We had a practice game in which we practiced whatever infield and outfield situations came up. And from 6:00 to 6:30, we practiced the heck out of the nuances of first base play.

Did we practice outfield technique? Absolutely. We practiced **specific** outfield techniques like throwing home and defensive situations.

Although my infield and outfield practice consumes less time than the 40 minutes of hitting infield in the traditional format, I'll bet my players each got more quality repetitions than the players in the 40-minute "hit infield" sessions did.

Note that the segments of my practices are as short as two minutes and the drills are never longer than ten minutes. Only my practice games go longer. Hitting infield is boring for the fielders who are not involved in the particular play. Batting practice is excruciatingly boring for all but the batter and catcher and an occasional fielder.

Note also the large amount of time I spend on base-running: 32 minutes. That, not blind aggressiveness, is the reason my base runners terrorize their leagues.

Do you see any **batting practice** in my schedule? The only batting we did was during the practice game. We also did a "chalk talk" about the benefits of waiting for a good pitch to hit for ten minutes at the end of practice. I guarantee you that you will accomplish more hitting improvement in three of those chalk talks than you will in an entire season of traditional batting practice.

In fact, I can almost guarantee you that your team will hit better if you **eliminate** traditional batting practice entirely and replace it with absolutely **nothing**. At least then your players will not have their game timing screwed up by slow-moving practice pitches. (Syd Thrift, one-time director of the Kansa City Royals Baseball Academy, says you should only practice hitting against game-speed pitches.) Nor will they ever be encouraged to chase bad pitches.

What not to do

It's easier to coach what **not** to do than to coach what to do. Furthermore, getting kids to stop doing something is often highly effective coaching. In youth baseball, players generally swing at too many pitches, cut off too many throws, think about too many things, anchor their foot too often when waiting for a throw, take too many practice swings between pitches, dive for too many balls, among other things.

Youth baseball **coaches** do a lot of stuff that their teams would be better off without. They give too many signs, teach too much mechanics, talk too much, and so forth. Less is more in many aspects of youth coaching.

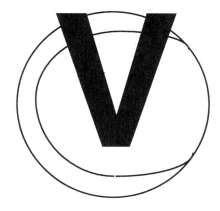

5 Fielding

This chapter is about general fielding—stuff that applies to **every** position. I will cover the skills specific to the individual positions in separate chapters.

Four-seam fastball grip

Fielders should always use a four-seam fastball grip, also called a "cross-seam" fastball, when they throw. A four-seam fastball is the fastest, straightest throw. You want speed for obvious reasons. You want straight to make the throw as easy as possible to catch.

First basemen, and to a lesser extent, other infielders, have to learn how each infielder's ball moves because none quite throw the perfect straight ball. But you want to minimize movement if you are a fielder.

I once caught a catcher overthrow as a center fielder backing up a steal throw to second in semi-pro baseball. I caught it in the air with my glove, but it had a sharp movement on it that caused it to slide at the last instant. The throw, which was going about 75 miles per hour, almost hit me in the face. Scared the daylights out of me.

The problem was that, unlike our middle infielders, I have never caught a hard throw from that catcher as an outfielder. I was not used to the movement on his ball. Plus he was also one of my pitchers so he was used to throwing moving fastballs in that role. In short, you want to straighten out fielder throws as much as possible.

Why it's called "four-seam"

When a four-seam fastball is coming at you, you will see four different seams of the ball go by during each rotation of the ball. A fastball rotates on a horizontal axis like the wheel of a car. Because of the spin put on the ball by the final snap downward of the fingers, it is like a car wheel going in **reverse** flying at you. That is, if you would videotape it and run it in slow motion, you would see the seams rotating up from the bottom to the top as it came at you.

The circle above is a baseball. The inner lines are the seams and the letter "V" represents your forefinger and middle finger. The bottom of the "V" is where the fingers connect with your hand.

Your fingers each have three joints: one where the finger connects with the hand, one in the middle, and one near the tip. In the four-seam fastball grip, the crease under the joint between the tip and middle of your forefinger and middle finger should be on top of the seams.

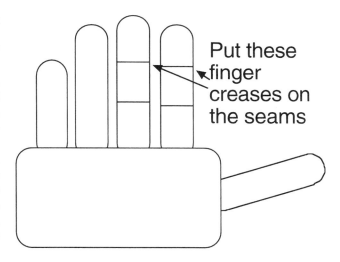

Put these finger creases on the seams

The ball should be held loosely, not tight. There should be daylight between the palm of the hand and the ball.

Oakland Athletics pitcher Storm Davis was visiting community groups and talking baseball with a fellow member of the A's. Davis heard his teammate give the discussion I just gave you about the four-seam fastball. Amazingly, Davis, who by then had a Word Series victory under his belt, had never been taught about the four-seam fastball. He tried it and found it made his fastball faster. I read his comments on this in my local paper.

Major Leaguers say, the four-seam fastball goes about **four** miles per hour faster than any other type of fastball. In his book, *The Physics of Baseball*, Professor Robert K. Adair says a four-seam fastball goes **two** miles per hour faster.

Why it goes faster and straighter

To go fast and straight, there must be turbulence around the ball. That's why golf balls and pitching machine balls have dimples. Baseballs do not have dimples, but they do have seams. As stated earlier, a four-seam fastball results in four seams going over the front of the ball per rotation of the ball.

The alternative is a **two**-seam fastball. Two-seam fastballs are gripped at right angles to the four-seam grip like this:

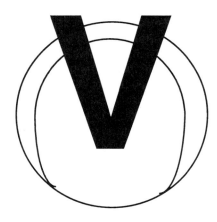

Two-seam fast balls **sink**. You don't want that from a fielder because it makes the throw harder to catch. With a two-seam fastball, only two seams cross the front of the ball during one full rotation. Four seams cutting through the air causes more turbulence than two seams, thus, more speed and straightness.

Why does turbulence do that? Sounds like it would do the opposite, doesn't it? I don't know. Scientists have not figured turbulence out.

Practice getting the grip

Former Major Leaguer Joe Garagiola said that when he was in the minor leagues, he and his teammates used to take their gloves and balls to the movies and practice getting a four-seam fastball grip during the movie. That is, they would spin the ball into the glove so the seams would be in some unknown position. Then they would reach into the glove in the dark, grab the ball, and move it with their fingers to a four-seam grip during the time it took to cock their arm to throw.

I tell my players to practice that while watching TV or riding in the car. It does not take much time to learn.

When your players are doing their warm-up throws you should remind them to use a four-seam grip. You'll see them thinking about it and moving the ball in their fingers. Many will actually look at the ball each time

they get ready to throw it. That's not a problem. They won't look at it in a game.

Smaller kids may need to use **three** fingers instead of two.

L-bend in the throwing arm

When you throw a baseball, your throwing arm should generally be shaped like a letter "L." Your bicep is almost parallel to the ground with the elbow a little higher than the shoulder and your forearm is perpendicular to the ground. Almost all photos of pitchers at the point of release will show that arm configuration.

Some players always throw sidearm. Some even throw submarine style (extremely-bent-over-at-the-waist sidearm). Some Major League submariners, like Dan Quisenberry and Kent Tekulve, were quite successful. However, either sidearm or submarine style is dangerous to the arm of a child.

The fix is to have the player lie on his back and throw. It is impossible to throw sidearm or submarine style from that position.

Do not throw **to** the player while he is on his back. Hand him the ball. Trying to catch while lying on your back is dangerous.

You do not have time to fix this in team practice. You need to talk to the player's parents and urge them to do it during free time.

Sidearm and submarine throws are not **always** a bad idea. Infielders often have to throw quickly and do not have time to change body positions. If they are bent over when they field a ball and have to throw in a hurry, they should throw from the bent-over position.

Make the throw easy to see

When one infielder or the pitcher is throwing to another infielder from close range, either overhand or underhand, he should try to make the ball easy to see from before he releases it. Things that can make it hard to see are the glove blocking the target's view of the ball or a throw that comes from behind a spinning fielder's body. The fielder who caught the hit often holds the ball up as if to say to the target fielder, "See it?" Then he throws or tosses it without his throwing hand ever disappearing from the target fielder's view during the throw.

Model it

I do not spend much time **teaching** players throwing mechanics. I try to model the correct way. Remember to avoid modeling a **short-arm** technique where you just use your wrist and a little forearm movement to throw because you don't want too much velocity with little kids.

Telling players the correct way to throw so they can work on it on their own seems to have no detrimental effect. If you tell a **pitcher** or **batter** about their mechanics, it will foul them up in games. But position players do not think much about their throws when they are hurried because they are mentally preoccupied with the rest of the play: catching the ball and figuring out where to throw it.

Pitchers and hitters, however, **are** preoccupied with their mechanics if you make them self-conscious about them. In general, I have not found throwing mechanics to be a problem in youth baseball. Except for the chronic sidearmers and submariners, the way kids throw without any coaching is generally "close enough for government work."

Fielding and the glove

Ever since the baseball glove was invented, coaches have been forced to teach fielding mechanics. **Barehanded** people generally do it right by instinct. I do not teach them much at the higher levels, but I do emphasize fielding mechanics with tee-ballers.

As I said earlier, I like to **force** the kid to do the right thing by the way I set up the drill, rather than **tell** him to do the right thing. With tee-ballers, I like to buy cheap, hollow, rubber balls at a local variety store. The best size is about the size of a softball or maybe a little bigger.

No glove

Then I tell the kids to take off their baseball gloves and I roll or skim the large rubber balls to them. They use roughly correct technique to field them without a word being said.

Again, you should model the correct technique. Have them roll the ball back to you and you field it correctly.

Correct grounder fielding technique means your feet are spread **wider than shoulder width** and your **back** is roughly **parallel** to the ground. You catch the ball **in front** of your body, not underneath it. With a glove, you form an "alligator" with your hands. The glove is the lower "jaw" of the "alligator" and your throwing hand is the upper "jaw."

Ready position and 'idling'

There are many different theories on the best ready position. In the infield, I recommend that your players get their glove down on the ground because failure to do that when the ball is hit is so common. In the outfield, you can stand up.

The other thing most people recommend, and so do I, is that the fielder should have **some movement** in his body when the pitch is delivered. Again, people differ on what the movement should be and I take no sides in that debate.

In the outfield, I always took a half step forward as the pitch was being delivered. As far as I'm concerned, your fielders can take whatever movement they want, but their body should be moving in some slight way as the batter is starting his swing. It's like the having the motor of a getaway car running and the car moving slowly at a bank robbery as opposed to having the ignition off.

Grounder-fielding position

Below is a stick figure drawing of the correct grounder fielding position Just to give you the rough idea while I am talking about it here. There are many books with far better drawings or photos of this technique. See the bibliography at the back of this book.

Whenever you write a nonfiction book, you are implicitly saying that all previous books on the subject did an inadequate job of covering it. This book is no exception, except when it comes to the photos and drawings of techniques in the other books. Those other books are great in that department. I did not write this one to give you better drawings or photos.

Grounder fielding front view

Grounder fielding side view

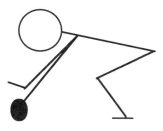

Hitches and hops

After securing the ball, the fielder should bring both hands to his stomach. Between the catch and the throw there are hitches and hops. After release is the follow through. It should all be a smooth, flowing, continuous motion.

Don't coach those things **verbally** in youth baseball. Just **model** them.

Eyes on the target

Some kids get into the habit of looking away from the target when they throw. You need to stop that. Tell them to look at the target **throughout** their throwing motion.

The web

Baseball gloves are misnamed. They should be called baseball **webs**. The main purpose of a baseball glove is to put a web between your thumb and forefinger so you can catch balls that are moving too fast to be caught bare-handed.

Gloves, the non-baseball kind, are meant to be used the **same** as bare hands. That is **not** the case with baseball gloves. But the fact that they are **called** gloves and **look** like gloves makes people think they are simply a protective cover for a bare hand that is to be used as a bare hand. Wrong.

Palmless glove

There are a lot of goofy-looking training devices in baseball. Here's an idea for another. Take an old baseball glove and cut out the entire palm. That will immediately cause the kids to try to catch the ball in the **web**, as they should. When you catch a ball properly in the web, right at the bottom, it sounds like a gun shot, even if the ball was not moving very fast.

If you tell the kids about that gunshot noise, and encourage them to strive for it in the warm-up period, you will see them concentrating on getting the impact point just right, which is great.

Bigger hand

Another purpose of a baseball glove is to enlarge your hand. When you are fielding a ball whose path you are not sure of, a larger thing to catch it with than a hand is helpful. The biggest glove of all is the one catchers use to catch knuckleball pitchers—because they do not know where the ball is going.

But what if the ball is going **neither** too fast to handle safely with a bare hand or is predictable in its path? Do you still want a large leather glove between you and the ball?

My late mother used to joke about getting me a job picking the fly manure out of pepper while wearing boxing gloves. If the baseball is **stopped**, or moving extremely **slowly** on a level surface, or floating slowly through the air with little spin, a baseball glove is about as helpful as the fly-manure-picker's boxing gloves.

Picking up a stopped ball

Stopped baseballs should **not** be picked up with the gloved hand, especially in grass. In fact, I drill a whole multi-step procedure for picking up a stopped ball because kids tend to act as if there were a penalty for touching the ball first with the bare hand.

1. Go to the vicinity of the ball and position your feet perpendicular to the path of your intended throw with your glove-side shoulder pointing at your

throwing target. In other words, line up your feet for the throw **before** you touch the ball.
2. Bend over the ball so it is **beneath your sternum. If** you do **not** do that, you will be in an awkward position to reach for the ball.
3. Look at the seams and pick it up so you have a **four-seam fastball grip** from the moment you touch it.
4. Throw it. Depending on the situation, you may throw from the bent-over position or you may stand up first.

I practice this by tossing a ball on the ground to the first of a line of players. I position a coach or other player some distance away for the drill subject to throw to. I vary throwing it to the right or left of the player to make him have to move his feet to get into throwing position first. The kids screw this up several times before they get it right.

Never allow a player to pick up a stopped ball with their glove. It is a bad habit which can result in them making several unsuccessful stabs at a stopped ball in a game. I have never seen this discussed in a baseball book, but I have often seen youth-baseball players doing that boxing-gloves-fly-manure sequence repeatedly in games.

Bunts and tosses

You may also want to field a slow-moving bunt or short toss from a teammate with your bare hand. If the ball is rolling with any speed, its momentum will carry it **up into** a properly placed glove. But if is really rolling slowly, the ball may bounce off the lip of the glove.

Wearing the glove

Another near universal mistake caused by the fact that a baseball glove is called a glove and looks like a glove is trying to make it **fit** like a glove. Let me quote *Little League's Official How-to-Play Baseball Book* (which is excellent):

> Don't **jam** [your fingers] in…The heel of your hand should be just **outside** the heel of the glove…the leather inside the glove stays **away** from the palm of your hand. [Emphasis added]

You really use the baseball glove somewhat like **tongs**. It has two sides: a thumb side and a fingers side. You get the ball between the two sides and squeeze those sides together. You most certainly do **not** use it like a glove. If you do, you will injure your palm.

The best way for players to become better fielders is to play catch or throw the ball against an object that will make it bounce back. When I was a kid, I used to throw it against steps because the irregular surface would make it bounce back at more challenging angles and speeds.

Open the glove

This may sound obvious, but the player has to **open the glove**. With small kids, that problem can be even worse. Some of them have gloves the same size as mine. That's generally good, but only if they can get them open to receive the ball.

Another fix is to play catch with an oversize ball like a softball or small soccer or basketball.

'Don't let the ball play you'

Youth baseball coaches often tell their fielders,

"You play the ball. Don't let the ball play you."

Excuse me, but what the heck does that mean?

Don't write and tell me. My point is not that more of us need to know what that cliche means. Rather my point is that if **I** don't know what it means, neither do most, if not all, of your players.

I suspect it's one of those things youth baseball coaches do to show off or to bluff baseball knowledge. It sounds very baseball savvy—like the guy who's saying it has spent many a year out on the old diamond.

I think the "Don't let the ball play you" line has something to do with my admonition that it is easiest to catch a bouncing ball the **level** or **falling** portion of its flight. Balls that are rising off the ground (short hops) are much harder to catch, especially after the first few inches which can be smothered by a glove.

Do youth-baseball infielders sometimes come in on a grounder and misjudge it, thereby placing themselves at one of its short hops? Yep, they do that. Is the way to fix it telling them "Don't let the ball play you?" Absolutely not. That opaque incantation just robs the player of self-confidence.

When they make an error, "letting the ball play them" or otherwise, just tell them learning to field grounders takes a long time and encourage them to get as many reps of practice (outside of team practice) as possible. The more grounders they field, the better they will get at judging the hops.

The way to get better at catching and throwing is to catch and throw thousands of times.

Run, don't reach

Fielders should catch grounders in the **middle of their body** whenever possible. That means they have to run to the right place whenever the ball is hit to their right or left. They tend to be lazy and run half way there and reach the rest of the way.

How do you fix this? Rant and rave about it. When they do it wrong, make them do it over correctly five times. The basic problem here is laziness. The solution to **laziness** is nothing but **discipline**. There is a couple of pertinent coaching sayings:

You get what you demand. What you tolerate, you encourage.

Reaching is only for when it is impossible to run to the right spot.

When you do infield drills, you should throw balls right at the player, and at varying distances to his right and left. When you find a weak spot, give him extra practice.

Call for pops

You should remind players to call for fly balls then give them practice doing so. This is a perennial problem, but it can be fixed with a couple of five- or ten-minute practice sessions early in the season.

Why catch it with one or more forced runners?

On the other hand, I have long wondered why anyone would ever catch an infield pop if there were one or more forced runners on base with less than two outs. Just let it hit the ground. Then throw out the lead runner. You may even get a double play if the batter is one of those jerks who walks away in disgust instead of running out all his hits. Jerk behavior is much more prevalent at the **teenage** level.

Listen to what Tim McCarver says about this in his book *Baseball for Brain Surgeons*.

I still think infielders should purposely drop the ball every now and then. I wish more infielders would consider dropping pop-ups and getting a force at second if they can replace a fast runner on first with a slow-footed batter. If the batter…doesn't bother running, the fielder can even pull off a double play by dropping the ball.

'Infield fly'

If there are **two** or more forced runners, and less than two outs, the ump is supposed to call an infield fly. But many youth umps are incompetent. If they do not **call** infield fly, it is **not** an infield fly, no matter where it is hit or the base runner-out situation.

Virtually all youth coaches and players are incompetent when it comes to the infield-fly rule. Indeed, I have often heard the statement in games that, "We don't enforce the infield fly rule at this level," as if that were some kind of nice-guy, be-kind-to-children behavior. It **is**, to the **defense**, if they take advantage of it.

In adult baseball, I once accidentally dropped a pop while playing first with a runner at first. The runner almost had a heart attack because he stayed assuming I would catch it. When I didn't, he had a long way to go and a short time to get there. I just picked the ball up and easily threw him out at second. If the ball had been closer to first, I could have stepped on first for the force then thrown to second for a tag out.

In Little League as a player in the fifties, I once charged hard on a humpbacked line drive from center field. There was a runner at first. I muffed it, but I muffed it **to** the second baseman. He stepped on second, then threw to first and got a double play. I suspect the batter must have loafed because he assumed I would catch the ball on the fly.

Keep it a secret

Don't let anyone **know** you plan to let the ball hit the ground. Make a big deal of saying "I got it! I got it!" Then just let it drop. Make sure you are between the foul-line and the impact point because infield pops tend to bounce toward the foul line.

In addition to the infield-fly rule, there is another little-known rule to prevent one version of this stunt. Little League Rule 6.05(l) says the batter is out if

an infielder intentionally drops a fair fly ball or line drive, with first, first and second, first and third, or first, second and third bases occupied before two are out. The ball is dead and the runners shall return to their original base or bases.

Note the phrase "intentionally drops." That rule does **not** apply if you do not touch the ball before it hits the ground.

I have never seen Rule 6.05(l) called in a game.

Do **not** do this, however, if there are **no runners** on base or if there are already **two outs**. In those two cases, catch the ball on the fly.

Tag on the ground

This is an area that I really emphasize. If you ask a kid who was on one of my teams what one phrase I used more than any other in coaching, he would probably say, "Tag on the ground." Kids are extremely resistant to putting the tag on the ground.

Unless the runner is far from a base, you should tag him by putting your glove with the ball in it on the ground, back to the runner, on the edge of the base to which the runner is approaching. You let the runner slide or run into the glove.

You do not reach out and touch someone at belt or chest level when you are trying to make a tag at a base. His body need never pass through that belt- or chest-level spot. But he does have to get to the base. "The base is on the ground. Put the tag on the ground," is one of my mantras.

To drill this, walk 360 degrees around a player who is at a base and keep tossing him the ball from every direction. He must then catch it and put it on the ground on the side of the base facing the next-lower numbered base. Sometimes, I add a player or coach who sits as if sliding and extends his foot into the tag each time.

You have to do this drill daily all season, like slid-

ing practice, unless you are coaching one of my former players.

No sweep tags at a base

Kids love to do sweep tags. That is, they catch the throw and sweep the tag down past the base like a matador. There have been cases even in the Major Leagues of runners taking advantage of that tendency. They deliberately do not extend their foot until the sweep tag has gone by. Safe!

A sweep tag requires both cooperation from the runner and great synchronization to be successful. F'get about it. The tag goes straight to the ground and stays there until the runner arrives. Absolutely no sweep tags allowed.

Wait at the base for the ball

A common youth mistake is to leave the base to go out and catch the ball, then reach back toward the base to make the tag. You have to do that if the throw is **off** line. But it is incorrect to do it if the throw is **on** line. Very simply, a flying ball move faster than a carried one. The tag will get to the ground next to the base faster if the fielder stays at the base and lets the throw come to him.

Don't even **reach** out for it with your feet at the base. Let the ball come all the way in. In his book *Men at Work*, George Will says Mark Belanger taught Cal Ripken, Jr. to keep his glove at the base and not reach out.

Always get two

Once, when I was a Little League catcher in 1957, I tagged a runner out at the plate. It was the game where we borrowed the good kids catchers mitt. I was so proud of myself getting that guy out that I turned to face the crowd—beaming and drinking in their applause and cheers.

Unfortunately, the runner at second was not so distracted. While I was taking curtain calls, he advanced to third.

So I try to teach tag plays as a three-step sequence:

1. Catch the ball
2. Tag on the ground
3. Pop your feet to get ready to throw to another base

Sometimes, I have the whole team simultaneously simulate catching an invisible ball, tagging the ground in front of the base, then popping up with the ball cocked ready to throw to another base. "Catch! Tag! Pop!" are the commands I use to run that drill.

In some cases, I actually have them **throw** the ball to another base. With a **catcher** practicing tagging a player out at the plate, I generally also have them come up afterwards and throw to **third**. Partly that's in commemoration of my screw up at the 1957 game, and partly it's because there often is another trailing runner when one comes home.

Elsewhere in the book, I say to forget two-throw double plays. I should have specified I was talking about two-throw, double plays where both outs are **force outs**. Two-throw double plays where at least one of the outs is a **tag** play **are** worth practicing at the youth level.

Get your players in the habit of coming up looking for **another** out every time they get a put out.

Run down

All fielders need to know how to execute a rundown. I once hung around to listen when my son was attending the Rob Andrews baseball camp. He was very big on keeping the number of throws down to just one.

Chase the runner and make a diving tag if you can. That would be **no** throws. That's my favorite. My second and final remaining choice is to make **one** throw.

Chase the runner. If you cannot tag himself yourself, charge him so hard that he has to commit to a base. I do not care which one.

Many, if not most coaches, teach that you should chase the runner to the **lower-numbered base**. I disagree, especially in youth baseball. Former San Francisco Giant Rob Andrews also says to drive the runner to the **nearest** base at all levels.

The only concession I would make to the lower-numbered-base approach is that if the fielder with the ball is **off the base path** and even with the runner, he should run at the side of the runner closest to the **higher-numbered base** so as to drive the runner back to the lower-numbered base.

Andrews says **not** to do any **pump fakes**. Makes sense to me. Just get the rundown over with as quickly as possible. Make the runner commit to whichever base so that he cannot change direction and either tag him out yourself or throw to the fielder at that base.

The fielder with the ball runs holding his throwing arm in an "L" position with the ball by his ear. When the runner has committed to the base in question and the fielder with the ball is sure he cannot tag the runner himself, he should throw to the fielder at the base.

Most youth coaches teach the rundown as an endless series of throws and catches and peel offs. Their concept seems to be that since we outnumber the runner we can wear him out. My concept is that youth baseball players are highly error-prone so there should be as few throws as possible.

When my oldest son was twelve and under, he did not care whether he got caught in a rundown because he escaped every single one. When he turned thirteen, he wisely decided that was no longer a prudent course.

You need to practice the rundown, but you must discourage throwing the ball at all and ban any throws beyond one. To an extent, this is a **deprogramming** situation because previous coaches have taught your players to execute this play with unlimited throws.

Do-or-die situations

A do-or-die situation is one where you have to throw the ball home or to a particular base before the runner or you **lose the game or your lead in the final inning**. In such cases, correct technique may need to be sacrificed for speed. Generally, the fastest way to field and throw a ball is with your bare hand and bent over if the ball was low when you caught it. Normally, a fielder should only field a ball bare-handed if it has stopped or is rolling slowly.

Practice this a little and refer to it as the "do-or-die technique." Then, if the situation comes up in a game, you can yell out to your players, "Do or die, guys! We MUST stop the runner on third from scoring!"

Watch runners touch the base

In youth baseball especially, runners often do not touch the base when they run by. The infielders should be trained to watch this and immediately call for an appeal after a play when a runner misses the base.

I cannot promise you that youth umpires will be sharp enough to have watched themselves, but if you appeal confidently enough, they may uphold the appeal based on your demeanor. Appealing is risk free so it should be done far more often.

Appeal procedure

By rule, you must follow a certain sequence when doing an appeal. I have seen umpires in adult baseball and semi-pro baseball stand mute when the team appealed at a base. After the inning was over, the umpire explained that he could not respond because the proper sequence had not been followed.

If time has not been called, simply throw the ball to the base in question. The fielder tags the base then tells the umpire the identity of the player who failed to touch the base or who left too soon.

If time has been called, the appeal must start with the pitcher on the mound in the set position. He then steps off with his throwing-arm side foot and throws to the base in question where the above procedure is followed.

You need to work on this a little bit in team practice. Have runners deliberately miss a base and leave early on a tag up to test if your players spot it, then have them execute the correct appeal procedure in both time-in and timeout situations.

Fake throws

When an infielder decides not to throw to a base, he should always **fake** the throw in the hope of getting a runner to try to take another base. The first baseman should fake a passed ball when the infielder fakes a throw to first to try to get the batter to take a turn toward second. Practice this in team practice.

Lots of fakes cause runners to become even more paranoid than they normally are and make them afraid to ever advance.

Diving for ground balls

One of the things that annoys me about youth baseball is kids diving for a grounder, but doing it in a way that indicates they never had any hope of catching the ball. They just did it for show to make the statement, "See, I did everything I could. I even dove for it."

While writing this book, I watched the 1999 Little League World Series tournament. Even the kids on those teams do that all the time. Usually, it appeared to me that the kid **could** have caught the ball if that had really been his intention.

I suspect the fix would be to practice diving to either side, perhaps into a local high-school long-jump pit. The problem appears to be that the kids are psyched out and do not **believe** they can make such a catch. That becomes a self-fulfilling prophecy. With practice, they would no doubt figure out that making such catches is not that big of a deal.

Accept it

Fielding, that is, catching and throwing, require enormous amounts of practice to produce discernible results after the first couple of years in a player's career. The sad fact is that you cannot spend time on fielding and throwing mechanics in team practices above the tee-ball level because neither your team as a group, nor your players as individuals, will get sufficient benefit from it. Remember that you only get about 40 hours total for practice in a youth-baseball season.

Furthermore, it is unlikely that any of your players and/or parents will have the desire and work ethics to do this on their own.

Every baseball coaching book says to practice this stuff, but few disclose the hard reality that unless you get thousands of repetitions, there will be no visible benefit. There are too many other practice activities that **will** produce benefits right now to waste time on stuff that won't.

Foul and fair

A ball that ends up outside the foul line before passing third base is foul even if it originally came down in fair territory. Third basemen often let a bunt roll down the line hoping it will go out of bounds if they have no play. To do that correctly, you should roll some balls near the third-base line before the game to see if the base path is graded so that the balls stay in or roll out.

A ball that hits the first or third base is fair.

A ball that goes past third is fair if it lands in fair territory on its **first bounce** regardless of what happens thereafter.

Coaches generally know these rules, but youth players often do not.

6 Pitcher fielding

Pitcher fielding is a neglected area in baseball coaching. The sole fielding training done by most youth-baseball coaches is hitting infield and outfield and the pitcher is typically **not** a part of that drill. Why would that be? Do batters never hit the ball to the pitcher?

It must be that pitchers are such good fielders that they do not need practice. They generally **are** among the best athletes on a youth-baseball field. And I would agree that they do not need **much** practice catching the ball. But they **do** need practice knowing what to do with it in different situations.

Safety

I did a big pitch for safety in the parent meeting chapter. All I want to say here is that the pitcher is in the **most danger** when it comes to fielding. He is right in front of the batter and a proper follow through puts him in a vulnerable position at the moment the ball is hit. The batted ball travels faster than the pitch. Every Major League season brings sickening video clips of pitchers getting hit in the face by line drives.

Pitcher Herb Score is thought by many baseball historians to have had as much potential as Hall of Famer and all-time great Sandy Koufax. Then, in 1957, he took a line drive in the eye from a hit by Gil McDougald and his career more or less ended.

Hall of Famer Bob Gibson, whose unusual follow-through left him in an extraordinarily vulnerable position, had his leg shattered by a line drive off Roberto Clemente's bat. Gibson got Clemente out on the play, but he was seriously injured.

The best fielding pitcher in history, Jim Kaat, won 16 consecutive Gold Gloves, more than any other pitcher. But that didn't save him from having several teeth knocked out by a one-hopper.

As I said earlier in the book, one of my players had an orthodontist father who would not let him pitch. Our family orthodontist says he has to work on youth baseball pitchers who had their teeth knocked out every season.

If youth-baseball organizations and coaches choose not to adopt the fielding safety recommendations of the medical groups for **position** players, they should at least consider doing so for **pitchers**. I have seen some years in which lower level leagues required the pitcher to wear a batters helmet (non-face mask). Pitchers should have to wear at least protective goggles and a mouthguard. A face-mask helmet would not be a bad idea.

Follow-through

A good pitcher follow-through leaves him vulnerable to being hit by a line drive or one-hopper. Teach the correct follow-through, but you must also tell the pitcher to get into a defensive posture as soon as he can after the follow-through. That is, he must square up facing home plate with his glove in front of him.

Get off the mound

When a ball is hit right back to the pitcher, he should get off the mound before throwing to first. He has plenty of time and the mound is an obstacle except when used for pitching *per se*.

Bunts

Rolling bunts should be fielded with both hands. The glove is put in front of the ball and the bare hand and glove are used like a dust pan and dust brush. You sweep the two hands together under your sternum gathering up the ball. Get a training video for catchers to see what this looks like if you have any question.

Pitcher fielding of bunts is not hard, but neither is it so easy that you need **never** practice it. You ought to toss the pitchers some bunts during your pitcher-fielding clinic and maybe during pre-game "hit infield" sessions, so they are not surprised by a game bunt.

The catcher calls which base to throw to when there are runners on and the pitcher fields a bunt. He should say "One," "Two," "Three," or "Home."

Bunt fielding is one of those skills where all you need are a few repetitions to put the correct behavior into the player's mind, but if you do nothing at all, he may panic when confronted with a bunt during a game.

When the bunt is in the vicinity of the catcher, first baseman, or third baseman, the player who has the best chance must call "I got it" the same as a pop fly. You have to practice this a little.

If a pitcher gets to a bunt late so he has no hope of getting the runner at first, he should still fake a throw to first in the hope that it will decoy another runner to trying to advance.

Pitcher cover first

Whenever the ball is hit on the ground or a line drive to the pitcher's left (the first-base side), he must immediately run along a prescribed path to cover first base. You do it on a line drive in case the infielder knocks it down or catches it and the runner at first is off base. Pitchers will not do this unless you practice it.

'I got it'

On many occasions, the first baseman will be able to make the play himself. In that case, the pitcher must pull up, get away from the baseline, and defer to the first baseman. The first baseman should say "I got it" to the pitcher when this is the case.

Although this sounds simple and obvious, you have to give each first baseman and pitcher a few reps of pulling up in this situation. If you give no reps at all of this situation, you will have collisions at first between the first baseman, pitcher, and runner.

Sometimes, however, the hit takes the first baseman sufficiently far away from the base that he needs the pitcher's help to get the out.

Do not run straight at the base

Once you convince the pitchers to go to first on a ground ball hit to their left, you must teach them **not** to run straight at the base. The reason is they will collide with the runner when they get there.

Rather they should head for the first baseline between first and home. *Little League's Official How-to-Play Baseball Book* says to go to a spot about **ten feet** from first base. Then you turn and run parallel to the first base line and on the inside of it.

Do not cross the base line

Another problem is pitchers drift across the base line when executing this play. Again, that will cause a collision with the runner. I have had to place a line of cones long the inside of the last ten feet of the first base line to drill the pitchers not to cross over the cones. Without a bunch of practice on this, about ten or twenty reps, pitchers will tend to drift over the baseline.

The pitcher should hold his glove in front of his chest as a target.

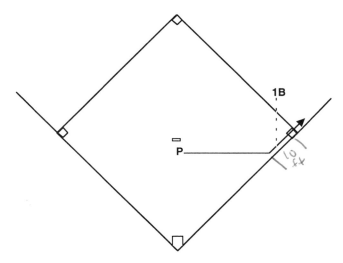

Toss before base

The first baseman must throw or toss the ball to the pitcher **before** the pitcher gets to first. The reason is the pitcher needs to **look** at the ball to catch it, then he needs to look at the **base** to step on it. If the ball arrives simultaneously with the pitcher arriving at first, he may well be unable to either catch the ball or find the base to step on it. He may even trip and fall and let the ball get past him allowing the runner to go to second.

Don't coach it, rep it

One of the differences between competent coaches and incompetent coaches is that incompetent coaches think they have to coach actively **every single aspect** of the sport. Other baseball coaching books tell you how to throw the ball to the pitcher.

I don't **know** how to throw the ball to the pitcher, and I don't **care**. I **do** know that if you give the first baseman and pitcher about twenty to thirty repetitions of the play, the first baseman will figure out the throw.

'Just catch the damn ball'

I attended the American Baseball Coaches Association convention one year. One of the speakers was Stanford head coach Mark Marquess. He was asked about the footwork by the shortstop on a double play. His answer was something to the effect that, "At Stanford we don't tell players where to put their left big toe in every situation. All we tell the shortstop on the double play is just catch the damn ball and throw it to second."

Pop your feet and look for other runners

After the pitcher gets the force out at first he must look for other runners who may be advancing. Often a runner on second will go all the way home on this play because the pitcher has his back to the plate. It might even be wise to make throwing to home or third after the put-out at first a standard part of your pitcher-cover-first practice routine.

Avoid coaching whenever possible

If a kid executes a baseball skill correctly with**out** any coaching, don't coach him. I would have thought that would go without saying. But most youth-baseball coaches coach every placement of every body part of their players in every situation. If it ain't broke, don't fix it.

Also, if a kid executes a baseball skill **almost** perfectly, but not quite, don't coach him. Coaching is not risk-free. It often harms the player. If he's already close enough for government work, leave well enough alone.

Some skills do not require **coaching** *per se*, just **practice**. The throw by the first baseman to the pitcher in the pitcher-cover-first play is a classic example of that.

If you **never** practice the play, your players will **not** execute it in games. But if you practice it just twenty to thirty times, they will get it and execute it successfully in games.

In a similar area, you are competent

You are probably a parent. Furthermore, you are probably a competent parent. Being a parent is very similar to coaching.

To a large extent, what I am urging in this book is that you coach the way you handle your other parent tasks.

Youth coaches tend to give verbal instruction on every single aspect of every skill. But as parents, those same guys would never dream of coaching their kid to walk or talk. They just model the behavior and encourage their kids.

Every single time a player does something "wrong," youth coaches feel they have to correct him instantly. Yet if I lived in your house for a period and did that to your kids on a day-to-day basis, you would tell me to get off the kid's back, and appropriately so.

Not every single body movement in baseball has to be coached, or can be. Not every single mistake needs to be pointed out. Some things get corrected without anything being said. Others may not get corrected, but the kid is still better off than if you criticize him for the transgression in question, which would make things worse.

In other words, when you think about it, what I am really saying in much of the "back off" comments in this book is that you should coach more like the way you parent. Let the kid figure it out on his own. Intervene only when necessary. Teach what can be taught. Model what is best taught by modeling. Drill and insist on those things which kids **must** do, but don't **want** to, like cleaning up or doing their homework.

Don't get me wrong. I am not from the Mr. Rogers-Barney school of coaching where kids can do no wrong and everyone gets a gold star for walking across the diamond without falling down.

'What did you learn?'

Ask a youth-baseball player after the season, "What did your coach this year teach you about baseball that you did not already know?" In the vast majority of cases, the honest answer will be, "Nothing." That is another way to define competence in youth-baseball coaching.

My players would give you a list of stuff and one of the things on that list would be the pitcher-cover-first play.

And it can't be just talk. There must be **proof** that the team in question really learned the skill in question. In the case of the pitcher-cover-first play, if you study the score books for my teams, year in and year out you will find a number of "3-1" entries. That's the scorekeeper's shorthand for the first baseman (player #3) throwing the ball to the pitcher (player #1) for the

out. Most years, you will not find a single other "3-1" entry for any other team all season.

It's not the world's biggest deal. The situation only comes up three or four times a youth season.

Because successful execution of this play is so rare, there ought to be applause when your team successfully does it. But there will not be. If you coach it well, which is not hard, your players will make it look so easy, no one will think any thing of it when it happens. They have seen that play on TV a million times. It's no big deal there.

Failure to execute looks bad

On the other hand, when the situation does come up, **failure** to execute the pitcher-cover-first play looks **bad**. The first baseman fields the grounder and looks up to throw to first—but no one is there.

The pitcher is standing on the mound, spectating. The second baseman could possibly cover in some situations, but he probably went to second or is backing up the first baseman's fielding. The batter strolls through first base with what should have been an easy out. The defensive team looks like idiots.

Chew out the pitcher?

The typical coaching response is to chew out the pitcher promptly and publicly for not knowing that he is supposed to cover first on all grounders hit to that side and not doing so on the previous play. This is disowning by the coach. What the coach **should** have done is announce to the crowd that it was **his** fault for never practicing that play.

Pop flies

In the Major Leagues, they treat pitchers as if they should have blue license plates. "He's handicapped. He can't hit. He can't catch. All he can do is pitch."

When there is a pop fly in the Majors, some infielder other than the pitcher comes over to catch it, even if it is falling right on the front of the mound. The implication is that the pitcher is such a lousy fielder that he cannot even catch a simple pop fly.

In youth baseball, the pitcher is often the best player on the field at **every** skill, so do **not** tell your team to behave like the pros and always have a fielder other than the pitcher take pops. Just treat the pitcher like any other infielder and have the player who is closest call for the ball.

When you practice calling for pops in the infield, make sure your pitchers are included in that practice session.

3-6-1 double play

If you coach an **elite teenage team**, you may be able to execute a two-throw, double-force play. If that's the case, you should practice the 3-6-1 double play to the pitcher. It is a variation of the pitcher-cover-first play and starts the same way. The ball is hit to the pitcher's left on the ground so he runs to cover first. In this case, he must stop there and stretch like a first baseman for the throw with his foot on the bag.

If you plan to practice this play, your pitchers should attend your first baseman's position clinic. But I must say again that the two-throw, double-force play has an extremely high degree of difficulty.

Hall of Fame second baseman Joe Morgan says in *Baseball for Dummies*, "When I first came up to the Major Leagues, I would work on starting the double play with our first baseman and shortstop for an hour and a half a day." Note that's an hour and a half a day just on **starting** the double play! You almost certainly have neither the time nor the talent to pull off a 3-6-1. So f' get about it.

Pitcher cover second and third

There is no set play when the pitcher covers second or third. But sometimes when those fielders are chasing the ball, the base is not covered and needs to be. In those cases, the pitcher needs to recognize the need and get there.

This should be covered in your half-field defensive drills. Here is a script for pitcher defensive-situation practice:

Do these for each of the eight possible men-on-base situations.

• grounder to left side of infield (at the first or second baseman)
• base hit
• comeback (sharp grounder to mound)
• line drive to pitcher
• dribbler to pitcher
• bunt to pitcher
• passed ball
• delayed steal (react to delayed steal)
• squeeze (with runner at third only)

Pitcher cover home

This is a very, common, important, and difficult play. On a passed ball with a runner at third, the pitcher must hustle to the plate. He must get a two-handed tag down (ball securely in palm of bare hand and bare hand deep in glove) on the ground on the third base corner of the plate. After the tag, he must pop his feet and be ready to throw to third.

You have to **practice this a lot**. Otherwise, the pitcher will fall asleep and forget to cover in which case the run will score easily.

There is **not** a lot of **technique** coaching that goes with this. You must give the pitchers and catchers many, many repetitions to practice. It's one of those plays where the players will panic if you only do it under game conditions.

First, do it against "air" as we say in football coaching. That is, no base runner and no stop watch. Then do it against a stopwatch. Finally, do it against a runner.

Key coaching points are run full speed as soon as you recognize it is a passed ball, stand between the tag spot and the catcher, put a two-handed tag on the ground, after the runner slides into it, pop up and look to get another out at third. This is a "Don't coach it, rep it" skill.

The 'Dayo' play

One play that is great fun for the offense and a colossal embarrassment to the defense is what I call the "Dayo" play. At this part of the book, I will discuss it to cover the pitcher's role in stopping it.

Home plate must always be covered by either the catcher or the pitcher when there is a runner at third. That's one of the Ten Commandments of Baseball.

Sometimes, the ball gets away from the catcher and the pitcher covers home. If the lead runner was at second, he will likely go to third. As long as the pitcher covers home, there is no problem with the catcher chasing the passed ball. But sometimes, the catcher is far away from home and the play seems to be over because the catcher is holding the ball and the runner cannot advance. However, what happens next is the problem.

The pitcher, figuring the danger is over, which it is as long as the catcher is holding the ball and standing between third and home, strolls back to the mound.

At this point, you will literally hear the players in my dugout start to sing *The Banana Boat Song* made famous by Harry Bellafonte and a scene from the movie *Beetlejuice*. The second line of that song begins,

Daylight come and me wanna go home.
Dayo. Daaaayo.
Daylight come and me wanna go home.

My base runners are trained and drilled about this situation. My runner will relax his body and reduce his lead to almost nothing to suggest to the catcher than he has abandoned all thoughts of advancing, but he will watch the catcher like a hawk.

Explode on daylight

If the catcher throws the ball to the pitcher from a location other than near home plate, my runner will explode full speed toward home just as soon as he sees daylight between the ball and the catcher's hand. Thus the name "Dayo."

The runner typically runs through a vacant home plate area without even a throw being made. The defense looks like idiots, catchers and coaches slam their gloves and clipboards on the ground, and the offense looks like men playing with boys.

Executed against us

Unbelievably, this play was executed successfully **against** us in 1992. My son was at catcher. He ended up half way up the third-base line chasing a runner who kept taking huge secondary leads back to third. The pitcher was on the mound.

I recognized the situation and said quietly to my son, the "world's greatest youth base runner," "Dan, Dayo."

He looked at me quizzically. A few seconds later, he threw the ball to the pitcher from his position half way up the third baseline. The runner exploded home and scored without a throw. My son slammed his mitt on the ground. The opposing coach, who was well aware of my reputation for baserunning, yelled "How about THAT, Jack?!"

I lamely shrugged and pleaded, "That's **our** play. We **practice** that." I asked my son what the heck he was doing in view of the fact that I explicitly said, "Dayo." He said, "I didn't know what you meant because we were not on offense."

I did not disown him publicly at the time. But I do so now. I taught him better than that. Must be his mother's DNA.

Actually, I should have said, "Dan, go back to home plate," or "Pitcher, cover home plate." By using code baserunning terminology instead of defensive terminology, I confused my son. BUT IT SEEMS PRETTY OBVIOUS TO ME WHAT "DAYO" MEANT AFTER ALL OUR PRACTICE ON THAT PLAY!

I'm sorry. Harkening back to my West Point training, my response to why I let that team pull the Dayo play against my team is, "No excuse, Sir." My son was only ten at the time. I was 46.

Pick another name

By the way, you cannot call it the "Dayo" play as far as a during game code word is concerned. There may be other readers of this book present and it will constitute a wake-up call to them.

The pitcher's role in stopping the Dayo play is to either stay at home or to remind the catcher to go there before he throws the ball to the mound.

Huge secondary leads at third

The particular team that did that against us was having their third-base runners take huge secondary leads all day. We had never seen that before.

Afterwards, we concluded that we needed to station the pitcher at home after each pitch and have the catcher meet the third baseman, hand him the ball, and have the third baseman walk the runner back to third. Then, when the catcher was back at home and the pitcher was back on the mound, the third baseman could throw the ball to the mound.

Catcher chasing pop foul

The catcher chasing a pop foul away from the plate is also a "Dayo" situation if there are less than two outs. The pitcher must cover home plate. If there is a smart runner at third, and no one is at home plate, he will tag up and jog home as soon as the catcher catches the foul pop. Practice this a couple of times.

Defensive assignments

I have already told you what a pitcher does on a ground ball hit to his left—cover first—and what he does on a passed ball or foul pop to the catcher—cover home.

On all other hits, he backs up second if there are no runners. If there is a runner at first, he backs up third. If there is a runner at second or third, he backs up home. Generally, when there are runners, he goes to the foul territory between third and home and backs up the appropriate base. He can figure out which base as the play develops.

Tell your pitchers to stay at least fifteen to twenty feet behind the guy they are backing up. If there is not that much room behind third or home because of the fence, they must play the carom of the ball that gets past the fielder in question. Trying to back up from a shorter distance is ineffective and dangerous.

Left fielder covering home

I said earlier that in semi-pro, I once prevented a run from scoring by covering home from left field! On that play, there was a runner at first and the batter hit a single to right field.

The pitcher stayed on the mound like an idiot. I disown him, too. I had told my pitchers repeatedly to get the heck off the mound when the ball was put in play with runners on. But semi-pro players are not very coachable. Getting them to show up on Sunday morning for a double header is a big enough challenge.

He should have been over behind third. I was there instead, as I should have been because the right fielder should automatically throw to third in that situation.

I had to cover home because the catcher decided to back up third also. Catchers **NEVER** back up third. If the pitcher had been where he should have been, he could have covered the surprisingly vacated home plate a lot easier than a left fielder.

Delayed-steal prevention

The pitcher must be alert to stop the delayed steal. One of the things I tell my delayed stealers to look for is a **pitcher who regularly turns his back on the runner** after he receives the throw back from the catcher. When we see that, we will probably execute a delayed steal.

The other indicators that a delayed steal is in order are a **catcher who lobs the ball back to the pitcher** or a **baseman who does not cover his base after each pitch.**

First, the pitcher must **not** turn his back on the lead runner after he receives the catcher's throw. Rather he must check the runner's secondary lead to see if it is too big. My delayed stealers are taught to take a longer and longer secondary lead after the pitches leading up to their delayed steal.

All occupied bases and bases ahead of the lead runner should be covered after the pitch gets to the catcher. If the pitcher sees either the catcher or an infielder neglecting his post-pitch duties, he must quietly tell him to straighten out.

At the teenage level, lobbing pickoff throws to one base when another is occupied may trigger a delayed steal by the other runner.

First-and-third defense

My teams are very big on the double steal, which is generally done with runners at first and third. Being conscious of that play because we use it so much, and practicing that play with some of our players playing the role of the opposing defense, made us pretty good at defending it. Although I hasten to add that it is a tough play to defend in youth baseball if executed well.

In the first-and-third play, the runner at first steals second and the runner at third breaks for home as soon as he is sure the catcher has really thrown to second.

There are several standard defensive plays to stop the first-and-third play:

• throw to middle infielder who charges in and throws back home
• throw hard to pitcher
• fake throw to second
• start to throw to second, then throw to third

Throw to middle infielder

We actually were successful on one occasion in 1990 with an **accidental** throw-to-the-middle-infielder defense at the 9-10-year-old level. But I think that success was a fluke.

We called the throw-hard-to-the-pitcher play before the pitch, but the pitcher screwed up and ducked instead of catching the ball.

My son, who was nine at the time, was playing shortstop. When the ball got past the pitcher, the runner at third broke for home. My son charged the throw and caught it, on a short hop no less, then gunned it home where we tagged the runner out. I do not recall whether we kept the trailing runner from advancing to third.

This was really quite a remarkable play for that level. I never saw another youth team pull that off and we never even tried except for fiddling with it in practice a few times. I recommend that you **not** use the throw-to-a-middle-infielder defense unless you are coaching an elite teenage team.

Throw hard to the pitcher

In the throw-hard-to-the-pitcher play, the catcher tries to make it look like he's throwing to second but he throws low so that the pitcher can catch the ball. The hope is that the runner at third will mistakenly think the ball is going past the pitcher and take off for home.

After the pitcher catches the ball, he runs at the runner from third base. He may be able to tag him out. Or he may have to drive the runner toward third, then throw to the third baseman for the tag out. In some cases, he may have to drive him toward home and throw to the catcher.

I think we made this work once. I do not understand why it did not work more often. Probably we need more reps in practice.

Pitchers afraid

This is a decent, relatively safe play. The biggest problem seems to be that the pitcher is afraid of a hard, short-range throw from the catcher. That's a bit annoying when you consider that the pitcher has been throwing hard at the catcher from the same range all day. True, the catcher is wearing protective equipment, but he also has a swinging batter distracting him.

The other problem is that the runners don't fall for the fake often enough.

Play code

We numbered our first-and-third plays. Because this play went to the pitcher who is player number one in scorekeeper shorthand, we called it Play #1. When we got a first-and-third situation, I would say to the whole infield, "If he goes, 656."

My players would ignore the first digit and add the last two digits together. The last digit of the sum was the player to whom we were going to throw the ball. 5 plus 6 is 11 which means throw to player #1.

The play my son executed in 1990 would be called play #6 because we threw it to the shortstop who is player #6. One code combination for that might be 833. (3 + 3 = 6)

This code gives you 100 different ways to call each play. You can also vary it by making the first two numbers the ones added to get the play or you could add the first and third numbers leaving the middle number as the dummy.

I'll cover the other first-and-third plays when I get to those positions later in the book.

Do something

Most youth coaches simply allow the runner at first to steal second. That offends my sense of the way the game ought to be played. I always call some kind of defensive play.

At times, it has been my impression that the mere fact of our saying, "If he goes, 342," intimidated opposing coaches and players out of running the play. They knew we were aware of the runner at third, that we had some secret play ready if the runner at first stole, and they were scared that whatever it was, it might work.

In contrast, my opponents often reacted to our having runners at first and third by saying, "Let him go." That absolutely did **not** intimidate us.

Sure, it could have been a trick, but it never was. Plus we were the best team in the league at executing the double steal so we were the worst candidates for being tricked.

'Check the runner'

When there is an unforced runner on base and less than two outs, the pitcher who fields a grounder must check the runner before throwing to first. You often hear youth-baseball coaches says that. And they are right when they do so. Unfortunately, they never taught the pitcher adequately what it **means** to check the runner.

In the typical youth-baseball game, the pitcher **looks at** the runner, then throws to first **regardless of what he saw** when he checked. The runner, who usually has too big of a secondary lead, advances to the next base because the pitcher was blind to his big lead.

The fix for this problem is a **competitive drill**. These can be run for longer than the five- or ten-minute normal drill limit because competition is fun. In a competitive drill, each side tries its best to beat the other. In a non-competitive drill, one side deliberately takes a fall just to give the other side practice at that situation.

You want to use competitive drills whenever possible because they are more fun, but for many skills, the competition gets in the way of teaching.

Put a runner at second or third (do both eventually) with no runner at first. Tell the players there are less than two outs. Fully staff the infield including the pitcher and catcher. Someone operates a stopwatch. Find out how long it takes your fastest player to get to first from the time his bat hits the ball.

The pitcher has a ball on the mound. A coach who stands in the batters box also has a ball. The pitcher throws a pitch to the catcher who catches it and holds it until the play is over. When the ball reaches the plate, the coach throws a grounder or line drive to the pitcher.

The object of the game is for the defense to keep the runner at second **and** get the batter out at first. Instead of having a batter run to first, which is tiring and boring, use a stopwatch to simulate the batter. If the pitcher gets the ball to first in less time than it takes your fastest runner to get there, the "batter" is out.

Keeping the runner at second and getting the "batter" out is a win for the defense. So is getting the lead runner out even if the "batter" reaches first safely.

If the runner advances to third or he stays at second and the "batter" is safe at first, the offense wins.

Show the full range of behaviors

Hopefully, the runners will show the full range of possibilities in their behavior at second on their own initiative. If not, the coach must order the runners to show the remaining behaviors which they did not show on their own initiative, so that the pitchers see all the possibilities. The full range of behaviors by the runner at second is:

- conservative secondary lead then break for third on the pitcher's throw to first
- aggressive secondary lead then break for third on the pitcher's throw to first
- run as soon as the ball is hit

The range of pitcher countermeasures includes:

- immediate throw to second
- immediate throw to third
- run at the second-base runner and tag him
- run at the second-base runner and throw to the base he is going toward
- fake throw to first then run at second-base runner and throw him out

Your runners and pitchers may come up with additional tactics. When and how do you attack the runner rather than throw to first? I don't know. The other baseball coaching books discuss that. But I **do** know that your players will figure out the best tactics if you give them reps. And I think that is the best course of action in youth-baseball coaching. They will also get **better** at the tactics in question from the practice.

When there are unforced runners at second and third with less than two out, guess which runner is most vulnerable to being picked off? The guy at **second** will take a huge secondary lead.

But unless your are coaching an elite teenage team, you probably cannot take advantage of that without letting a run score. The top priority in a unforced-runner-less-than-two-out situation is preventing the lead runner from advancing. Because of the high incidence of passed balls, a runner on third often, or maybe usually, translates into a run. Getting an out is secondary.

Runner may still go to third

Part of this play is preventing the runner from advancing even when the pitcher does his job correctly then throws to first. The first basemen have to practice throwing to third after getting the force.

It may be that the best baserunning tactic is to take a conservative lead at second then explode to third as soon as the ball leaves the pitcher's hand. Often in youth baseball, the defense is simply not physically capable of stopping the base runners in certain situations. This may be one of them.

If that's the case, you need to look at your numbers to see which is worse, runners at first and second with the same number of outs as before or a runner at third with one more out than before.

There are 24 different possible combinations of runners and outs. The authors of the excellent book *The Hidden Game of Baseball* worked out the likely runs scored after each. Here's the table based on Major League games.

Runners at	Number of outs		
	0	1	2
0	0.454	0.249	0.095
1	0.783	0.478	0.209
2	1.068	0.699	0.348
3	1.277	0.897	0.382
1+2	1.380	0.888	0.457
1+3	1.639	1.088	0.494
2+3	1.946	1.371	0.661
1+2+3	2.254	1.546	0.798

← # RUNS

Looking at the table, we see that it is better for the defense to have a runner at third with one out (.897) than runners at first and second with no outs (1.380). It is also better to have a runner at third with two outs (.382) than runners at first and second with one out (.888).

But remember those figures are based on **Major League** games. The fielding is relatively better in the Major Leagues than the baserunning compared to youth baseball. I know of no source for youth-baseball statistics, but I know the incidence of runners stealing home on passed balls is far higher in youth baseball than in the Majors.

It may well be that the percentage play in youth baseball is to hold the runner at second even if it means letting the hitter be safe at first, then hoping to get two or three "any base" fielder's choice outs on the ensuing batters.

The answer depends on the hitting success of the opposing team, the catching success of your catcher, and the distance between the backstop and the plate. If your pitcher and catcher can avoid passed balls, or cover the plate well when they occur, getting the out is a higher priority than keeping third empty.

1-2-3 double-force play

I have said that two-throw, double-force plays are all but impossible in youth baseball unless you coach an elite teenage team. One that might work however is the 1-2-3. The reason is that the ball gets to the fielder, the pitcher, extremely fast.

I have never seen the play executed in a youth game. But I have never seen it **not** executed when the situation came up either. I don't think I ever saw the situa-

tion—bases loaded, no-outs or one-out, and a grounder to the pitcher.

You should try it with your kids to see if they can get the out at home and get the ball to first before the stopwatch says the fastest runner on the team would have arrived there. It's mainly a matter of being awake and conscious of the possibility of the play before the pitch.

Pitcher as cut man

The pitcher is the cut man on hits to center with a runner at second. This is not the way they do it in the pros, but they have far more territory behind the plate where the pitcher can back up the catcher. In youth baseball, there is hardly any room behind the plate so the pitcher is best used as a cut man on throws home from center.

He should stand just behind the mound. He holds both arms up high to show the center fielder that he is the cut man. The cut man should not get short hopped. He should move toward the throw if necessary to avoid a short hop.

The cut man's job is to change the direction of the ball, **not** to relay it. He only catches the ball if it is off line or if the fielder in charge tells him to cut and throw to another base. If the throw is on line, he lets it go through to the catcher, although he should **pretend** to catch it and throw it to a base to screw up the runners. He will generally know whether it is off line because the catcher will have lined him up before the throw.

The correct way to relay the off-line throw to the catcher is diagrammed in the first base chapter.

Pitcher-fielding position clinics

You should hold at least one pitcher fielding clinic and preferably two. Here are suggested practice schedules for those clinics:

Clinic #1

5:30	Pitcher cover first then throw to third and home
5:35	Field bunts and throw to all four bases (also fake throws and chase lead runner)
5:40	Two-handed tag on the ground at home
5:42	Pitcher cover home on passed ball or pop up to catcher
5:50	Delayed-steal throw to second, third, and home
5:55	Face runner after receiving throw from catcher
5:57	First-and-third defense play #1
6:00	End

Clinic #2

5:30	Pitcher cover home on passed ball and pop to catcher

5:35   Two-handed tag on the ground at home
5:37   Half-field defensive situations
5:47   Defense against overly large secondary lead
5:55   Check the runner then throw to first

You would also have a pitcher **pitching** clinic or two in addition to this pitcher **fielding** clinic. At the **teenage** level, you would also need to do a pitcher clinic on the **balk rule** and **holding runners** close. I will discuss those clinics in the appropriate chapters.

Tee-ball pitchers need all of the above clinic segments except those items relating to steal prevention. The pitcher-cover-first situation is more common in tee ball than at any other level of baseball. Tee-ball pitchers do not need to cover home on a passed ball, but they **do** on a caught foul pop with less than two outs.

7 Catcher

At the 9-12 age levels, the catcher is the most important defensive position because they **steal** at those levels and pitchers, who would normally be more important, only work two or three innings. Catchers can go the whole game, although they usually also pitch some, too. **Above** that level, the **pitcher** is most important. **Below** that level, the **pitcher** as fielder and the **first baseman** are most important. At the teenage level, the catcher is the **second** most important defensive position.

Equipment

It is important that your catcher's equipment **fit** your catcher and be in good condition. Unless he owns his own equipment, it is unlikely that his equipment either fits or is in good condition. You should request better-fitting, adequate quality equipment from your league equipment manager.

If none is forthcoming, you should tell the catcher's **parents** about the problem and urge them to buy their own equipment. Give them the league equipment manager's name and number if they are not happy with that solution. This will not help your campaign for league president, but you have a moral, ethical, and a legal obligation to your kids to see that they are properly protected.

Regarding shin guards, the clips go on the **outside**. I wish I had a dollar for every time some coach or father sent his catcher to the plate with the clips on the inside. It's not life or death. It's just ignorant. The shin guard clips go on the outside so they do not get tangled if the catcher's legs come together.

Typically, with league-issued equipment, you need to **cross** the shin guard straps to get the fit snug. That is you clip the top strap to the next lower clip and vice versa.

The chest protector should fit snug against the throat and chest.

Often, the catcher's helmet is too small, but because it is attached to the mask with elastic straps, catchers wear it anyway. This results in a large gap between the face mask and the helmet. That gap is unprotected child head. It must be corrected.

Passed balls

In the pros, the catcher's main job is to call the game. That is, tell the pitcher what pitch to throw and to what location. Youth baseball ain't the pros.

Youth pitchers only have one pitch, two at best. And their control is so poor that they cannot often hit the spot the catcher, in his wisdom, thinks they should hit.

All **tee-ball** catchers do is get put outs at home. Above the tee-ball level, the youth catcher's main job is to **prevent passed balls**. Preventing passed balls requires a good stance and athletic ability when the pitch is wide or high. When the pitch is in the dirt, preventing passed balls requires good blocking technique and the discipline or habit of using good technique.

The stance and technique are coachable.

Stance

Catchers have three stances:

- giving signs to the pitcher
- catching the pitch with no runners on
- catching the pitch with runners on

To watch a typical youth baseball game, you would think there was only one. If it were the runners-on stance, that would not be a problem. Unfortunately, it is the giving-signs stance.

Giving-signs stance

In the giving-signs stance, the catcher has his feet together and is up on the balls of his feet. The right-handed catcher shields the view of a third-base runner and third-base coach by holding his mitt out in front of his left knee. (A left-handed catcher would do the opposite. As far as I can tell, there is no basis for the widespread aversion to left-handed catchers. I had one. I saw no difference because of his handedness.)

With his bare hand, the catcher gives the pitcher signs. In youth baseball, one finger for a fast ball and two for a change should be enough. At the sub-teen level, throwing other pitches is not advisable because of the danger of the pitcher injuring his arm.

A common mistake is to hold the fingers too low so they can be seen by opposing coaches or base runners. The sign should be up in the crotch, not below it. The thighs are opened just wide enough so the pitcher can see.

At the higher youth levels, a catcher may need to disguise his signs so that a runner on second cannot steal the signs and signal them to the batter.

The main reason for a catcher giving a sign at all is that breaking balls are hard to catch if the catcher is not expecting them. The catcher does not need to know in advance whether the pitcher is throwing a fast ball or change, if that's all the pitcher has. But he **does** need to know in advance whether the pitch is a curve or slider or screw ball if the pitcher has any of those pitches.

I like the catcher to give signs at the lower levels to take some pressure off the pitcher. "Get the sign and throw that pitch," I tell them. "If the batter hits it, it's not **your** fault. **You** didn't pick the pitch."

One year when I taught my pitchers only **two** pitches—fastball and changeup—I gave them **three** signs:

- fastball
- changeup
- shake your head no

The latter sign just told the pitcher to pretend he was rejecting the catcher's pitch call. We were just having a little fun and messing with the batter's mind.

There **is** a little strategy at calling the pitches at the subteen level.

If he can't hit the fastball, call for nothing but fastballs

In sub-teen baseball, many bottom-of-the-order batters cannot hit the pitcher's fastball. When that is the case, call for nothing but fastballs.

The reason is most pitchers have their best control when they throw the fastball. That's the 85% fastball.

Do **not** call for a changeup to a weak hitter. It's probably the only pitch he can hit.

The hyper heater

Some pitchers have hyper heaters—extremely fast fastballs. When my oldest son was ten, he had a fastball so terrifying some batters would jump back out of the batter's box before he released the pitch.

In adult baseball, I once faced a former triple-A professional pitcher. His fastball was in the nineties. It made a spitting, hissing sound as it approached the plate. I only heard that sound on two previous occasions. Once, while coaching first base in an adult game, a line drive almost took my head off. In the Army, a 105 mm howitzer crew once accidentally fired a shell right over the forward-observer location that I and a couple dozen others were occupying.

I was wearing a cast on my left hand the day I faced the AAA pitcher. It had been broken by a pitch the previous weekend, but my team only had nine guys counting me the following week. I also had on my face-mask batting helmet. Seeing my cast and mask, the former AAA pitcher thought it would be cute to deliberately throw his first pitch as hard as he could into the backstop. It made a crash so loud I suspect some neighbors may have called the cops to report a car accident.

Did he intimidate me? I wasn't much of a hitting threat to begin with having a cast on my left hand. But I did mutter an expletive after that ball hit the back-

stop. Then I bunted back to the pitcher to start a double play.

So if your pitcher has a pitch that bears some resemblance to that one, it would probably be a good idea for him to knock a board out of the backstop to start the game and to throw it a few other times during the game, like at the start of a bottom-of-the-batting-order player's at bat.

For a pitcher with one of hose, I would have three signs:

- 100% fastball
- 85% fastball
- changeup

Change speeds with good hitters

Against the top of the order, you probably cannot call all fastballs unless your pitcher has excellent control. In adult baseball I faced a former AA professional pitcher several times. He threw me nothing but fastballs. They were in the high eighties, which was not beyond my ability to catch, but every single pitch was in the black (around the edge of the plate).

I was looking for a hitter's pitch, but he only threw pitcher's pitches. Plus they were so fast you had to decide earlier whether to swing. Darned near injured myself trying to check a swing against the guy once.

I finally managed to hit a weak ground out to second against him. Got a standing ovation from my dugout mates who had struck out, as had I in all previous at bats against the guy. The grounder looked like a hitter's pitch, then moved in on me so I hit it off the handle.

If your pitcher has that kind of control, you may be able to call all fastballs even against good hitters.

One of our family's favorite youth-baseball moments came when my son was ten and pitching in the bottom of the last inning. We were ahead by one, but the opponent had the bases loaded. With two outs and a three-two count, my son was facing a top-of-the-order batter. On his own initiative, he chose a changeup which floated in as if it were a high fastball then fell right into the middle of the strike zone for a called strike three.

Our parents and players exploded in cheers. The opposing coach went ugly nuts screaming at his players and spoiling the moment for us to an extent. He should have just tipped his hat to my son for having the smarts to pick that pitch, the guts to throw it, and the athletic ability to put it where he wanted it.

Calling pitches at the teenage level

Teenage pitchers often have a larger repertoire than fastball and changeup. They also have better control so the catcher should call for pitches both by type and location.

One of the age-old admonitions to pitchers is

- Throw strikes
- Change speeds
- Work fast
- Hold the runners close

That's generally good advice, although the admonition to throw strikes may be misinterpreted by some to mean throw all pitches in the strike zone. You can often get strikes on pitches **outside** the zone, too.

Catchers should keep the pitcher moving. A slow tempo will put the fielders to sleep. Many times in youth baseball, the **catcher** slows down the tempo by walking toward the pitcher after every pitch. Get the ball back to the pitcher quickly.

Read McCarver

The great philosopher Clint Eastwood once said, "A man's got to know his limitations." One of my limitations is I am not very knowledgeable about sophisticated pitch calling with pitchers who have pinpoint control and a repertoire of several breaking balls. So for that I refer you to Tim McCarver's book *Baseball for Brain Surgeons and Other Fans*. McCarver was a Major League catcher and is now a baseball TV analyst.

Hitter's perspective

I do have a few comments to make from a hitter's perspective, though. Although I occasionally faced former pros in adult and semi-pro baseball, the majority of the pitchers were simply grown-up Little Leaguers.

In the over-30 baseball leagues, the pitchers generally threw in the 70-to-80-miles-per-hour range. But they were crafty. They would throw fastballs, curves, sliders, knuckleballs, you name it.

In the over-40 all-star game, I faced a guy I had never seen. I was National League. He was American. His average fastball went about 65 mile per hour. From the dugout, we couldn't believe he was an all-star and we couldn't wait to face him.

Then, when he got us out, we came back to the dugout muttering and expressing our feeling that we couldn't wait to face him again.

Because it was an all-star game, he only got to pitch for two or three innings (out of nine). Thank God. He was the biggest junk ball pitcher I have ever seen. He threw every pitch ever invented. After showing you his 65 miles per hour fastball, he would throw a 55 miles per hour changeup—about the speed of a ten-year old. And every once in a while, he would throw his 100% heater, which was about 72. But it was far more effective because of the junk that preceded it.

Semi-pro pitchers

Contrast that with the semi-pro pitchers. They were typically 18 to 22 years old. They could throw in the low eighties. Most had a curve, but they could not throw it for strikes.

They would see my over-30 teammates the first two seasons I played semi-pro—many with gray hair—and figure they could throw fastballs by us. They could not. They also figured they could hit the crap out of our over-30 pitchers because they only threw in the seventies. They could not.

We over-30 guys can hit fastballs in the eighties, especially when the pitcher falls behind in the count and has to throw what the pros call a "mistake pitch" down the pipe. But the semi-pro kids could not hit well against multi-pitch older pitchers, especially when the hitters were behind in the count.

Curveball

I generally would not swing at a curveball the first time I saw it from a particular pitcher. But if I saw it again from the same pitcher in that at bat or that game, and it was a hitter's pitch, I could recognize it and hit it.

That suggests that a curveball should be called for and thrown for a strike when needed in an early at bat against a particular batter. But if you need to use it **again** against that batter, better you should call for it when it can be thrown for a **ball** and hope the batter chases it.

The more pitches a batter sees from a particular pitcher, the greater the probability he will get a hit, and that is especially true of off-speed pitches.

I have read that some excellent players cannot make it in the Majors because they can't hit a curveball. I never faced curve balls as fast as the pros throw, but I always felt the curve was an easy pitch to hit, as long as I got to see at least two of them from the same pitcher.

Knuckleball

I have seen a few knuckleball pitches. Not only did I miss them, I looked like an idiot doing so. I have read that some Major Leaguers won't swing at them because they are afraid they will mess up their finely-tuned swing. It's a great pitch if it's a strike or the batter swings at a ball. But I would be leery of calling for it unless I was not worried about passed balls.

Also, in youth baseball, many knuckleball pitchers have not quite perfected it. An unperfected knuckleball is about like a slow-pitch softball pitch. If that describes your pitcher's knuckler, tell him to keep working on it and forget about it in games.

Sliders

I never could make good decisions with sliders. The well-located ones all look like fastballs down the pipe to me. Then when I swing, they are low and outside. I probably hit a few that hung, thinking they were high, inside fastballs. But I chased a bunch that were where the pitcher wanted them. If your pitcher can throw that pitch accurately without injuring his arm, and there are other batters like me, call for it.

No-runners stance

Back to stances. When there are no runners, the catcher can get into a relaxed stance. The only downside to getting too relaxed is you may miss out on catching a bunt or foul pop, although the latter is less likely for youth catchers because of the small foul territory and the many overhead backstops.

With no runners, some catchers do a split (ouch). Others catch from their knees.

Whatever the catcher wants is fine with me, although if there were roofless catcher foul-pop territory, I would want him mobile enough to make those catches.

With no runners on base, the catcher should put his throwing hand behind his back.

Runner-on-base stance

In the **correct** stance, the catcher has his heels touching the ground and his thighs parallel to the ground. He is **not** up on the balls of his feet with his feet together the way he is when he gives signs.

His feet are spread shoulder-width apart. The ball of the throwing-side foot is even with the arch of the glove-side foot.

The glove arm is bent at the elbow. His throwing hand is balled into a relaxed fist and hidden behind the catcher's mitt as the pitch approaches to protect it from being hit by a foul ball, but to have it close to the mitt for a quick throw to a base. His glove elbow is **above** his glove-side knee, otherwise he will have trouble catching balls to his glove side that are outside his knee.

This is uncomfortable and a strain to youth baseball players, so they resist it. This is the situation that **drills** were invented for: instilling a necessary habit that players resist. Just make the catcher get into the correct stance again and again throughout the season or they will use a poor stance.

Virtually every baseball book has a good drawing or photo showing a good catcher stance. There are also many good catcher videos that show the correct stances.

Pitcher need not see palm of mitt

Another common misunderstanding is the notion that the catcher has to show the **palm** of his mitt to the pitcher. Some mitt manufacturers contribute to this by sewing day-glo strips around the palm of the mitt.

For the catcher to show his palm to the pitcher requires the catcher to rotate his hand back to an extreme position 90 degrees from his forearm. That's tiring. It's also unnecessary. Just have the catcher hold the mitt in a natural way. That means the pitcher sees only the forward edge of the mitt. He can throw to the forward edge just as easily as the can throw to the palm.

Also, holding the wrist at right angles to the fore-arm makes it stiff and makes it harder to catch the pitch. The wrist must be relaxed.

Depth of set-up point

Youth catchers almost always set up **too deep** in the catcher's box. I suspect they are afraid and fail to take into account that the batter strides forward when he swings. They should be close enough to reach out and touch the back leg of the batter. If you get called for catcher interference, move back. Otherwise stay up there.

This is extremely important at the levels at which stealing is allowed. Most passed balls are caused by pitches in the dirt. The farther back the catcher is, the more pitches hit the ground. Remember the catcher's main job in youth baseball is to prevent passed balls. Playing back too far also reduces the number of foul tips you catch.

Catch it in the web

You should catch the ball in the web of the catcher's mitt, same as if you were wearing a fielder's glove. The catcher's mitt is worn the same as a fielder's glove, that is, with the heel of the hand sticking out of the mitt and the fingers only partly in so that the mitt is used like tongs with a web.

Framing

Framing is catching the unswung-at pitch that is just outside the strike zone in such a way that it tricks the umpire into thinking it was a strike. I don't know that you need to teach this. Intelligent kids figure it out for themselves. If you also teach it on top of their own figuring it out, the catcher may overdo it, which looks ridiculous and antagonizes umpires. The whole idea of framing is a bit dishonest, but it's sort of involuntary around the edges of the strike zone.

Throwing to second

For the first half of the 1992 season, we automatically stole second on the first pitch against everybody. But about half way through the season, I had to tell my players not to steal against Al Cuthbert's son. Why? He had been practicing and finally got it.

I saw that phenomenon with other catchers over the years, too. What's that tell you? It should tell you that throwing to second takes time to learn. Your catchers need reps to get it. I would guess the typical youth catcher needs to throw to second about 150 times to get the distance and accuracy right.

You must set aside time for the catchers to practice this throw so they get their 150 reps **before the first game**. You should put a stopwatch on the throw after the initial period of getting comfortable with the mechanics of the throw.

To succeed at throwing out a would-be stealer, you

must be quick. The catchers will not get into the habit of being quick unless you use a stopwatch. You can also use live runners, but your catchers need more reps than your base runners will be willing to give them. Use a few live runners at the outset to find out what stopwatch time you are looking for.

Experts say the key is the catcher's **feet**. They must be quick. Catchers also have different throwing styles. I would not teach the mechanics of the throw verbally. But I always show my catchers a training video and they see the mechanics there.

At the 9-10 year old level, I had to teach some of my catchers to make the throw a long hop. That is, they were to aim at the ground about 15 feet in front of second base.

Keep your mask on!

One the most common mistakes I see in youth baseball is the catcher **taking his mask off for a steal throw**. Some even do it on pitches that they field cleanly.

On 8/17/99, I was watching the Southeast Regional Little League Championship on ESPN 2. One of the catchers took his mask off in a steal-preventing situation. No! No! No! The catcher takes his mask off only to catch pops, bunts, or throws, not thieves.

Most base runners are chicken. A well-executed throw on the "coming down" before the half inning starts can do more to prevent base runners from stealing second than a game throw. Most base runners are abject cowards when it comes to getting thrown out. So are most youth coaches. They are easily intimidated by a strong-armed catcher.

How to stop the unstoppable base runner from stealing second

The opponent has a super base runner at first at the teenage level. He **always** steals second on the first pitch after he gets to first. Here's a way that might stop him. The defensive coach give a verbal coded signal to his team. On the pitcher's first body movement, the runner takes off. At the moment the pitch arrives at home, a player or coach in the defensive team's dugout bangs two bats together simulating the sound of the pitch being hit. The catcher catches the pitch and throws a **pop-up** to the second baseman, who very theatrically yells, "I got it! I got it!"

Equally theatricially, the whole defensive team starts yelling, "Throw it to first! Throw it to first!" The runner, thinking it's a pop-fly hit, desperately tries to get back to first.

I got this from high school baseball coach Cliff Petrak, author of the book The Art and Science of Aggressive Baserunning. He said that once when he did it, and tagged the speedy runner out when he was going back to first, the opposing third-base coach/manager demanded demanded of his first-base coach, "Why didn't you tell our runner to stay at second?" "I heard the ball hit the bat," was his explanation. Petrak's league subsequently outlawed banging bats together at the moment a pitch reaches the plate. So I suggested to Petrak that he hit a **ball** in the dugout with a bat at that moment.

High pitch

When the pitch is high, the catchers should make sure his mitt deflects it **down** in front of him. You still try to catch it in the web of the mitt, but you tilt the mitt so that if you just bat the ball, it is batted **down**, not up and in **front** of you rather than behind. Drill this to get the catcher into the right habit.

Blocking the ball

Blocking the low pitch is extremely important. I had enormous difficulty motivating players to do this correctly. They do not **want** to block the ball correctly. Rather they want to reach for it with their glove only.

In 1992, I badgered my catchers endlessly to block balls correctly. But they would not. One said he **couldn't** do it that way.

The following year at the tryout, I saw him try out for catcher. With all the coaches in the league watching, the player who told me he could not block the ball correctly blocked every single one as if he were Johnny Bench. He could do it all along. He just did not **want** to until the tryout.

Blocking technique

To block a low pitch, the catcher drops to his knees, sits on his heels, puts both hands between his knees, palm of mitt wide open and facing pitch, hunches his shoulders forward, and puts his chin on his chest. In fact, the whole body from the knees to the face is in the shape of a letter "C" over the ball so that it bounces back out in front of the catcher if he does not catch it.

When blocking, you really abandon most hope of catching the ball in the mitt. You're just trying to keep it in front of you.

If the low pitch is off to one side, you need to step that direction so as to get the center of your body in front of the pitch if possible. In that case, you try to get your body position as close to what I just described as possible, but the need to step sideways will hamper your ability to do that.

I suggest you try everything to get catchers to block the ball. One thing I have done is a competitive drill. Make a target on a backstop or wall using chalk. The target is a square about as big as a catcher can protect at the outer limits. Put a pitcher as far away as is normal in your league.

The pitcher tries to hit the target. If he does, he wins. The catcher tries to catch or bat down in front of him every pitch. If the ball hits the target or is deflected backward by the catcher, he loses.

In this competitive drill, the catcher is acting like a

hockey goalie and the pitcher is acting like a hockey shooter.

Bucket of balls and pitching machine

Another drill would be to take a bucket of balls and a pitching machine and work on blocking a particular location over and over. Preferably, this would be a bucket of **poly balls** and a poly ball pitching machine.

The first bucket might be aimed it the plate. The next bucket aimed two feet to the right of the plate. The next, two feet to the left. The next, two feet above the catcher's head. Curveballs and sliders should be part of the mix because the catcher has to block them a little differently.

The main point is to give your catchers a zillion reps of correctly blocking hard-to-catch pitches so passed balls will be minimized in games.

Throw to third

You do not need to practice the throw to third as much as the throw to second, but that doesn't mean you don't have to practice it at all. In throwing to third, the youth catcher usually has the added complication of a right-handed batter in the way. So when you practice, make sure you have a right-handed batter in the batter's box. If you do not, the catcher will learn an absolutely wrong way to throw to third.

Deking the runner

My son used to try to decoy the runner at second into trying to steal third. One technique he used (not my idea) was to let the pitch hit the back of his mitt. That would cause the ball to fall right in front of him where he could easily pick it up, but he would do some frantic body language to suggest that he was in a panic.

He also would sometimes catch the ball, but come up out of his crouch wildly spinning as if he were looking for the ball. In fact, the only thing he was looking for was for the runner at second to break for third.

I don't think he ever got more than one or two runners doing that. I thought it was funny and although possibly ill-advised, it was the kind of aggressiveness that should be encouraged.

Catcher pick-offs

Youth baseball runners are often vulnerable to catcher pickoff throws. However, because of the low throwing accuracy and fielding percentages in youth baseball, you generally have to let those golden opportunities go by. Otherwise, you will throw the ball into the outfield and allow runners to advance.

My approach to catcher pick-offs is to work on them in practice, but prohibit them in games unless we can achieve a satisfactory success rate in practice. It depends on the kids you have that season. My son could do the throws and we occasionally had first and third

baseman would not muff the catch. But some years, like 1997, we simply could never throw to third because either the throw or the catch would be bad.

Catcher pick-offs need to be practiced with the basemen and backing-up outfielders. One of the problems with catcher pick-offs is basemen not expecting them. Signs and acknowledgments must be worked out if you plan to use catcher pick-offs.

You might have the catcher yell out an obvious signal. For example, let's say the runner at first is taking overly long secondary leads. The catcher could yell to the first baseman, "501." What does that mean? It could mean nothing. Just the fact that the catcher and first baseman seem to have a pick-off play on will probably shorten the lead of the runner.

Play #2

In play #2, the catcher throws to himself because **he** is player #2. How does he throw to himself? He leaves the ball in his mitt and throws hard to second with an empty hand.

If he tries to fake a throw with the ball in his hand, either he will fake hard and it will come out or he will injure his arm or he will have to fake softly and the fake will not be believable. With an empty hand, he can fake as hard as possible.

He must **look** at second, **throw** toward second, then charge up the third base line to tag or throw out the runner. Even if he does not succeed, he has prevented the run from scoring and at least managed to avoid looking like a powerless wimp, which is what happens when the coach just says, "Let him go" regarding the runner from first base.

Play #5

In play # 5, the catcher throws to player # 5, the third baseman. This is the play we had the most success with. Indeed, in spite of all my emphasis on the first-and-third double steal in my youth practices, I got picked off third by this play **myself** when I was playing adult baseball in 1994.

In 1992, we used this play in a game against a Tassajara team. The teams in our local league knew about both our baserunning expertise and our baserunning-defense expertise. But the Tassajara teams only played us intermittently so they had no clue about our skills in those departments.

They got a first-and-third situation. I called for play #5. The runner at first went. The runner at third took a couple of hops toward home ready to take off if we threw to second. My son was the catcher. He leaped out from behind the plate very theatrically as we had practiced, cocked his arm to throw to second while intently staring at second, then suddenly threw the ball to third.

The runner didn't know what hit him. Third baseman Joe Swec caught the ball and easily tagged the paralyzed runner out. The Tassajara adult third-base coach burst out laughing at the sight of his runner looking like a deer caught in headlights.

Throw to a middle infielder

As I said in the pitcher-fielding chapter, I do not believe the throw-to-a-middle-infielder play against the first-and-third double steal is viable in youth baseball. Again, it might work on an elite teenage team. Try it in practice and see.

Pitch-outs

Forget about it. I suspect they are a waste of time even on elite teenage teams. Maybe you can use it sparingly on an elite teenage team if you perfect it in practice.

Catch foul pop

Turn your back to the field. Take your mask off, but continue to hold it in your hand. When you figure out where the ball is coming down, you can toss your mask away. If you do it too soon, you may later trip over it.

That mistake cost the 1946 New York Giants a World Series. With the score tied in the bottom of an extra inning, Washington Senator Muddy Ruel hit a foul pop. Giants catcher Hank Gowdy tripped over his mask and missed the catch. Ruel then hit a double and subsequently scored the winning run.

Catch the ball above your face. Do **not** try to make a basket catch.

Foul pops have a lot of spin on them and they tend to move away from fair territory then move back to the foul line along a sort of boomerang path. They are easy to misjudge.

Keep them in front of you. If you think the ball is straight above you, and misjudge, it's harder to move backward than forward. I do not know of a way to get the correct spin on the ball to practice this. Just toss them, but make sure the catcher uses correct technique so he can deal with the spin in a game.

After the catch, pop your feet and look for a runner who tagged up and is now advancing.

Do not catch a foul pop of a two-strike bunt unless you can double a runner off. The batter is already out. Catching it might enable a tagging runner to advance.

Bunt defense

As with the pitcher, the catcher should sweep his two hands together to field a bunt. He often has to **call for** the bunt if it is near the pitcher.

If the bunt is near the first baseline, after he picks it up, he must shuffle a couple of steps toward the mound to get a clear path to throw to first. He usually has the time.

A bunt near the line may roll out of bounds. The coach or catcher should roll a ball down each line before the game to see how it's graded. But if you have time to get the guy out, you want to **prevent** it from going out of bounds. For some reason, infielders always seem to take the let-it-go-foul option when it appears probable.

On a bunt hit down the third-base line, the right-handed catcher will round the ball. That is, he will turn his back on the first baseman as he approaches the ball, then his back is facing the shortstop, he will gather up the ball and throw it to first. A left-handed catcher will round bunts hit down the first-base line, or let a right-handed pitcher take it.

Dropped third strike

If the catcher drops the third strike at higher levels, he must tag the runner or throw him out at first unless the runner just walks away toward the dugout. I saw a Major Leaguer just walk away the other day on TV. When I was a kid, he would have been shot.

This must be practiced, but it only needs a few reps. First, you need to plant the seed in the catcher's mind, especially if this is his first year at the level where dropped third strikes matter. Give him practice making the tag and practice making the throw. As with a bunt near the first-base line, the catcher needs to shuffle away from the line to get a clear throw to first.

If there are other runners on second or third, they may advance on this play so it is a pop-your-feet play in the case of a tag. If a runner is on third and there are less than two outs, the catcher needs to be mindful of the need to check the runner and cover home after the throw to first. If a runner is on second only and there are less than two outs, he needs to check the runner before throwing to first.

Knockdown pitch

In his *Baseball Playbook*, Mississippi State coach Ron Polk has a catcher signal to the pitcher for a knockdown pitch. You cannot do that in youth baseball because getting hit by a ball can kill a child. I am not saying you have to avoid pitching inside, only that you may not tell one child to throw the ball **at** another.

I believe the pitcher is entitled to aim pitches at or near the strike zone or any spot where the batter has shown a propensity to swing. Some youth baseball batters really crowd the plate, in which case the danger of being hit by an inside pitch is on the batter and his coach.

Faking out the runner coming home

If the ball is being thrown to a base that a runner is approaching from **behind** the runner, it sometimes makes sense for the fielder at the base to adopt a posture that suggests no ball is coming. The fielder should relax, maybe put one hand on his hip. This makes the runner think there is no ball anywhere near, even though it may be right beside him.

Then the fielder, in this case the catcher, suddenly grabs the ball and puts the tag on the ground. The runner may have slowed up or failed to slide because he thought there would be no play at the plate.

I once threw a batter out at second from the right-field line. On that play, our second baseman pretended no throw was coming. At the last instant he grabbed the ball and put the tag down getting the runner out. It's a smart, neat play.

The opposite play, however, pretending the ball **is** coming when it is not, is obstruction (Little League Rule 2.00).

Tag at the plate

The catcher holds the ball tightly in his bare hand and puts his bare hand deep in the palm of the catcher's mitt then tags the runner with the back of the mitt. He should get into the habit of immediately looking to third or second to see if he can throw out another runner.

The catcher's left foot should point toward third base to minimize leg injuries. That places the shin guard squarely at the incoming runner. It also puts the hinge that is the knee joint in its swinging position versus the incoming runner. If the left foot is pointed in a direction other than toward third, the force of the runner sliding into it from the side may injure the leg or knee.

At the time of the tag, the catcher's chest is on his left thigh and his right knee is on or near the ground.

Blocking the plate

A lot of youth coaches think one of their main jobs is to **toughen** boys in preparation for manhood. Often, that toughening takes the form of teaching the child to engage in a violent act. In baseball, one of the classic violent acts is the catcher blocking the plate in the face of an approaching runner.

First, I want to remind you that children sometimes **die** from chest impact. One of the typical causes of a child dying in baseball each year is a two-player collision, either on the base path or in the field.

In my area about ten years ago, it was common at a local high school for one boy to suddenly punch another for "fun." One boy of 16, as I recall, received such a punch, said, "That was a good one," and fell over dead.

Some would argue that catcher's are protected by their equipment. No. Catcher's **shins** are protected by their equipment. The chest protector offers little protection and they typically take their mask and helmet off to receive the throw. (I'm not sure that's such a hot idea. Catchers who wear street-frame glasses under their masks should leave their helmets on for tag plays. Wrap-around-frame sports goggles will not fit inside most catcher's masks.)

If you encourage a catcher to block the plate, and he dies from the ensuing collision, you will regret it every day of the rest of your life. You may be sued for it.

In fact, the catcher **should** block the plate, once he is in possession of the ball. It is **obstruction** to block any base when you are **not** in possession of the ball or fielding the ball. (e.g., Little League Rule 2.00) But there is a right way to block the plate and a wrong way. Be very careful that you teach it the right way.

The most macho catcher I know of is Johnny Bench. He is a Hall of Famer who was named the greatest catcher of all time by the *Sporting News* in 1998. He won ten consecutive Gold Gloves, was a 14-time all-star, an NL MVP, and a World Series MVP.

Once, in a 1969 Major League game against the Dodgers, he was upset with the slow speed at which his pitcher, Gerry Arrigo, was throwing. To make the point, he caught one fastball **bare-handed** and threw it back to the pitcher harder than the pitcher had thrown it to the batter.

Bench says to let the runner see part of home plate so they think they can slide and catch the corner of the plate with their foot. He says do NOT stand squarely in front of the plate on the third-base line so that you give the runner no choice but to run into you.

"I wanted him on the ground, not in the air banging into my shoulder," says Bench in his *Complete Idiot's Guide to Baseball*. He placed his left foot **inside** the third-base line until he caught the ball. Then, when he caught it, he would step **on** the line to make the tag, still making sure his left foot was pointed at third base.

On a throw from right field, the catcher generally has to do a sweep tag like a first baseman who is drawn off the bag toward home. Do NOT teach catchers to block the plate when the throw is coming from right field. To do so is to hang a sign on your catcher that says, "Please blind-side me."

The most famous attempt to block the plate was Ray Fosse versus Pete Rose in the 1970 All-star game. Rose said, "I was going to slide, but I saw he had the plate blocked, so I determined that the only way I could score was to bowl him over. And that's what I did." (This story is often told as if Rose ended Fosse's career with that collision. In fact, Fosse had his best year at the plate that year and caught more games per season in the next three years than he did in 1970.)

Dive tag

Sometimes, the catcher gets the ball just barely in time to dive at the left front corner of the plate. You need to give the catcher a few repetitions of doing that to put it into their head. Otherwise, they will always feel that they have to run to the corner of the plate, which is often too slow.

Tag away from the plate

Sometimes, the catcher has an opportunity to tag a runner away from the plate. In that case, he just holds the ball the same way, but tags the nearest body part of the runner. Between third and home, the runner may try to run into the catcher to jar the ball loose.

Give the catcher a couple of reps of the away-from-home tag. Tell him to brace himself up the third-base line, or do an ole´ tag, if it appears someone wants to play football.

1-2-3 double-force play

As stated in the chapter on pitcher fielding, you should practice the 1-2-3 double-force play just to put it in the player's heads. The situation rarely comes up. You need bases loaded, less than two outs, and a quick grounder to the pitcher.

Because the pitcher gets the ball so quickly and is so close to home, this is probably the only two-throw, double-force play a normal youth team has any chance of pulling off.

In the 1-2-3 double-force play, the catcher needs to turn the pivot somewhat like a middle infielder. That is, instead of standing **on** the plate like a first baseman, he should set up **behind** the plate. As the throw arrives, he steps forward dragging his foot over the plate catching the ball and then throwing to first. By starting behind the plate and stepping forward while catching the throw, he enables himself to quickly get a couple of steps inside the first-base line so he won't hit the batter and gives his throw to first more oomph.

2-3-2 double play

My youth teams have done a total of **two** two-throw double plays in my entire career. I already told you about one, where we got a 6-4-3 against an extremely slow batter.

The other one occurred on my oldest son's AAA team when he was eleven. I was a helper father on that team.

Dan was the catcher, the opponent had a runner at third. The batter bunted. Dan fielded the bunt, checked the runner—really checked him—then threw to first. The runner at third broke for home on Dan's throw. The first baseman caught the ball getting the force out then threw back home. Dan caught the ball and tagged the runner out.

The home-plate umpire, a grown-up who, as a football coach, had cut Dan from his team three years before, shook Dan's hand to congratulate him on the play.

The key to the play was that Dan **really** checked the runner. He not only looked at him, he gave him a menacing look that said, "Take too big a lead and you die!"

The typical youth player might **look** at the runner, but he would not really **see** whether the runner had taken too big of a lead. Of course, this look by my son was preceded by Dan demonstrating his arm on many other plays, which was also a factor in the runner's decision to retreat toward third in response to Dan's unspoken threat to pick him off.

The first baseman also did a nice job of not panicking and making a quick catch and accurate return throw to Dan. The team had not practiced that play at all, but Dan had practiced really checking runners on my various teams over the years.

Using a cut man

Around the 1970's I think it was, some TV color man complained that, "today's players don't do the little things like hit the cut man." This apparently really caught the fancy of the public. Ever since, youth-baseball coaches have been demonstrating how baseball savvy they are by yelling, "Hit the cut man."

One of the advantages of writing a book is you can address pet peeves. Indeed, virtually all how-to books are written because the authors had a pet peeve about the subject matter. Hitting the cut man is one of mine.

First, there are **three different "men,"** not just a cut man. They are:

• relay man
• trail man
• cut man

Youth coaches seem to think the purpose of a cut man is to catch the ball and throw it along the same course it was already on. They seem to think its purpose is the same as that of a booster rocket. That is incorrect.

Relay man

The person who simply continues the ball on the same course is the **relay** man. A relay man is used when the ball either would **never** get to the intended base, or would get there **slower** than if it is relayed. When does that occur in youth baseball?

Hardly ever. Maybe in a field with no outfield fences.

Brings the ball to a dead stop

Think about what a relay does. It brings the ball to a dead stop for about one second.

I once had an argument with a fellow coach about whether a relay man was faster than just letting the ball bounce its way to the target. I said letting it bounce was faster.

To settle it, we had a **race**. My no-cut-man side won every time—by a wide margin. It's common sense if you stop and think about it. During the second that you are stopping the ball with the relay man, my bouncing ball is traveling at about forty miles per hour or about 60 feet per second. That means on the first leg of the race, we are tied. But on the second leg of your side, you are giving me a 60-foot head start.

Need a relay at some distance

Let's say the ball leaves the hand of a twelve-year old at 60 miles per hour. Because of air resistance, it slows to 50 miles per hour by the time it first hits the ground. Each bounce takes probably about ten miles per hour off the speed.

Clearly, there is a distance at which the relayed throw will finally beat the unrelayed throw. That distance varies according to the arm strength of the outfielder making the initial throw and the field conditions. High grass or a soft infield slow the bouncing ball more. Wet grass causes the ball to bounce very low and therefore start rolling sooner.

Test

You should put two balls in the deepest corner of your local fenced outfield and have two outfielders throw home. One gets a relay man and one does not. See which ball gets to home first. If there is a point at which the relayed ball wins, you should have a relay man on any ball hit that far or farther.

If your outfield has no fence, then there will always be a distance at which you want to use a relay man for a throw to home, but it's farther out than the usual distance at which a youth baseball "cut" man gets involved. In general, what I am saying, is let the ball bounce to its destination. It's faster.

Also, remember that this is youth baseball, where **fielding percentages are awful.** Every handling of the ball means a marked deterioration in the probability of an error-free play. Do **not** encourage your players to handle the ball unnecessarily. Of course, if the throw to the relay man is **off line**, he does change its direction.

Trail man

A trail man is a backup relay man on balls hit really far. With a trail man, the outfielder just heaves it as hard as he can on line. If he overthrows the relay man, the trail man becomes the relay man on that throw.

Cut man

The cut man stands as far in front of the target base as the distance from the pitcher's mound to home. **The purpose of a cut man is NOT to relay the throw, but to change its direction.** There are two circumstances that warrant changing the direction of the outfielder or relay/trail man's throw:

- it is off line
- there is a better play at another base

The cut man works in conjunction with the target baseman, who lines him up and tells him which base to throw to. In this chapter, I am talking about catchers. The catcher is a target baseman. He yells out to the cut man, "Left," "Right," or "Stay." Each "Left" or "Right" command means take **one step only** in that direction.

No cut

The cut man only cuts the ball if he is told to. If he hears nothing as the ball approaches, he **pretends** to catch it and throw it to a base.

The catcher needs to make a high-speed judgment call. If the ball is off line, he must figure out, "Is it so far off line that I cannot go get it and get back to home before the base runner arrives?" If he cannot, he yells "Cut home." It means catch the ball and throw it to home.

If there is a better play at third or second, he yells, "Cut three" or "Cut two."

You have to practice the catcher making use of a cut man without live runners then with live runners. It's very tricky. Also, your players almost certainly need to be deprogrammed of the always-cut-the-ball nonsense they were taught by previous coaches or which was tolerated by those coaches. Deprogramming takes time.

In the 1999 Little League World Series final game between Phenix City, AL and Osaka Japan, there were two instances where the Phenix City Team cut the ball. On one occasion, the announcer questioned whether they should have.

In the 1999 Little League World Series games leading up to that final, I repeatedly saw an outfielder throw to a cut man who relayed the ball. In every single case, it appeared to me that the throw should **not** have been cut. In a game between the Central and West teams, a double off the left-field wall took about 2.89 seconds to get from the left fielder to the cut man then to second base. This was at the Williamsport stadium. Take a similar kid and have him throw the same distance, probably on a hop, and I'll bet the ball will arrive significantly sooner with**out** the cut.

There are a million dumb things that dumb youth baseball coaches do. Hitting the cut man far too often is one of the mistakes committed by **smart** youth baseball coaches, like those in the Little League World Series. Time the throw in question with and without the cut and I guarantee you that you will all but abolish hitting the cut man on your team.

The fence at Williamsport's Lamadie Field is 205 feet all around. That means the throw to the plate is about 200 feet max. I doubt there are very many Little League all-stars (all Little League World Series players were chosen for their league all-star team) who cannot throw the ball 200 feet.

Given that, there arguably should **never** be a relay at Lamadie Field. The ball will always arrive at the target base sooner without it. If the ball is off-line, that's another matter. It must be cut to redirect it to the target base.

In short, my message is **DO NOT HIT THE CUT MAN!** Hit the relay or trail man if there is one. There generally should **not** be in most youth baseball plays because the outfielder can make the throw without them. No outfielder or relay/trail man should ever throw TO the cut man. They should always throw THROUGH him to the target baseman.

The whole hit-the-cut-man concept would be better explained as simply saying, "Throw only line drives.

No rainbows (high arching trajectory throws)." If the throw is low, as it should be, the cut man will be able to reach up and grab it if he needs to. But the thrower's focus absolutely should be on the target base, **not** the cut man

Handling the pitcher

The catcher may be able to make the pitcher more effective. Note the word "may." Just because you are the catcher doesn't make you smarter than the pitcher. Depending upon the personalities of the pitcher and catcher, the catcher may be able to go out to the mound and calm the pitcher down. But catchers should not go out to the mound whenever the pitcher is struggling just because they think it's the thing to do. Some pitchers, most notably Hall of Famer Bob Gibson, **hate** visits from the catcher. It is very much a function of the people and situation involved.

The goal of such psychological sessions is to calm the pitcher down and to help him turn off his conscious brain and let his subconscious do the pitching. "Trust the Force, Luke." If your catcher has a good chance to succeed along that vein, he should try. Otherwise, he should stay at the plate.

Catcher's battle station

In general, the catcher does not leave home plate. There are one, maybe two exceptions. When there are no runners on base, the catcher backs up the throw to first base. To do that, he runs down to the area behind first base with the batter. As always with backing up, he should be at least 15 to 20 feet behind the base.

In youth baseball, however, there is often not that much room between first base and the fence. In that case, he should **not** be on line with the throw and should play the carom off the fence if the ball gets past the first baseman.

Catcher-cover-first play

There is a bit of a trick play you can use in that situation. I always wanted to try it, but never did. With no runners on, the batter hits a single to right. The first baseman makes a big show of going out toward the right fielder so the runner can see him when he rounds the bag. The right fielder relaxes his body and prepares for a leisurely throw to second. The runner relaxes for an equally leisurely walk back to the unguarded first base, or so he thinks. Then the right fielder suddenly guns the ball to first, which is covered by the **catcher**.

Covering third

Some baseball books say that the third baseman and catcher should trade bases on a **bunt** down the third-base line with one runner on first. I don't like that. I prefer that the **pitcher** take care of third in that situation.

Once he sees that the ball is not hit to the his left, the pitcher should be moving to the foul territory behind third. He can easily cover third if the third baseman is unavailable. He has a better glove for the purpose. Also, the catcher understands the tag at home, which is different than any other base, better than the third baseman.

So the catcher only has two battle stations: first base back-up or covering first when there are no runners, and home plate in all other situations.

Intentional walk

I have rarely seen the intentional walk used in youth baseball. It probably makes more sense in youth baseball than it does in the pros, so it should be used more. The decision is a probability-and-statistics calculation on what the batter is likely to do compared to what the next batters are likely to do. In view of the lack of data on batters in youth baseball, it's hard to be confident it is the right decision.

In general, it makes sense to avoid pitching to a great hitter. On the other hand, it makes sense to avoid putting a great base runner on if there is no other runner blocking his path. The more outs there are, the greater the probability that the walked runner will not score. The weaker the next hitter the more sense an intentional walk makes.

Go back over previous games and see if it looks as thought you might have turned any losses into victories if you had intentionally walked any likely candidates.

When the intentional walk is called, the catcher must be careful not to commit a **catcher balk**. Little League Rule 4.03(a) says, "...the catcher must stand with both feet in the catcher's box until the ball leaves the pitcher's hand." I know a guy who was a college pitcher and lost a key game on this balk.

Catcher as leader

Many coaches say the catcher has to be a leader. It is true that the catcher is physically located in a good position to be a leader. But some people are leaders and some people are not.

If your catcher is a leader in terms of his personality, great. But that would be a nice coincidence. If the catcher is **not** a leader, do not try to force him into that role. The pitcher and other infielders are close enough to provide leadership. So is the coach in youth baseball where foul territory is minuscule and there is little crowd noise.

Special catcher practice

In this chapter, I have identified several skills which can only be achieved with an extraordinarily high number of repetitions.

- runners-on-base stance
- blocking the low pitch
- throwing to second (with batter in one or the other batter's box)

Accordingly, you need to practice these skills every day and in every pre-game. I suggest having the catchers arrive fifteen minutes early or having a special catcher coach who works only with the catchers during segments of team practice where the catcher's skills are more important than the skill being worked on. I suggest seven-and-a-half minutes each on throwing to second and blocking low pitches. Start each repetition with a good stance.

Catcher position clinics

Once or twice during the season, you should hold a catchers position clinic. Here are the curricula:

Clinic #1

5:30   Sign-giving and runners-on stances and proper depth in catcher's box
5:35   Pitch-calling strategy
5:38   Two-handed tag on the ground at home
5:42   Throw to each base with mask on and with a batter on one of the batter's boxes
5:47   Intentional walk catcher balk avoidance
5:50   Catching high pitches
5:55   Blocking the low pitch
6:00   End

Clinic #2

5:30   First-and-third defense
5:35   Foul-pop-catching technique
5:37   Line up cut man and direct throws to second, third, and home
5:40   Bunt defense
5:44   Appealing the plate ump's called on a checked swing
5:45   Dropped third strike (if batter may run at your level)
5:50   Making runner coming home mistakenly think no throw is coming from left field
5:55   Dive tag
5:57   1-2-3 double-force play

8 First base

First base is the most important position at the tee-ball and farm levels. At the 10-12 level, he is probably about third after the pitcher and catcher. At the teenage level, he is probably tied for third with the shortstop.

His main job is to catch throws, with inaccurate throws being the challenge, especially those in the dirt.

Who should play first?

At the sub-teen levels, your first baseman should be one of your best fielders, if not **the** best fielder. In the pros, the prototypical first baseman is tall and left handed and a good hitter. Don't worry about any of that in youth baseball.

Where to play

Unlike the pitcher and catcher, the first baseman has considerable latitude as to where he stands when the ball is pitched.

Where a first baseman plays is a function of:

• pitch speed
• batter tendencies
• range of second baseman
• ability to move to right or left
• infield surface and condition
• count on the batter
• game situation
• runner to be held (teenage level)

Pitch speed

The faster the pitcher, the more likely the batter is to hit the ball to the opposite field, and the slower the pitch speed, the more likely the batter is to pull the ball.

Batter tendencies

Some batters, like Ted Williams, always pull the ball. Some youth batters tend to be behind the pitch and hit to the opposite field. If the batter fouls the ball off, that often tells you whether he's pulling the ball or hitting opposite field.

Batters are stronger when pulling so you may want to play deeper against left-handed hitters. You can also play deeper if the batter is a slow runner, but you may have to play tighter if he is fast or he will get an infield hit.

Not too close to the line

The rule sort of is that the more the batter is likely to hit down the line, the closer you get to the line. However, there is a definite limit. If the batter is likely to hit down the line, you must be close enough to line to get to all **fair** balls. But there is little point to being closer.

True, being closer might enable you to catch a foul line drive or pop, but that's a low percentage play. Not opening up too big a gap between the first baseman and the second baseman is more important than aligning yourself to catch foul balls on the fly.

Range of the second baseman

The greater the range of the second baseman, the closer to the bag the first baseman can play, and vice versa.

Lateral movement

If the first baseman has less ability to move to one side or the other, he needs to shade toward the side he has trouble moving to.

Infield surface and condition

The infield is either fast or slow. If it is fast—as with a hard-packed skin diamond or Astro turf—the fielders should play deeper to get more time to see the hit. If it is slow—as with a grass infield or soft skin diamond —the infielders must play closer to home so they can get to the slow-moving ball in time to get the batter out.

Count

Many batters will shorten their swing and tend to swing behind the pitch when they are behind in the count (two strikes). That suggests the first baseman should move closer to the first base line against a right-handed batter.

Game situation

If you are expecting a **bunt**, the first baseman should play closer to home plate. In the pros, the first baseman who fields a bunt tries to get the runner going to second. Forget that in youth baseball unless the batter really bunts it hard. On a normal bunt, throw to first, which should be covered by the second baseman on this play.

If the runner at third is crucial, throw home instead of to first base. In a do-or-die situation—that is the runner at third is the tying or go ahead run—you may have to field the bunt with your bare hand in order to have any chance of throwing it home in time. If the bunt is near both the pitcher and the first baseman, one of them must call for it just like with a pop.

If a double could score a runner from second, the first baseman should move closer to the line to prevent the double. That would especially be true when you are ahead in the last two innings and the winning or tying run is at the plate.

If you are ahead in general, you should play deeper because it increases your ability to prevent base hits.

With two outs, you generally play deep because you only need to get the force at first.

With the tying or winning run at third, you need to play close enough to get the ball home before the runner.

Hustle to first

The first baseman really has to hustle to get to first. It's only a short distance, but he has to look at the bag until he is touching it, then he has to look for the ball. If he loafs, the ball may be flying toward his face before he looks for it or too late to get his glove up in time.

Holding runners on (teenage level)

Do not hold the runner on if there is also a runner on second.

Communicate with the pitcher if the runner is taking too big of a lead and if you are not holding the runner on.

The feet position for holding a runner on is often screwed up. Your right foot points at the pitcher and is against the corner of the bag which is closest to the pitcher. Your left foot also points at the pitcher, is shoulder width from the right and is on or near the base line.

Once, in the 13-year old league, I faced a team where the first baseman always put his left knee down so that his left calf covered the entire base when trying to pick-off my runner. This struck me as obstruction. The penalty for obstruction is that my runner is awarded second, regardless of whether he is safe or out on the pick-off throw at first.

In the waiting stance for a pick-off throw, the first baseman's belt buckle and sternum face the pitcher. You crouch comfortably so you can move in any direction in case of an inaccurate throw from the pitcher. Give the pitcher a waist-high target with your mitt.

If the pitcher throws to you, put the tag on the ground on the corner of the base closest to the center fielder.

If the pitcher throws to the batter, crossover step with your left foot then hop into a fielding position facing the batter. If the runner steals, yell, "He's going!" so the catcher knows to throw to second.

Digging balls out of the dirt

The first baseman should **not** wave at the ball. He just puts his mitt in the best place and holds it still.

Shooting dirt ball after dirt ball with a pitching machine would give the maximum number of reps. I would

use real baseballs and pad the player up with full catcher's equipment, except that he would use his first baseman's mitt, not a catcher's mitt.

Poly balls are not such a good idea because, unlike the catcher practicing blocking the ball, the first baseman needs to **catch** it, not just block it and poly balls do not bounce the same as real balls.

Make sure you give the first baseman some practice fielding **long-hop** throws. They are generally easy to catch, but he should see a few before his first game so they do not panic him. When my third baseman and shortstop have weak arms at the sub teenage levels, I often coach them to throw long hops deliberately to first.

Force play

Another common youth first baseman mistake is for the player to put his toes and the ball of his foot on the ground and his **heel** on the base. Then, when he stretches, he pulls his heel off the base and the runner is safe. The **toes** go on the base, not the heel.

A common mistake is that the first baseman places his base foot **parallel** to the edge of the base with the bottom of the entire foot in contact with the base. This reduces his stretch. The **toes** of the base foot must be pointed at the incoming throw.

Foot position to receive the infielder's throw

Always use your throwing-side foot to tag the base. Always using your throwing-side foot is simpler and therefore probably easier to learn.

Find the base before you look for the throw

Some first basemen try to watch the hit and the infielder continuously from the time the ball leaves the bat. They simultaneously try to find first base by Braille, groping around with their foot. That is incorrect. Step one is to find the base with your **eyes** and run to it. Then, and only then, do you look for the infielder and the throw.

Don't stretch until you see where the throw is

Another common mistake is that youth first basemen often stretch **before** the infielder releases the throw. Do NOT let your players do that.

The first baseman must keep both feet together until he sees where the throw is going. Then he stretches toward the throw, not toward the infielder who threw it. If you stretch **before** you see where the throw is going, and you guess wrong, you are in a very bad position to catch the ball and still keep your foot on the bag.

Unlike most catching techniques, the glove arm

should be straight on a force play or failure-to-tag up play so as to move the glove as close to the infielder who threw it as possible.

If the throw is off line, forget keeping your foot on the bag and go get the ball. There is an old saying in baseball: "First the ball, then the play." That is, you must catch the ball before you worry about getting someone out.

The only thing worse than pulling your foot off the bag is to let the ball get past you. If you pull your foot off the bag, the runner is safe at first. If you let the ball get past you, he will generally advance to second on the overthrow. If the ball goes out of play, all runners will be awarded at least one base and sometimes two.

Where does the foot go?

The foot goes on the edge of the base closest to the infielder who is throwing the ball. It does **not** go on the middle of the base. The **batter** often steps on the middle of the base. (He ought to step on the front edge, but that's for another chapter.)

This is a common mistake in tee ball and farm. By the time they get to the 10-12 level, most first basemen have been stepped on and thereby learned their lesson.

Around-the-clock drill

Give your first baseman practice stretching for throws all around the clock. To do this, I stand about fifteen feet away at various positions on line with third, short, and second and throw the ball to each position on a clock dial with the first baseman at the center.

Twelve o'clock is the one where he jumps straight up catches the ball, then comes back down and lands on the bag. On some twelve o'clock throws, the correct technique is to stretch on the other side of the bag back into foul territory. That can sometimes save having to jump. Six o'clock is a low throw, but not one that hits the ground. On that throw, his arm needs to give a little to keep the ball in the mitt. Three o'clock is the one where he has to do a sweep tag. And so on.

Make sure some of the throws are far enough out that the first baseman is forced to take his foot off the base. This is to make sure he knows the ball is more important than the base.

Although the first baseman has a glove designed for one-hand catches and often needs to make one-handed catches, he should try to catch the ball with two hands as often as possible just like everyone else.

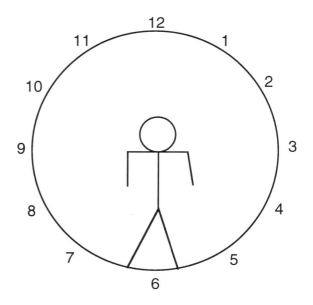

Tag the runner

Sometimes, the first baseman will field the hit himself and be in a position to tag the runner more easily than stepping on the base. Because of this, you should give the first baseman a little practice at doing this just to put it in his head.

If the throw from an infielder draws the first baseman's foot off the bag and toward home, the first baseman should sweep the tag around to his left and behind him because the runner will likely be going by at the time. You have to practice this a little to put it in the first baseman's mind.

First baseman as cutoff man

On extra-base hits to right field, the first baseman is the cutoff man to home. He is no longer needed at first because, by definition, the batter will get to second on an extra-base hit. He should be as far from home plate as the pitcher's rubber.

He holds both arms up high to show the right fielder that he is the cut man. The cut man should never get short hopped. He should move toward the throw if necessary to avoid a short hop.

Remember the cut man's job is to change the direction of the ball, **not** to relay it. He only catches the ball if it is off line or if the fielder in charge tells him to cut and throw to another base. If the throw is on line, he lets it go through to the catcher, although he should **pretend** to catch it and throw it to a base to screw up the runners. He will generally know whether it is off line because the catcher will have lined him up before the throw.

If the throw is off line, the first baseman should catch the throw on his glove side with his shoulders parallel to the path of the throw. The worst thing he can do, which is common in youth baseball, is to catch the throw on his throwing arm side then turn 360 degrees before throwing it to the catcher.

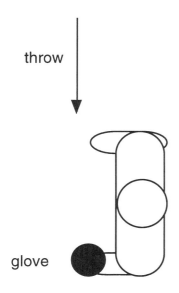

Correct position for relay or off-line cut

Here is a typical incorrect position that is going to force the fielder to turn 270 degrees in order to relay the throw, which takes much longer.

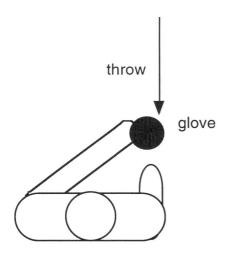

Incorrect position for relay or off-line cut

In the Major Leagues, they also have the first baseman act as cutoff man on throws from center field. I disagree as far as youth baseball is concerned.

The reason they do it in the Majors is that there is a deep foul territory between home plate and the back stop. In the pros, the pitcher goes back there to back up

the catcher. But in youth baseball, the area between the plate and the backstop is minuscule so there is no room for the pitcher back there. Better he should stay near the mound to cut the throw from center off when the lead runner is on second.

Pitcher-cover-first play

I have already covered this pretty thoroughly elsewhere in the book. The first baseman's job on this play is to field the grounder and toss or throw it to the pitcher as he runs toward first. He should try to enable the pitcher to see the ball as early as possible when it is still in the first baseman's hand. The pitcher must get the ball **before** he gets to first so he can take his eyes off the ball after he catches and look for the base.

This will take twenty or thirty repetitions to get it down.

Make him do a few reps of making a **diving** stop on a ball then throwing to the pitcher from the ground.

After the first baseman throws to the pitcher and the pitcher steps on the base, he should direct the pitcher to throw to another base if there is a runner trying to advance.

If the first baseman can field the grounder and step on first himself, he should call the pitcher off verbally only by saying "I got it," then step on the base. He must **not cross the base line** or he will collide with the batter. He must not physically wave the pitcher off with his mitt. Some first basemen who did that caused the ball to fall out of the mitt.

In the 1999 Little League World Series final game, the Phenix City, AL team tried to execute this play, but they were too slow. I do not know if they would have been more successful if the first baseman had said, "I got it," and taken it himself. But examining the video, I believe the first baseman would have gotten the out. That is an example of overcoaching one play and undercoaching an alternative version to get the same out. In general, the first baseman should be biased in favor of stepping on the base himself.

After stepping on first, the first baseman should immediately pop his feet and look for another runner to throw out after getting the force out. Give him a couple of reps to practice this "3U" play (Player #3 getting the out unassisted).

When he needs to go full speed to get to the base in time, he should do a **figure-four, feet-first slide** into it like a base runner. He must then pop up and look for another runner to throw out. Give him a couple of reps of this sliding "3U," too.

General fielding for a first baseman

The first baseman should be given practice catching or knocking down balls hit to the edges of his range. Put a cone on the infield at the spot where you want him to stand. Then fire balls to his right, left, and over his head out of a pitching machine. Let him get multiple reps at stopping line drives hit at the limit of his reach.

Youth baseball players tend to underestimate their range. They also tend to give up on a ball too soon, but dive in the dirt after to make it look like they really tried to get it. This drill builds confidence and gives the first baseman a better understanding of his range.

Stay out of the base path

When the fielder is not in possession of the ball or fielding it, the runner has the right of way. Getting in his way is obstruction. If the defense commits obstruction, the runner is awarded at least one base beyond the one he had safely reached when the obstruction had occurred.

At each base, there are two paths the runner might take: **straight in** and **rounding**. The first baseman must not be in the base path the runner chooses, and he can and should generally avoid being in **either** base path.

Demonstrate this problem once with your players. Otherwise they tend to stand wherever they feel like and watch the action in the outfield.

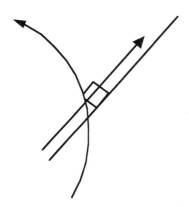

Straight and rounded base paths at first
Keep off unless you have the ball or are fielding it

Pops near the fence

If the pop is near the fence, **go to the fence first**, touch it so you know where it is, then go get the ball safe in the knowledge that you will not bang into the fence. Give your first baseman a few reps of practicing this.

'Get two?'

Forget about the 3-6-3 and 3-6-1 double-force plays. This is too hard for youth players unless you coach an elite teenage team. However, it may be best to go for a 3-6 put-out (force at second by shortstop) rather than a 3-1 (pitcher cover first). Practice this play.

The right-handed first baseman should either catch the grounder with his back to second then pivot 180 degrees and throw there or he should catch it frontally,

then turn his upper body toward second base for the throw. Use whichever technique the first baseman is most comfortable with. The frontal technique has an increased probability of stopping the grounder.

First base position clinics

I already gave you the script for one first base position clinic in the practice organization chapter. Here's that clinic and another:

Clinic #1

6:30	Foot placement at base for infield throw and pickoff (no ball)
6:35	Same with live ball
6:40	Sweep tag for when throw draws the first baseman off the base toward home
6:45	Around-the-clock drill
6:50	Going back on a pop
6:55	Pitcher-cover-first play
7:00	End

Clinic #2

6:30	Where to line up before the pitch in different situations
6:35	Bunt defense (no runners, runner at 3rd)
6:40	Holding runners on (teenage)
	Dig balls out of dirt (Sub-teen)
6:45	Cutoff man duties
6:50	Pop near fence
6:55	3-6 force play and 3-2 force at home
7:00	End

Try to find a way to give your first basemen extra reps of digging balls out of the dirt. It's difficult, but learnable. A first baseman coach who can take the first basemen aside during practice may be the answer. A father who will work with his son outside of practice may solve the problem. A special practice on a day off for the other players may work.

Still like rotation?

Earlier in the book, I said I oppose rotating players among the nine positions. Now that I have given you three position chapters, I want to stop and point out the extent of each.

It took me ten pages just to explain pitcher fielding. That chapter did not cover **pitching** itself, just the **fielding** part of the pitcher's job.

It took me thirteen pages to cover the catcher position. Furthermore, in that chapter, I identified three areas that I said take many, many reps to achieve satisfactory performance.

In this chapter, it took me six pages to explain how to play first base, and I identified one skill that takes many, many reps.

If you specialize the kids by position, it will be a struggle to teach the pitchers, catchers, and first basemen all the skills in these chapters by the end of the season. To the extent that you succeed, you team will perform excellently and your kids will feel a great sense of accomplishment at having learned a great deal and improved greatly in their defensive performance.

On the other hand, if you **rotate**, your kids will spend the entire season overwhelmed by the job of trying to learn nine different positions, some of which have extremely difficult-to-master aspects. They will make far more errors, especially mental errors, than if they had stayed with one position. They will be jacks of all positions and masters of none, ostensibly to serve some vague purpose about letting them experience different things. One of the things that they are sure to experience more of in the rotation system is **failure**.

9 Second base

Second base is the closest thing the infield has to right field. It is considered the place where weak infielders are put. Many coaches who claim they rotate everyone among the nine positions really only rotate the weak players through second base and sometimes third base (and catcher at the sub-stealing levels).

Having acknowledged that reality, I must add that, except for the short distance of his throw to first, second base is no less demanding than any other infield position. It **is** the place for the weakest infielder, but he ought to be a better ground-ball fielder than any of your outfielders.

Get two? Get real

In the pros, the second baseman is best known for turning the double play. Forget that. Two-throw, double-force plays are almost impossible in youth baseball, except on an elite teenage team.

I saw two 6-4-3 double-force plays in my entire youth baseball career. One involved an extremely hard-hitting, extremely slow-running batter. The other, in 1991, involved a ball hit almost directly to second base.

In his book, *Managing Little League Baseball*, Ned McIntosh says, "Double plays are so rare in Little League Baseball that they should be given minimal practice time, in my opinion." I think he is really referring to two-throw, double-force plays. I have seen many **one**-throw double plays and I am sure he has too. McIntnosh goes on to say, "As a matter of fact, there is a danger in overdrilling the double play to the point that the pivot man will feel that he *has* to make the play at first and will rush the play, with resulting fielding and/or throwing errors." [Emphasis in original] Good point. I wouldn't know because I never went down that path to begin with.

I never practice the two-throw, double-force play, but I do practice **one**-throw double plays. In that 1991 case, it could have, and probably **should** have, been a one-throw double play with the shortstop saying "I got it," and stepping on second himself, then throwing to first.

The one-throw, double-force play

You need to practice this play a little just to put it in the kids' minds. Yell out "One-throw double play" and throw a grounder to the second baseman. Make sure it is close to the bag. If the pitcher is on the mound, tell him to let it go through. The second baseman fields the grounder, steps on second, and throws to first.

I saw a one-throw double play in the Central versus West playoff game of the 1999 Little League World Series. With a runner on first and less than two out, the ball was hit to the shortstop who caught it right next to second. The shortstop then stepped on second and threw to first. The play at first was close.

I always practice this in my pre-game warm-ups. Opposing coaches and parents must think I'm some kind of nut. But in one game, shortly after they saw me practice it in pre-game, we got a 6U-6-3 one-throw, double force play against them.

Get one at first

You almost do not have to practice getting one at first. For one thing, if the kid is a veteran infielder, he has done this a zillion times with the coaches on whose teams he previously played. Plus he is going to do it hundreds of times this season in pre-game and pre-inning warm-ups.

Back up the throw to the pitcher

One of the middle infielder responsibilities that is unique to youth baseball is the need to back up the throw from the catcher to the pitcher. I recommend that you **designate the second baseman to do this all season**. He does not need to cross the path of a runner at second.

After each pitch reaches the catcher, he needs to hustle to a spot in front of second base on line with the pitcher and catcher. He should be at least 15 to 20 feet behind the pitcher as with any backup duty so the ball does not explode out at him as it would if he were too close behind the pitcher.

Catcher pick-off

When there is a runner at second, the second baseman should go to the base itself after each pitch gets to the catcher in case the catcher or pitcher wants to make a pickoff throw to second. This is generally not a high-percentage play, but with a base runner who takes overly large secondary leads, or who takes his eye off the ball when going back to the base, and with competent fielders, it can work. It must be practiced both to see if your team can do it and to get better at it.

Who covers second on a steal throw?

The best fielder of the two middle infielders should cover second on a steal throw from the catcher. It would be best to keep this constant all season, but illnesses and absences sometimes force you to assign the responsibility to a different player for a game or two. Also, the shortstop or second baseman is also often one of your pitchers, so someone else has to cover second while the normal guy is pitching.

The pros vary who covers according to the handedness of the batter and other considerations. That's not necessary in youth baseball and it is likely to confuse the players. Just have the same player do it all season. I recommend the shortstop. Keep it simple.

Stand in front of the bag

The middle infielder who takes the throw should **stand on the home plate side of second**. He should **not** straddle the bag or stand behind it.

I know they straddle it in the pros. They also have extremely accurate throws from the catchers in the pros. Youth throws are far less accurate and having your feet straddling the bag is likely to trip you when you have to scramble for an errant throw.

If he stands behind the bag, he gives the ball a chance to bounce off the base or the runner.

Tag, not force

Make sure he is not keeping one foot on the base as if it were a force play. Infielders at second and third tend to anchor one foot on the base as they await a throw, even thought the play in question is not a force play! This inhibits their mobility and often causes them to forget to put the tag down. In youth baseball, runners often are safe at a base where the throw beat them because the fielder tagged the base with his foot instead of the runner with the glove.

Glove is tag only if it contains the ball

I have seen some youth infielders tag a runner with their glove when the ball was still in their other hand. That is not a legal tag, although they fooled the teenage ump in one game where I saw that. Explain and demonstrate this to your players, especially rookies.

Back up the steal throw

Whichever middle infielder takes the steal throw from the catcher, the other backs him up. Remember to make them get at least twenty feet behind the bag in center field.

Bunt

On a bunt, the second baseman covers first. Because of the distance, he really has to hustle to get there on time. Head for first as soon as the batter shows bunt. When you arrive, put your throwing-side foot against the base and face the fielder who his handling the bunt. Give him a chest-high target.

Pops

The second baseman needs to learn to work with his neighbors on pops. Generally, he should defer to the outfielders because it's easier to come **in** on a ball than to go **out**. Sometimes the second baseman needs to catch the ball because he can get to it, but the outfielders cannot.

The coach should give the second baseman and his neighbors practice calling for pops. That is throw balls up in the seam between the second baseman and the first baseman, the pitcher, the shortstop, the right fielder, and the center fielder.

Force at second

If the ball is hit to the second baseman when there is a force at second, he needs to get the lead runner if possible.

As always with short throws, **show** the ball to the target baseman as early as possible so it doesn't explode out of hiding at him.

Receiving the force throw at second

The second baseman can receive the force throw at second the same way the first base man does at first. But often he does not have time to look at the base because both the ball and runner are coming so fast. In that case, he catches the ball wherever then drags his foot over the base or steps on it.

This is akin to what the pitcher does on the pitcher cover-first play. It is important that you tell your players that they do **not** have to find second base **before** they receive the throw. Either sequence is fine. Make them practice it both ways so they are comfortable with both.

Where to align before the pitch

As with first base, where you line up is a function of:

- pitch speed
- batter tendencies
- range of first baseman
- ability to move to right or left
- infield surface and condition
- count on the batter
- game situation
- runner to be held (teenage level)

In general, the second baseman should play deep. That increases the time he gets to react to the ball. He can afford to be deeper than any other infielder because he has the shortest throw to first.

The exception to the play-deep rule is when he has to throw to a base other than first. If the tying or winning run is on third, the infielders have to throw home. Furthermore, they have less time than they have to throw to first because the runner at third, especially at the teenage level where runners can take a pre-pitch lead. In that situation, the infielders must be as close as they need to be to get the throw back home before the run scores.

Shift toward batter tendency

If a batter tends to hit the ball to a certain side against the pitcher on the mound, you may want to shift a little that way. In general in youth baseball, where scouting is minimal at best, I would be inclined to play straight away unless there was a distinct tendency, like a batter always being behind a pitcher and hitting everything down one line or the other.

What is 'straight away?'

We coaches sometimes tell players to play the batter "straight away." What exactly is that?

Generally, the pitcher can cover part of the infield. His range is narrow because he is so close and has so little time. Below is a diagram of how I think the infield divides up. I have given the pitcher responsibility for a narrow wedge in the middle then divided up the remaining area equally between the four other infielders.

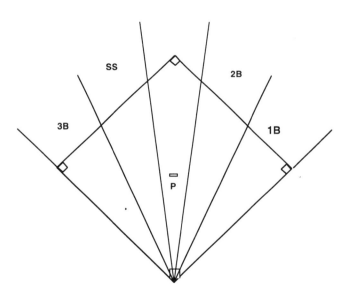

To play straight away, you simply position yourself in the center of the pie slice for which you are responsible.

No shade toward second to set up double play

In the pros, the second baseman shades toward second in a double-play situation. In youth baseball, the two-throw, double-force play is all but nonexistent so your second baseman should **not** shade toward second.

Play in if grass infield

As a general rule, grass infields cause rapid deceleration of ground balls. Accordingly, the infielders need to play closer to home. There have been fields where I had them play **on** the infield grass in normal situations because batters were getting infield hits when we played at normal depth.

Holding runners close (teen level)

At the teenage level, where runners can take a pre-pitch lead, the middle infielders must hold the runner close with various fakes and the occasional pick-off throw. Pick-off throws to second by the pitcher are signalled in advance. This has to be practiced a fair amount and emphasis must be on **both** players knowing that a pick-off is coming. There should be both a sign by the initiator and an acknowledgment sign by the other player.

Force at home

Youth coaches practice the second baseman's throw to first incessantly. In fact, your predecessors probably did it so much with your current second baseman that you can skip it. But they do not practice force throws to second and home. **Those** are the ones you need to practice. With the throw to home, you must emphasize quickness.

Fake ground balls

If there is a runner at first and a fly ball is hit to someone other than the second baseman, the second baseman might pretend that he is fielding a ground ball. If the runner at first is poorly trained and does not look at the ball, the fake fielding of a grounder may cause him to bolt for second and thereby possibly get doubled off first after the fly is caught.

The 2nd baseman's battle station once the ball is hit to someone else

The tricky part of playing second is knowing where to go when the ball is hit to **someone else**. Here are the rules:

- Bunt—Cover first
- Ball hit to pitcher or first baseman on first base side of infield—Back up player fielding ball
- Ball hit to third-base side of infield—Cover second
- Ball hit to shallow right field—Cover second
- Ball hit to deep right—Relay throw to second if needed
- Ball hit to shallow center or deep center with outfield fence—Back up second (Shortstop is generally the better fielder so he covers the base)
- Ball hit to deep center (no outfield fence)—Relay man
- Ball hit to shallow left field—Back up second

• Ball hit to deep left—Cover second

Relay duties

The second baseman is a relay man on hits deep into the corner of right field or hits deep into center or right at a field with no outfield fence.

How far out does a relay man go? It's a judgment call. Generally, he wants to catch the outfielder's throw in the air. So he needs to get the appropriate distance from the outfielder in question based on the strength of the particular outfielder's arm. It will vary according to who is playing center or right at the moment. Halfway will be about right in most cases.

He puts both arms high into the air to give the outfielder a target. As the ball approaches, he positions himself so as to catch the ball on his glove side. If the second baseman is right handed, his back will be toward the first base line and he will be facing left field.

This hit will generally be an extra-base hit so he has to throw to third, or home. After he catches the ball, he should turn and power the ball about two feet above the head of the guy with his arms up. That will be the cut man. A fellow infielder may also tell the relay man where to throw saying, "Three! Three! Three!" or "Home! Home! Home!"

Middle infielders are a relay-cover-back-up tandem

The two middle infielders, the shortstop and second baseman, are a tandem, a duo. They work together. On a base hit, they line up with the outfielder's throw and second base. The middle infielder nearest the ball either relays (on a deep hit) or covers second (on a shallow hit). The middle infielder farthest from the ball either covers second (on a deep hit) or backs up second (on a shallow hit). See the diagrams at the end of this chapter.

Second base position clinics
Clinic #1

6:30	One-throw double play
6:33	Decision to throw to first or second with runner
6:38	Back up the catcher throw to the pitcher
6:40	Back up second after pitch if runner and no hit
6:42	Cover second on steal throw from catcher
6:47	Tag on ground
6:50	Back up steal throw
6:55	Cover first on bunt
7:00	End practice

Clinic #2

6:30	Call for pop in seam between each neighbor
6:35	Force at second throw from catcher, pitcher, short, and third

6:40	Where to align before the pitch in different situations
6:45	Where to go when ball not hit to you in different situations

- pitcher cover first
- grounder to short or third
- hit to shallow right
- hit to deep right
- hit to center with outfield fence
- hit to deep center with no fence
- hit to shallow left
- hit to deep left

6:55	Relay
	Pickoff (teenage level)
7:00	End practice

On his own, the second baseman should practice catching grounders hit to his left, right, and directly at him. If he has a weaker side and cannot fix it, he should cheat to that side in his pre-pitch alignment. Most players are weak on their throwing hand side where they have to field backhanded.

Relay on hit to deep right field

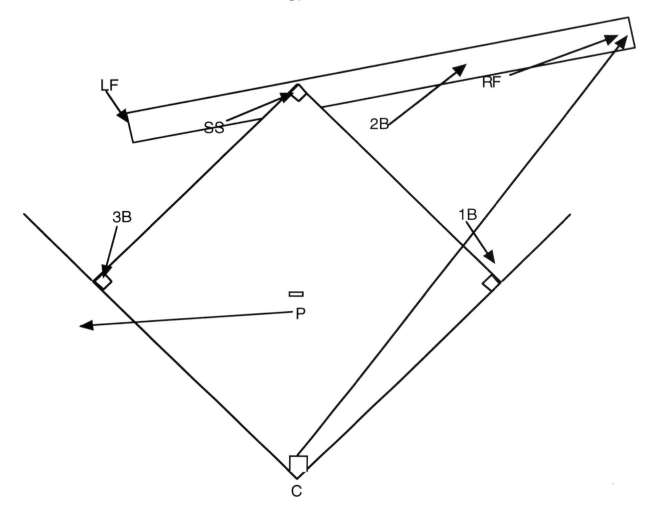

On a shallow hit to right, the same line of players lines up the same way except that the second baseman is on the base and the shortstop is backing up.

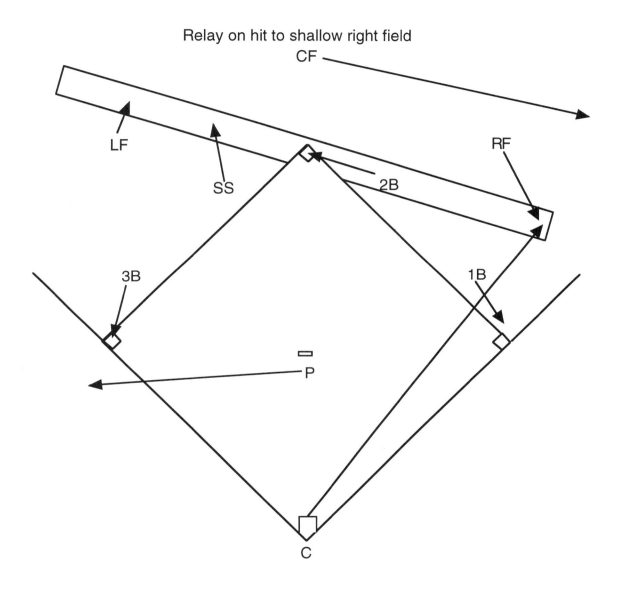

Relay on hit to shallow right field

10 Shortstop

Shortstop is traditionally the place for the **best** infielder. At the six- to twelve-year old level, I would disagree with that. **First** base is more important there. I would not put the shortstop on a par with the first baseman until the **teenage** level, and even then I would say they are **equal**.

The reason the shortstop is more important at the high school and higher levels is that the throws are so accurate at those levels that the first baseman generally has a routine catch to make and the shortstop has to execute the double play. In **youth** baseball, the first baseman has to make many difficult catches and there are no two-throw, double-force plays.

Another theory of placing talent is the strong-up-the-middle theory. Again, that pertains to higher levels where the routine is truly routine. In youth baseball, very little is routine. So you must place priority instead on things the higher levels take for granted, like the force at first.

Infielders are born not made

Some of your players are infielders. Most are not. There is no shame in not being an infielder. **I** am not an infielder. My oldest son is. It takes some sort of fine-motor coordination.

Basically, infielders can catch grounders and throw quickly and accurately to the appropriate base. We non-infielders tend to muff grounders and we take too long to throw to a base. Identify the infielders by audition, then assign the best to first and the second best to shortstop.

At the higher levels, the shortstop is not considered to be a player who needs an arm. But at the youngest youth levels, he does. Many youth players do not have the arm to throw to first from short. Do not subject those players to continuous failure by making them play shortstop. If you have to used a weak-armed player at short, you may be able to teach him to **long hop** the ball to the first baseman if the field surface at that location is reliable. One of the fields we had to play on, Los Cerros East, had a sand surface in patches and the ball would not bounce off it. On a field like thant, you are forced to use only strong-armed infielders at short and third.

Almost the same as second base

In general, the shortstop position is the same as the second-base position. The shortstop has to get his throw to first faster. The second baseman can knock the ball down and still pick it up and get the put-out at first. If the shortstop just knocks it down, he needs to consider whether he really still has a play at first before he throws.

On a **bunt** with a runner at first, the shortstop covers second. With runners at both first and second, you may want to run a **rotation play**. In that play, the shortstop goes to third.

The second baseman can play a little deeper than the shortstop because of his shorter throw.

But otherwise his position is largely a mirror-image of the second baseman. Accordingly, I will not repeat that information here. Use the second-baseman chapter, modified for the obvious mirror-image differences, to coach your shortstops.

Turning the double play at the elite teenage level

Elite teenage teams can turn that play. My second semi-pro team turned about two a game.

However, I did not coach them to do that. They had apparently learned it in high school. So I do not consider myself an expert on coaching the double play. Read the other more high-level books on baseball coaching for that information. See the bibliography in the back of this book for the names of other good baseball books.

Shortstop position clinics
Clinic #1
6:30　One-throw double play
6:33　Decision to throw to first, second, or third with runner
6:40　Go to second after pitch if runner and no hit
6:42　Cover second on steal throw from catcher
6:47　Tag on ground
6:50　Throw to first from deep in the hole
6:55　Cover second and third on bunt
7:00　End practice

Clinic #2
6:30　Call for pop in seam between each neighbor
6:35　Force at second throw from catcher, pitcher, short, and third
6:40　Where to align before the pitch in different situations
6:45　Where to go when ball not hit to you in different situations
　　　• pitcher cover first
　　　• grounder to short or third

- hit to shallow right
- hit to deep right
- hit to center with outfield fence
- hit to deep center with no fence
- hit to shallow left
- hit to deep left

6:55   Relay
        Pick-off (teenage level)
7:00   End practice

11 Third base

Third is not a mirror image of first, although there are some similarities, like the need to learn to play near the fence. There are few force plays at third. The third baseman has to make the **longest throw** in the infield.

At the lowest levels, many players on the team cannot physically throw from third to first. They must **not** play third. Some hard-core believers in the rotate-through-every-position approach might actually put weak-armed players at third. This will embarrass the players in question and antagonize everyone else associated with the team. It's suicidally dumb.

Pre-pitch alignment

The normal position is behind the base line, but as with the other infield positions, it depends on the game situation, field conditions, and strengths and weaknesses of the third baseman.

Knock it down is better than let it through

At second, you can knock the ball down and still get the force at first. At short, you generally have to field it cleanly to get the out at first. But if you fail to field it cleanly, it just goes into left for a single. At third, however, a ball that gets past the third baseman to his right may go for extra bases because it gets into the corner where there is no left fielder.

Bunt

You need to get a jump on the bunt. Watch carefully for indications the batter is going to bunt then charge hard if that's what it appears to be. Many third baseman emphasize the importance of looking for bunt tip-offs and getting a good jump on the bunt.

There is a play called the **fake bunt and slash** which may beat you if you charge the bunt, but you have little choice.

The classic third base bunt play is when the third baseman charges the bunt, fields it bare-handed on a dead run and while still bent over, throws a submarine shot to first.

My son actually did that once when he was nine. I have no idea where he learned it. I have never seen it done on another occasion in youth baseball. Hall of Fame third baseman Brooks Robinson says one of the keys to this play is to field the ball when your glove-side foot hits the ground, then throw on the next step.

You might try practicing it, but I suspect it's too hard. Better they should just field the ball in whatever way and stand up and throw in the normal way.

The third baseman's battle station

The third baseman's battle station is easy: third base—**always** third base. Whenever the ball is hit anywhere other than to the third baseman, he covers third. He is **never** a **relay** man. He is **never** a **cut** man. He **never backs up** anyone. He **always** goes to the **base**.

So how come I have often seen a ball carrier be able to advance to a vacant third base? It has never happened on one of my teams in recent years, but it happened a few times in my early years as a coach, often when my son was playing third.

He was very active and running all over to back up or make plays. I was the same way when I played third as a kid—too often backing up the catcher or some such and thereby allowing runners to advance to third.

The third baseman must always go to third. The reason is that it is a very important base and as the next-to-last base, there are almost always runners still heading toward it. In contrast, any time a batter hits a double, **first** base becomes irrelevant.

Some experts say the third baseman covers home on a slow roller hit down the third base line with no runners on. The catcher and third baseman trade places in that case. Forget that. We don't need that sort of cuteness in youth baseball. The third baseman has plenty of time to field a slow roller and get back to third when there are no runners other than the batter. Or the pitcher can cover third.

Some experts have the third baseman serve as cut man on hits down the line. For youth baseball, simplicity is a priority so I always tell the third baseman that he covers third, period. The shortstop can serve as cut man on hits down the line, although if there is an outfield fence, you probably don't need a cut man for that throw because it is so short.

Some experts have the third baseman act as cut man on hits to right and center so the first baseman can stay at first and prevent the batter from going to second. The shortstop covers third in that case, although they say it's not important because runners on second and third should score on a base hit.

The main problem they see is stopping the batter from getting to second. I do not think youth runners are so sure to score from second on a base hit. Both they and their third-base coaches are chickens and can often be held to a one-base advance. Furthermore, the cut play is rarely executed successfully in youth baseball, so I would always place a priority on covering all live bases (those ahead of the batter) over getting into position to try to do the cutoff play to an unexpected base. All those approaches are too complicated for youth baseball. Have the third baseman always cover third.

Take anything you can get

The third baseman takes any ball he can get to. He is always running toward first more or less whenever he is near a neighboring player, and that player is running **away** from first. So the third baseman always has the easier throw. In other words, he never defers to the shortstop, pitcher, or catcher on a ball hit in the seam between them.

The only exception to this rule is that the third baseman should not dive for a ball to his left. Better the shortstop, who is generally playing deeper, should catch it standing up than the third baseman catch it while lying the dirt.

The fake throw to first

This is not a common or high-percentage play, but a number of writers have commented on the fake throw to first play at third. This works when there is a runner at second and the third baseman fields a grounder after moving in and toward the third-base line.

As with the fake throw to second by the catcher, I recommend that the baseman leave the ball in his glove and **fake** a hard throw with his **empty bare hand**. If you try to fake with the ball in your hand either it will come out or you may hurt your arm trying to stop after a hard fake.

After the fake throw to first, you turn around and tag the runner from second out as he rounds third base. If this play works, you look smart. If not, you look dumb. But getting the out at third is better than at first. Of course, it's also an excellent play if you conclude you have little chance to get the runner at first.

Holding the runner on (teenage level)

For some reason, a lot of people have it in their head that you do not need to hold runners on at third. I guess they figure they can't steal home.

Yes, they can. Furthermore, a steal of home is not the only danger of a long lead at third. Long leads at third let the runner score more easily on a passed ball, grounder, or delayed steal.

Right-handed pitchers are in a great position when they are in the stretch to throw deceptively to third. They are like left-handed pitchers throwing to first, which is well known to be a difficult move to read. But if third baseman does not cover the base, the advantage of the right-handed pitcher facing third is lost.

When the pitcher is right-handed, third basemen need not stand at the base like first basemen when holding a runner. They need only be close enough to get

there before the runner in case of a pick-off throw. This needs to be practiced.

Knowing the pitch

It is common for shortstops to watch the catcher's sign and warn the third baseman of off-speed pitches against right-handed batters. Right-handed hitters often pull off-speed pitches down the third-base line. The shortstop and third baseman need to work out a verbal secret code for that. If the opponents figure it out, the batter will have an advantage.

Position clinics
Clinic #1

6:30	Foot placement at base for infield throw and pick-off (no ball)
6:35	Same with live ball
6:40	Slow roller play at first
6:45	Around-the-clock drill
6:50	Going back on a pop
6:55	Fake throw to first then throw to other base or tag runner at third
7:00	End

Clinic #2

6:30	Where to line up before the pitch in different situations
6:35	Bunt defense (no runners, runner at 3rd)
6:40	Holding runners on (teenage) Force at home (Sub-teen)
6:45	One-throw, double-force play
6:50	Pop near fence
6:55	5-4 force play
7:00	End

12 Right field

Much maligned though it may be, right field is a position no less than any other. Good athletes who have never played right field screw up when they play it for the first time because they do not know the details of how to play the position. Dave Winfield said, "Right field is where you put your best guy, the guy who has the big arm, keeps the runner from advancing from first to third…"

Andre Dawson, who won four Gold Gloves in center field and four more in right field, said, "Center field was easier."

Great right fielders

Some of the best baseball players in history have played right field, including:

- Roberto Clemente (Hall of Fame)
- Ruben Sierra
- Dave Winfield
- Dwight Evans
- Babe Ruth (Hall of Fame)
- Carl Furillo
- Enos Slaughter (Hall of Fame)
- Reggie Jackson (Hall of Fame)
- Darryl Strawberry
- Al Kaline (Hall of Fame)
- Hank Bauer
- Jimmy Piersall
- Stan Musial (Hall of Fame)
- Tony Gwynn (future Hall of Fame)
- Andre Dawson
- Jesse Barfield
- Bobby Bonds
- Mel Ott (Hall of Fame)
- Manny Ramirez
- Larry Walker
- Sammy Sosa
- David Justice
- Frank Robinson (Hall of Fame)
- Roger Maris
- Hank Aaron (Hall of Fame)

Whatever team you or your players like, I guarantee you that team has a right fielder. Maybe coaches who have players or fathers who are unhappy about playing right field should contact their local pro team and ask their current starting right fielder to explain why the child should welcome the chance to play the position.

Eyes

When the pitcher throws his pitch, focus your eyes on the strike zone.

Sometimes the first baseman or an umpire will block your line of sight. If it's the first baseman, you need to move a step or two to one side so you can see the strike zone. If it's the umpire, you can ask him to move a step or two to one side and he usually will.

Hits curve toward the foul line

Balls hit to right and left fields curve toward the foul line. The closer the trajectory is to the foul line to begin with, the more pronounced the curve. In other words, a ball hit to right center curves a little bit toward the first-base line. But a ball hit down the first-base line curves a lot.

In his book, *The Complete Idiot's Guide to Baseball*, Hall of Fame catcher Johnny Bench says this only happens on balls hit by right-handed batters to right field and by left-handed batters to left field, in other words, pulled hits. Hall of Fame or not, he's only half right. And he actually played 111 games in the outfield in the Majors.

In fact, **all** balls hit to right or left curve outward. In his *Baseball Playbook*, Missippi State coach Ron Polk says, "The left fielder and right fielder must be aware that a pulled line drive down the line can break toward the line just as opposite field line drives do." He uses the phrase line drives because the quote was under a line-drive subhead. **All** balls hit to left and right curve.

I assume this is caused by the angle between the path of the pitch and the bat. The closer that angle is to 90 degrees, the less curve on the hit. That's why fungoes do not curve. They are almost always hit at a 90-degree angle. The more the angle of the bat to the pitch path is greater than 90 degrees, the more sideways spin is put on the ball at impact. That sideways spin causes the ball to curve outward. Here's a diagram:

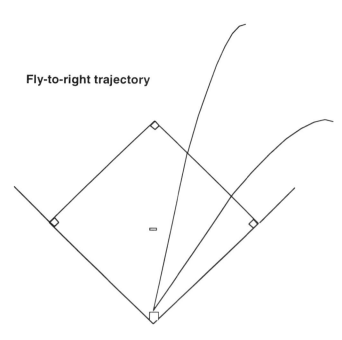

Fly-to-right trajectory

Ground balls too

Ground balls hit to right also usually curve toward the first-base line, especially on the first bounce. The reason is the same: sideways spin imparted by the angle of the bat to the path of the pitch. Here's a diagram:

Base-hit-to-right bounce trajectory

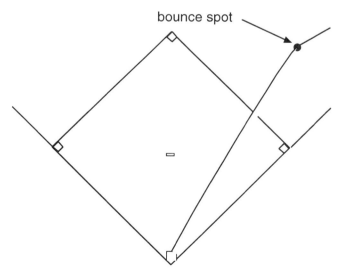

bounce spot

Playing a fly ball in right

When you play a fly ball in right, you must keep your body between it and the foul line. The ball will come to you if you do. But if you go straight to where the ball appears to be heading, you will find it is not

there. It will have drifted toward the foul line, probably out of your reach.

You can only learn to play the curve of the ball through **experience**, but you will learn faster if you are told about the curve verbally in advance.

Fungoes cause bad habits

Coaches should **not** hit fungoes to right or left fielders. Fungoes go straight. They do not curve. As a result, they cause right and left fielders to pick up the bad habit of running to where the ball **appears** to be hit. Then, in a game, when the ball hit to left or right curves toward the foul line, the fielder will misplay the hit.

If you cannot hit fungoes to right and left fielders, how do they get experience?

You might be able to show them a true look by having a batter hit opposite field or pull to right. The batter would stand at the plate in the normal fashion. A pitcher or coach would feed him balls from a short distance, preferably from behind a screen. The pitches would be thrown to the right-field side of the plate.

The way most coaches give right and left fielders practice shagging curving hits is to station them out there during batting practice. I hate batting practice and never have it so I do not recommend that method, although I acknowledge that it does work for showing right and left fielders the way a batted ball curves in those fields.

Cardinals manager Tony LaRussa requires his outfielders to field balls hit by batters during batting practice for 20 minutes a day in spring training and five minutes a day in pre-game warm-ups. He says, "You can take 1,000 fungoes a day and it won't be as good as ten minutes a day pretending you are in a game, taking balls off the bat during batting practice."

Pitching-machine curve balls

Shooting curve balls to right and left field from a pitching machine might work. Make sure it is set to make the ball curve in the correct direction, that is, toward the foul line.

Outfielders must talk to each other

Outfielders need to learn to communicate with each other using **two words**: "Back!" and "In!" Do not use words like "Deep!" or "Short!" because they can have other meanings.

The hardest ball for an outfielder to judge is one hit directly at him. It takes a second or two to figure out whether the ball is going to fall in front of him, come right to him, or go over his head. Accordingly, the outfielder should not move until he is sure he knows where the ball is going.

Unfortunately, if you wait that long to start moving, you will not get to the short or deep balls. The other two outfielders, on the other hand, have excellent angles from which to see the trajectory of the ball. They know almost immediately whether the outfielder to whom the ball is hit must move in or back. So you must train your outfielders to help their teammate by yelling "Back!" or "In!" as soon as they recognize which it is.

One problem I have seen with inexperienced outfielders is they try to yell **too soon** and get it wrong. Even the fielders in the non-ground-zero outfields must wait the better part of one second themselves to see where the ball is going.

Give all three of your outfielders practice yelling "Back!" or "In!" so they learn to wait a second before doing so and so they get into the habit of helping their outfieldmates and of making use of that help when the ball is hit to them.

Don't bounce when you run

If you run incorrectly in the outfield, a fly ball will appear to jerk or bounce in your vision with each step. That makes it very hard to catch.

Numerous baseball books say you can fix this by running on your toes or the balls of your feet. I tried. That did not work for me. Maybe it will work for your players. But I **did** learn to run without the ball bouncing in my vision. I do not know how to explain it. The best I can do is to say you have to smooth out your running. Again, it is something you learn from experience and you will learn faster if it is explained to you in advance.

'Nice catch'

One of the lowest moments in my baseball career came when I was eleven. I was playing right field. The batter hit a ball right at me. I thought it was short and took two steps forward. In fact, it went over my head for extra bases.

One of the fathers helping coach our team yelled out immediately after the play, "Nice catch, Reed!" in a voice dripping with sarcasm.

Exile

When I came back to the dugout, I sat at the end of the bench by myself. No coach or player spoke to me. I did not cry, but I was about as close to it as possible.

More than forty years later, I still remember the name of the man who yelled, "Nice catch, Reed!" I was going to put it in the book, but I figure he's dead or drooling now.

Neither that man, nor my coach, nor my teammates nor myself had the proper perspective on that play back in 1958. Here's the proper perspective so you do not give any of **your** players a forty-year bad memory.

Right at me

That ball was hit right at me. As I said earlier, that's the toughest ball to judge. My fellow outfielders should have yelled, "Back!" No one ever taught them to do so. I should have stayed put until I knew where the ball was going. No one had ever taught me to do so back then.

Curt Flood used to use the bill of his cap as a range finder according to Tim McCarver's *Baseball for Brain Surgeons*. If the ball rose **above** the bill of his cap, he ran **back**. If it stayed **below** the bill of his cap, he would charge **in**. That reminds me of a trick batter's use. If the ball rises **above** the pitcher's hand on release, it's a **curve**. If it comes **down** from the hand on release, it's a **fast ball**.

Even if I had stayed put, the ball **still** probably would have gone over my head. It was well hit. Had I gotten a better jump on it, I might have held the batter to one less base.

The only way I could have caught that ball in the air would have been to make an instant correct read as the ball came off the bat, take off at a dead run keeping outside the ball to take into account the curve, and make a Willie Mays-style back-to-the-plate catch.

Rare catch

I have never seen a Little Leaguer make such a catch. I doubt that the man who yelled, "Nice catch, Reed!" ever made such a catch, or could have.

As it turned out, I got to redeem myself on that play—in 1992 when I was playing semi-pro baseball.

Willie Mays impersonation

In 1992, I was playing right field in a semi-pro game at Dublin High School in Dublin, CA. The batter hit a ball right at me. As in 1958, my outfieldmates gave me no verbal help as to the trajectory of the ball. And as is 1958, I erroneously took two steps forward when I should have just stood still and waited until I could figure out the trajectory.

But everything I did thereafter was different from 1958—starting with my muttering an expletive to myself when I realized the ball was hit over my head.

I figured it was an inside-the-park home run. There is no outfield fence at the Dublin J.V. field. But I thought if I hustled, I could pick the ball up off the ground and maybe hold the batter to a triple.

I took off running full speed toward the right field foul pole. The ball was hit to straightaway right, but in my old age, I knew it would curve toward the foul line.

Watch the ball with one eye

When I was an end in high school football, I read a booklet that said you should watch the ball with just **one eye** when you are running a pass route that takes you directly **away** from the quarterback. It said that if you tried to watch it with two eyes, you would have to turn your head, which, in turn, would cause you to turn your upper body, which, in turn, will slow you down.

The correct technique is to follow the ball out of the corner of one eye until it gets close enough to catch. In football, this also helps you prevent the defensive back from realizing that the ball is on the way to the receiver in question.

I did that in football and found that it worked. I also did it in baseball when playing outfield, where it also worked to enable me to maintain top speed when chasing deep balls.

I got a huge cheer from my teammates when I made the catch at Dublin. I suspect part of the reason was that they did not think I was looking at the ball because my head was facing the direction I was running and I had my back to the plate and the ball.

Pro outfielders actually do **not** look at the ball while they run for a really deep hit. I cannot do that. I doubt any youth player can either. Pros are aided in part by their many years of experience. They may also be aided by the **sound** of the ball coming off the **wooden** bat. I do not think the aluminum-bat sound provides as much information.

Not that hard

Willie Mays once made the comment that his famous catch was not that difficult, that it was "…just a football catch." I agree that it was not a difficult catch if you go to the right place, run smoothly, and don't turn your upper body.

When you think about it, if you and the ball are going the same direction, the differential in speed between you and the ball is fairly small so the ball seems to be coming in slow motion. The difficult catches are where you are standing still and the ball is whizzing by you at 100 miles per hour.

I think the Mays catch is famous not because it was difficult, but because it was **unusual**—they tore the Polo Grounds down and few current ball parks have a center field that deep—because it came in a **World Series**, and because he made a **great throw** after the catch.

People **think** it was difficult, but most players could make that catch if they had the running room and a little practice. Heck, if **I** made it, how hard can it be?

Wind aided

My Willie Mays catch was wind aided. In track, your record does not count when you have a tailwind. At Dublin, the wind was blowing in from right field toward home plate. (Dublin is just west of the Altamont Pass, the windmill capital of the world.)

Initially, I figured I had no chance to catch this ball in the air. But as I ran toward the foul pole keeping one eye on the ball, it began to occur to me that I might have a chance because the ball was hit high and the wind was slowing it down.

As the ball came down, it was just beyond my normal reach, so I had to do a little jump and extend my glove hand to make a one-handed basket-style (palm facing upward) catch.

Unlike Willie Mays' September 29, 1954 World Series catch of Vic Wertz's 450-foot drive at the Polo Grounds, there were no runners on base when I made my catch. I just jogged around and threw it back to the pitcher. Also, the ball I caught probably only went about 350 feet, not 450.

In the '54 World Series catch, there were runners on first and second. Mays' quick throw held the runner at first. The runner at second managed to advance to third.

Why the difference between my '58 and '92 performances?

I was ridiculed and shunned for my failure to make that catch in 1958; cheered in 1992. In fact I heard the same phrase afterwards. The semi-pro batter said, "Nice catch," when we passed at the end of the inning. Only he said it without sarcasm.

One difference was I knew to adjust for the curve of a ball hit to right field. No one taught me that in Little League. I figured it out years later from experience and from reading baseball books.

Another difference was I learned how to run in a gliding manner so that the ball did not bounce in my vision. No one ever taught me about that in Little League either. My Little League coach was a fast-pitch softball **catcher**.

It took me until part way through my adult playing career to figure out how to run smoothly when chasing a fly ball. Again, it was experience and reading about the bounce in baseball books that straightened me out.

Watching the ball out of the corner of one eye, which I did not learn until high school, enabled me to chase the ball at the faster speed necessary to get to this hit.

Of course, I was also helped by the wind, which I do not recall being present in 1958.

In short, there was no way I or any other similarly trained Little Leaguer could have made that catch. To train a youth baseball player so he could make that catch, you would probably have to have at least one or two long (hour or so) sessions where you kept hitting or shooting (with a pitching machine set on curve) flies to right. Place a cone or some other marker in the middle of right field, then just hit ball after ball deeper than that spot.

Furthermore, you would have to teach your other outfielders to yell "Back!" or "In!" in order to help the ground-zero outfielder get the necessary early jump on the ball.

Infielders and pitcher should point at flies

When a fly ball is hit on TV, you will see the infielders and pitcher immediately point at it. That's because it is hard to see the ball come off the bat in the outfield many times. The pointing by the infielders help the outfielder find the ball.

There were many times in my adult career when I could not see the ball come off the bat. Usually it was because the background was hazy. With good contrast like trees, I had no trouble. Sometimes, I never found the ball until it hit the ground. On many other occasions, I would do a big "I don't know where it is" in body language and some of my teammates would point, then I would find the ball and make the catch, albeit awkwardly.

This appears to be less of a problem in youth baseball, probably because the youth outfielders are much closer to the plate. But I still recommend that you train your infielders and pitchers to point to the fly ball and give them a little practice doing it.

You could have your outfielders turn their back to the plate, throw a fly ball to them, then yell, "Now!" and have the outfielder find the fly with the help of the teammates' pointing. If you do this, you'd better have the outfielders wear face mask batting helmets in case they do not find the ball before it finds them.

Drop step first on deep ball

If the ball is hit over your head, your first step is a drop step with the ball-side foot. A drop step just means you step straight backwards. Then you crossover with the other foot and go to the ball.

Teach it or accept it

You can find the time to teach your players how to make that play, although it will take an extraordinary effort to do so. Or you can let it go and just accept the fact that your players will never make that catch.

But do NOT do what was done to me when I was eleven. Do NOT blame the kid for not making a tough catch that neither he nor his outfieldmates was trained to catch, a catch that probably none of the adults present ever made or could have made.

Wet versus dry grass

The ball bounces differently on wet grass than dry. I am amazed that I have never heard TV color men discuss this.

Wet grass occurs more often in youth baseball because we typically start our games at 8 AM or 9 AM on Saturday mornings, when there is still dew on the grass. Also, youth leagues rarely cover the field with a tarp.

The notion that wet grass is different is not just my theory. I once asked some pro minor leaguers at a clinic about it. They laughed and said something to the effect that, "You **bet** the ball bounces different when the grass is wet."

Like a hockey puck

On **dry** grass, the ball generally bounces **up** at the same angle it came **down**. On **wet** grass, the ball behaves like a **hockey puck**. That is, it skids low along the grass. Here's a diagram:

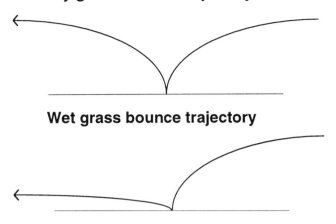

Dry grass bounce trajectory

Wet grass bounce trajectory

The ball also seems to pick up speed after it bounces on wet grass. That is physically impossible. What probably happens is that a ball bouncing on dry grass slows down, but a ball bounces on wet grass slows down **less**, so it appears to pick up speed when compared to the bounce we are used to.

The bottom line is that you must approach a wet-grass bounce much more cautiously. You need to hang back to deal with the low post-bounce trajectory and to deal with the unexpected speed after the bounce.

Moving laterally

To move laterally (sideways) in the outfield, your **first** step is a **crossover** step with the leg farthest from where you want to go. That's because a crossover step covers more ground faster than an open step with the leg nearest the ball. Practice this to get your players in the right habit.

Gambling in the outfield

Outfielders are the last line of defense. Balls that get past an outfielder can do a lot of damage. They are usually extra-base hits and can permit a runner who was on base to advance two or three bases.

Accordingly, outfielders have to approach a ball differently than infielders in most situations. If you watch a few youth baseball games, you will see that a great many youth outfielders do not know this. This may be a result of rotating players through numerous positions. More likely, it's just a result of their not being trained at all in outfield play.

Two zones

Divide right field into two zones:

• gamble
• play it safe

In straightaway right field and near the first-base

line, you should rarely gamble because if the ball gets behind you, there is no back up. In right center, however, the center fielder should be backing you up. Here's a diagram:

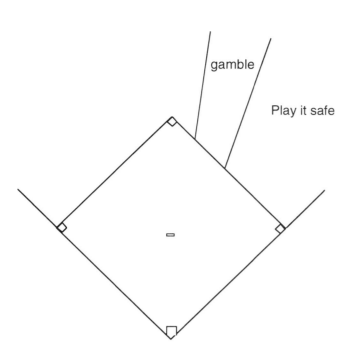

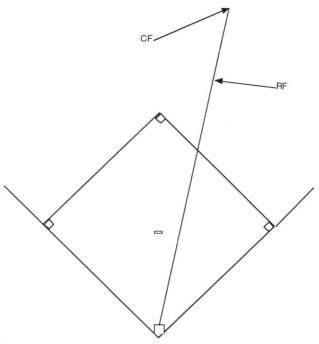

Right-handed right fielder versus right-center hit

What is gambling?

What do I mean by gambling? One technique that constitutes gambling in the outfield is cutting off a grounder the way infielders do. Infielders take the **shortest route** to the path of a batted ball. That is usually perpendicular to the path of the batted ball.

Infielders do this because they need to in order to have enough time to throw the runner out at first. Also, if the ball gets past them, it will generally be caught by an outfielder and the batter will be held to a single.

In right center, the right fielder (assuming he is right handed) can go ahead and try to cut the ground ball off like an infielder because the center fielder should be backing him up. On this play, the center fielder must **not** try to cut the ball off. If he did, the two outfielders might collide, plus there would be no back up. Here's a diagram:

Shoestring or leaping catch

Another form of gambling is attempting to make a shoestring catch or a leaping catch. Again, if the ball is in right **center**, it should be OK because of back up by the center fielder. But in straightaway right or along the first-base line, either technique would have an unacceptably low probability of success in most situations.

Collision with infielder

In general, if both an infielder and an outfielder can get to a particular fly ball, the **outfielder** should call for it because it is easier to come **in** on a ball than to go **back** on it. You need to practice this with your infielders and outfielders to prevent collisions.

A common mistake in the outfield is to call for a ball **too soon**. Practice should take care of this.

Widespread ignorance on gambling decision

Most people are ignorant about the outfield decision to gamble or not. The typical yahoo wants the outfielder to gamble on every play. People who believe in that think it's unmanly or something not to aggressively go after every ball hit to your area. Pete Rose said in his book *Pete Rose on Hitting*,

> *I don't want nonaggressive players on my team.*
> *I'd rather have an outfielder who tries for the shoe-*

string catch too often and lets a few of them get by him than have an outfielder who never tries for the game saver.

You need to read that statement very carefully. Note that he uses the phrase "game saver" at the end. There is no question that all players must gamble in what is called a "do-or-die situation." The fallacy with Rose's statement is that he suggests that only by "let[ting] a few of them get by him" can an outfielder try for the "game saver." That's bull.

In a do-or-die situation, you play aggressively. In a **non**-do-or-die situation, you do **not**. You do not need to screw up several non-do-or-die situations in order to use actual games to practice do-or-die technique. You use **practice** to practice do-or-die technique.

Calculated risk

This is a mathematical issue, not one to be decided by the opinion of Pete Rose or John Reed or anyone else.

Let's say you are in right field during an early inning with no runners on, no score, and no outs. The batter hits a ground ball down the line.

If you take a path perpendicular to the path of the ball and lay out to make a desperate effort to stop it, you may be able to cut the ball off and hold the batter to a single. But if you miss, and end up lying on the ground in foul territory while the ball goes to the corner, the batter will probably get a triple.

In the pitcher-fielding chapter, I gave you a table that shows the run values of various combinations of runners and outs. Refer back to that for the following.

If you play it safe and thereby hold the runner to a double, you are in the runner-at-second-with-no-outs situation. As the table shows, that has a run value of 1.068. If your gamble wins, you hold the batter to a single, which has a run value of .783. But if your gamble fails, you have a runner at third with no outs. That situation has a value of 1.277.

Decision tree

You can depict the gamble-or-play-it-safe choice in a diagram called a decision tree. Here it is:

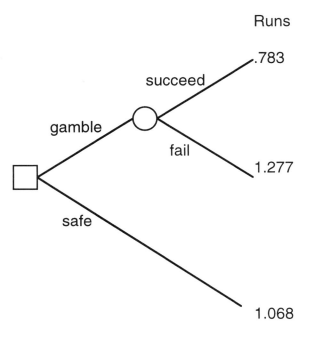

Runs

.783

succeed

gamble

fail

1.277

safe

1.068

The key question then is, "What probability of success do you need to make the gamble worth it?" You can calculate that probability using algebra. You've heard the phrase "calculated risk." But the people who use that phrase rarely do the actual calculation. Here is the actual calculation.

Let's say the probability of **success** you need to make the gamble worthwhile is P. That means the probability of **failure** on the gamble is 1-P because the probability of either success or failure is 100% or 1.000.

The **breakeven point** is the point at which the weighted average of the probabilities and outcomes of the gamble course of action **equal** the play-it-safe outcome. Here's the algebraic formula that states that and its solution:

$$.783P + 1.277 (1-P) = 1.068$$
$$.783P + 1.277 - 1.277P = 1.068$$
$$1.277 + .783P - 1.277P = 1.068$$
$$1.277 - .494P = 1.068$$
$$1.277 - 1.068 = .494P$$
$$.209 = .494P$$
$$P = .209/.494$$
$$P = .423 \text{ or } 42.3\%$$

In other words, you would only gamble on a grounder hit down the line in this situation if your success probability were greater than 42.3%.

Of course, sometimes you are in a situation where you absolutely **must** hold the runner to a single, for example there is a runner on second and it is the bottom of the inning of an extra-inning game. In that case, the weighted averages do not matter because if the runner at second touches the plate, the game is over. In that case, the right fielder must do whatever it takes to keep that runner from scoring from second.

How do you know the probability?

Experiment in practice to see what your success rate is. Mark a spot in the beginning of right field then hit ball after ball down the right field line. Keep track of the fielder's success rate and make sure he knows his success rate.

There are two reasons to do this:

• do-or-die situations
• to learn your success rate for normal situations

Should you do algebra every time the ball is hit down the line? Of course not. This is just a learning exercise to illustrate that it is **wrong** to adopt an aggressive-play-is-always-best policy.

Gambling path to a grounder

What exactly are the gambling path and the play-it-safe paths? Here you go:

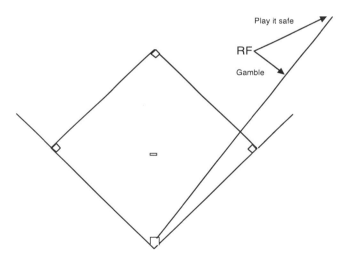

In the play-it-safe mode, you take a path that you are **certain** will result in your catching the ball. Basically, you are going to a point where the ball is traveling sufficiently slowly that there is virtually no chance that it will get past you. Again, this is a matter of experience.

Right fielder always takes the cut-off route to his right

On balls hit in the right-center gap, the right fielder should take the cutoff route. If he is right-handed, he is running toward his throwing-arm side, he will be able to get off a stronger, faster throw.

If a right-handed **center** fielder were to take the cut-

off route, he would then have to pivot 180 degrees and throw against his momentnum.

Also, the right fielder is heading in the direction of the action in two-thirds of the situations. Once a ball gets to the outfield, nothing is happening at first base. The outfielder needs to throw to second, third, or home. The right fielder is heading in the direction of second and third.

The only situation where you might want the center fielder to take the cutoff route would be when you had left-handed center and right fielder and a runner at second. In that case, the ball needs to go home and the left-handed center fielder running toward his throwing arm side will be able to make a quicker, stronger throw. However, in the interest of **simplicity**, I recommend that you **always** have the right-fielder take the cutoff route and the center fielder take the backup route on balls hit to the seam between the two fielders.

Counterclockwise-spin technique when going to left

I and many other right-handed right fielders use a counterclockwise-spin technique on some balls hit to our left. To me, it's natural and easy. I never **learned** how to do it. I just started doing it without thinking and it worked from the first time.

Others who have seen me do it thought it was some kind of spectacular razzle dazzle. So I hesitate to advocate it. But I am not the only one who does it, so you might want to suggest that your outfielders try it.

A similar, but clockwise, spin would also work for a left fielder who was left-handed and running toward his right. An appropriate-direction spin could work for a center fielder, but it should only be attempted if there is not an adjacent outfielder who is running toward his throwing arm and has an equal opportunity to get to the ball.

When a right-handed right fielder is running to his left, which is his glove side, he is not in a good position to face inward and throw the ball back to the infield.

What I do in many cases, is sort of let the momentum of the ball hitting my glove spin me like a pinwheel in that counterclockwise direction. During the spin, I take the ball out of my glove and cock my throwing arm. As I reach about the 270-degree point, I throw to second, third, or home. At that point, the momentum of the counterclockwise spin adds velocity to my throw, like a discus thrower.

You might think it would be hard to throw with any accuracy. **I** would think that. But in my experience, it is not. That may not be true for every individual. I think your body can make the throw accurately coming out of a spin, but you have to trust your body. You cannot **think** about this throw. You just **do** it.

I have never thrown one inaccurately out of the spin. I **have** thrown inaccurately out of the regular throwing motion.

Try it in practice to see if your outfielders can do it.

When not to catch a catchable foul fly

Is there ever a time when you should **not** catch a catchable foul fly as a right fielder? Yes. When there is a runner at third and fewer than two outs. If you catch the ball in that situation, the runner at third will almost certainly score. Trading an out for a run is an **offensive** strategy, not a **defensive** one.

Where to align before the pitch

The neutral alignment would be half way between the outfield fence and the infield dirt and half way between first and second bases. But batter tendencies usually warrant shifting. Also a near-foul-territory fence allows a right or left fielder to play farther away from the line because he has no chance to catch a foul fly on the other side of the fence.

The coach should track where the batters hit the ball during a game so that he can direct the outfielders to shift when that batter comes up again.

If you play the same team more than once during the season, which is typical, you can refer to past game charts to see where batters tend to hit the ball. In many cases, you can even determine that a shift is necessary **during** an at bat. If the batter fouls a couple of pitches down the first-base line, the right fielder should probably shift that way.

The same is true of the **depth** of the right fielder. In youth baseball, you have a wide mix of talent levels. That's much different from the high school and higher levels. In youth baseball, the top of the order can generally hit the ball deep. But the bottom of the order often has no power. Accordingly, the right fielder should move in when the bottom of the order is up in most cases.

Who's pitching?

Who is pitching is also important. The **faster** the pitcher, the more likely the batter will hit toward the **opposite field**. The **slower**, the more likely the batter will pull the ball. Again, this is more pronounced in youth baseball than in the baseball you see on TV because of the wide range of ability levels on each team.

At the higher levels, it is standard to play all hitters to pull. At the youth level, I do not recommend that. Rather see what's happening with the pitcher and batter in question.

I question the whole idea of putting the weakest fielder in right, which is, itself, a manifestation of the assumption that everyone pulls. At the youth level, many batters hit opposite field because they are late with their swing. Using a bat that is too heavy is the most common cause of that. Slow hands is another.

Once, in semi-pro, we played a high-school team that joined the semi-pro league *en masse* in the off-season (Watsonville, CA if I recall correctly). The high-school coach played on their semi-pro team.

Although they were mostly right-handed batters, I was busier than a one-armed paper hanger in a windstorm in right field that day. I made so many catches my teammates were calling me the "Miller Lite Player of the Game." How come? That high-school team was well coached and were trained to hit opposite field either to hit behind the runner or to make the most of an outside pitch.

So don't be too quick to assume that every batter pulls.

What pitch?

When I played adult baseball, my second baseman used to watch the catcher's signals then signal me what pitch was coming. If it was an off-speed pitch, I would shift in and toward the pull side. If it was a fast ball, I would shift back and toward the opposite field.

No tip-off

You have to be careful when you do this that you do not tip off to the offense what pitch is coming. I scraped a spot bare in the middle of right field as a starting point, then I would wander around before each pitch. I figured that the offense, who could not see my mark on the ground, could not tell whether I was shifting or where to.

The offense **could** see my shifts if they lined me up visually with some fixture in the dugout, like a chain-link fence post, and another, like a tree or outfield-fence mark, behind me in the outfield.

Jesse Barfield said he watched the way the catcher shifted before the pitch. Generally, Barfield would shift the same way. In youth baseball, that might not be a good idea because where the catcher wants the ball and where the youth pitcher throws it are usually two different things.

Range of the other fielders

The range of the neighboring fielders also determines pre-pitch alignment. Outfielders with great range should shade toward outfielders and infielders with less range and vice versa, that is, shade away from neighboring fielders with great range.

The count

The count matters at the higher levels. It **should** at the youth level and would if the batters were better trained. If you are coaching a youth level where the batters **are** trained to shorten up when they are behind in the count, you can play shallower and more opposite field when the batter has two strikes.

Right fielder Dave Winfield **faced** the direction he thought the batter was most likely to hit. For example, if he thought the left-handed batter was likely to pull the ball down the line, his pre-pitch position was to face slightly toward the first-base line so he could get a faster start in that direction.

Field conditions

Field conditions also determine where you align before the pitch. When the grass is wet, align deeper so you can stay safely back from a bounce.

Grass is usually high in youth baseball. Sometimes it is extremely high That means grounders get eaten up by the grass. That is, they rapidly slow down and even stop before you can get to them.

To the extent that you expect a grounder on such a field, you should play in. Because of the danger of a fly, which is unaffected by grass length, don't overdo this. The more important outfield tactic when there is high grass is to charge the ground ball hard regardless of where you aligned before the pitch.

Field dimensions

Sometimes, the field dimensions determine where you line up. My semi-pro team sometimes played at the California High School J.V. field. Right field was so short there that a stripe was painted on the outfield fence half way between the first-base line and center field. If you hit the ball over that part of the fence, it was only a ground-rule double.

At that field, I played so shallow I could force runners out at first. Another field I played at, Sycamore Valley in Danville, has a right field which goes up a hill fairly close to home plate. Again, I played shallow. In general, your right fielder should split the difference between the outfield fence and the infield dirt.

When there is no outfield fence, which was most of the time in my experience, you need to play as deep as the hitter can hit.

Do or die

The alignment of the right fielder is greatly affected by do-or-die situations. The vast majority of youth coaches screw this up.

A do-or-die situation is one where you have to either get a fly or force out or prevent a runner from scoring. Typically, that is in the last inning of a one-run or tie game or an extra inning.

In the outfield, if there are two outs, the outfielders should play where they are most likely to catch a fly ball if it is a do-or-die situation.

If there are less than two outs, they may want to play in. For example, in the bottom of an extra inning with a runner at third, the defense **must** stop the runner at third from scoring or they lose.

They cannot catch a **deep fly** because the runner will tag up and score before they can throw the ball home. So they have to play shallow enough that if they catch a fly there, they are close enough to home to throw the runner out after a tag up.

Catch the fly on the run

In this situation, the right fielder should probably catch the ball while running toward home. So although he should play shallow in order to be close enough to home to beat the runner, it needs to be a **deep** shallow because he does not want to be going **back** on the ball when he catches it.

In this situation and alignment, if the ball is hit over your head, you just walk to the dugout because the game is over. You see this occasionally on TV in the Major Leagues.

You need to practice the do-or-die situation with a runner at third and less than two outs. And the coach needs to make sure he yells "Do or die" to his team when these situations come up. Of course, if the team should get two outs before the runner at third scores, the coach must yell, "Normal! No more do or die!" to his outfielders and get them back to normal alignment so they have the greatest chance to catch a fly ball in the air.

Technique for catching grounders

There are three ways to catch a grounder in the outfield. Here they are along with the situations when you use them:

Situation	Technique
no runners on first or second	down on one knee
runners on 1st and/or 2nd	like an infielder
must stop runner to win	do or die

When there are no runners on first or second, you do not need to make a fast throw, so you can go down on your throwing-side knee to make a more certain stop of the ground ball.

The glove is between the knee that's down and the heel of the foot of the other leg. This, along with the upper body, creates a large blocking surface in the event of a bad hop.

Of course, this applies only to a rolling or low bouncing grounder. If it's a one- or two-hopper bouncing up five or six feet in the air, you stay up on two feet.

This assumes you are **in front** of the grounder. If it's hit in the gap or down the line, you need to take the angle discussed previously and use the backhand or catch on the run glove technique.

You do not worry about a runner at third base (in a non-do-or-die situation) on a base hit to the outfield because he will surely score.

Runner at first or second

If there is a runner at first or second, the outfielder needs to throw in a hurry to prevent the lead runner from advancing two bases. Actually, whether you want to try to prevent the lead runner from advancing two bases varies according to the quality of your outfielders. I'll discuss that later.

To make a faster throw, you must take the grounder like an infielder. That is, you set your feet apart in a wide base, form two hands in an alligator configuration, catch the ball in front, bring it up your chest, crow hop, and throw.

Do-or-die grounder technique

You should rarely see the do-or-die grounder technique. But in fact I see it all the time in youth baseball. It is **incorrect** to use the do-or-die grounder fielding technique in a non-do-or-die situation.

In the do-or-die grounder fielding technique, you run at the grounder more or less upright keeping the ball on your glove side. At the appropriate moment, you bend over and scoop up the grounder with only your glove hand, and, while still on the run, fire it to the appropriate base. You only use this technique when you **must** prevent the runner on second from scoring or you will lose the game.

Youth-baseball outfielders tend to use this technique all the time. That's very bad because it increases the probability that they will miss, in which case they are running away from the direction the ball is going. The runners may get not **one** extra base, but **two** as a result.

In the vast majority of cases, there is no benefit whatsoever to using the do-or-die technique on a routine grounder to the outfield. Typically, the runners are slowly rounding the next base and are not going anywhere regardless of what technique the outfielder uses. So why risk giving up extra bases with an inappropriate do-or-die technique?

Catching flies

I've been discussing a bunch of fairly sophisticated stuff so far in this chapter. But in youth baseball, the challenge is often just to get the kid to even **try** to catch a fly. Youth baseball players often shy away from ground zero and deliberately let flies fall to the ground before they go after them.

85% drill

The solution is what I call the 85% drill. It's a variation of the one-step drill I described elsewhere in the book.

Almost every kid will catch a fly ball if it's trajectory is short enough. For example, a tee ball player will catch a fly thrown from five feet away if that fly never gets higher than about six feet above the ground.

What you need to do at each level is find the combination of distance and trajectory at which the player in question will succeed about 85% of the time. Then, every time he succeeds, have him back up a step or five or ten feet and do it again. If he fails, have him move closer a step or five or ten feet.

Success

This will result in his spending most of the time making catches at a distance where he **succeeds** about 85% of the time and at a slightly longer distance where he is stretching and trying to improve. Progress can easily be seen if you mark the original distance.

Contrast this with the typical youth coach technique of putting the outfielders in the outfield and hitting fungoes at them. In most cases, there will be kids in that drill who are **afraid** of fly balls. They will never make or even attempt a catch and their confidence will go down, down, down.

Remember that the ability level of youth baseball players varies enormously within each team, especially below the eleven-year old level where they do not divide into different ability levels. So the 85% drill must be run in accordance with each **individual** player's ability, not the team average.

This is really the top priority at the lower levels. Until the kids can catch, the various tactics and strategy do not matter.

Not basket catch

Young baseball players tend to try to catch flies basket style. That is, holding the glove waist high with the palm facing up. That's incorrect. Don't even let them start that way.

They should have their glove little finger up in front of their throwing arm shoulder. The glove should be in front of the face above the head. The throwing hand should be right next to the web of the glove to help trap the ball in the glove and to remove it quickly.

In his book *Defensive Baseball*, Rod Delmonico says to catch the ball above your glove-side eye. He says catching it on your throwing side causes you to short-arm the ball like an infielder. I have always heard it taught the other way. For example, Walter Alston says to catch it on the throwing-arm side in his *Complete Baseball Handbook*.

I cannot say which theory is correct. Delmonico is a very successful college (TN) coach. Alston was a Hall of Fame manager of the Dodgers. Apparently, it is not important which side you catch it on.

Soft balls

You can reduce your players' fear by using soft baseballs. Those are the only kind I use in practice. Poly balls are the softest, although they are so light they blow around if there is any wind.

Father-son activity

Doing the 85% drill is really more of a **father-son** exercise than a coach-player exercise. That's because it takes many, many repetitions. So train your fathers to do this with their sons and encourage them to do it **a lot**.

Throwing two bases ahead of the lead runner on a base hit

On a non-extra-base hit, the outfielder who gets the ball should throw two bases ahead of the lead runner—**without hesitation**. (A runner at third is never the lead runner on a ground ball from an outfielder's perspective. He will always score on a base hit regardless of what any outfielder does.) This is basic outfielding.

Many youth coaches tell their outfielders to always throw to the pitcher or to second. I hate that, but I must admit that in the case of many youth right fielders, throwing to second is probably a better idea.

For reasons unknown to me, many youth outfielders cannot throw accurately to third from right, or home from any field. If you have such an outfielder, work with him to try to achieve the strong, accurate throw to third or home from right. But if you cannot achieve it in practice, you'd better tell him to throw it to second in every case.

Stop the runner

In 1993, I was a helper father with my oldest son's team. They were 11 and 12.

One game, the manager and his assistant left town on business and made me temporary head coach. One of the things I did in pre-game warm-up was emphasize the outfielders throwing two bases ahead of the lead runner **without hesitation**. We were only able to get a few repetitions, but it planted the seed in their heads.

Later, during the game, the opponent had a runner at first. The batter hit a base hit to right. Just as I had during the pre-game warm-ups, I yelled "Three! Three!"

The right fielder caught the hit on one hop and gunned it straight to third base—without hesitation. The runner was forced to stop at second, the first time I had seen a runner stop at second in that situation all season.

We won that game by one run. That was one of those few games each season where I felt we won because I was the coach that day. That play and some others that took place clearly made the difference. I'll tell you about the others later in the book.

The father of one player was so impressed that he telephoned to compliment me that evening.

Sliding catch

One technique for catching low flies, instead of the shoestring catch, is the sliding catch. I never did it. But some of my teammates did. I suspect that practicing it would help. You might do that on a slip 'n slide or on cardboard with no shoes on. It is preferable also because if you miss, the ball is likely to hit your body and therefore stay in front of you.

Tony Gwynn is a notoriously weak-armed right fielder. For years, opposing runners took extra bases on him all the time. So he had to work extra hard on finding ways to throw harder and faster.

He found that he could get the ball back into the infield faster if he made a **sliding catch** when going toward the foul line. He throws left-handed.

When he was a **left** fielder, Gwynn compensated for his weak arm by playing shallow. But he found he could not do that in right because more damage was done when the ball got by a right fielder than when it got by a left fielder.

Gwynn also taught himself to throw while running full speed. In 1984, a pennant-winning season for the Padres, Gwynn made a leaping catch against the wall then, after a 360-degree spin, doubled a runner off first. His team won that game 7-6 in extra innings.

Tony Gwynn says he is more proud of his five Gold Gloves than he is of his many batting awards. Gold Gloves are awarded annually to the best three outfielders in each league.

Diving catch

Diving catches are very dangerous. It is also questionable whether diving is **ever** the best technique. Once your feet stop pushing off the planet earth, you slow down. The fastest way to get to a particular spot is to **run through it**.

Of all the people on earth, which ones are most interested in getting to a particular spot as fast as possible? World class sprinters. They have studied speed every which way with every pertinent scientific instrument. They have tried every technique they thought might work. Do they dive across the finish line?

Nope. They run through it.

In football, we tell receivers to keep their feet on the ground. The only time they are supposed to jump is to fight a defender for a ball or to catch a line drive that is too high up to reach with their feet on the ground. Otherwise, we tell them to run under the ball. No diving.

There is one logical argument in favor of diving. When a ball is falling, catching it closer to the ground gives you a fraction of a second more time to get to it.

Infielders often have to make diving catches on balls hit to either side. They have no choice. They were never running to begin with. But outfielders are always running before they get to a ball.

Sneak a peek at first

With no runners on, the right fielder should throw a base hit to second, which is two bases ahead of the lead runner, who is also the batter. However, he ought to sneak a peek at first, sometimes the batter-runner gets sloppy and takes an overly big slow turn at first. The right fielder may be able to pick him off. Carl Furillo was famous for this play.

Throw to catcher at first

You can increase the chances that play will work by having the first baseman run out toward right field on a no-runners single. The batter-runner, seeing the first baseman leave the base and go out into the outfield assumes it's safe to linger off base. Meanwhile, the catcher, who has been trailing the batter up the line, covers first base.

The right fielder makes a leisurely move as if he is going to make a casual throw to second, then suddenly fires the ball to the catcher at first. The pitcher should have moved into position to back that up. The catcher should stay away from first base until the last second to avoid alerting the first-base coach as to what is going on.

Enos Slaughter once successfully executed this play against batter Connie Ryan with Stan Musial when Musial was playing first. On that play, Musial had dived toward second in a vain effort to catch the hit.

Back up the throw to first

The right fielder needs to back up throws to first from the catcher and the pitcher. These are less likely, but not unheard of at the sub-teenage levels.

The catcher may throw to first on a

- bunt
- dropped third strike
- catcher pick-off after a pitch

The pitcher may throw to first **before** he gets on the rubber. **These** catcher and pitcher throws to first can all occur at **all** age levels. At the teenage level, the pitcher may also throw to first **from** the rubber when the runner takes a lead.

The right fielder will have a hard time getting to a **pitcher** pick-off unless he gets advance notice of it. Although if there is a fence behind first base, it is likely that the right fielder will be able to get to an errant throw from the pitcher in at least enough time to stop the runner from advancing to third.

The right fielder should also back up a throw to first from third or shortstop. Although again it is tough for him to get to the ball quickly unless it bounces off a fence.

Back up fielding of hits

When the ball is hit to the first or second baseman, the right fielder does not back up the throw to first. One reason is the angle is too extreme. But the main reason is that he must back up the infielder's efforts to field the batted ball.

Base hit to left field

On a base hit to left field with no runners, the right fielder backs up the possible throw from the left-fielder to second base. If there is a runner at first at the start of the play, the right fielder assumes that the left fielder will throw to third and backs up a possible throw from third to second. That is, he gets online with second and third bases at least twenty feet away from second.

General backing up

All outfielders should always be alert for opportunities to back up. I already told you how I once covered home plate and prevented a run from scoring in a game where I was the left fielder.

In another game in 1990 at Golden Gate Park in San Francisco, I saw that the first baseman might be making a throw to second. I forget the situation that led to that, but there was a runner advancing from first to second at the time. I sprinted from right field to shallow left center just in case. The left fielder and center fielder were doing what most outfielders do—spectating.

The first baseman's throw to second was inaccurate. I was just able to make a sliding stop of it in left-center. The runner popped up to go to third, but was stopped by his screaming third-base coach. "Where'd **he** come from?" the runner asked the coach, referring to me. I had about one base-saving play like that per season while playing right field.

There are few opportunities for heroism in the outfield, that's why I have always hustled my butt off to go where I might be able to make a play. I have never understood why other outfielders just stand way out there and watch the game.

Cover first or second bases

Sometimes, a right fielder may find he is the only one available to cover first or second base. At the Major League level, this is **designed** on some plays where the first baseman is the cut man and the batter has not yet reached second base. At the youth level, I do not think you should have the first baseman ever act as a cut man unless the batter has reached second. But even if you teach that the first baseman never leaves first, sometimes people forget in the heat of battle.

Show off your arm in pre-game warm-ups

An ounce of prevention is worth a pound of cure. Accordingly, it is smart to show off a strong outfield or catcher's arm in pre-game warm-ups. Often, the opposing players and coaches see it and resolve not to try to run on you during the game. I had a pretty good arm and often heard opponents comment about it when I threw to third or home in pre-game warm-ups.

I only got about one outfield assist (throwing a guy out at a base) per season. I'd like to say it was because opposing runners didn't try to take extra bases on me because they knew I had a strong arm. In fact, that was rarely the case. I **did** have a strong arm, but opposing runners were not smart enough to notice outfielders' arms in most cases in the leagues I played in.

The main reason I only had one outfield assist per season was that outfield assists are very hard to come by. In 1995, Raul Mondesi of the Dodgers won the Gold Glove in the National League. He played in 142 games that year and had 16 assists or one per every 8.9 games.

Outfield assists are easier to come by in youth baseball because youth runners are really dumb. In 1998, my right fielder had two assists in one inning—both at home plate!

Intimidating base coaches out of sending the runner by demonstrating a strong arm is also easier in youth baseball because the typical youth base coach is a total chicken about sending runners.

There is another school of thought. Once, a minor-league pro played a game at Foothill High School in Pleasanton, CA with my semi-pro team. He was getting ready to go to spring training and wanted to get into baseball shape. He was a professional center fielder and had an atomic cannon for an arm. But in pre-game and pre-inning warm-ups, he acted as if he had a very weak arm—one-hopping throws to the right and left fielders.

He was trying to decoy one of the opponents into trying to take an extra base on him. During the game, a guy tried to go home on him and he unleashed a rocket to the plate from deep center.

In **youth** baseball, I think the **prevention** tactic is a better idea.

Line it up

As you approach a batted ball, either a grounder or a fly, you should try to come at it so you are going toward the target base. On grounders, this is sometimes called "rounding." Instead of going straight to a ground ball, you circle back a bit so that when you get to the ball you are lined up with the base at which you plan to throw.

In semi-pro, I once got an attaboy for lining up a catch of a fly. There was a runner at third with less than two outs. The batter hit a fly to shallow right center. If I had gone **straight** to it, I would **not** be in a good position to throw home to prevent the runner from scoring after a tag-up. So I looped out toward center so that the plate, the ball, and I were in a straight line. Here's a diagram with a black circle marking the spot where the ball is coming down:

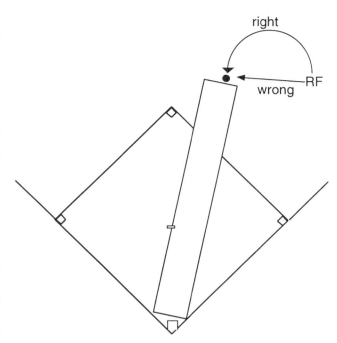

The basic idea is that sometimes, when you have time, you can and should approach the ball from a direction that aids your throw to a base. In the semi-pro play in question, the runner **did** tag and I made a good throw, but our second baseman cut it off then made a bad throw. In fact, he should not have cut it off at all. As I said when I was talking about the infield, there are far too many cutoffs of on-line throws that will get to the destination quicker if they are left alone.

Steps for catching a fly

Former Major Leaguer Duane Anderson taught me the ideal steps for catching a fly ball in the outfield. I used what he taught me in the semi-pro play I just described.

When possible, you want to not only line yourself up with the base toward which you intend to throw, you also want to get a step back **behind** where the ball is coming down.

As the ball arrives, you take a step forward with your glove-side foot, toes pointed at the target base, and catch the ball in front of your throwing-side ear. In one continuous motion, you grab the ball with your throwing hand and crow hop onto your throwing-side foot. Your throwing-side foot now will point outward at about a 45-degree angle and your glove-side shoulder will point toward your target base.

You actually gain a little altitude on your crow hop step because you need a little extra time to do a full windup with your throwing arm. Infielders do not gain altitude on their crow hop because they are making a quick, arm-only throw. Outfielders need to get their whole body into the throw and that requires a fraction of a second of extra airborne time during the crow hop.

Your third step with your glove-side foot is like a pitcher's stride as you throw the ball hard to the infield and your throwing side foot is pushing as off the pitcher's rubber.

This is not something I can really describe adequately in a book, even with photos. (There is a photo sequence of this on page 78 of Rod Delmonico's *Defensive Baseball*.) The best thing I can tell you is to attend a professional **minor league** or **major college** baseball game. Get there early so you can see the pre-game warm-up. Watch the outfielders. They will be doing this. You might take a video camera to tape it and use it as a training video for your players.

Why not go to a **Major** League game? Those guys frequently use lousy technique, like Rickey Henderson's "Snatch" method of catching flies. There may also be an outfield training video somewhere that shows this sequence.

Dwight Evans, who is a state-of-the art right fielder, takes his crow hop **as he is catching** the fly, not immediately afterward like everyone else.

I must warn you that, on several occasions, I tried to teach youth baseball players the step-hop-throw sequence, with no success. Although I am sure they would have gotten it if I had given them more repetitions.

Do-or-die fly technique

There is also a do-or-die version of this. In that, you charge the fly ball at a dead run and throw from a dead run after you catch it. I usually end up doing a shoulder roll on the ground after one of those all-out throws. I have never seen a pro do that, so I guess I am doing something wrong.

Sprint, don't jog

You often see an outfielder jog or drift under a fly. That's wrong. He should always sprint to a point behind the ball whenever possible, then step toward the infield as he makes the catch. That increases the probability of a successful catch, and, if there is a runner on first or second, increases the probability that he will prevent the runner from advancing two bases.

Sun

All fielders need to learn to catch balls coming from the direction of the sun, but outfielders have more occasion to use that skill than other positions. The recommended orientation of baseball fields is that the catcher face east-northeast. That puts the morning sun at the right-fielder's back, but it puts the **afternoon** or **evening** sun in the right fielder's face. Of course, not all fields are oriented the optimum direction.

There are three ways to deal with the ball coming out of the sun:

- flip-down sunglasses
- block the sun with your glove or throwing hand (glove is bigger and therefore better)
- stand off to one side or the other so that the sun is not behind the ball

I am dead set against the flip-down sunglasses. They are unbelievably **dangerous** if a kid should fall on his face. They ought to be outlawed at all levels.

You can use your glove or throwing hand to block the sun. Hold it away from your body and block the sun. Eventually, the ball will appear from behind your glove or hand and you can catch it. If the sun is low, you may need to block it with your glove just to see the pitch get to the plate.

The normal fly-catching position is to have the glove in front of your throwing-side ear. But when the sun is a factor, it is better to stand off to one side or the other and catch the ball away from your body so your line of sight to the ball does not also go to the sun.

A little practice as all your players need. They should wear regular sunglasses for this purpose, not flip downs, because they are going to be looking in the direction of the sun repeatedly and you need to protect their eyes. Show them the two techniques and have them practice each. This skill is a bit like riding a bike. Everyone can learn to do it, but it's hard to learn solely by hearing it explained. You have to go out and do it.

The main purpose of a little practice is to prevent the player from panicking when he encounters a sun ball in a game.

Bright sky

Sometimes, the whole sky is sun bright when there is overcast with a sun behind it. You cannot use either the glove, hand, or stand to one side techniques. The bright area is too big. In that case, the best technique is probably to wear safety sunglasses, not flip-downs.

Lights

I have only played in one night baseball game. But in many hot weather areas, it is standard to play under the lights. The first time I looked up to catch a fly ball in that night game, I was astounded. It was as if there were 40 suns. Fortunately, that was pre-game warm-ups. I got used to the lights before the actual game.

As with the sun on a clear day, you can block out the lights with your glove or hand or by standing to one side. And as with the sun, you should give your players some practice catching flies under the lights so they don't panic when they first see them in a game.

When the sun is a problem, you should also pull the bill of your hat down as low as possible.

Wind

Outfielders frequently grab a handful of grass and toss it to see which way the wind is blowing and how hard. The wind greatly affects fly balls. You have to position yourself differently to catch a fly ball on a windy day. Balls hit into the wind will not go as far. Balls hit with a tailwind will go farther. Cross winds change the direction of the ball. Try to give your fielders practice catching flies on windy days.

No rainbows

All throws on the baseball field must be line drives. The ball will go **farther** if you throw a high arc, a rainbow-shaped trajectory, but it takes too long.

I tell my players they must always throw as if there is a 12-foot high glass ceiling over the field. Youth players tend to think the ball should get all the way to its destination **on the fly**. No. It should get to its destination **fast**. From the outfield, that almost always means that the outfielder should one- or two-hop it.

Earlier, I said my players would probably tell you the phrase they heard most from me was "Tag on the ground." The phrase they heard second-most was probably, "No Rainbows!" They heard that every time I saw a rainbow throw.

Another problem with high throws is that they eliminate the possibility of relaying an off-line or weak throw or redirecting the throw to another base.

Fence

If your field has a fence along the foul line or to designate home runs, you must give your right fielders practice catching balls near the fence and bouncing in the corner. Teammates should warn them when they are close. If there is a warning track, outfielders should learn to read it during pre-game warm-ups. That is, they need to know how many full-speed steps it is from the start of the warning track to the fence.

Fences have been the scene of a lot of baseball heroics over the years. Nowadays, the pros even make the fences the right height to enable outfielders to rob batters of home runs.

Forget that. Fences are very dangerous. The extremely promising career of Dodgers center fielder Pete Reiser was ended by a collision with the outfield fence. Reiser made the catch, but was in a coma for ten days. Ted Williams was never the same after he ran into the fence in an all-star game. Bobby Valentine, manager of the 1999 Mets, was a star player until he hit the center field wall at Anaheim stadium on May 17, 1973.

Do **not** teach your players to run into or climb fences. Leave that to the pros and their padded walls.

Don't slight right field

This is the longest fielding chapter in this book. One reason for that is it happens to be my position, so I know more about it. Another, more important reason is that I want to show coaches how complicated it is so they can sell their players and parents on the idea that it is not a substandard position.

It's true that the outfield is the best place to put weak players because there is less happening out there. But that does not mean the right field is not a position in which players can take great pride. If you do a good job of coaching your right fielders, you will find that the relatively weak athletes who play there on non-elite youth teams play the position better at the end of the season than much better athletes who have not been trained to play right and who do not have experience at playing right. The better athlete will misplay the curve on the hit. He will not know his backup assignments. He will collide with his neighbors. He will gamble inappropriately. And so forth.

Coaching a weak athlete to the point where he can outplay the better athlete is a great thing for a youth coach to do and right field gives you the best opportunity to do it.

Because outfielders need more repetitions than coaches can give them, encourage fathers (or whatever adult is likely to play catch with the kid in question) to attend the position clinic so they can learn some of the drills that their sons and daughters need to work on.

Position clinics (age 6 to 9)
Clinic #1
6:30 One step play catch
6:35 Yell "Back!" and "In!" to teammates
6:37 Catch grounders on asphalt using one knee technique
6:42 Throw ball to second base
6:47 Back up throw to first base
6:52 Catch fly and throw behind runner who did not tag up
6:57 Calling for shallow pop
7:00 End

Clinic #2
6:30 Sliding catch (on cardboard)
6:35 Sun techniques
6:38 One-step play catch
6:45 Back up throw to second from left field
6:48 Catch grounder regular technique
6:53 Ready position before pitch and step toward plate on pitch
6:57 Backhand catches of grounders and flies
7:00 End

Position clinics (10 and up)
Clinic #1
6:30 Chalk talk:
curve toward foul line
ground ball bounce toward line
need to run smoothly
ball hit right at you
wet and dry grass
gambling on various catches
when not catch catchable foul fly

where align before pitch

6:35	Yell "Back!" and "In!" to teammates
6:37	Drop step first on deep ball
6:38	Watch ball over your head with one eye
6:40	Lateral move (crossover step)
6:41	Cutting off ball hit to right-center seam
6:45	Calling for shallow pop
6:47	One-knee grounder technique
6:48	Regular grounder technique
6:49	Do-or-die grounder technique
6:50	Do-or-die fly technique
6:53	Throw two bases ahead of the runner
7:00	End

Clinic #2

6:30	Sliding catch (on cardboard)
6:35	Back up throw to first by

> catcher
> pitcher
> shortstop
> third baseman

6:41	Back up first and second baseman fielding (deliberately let ball go through)
6:45	Back up throw to second from left field
6:48	Line up fielding for throw

> grounder
> fly

6:53	Fly-catching steps
6:57	Sun techniques
7:00	End

13 Center field

Center field is generally the place for the **fastest-running outfielder**. Center is the position I played second most. I thought it was great fun. You can gamble all over the place because you have back up from the right and left fielders. Plus center is busier. I once went 18 games without getting a fly in right. In center, if nothing else happens, you at least get the occasional overthrow by the catcher on a steal.

Strong up the middle

One theory of baseball defense is that you should be strong up the middle, that is place your best fielders at second, short, and center. As I said earlier in the book, I do not think that applies to youth baseball because of the great importance of first base and catcher.

In the pros, they put the **strongest arm in right**, the **weakest arm in left**, and the **fastest, best all-around guy in center**. I would agree with that in youth baseball, as long as you staff the infield first and only choose the outfielders from what's left.

I covered a lot of general outfielding information in the previous chapter on right field. You should read that and supplement it with the information in this chapter which is specific to center field.

Great center fielders

Here are some of the great center fielders:

- Willie Mays (Hall of Fame)
- Joe DiMaggio (Hall of Fame)
- Tris Speaker (Hall of Fame)
- Kirby Puckett
- Duke Snider (Hall of Fame)
- Ken Griffey, Jr.
- Cool Papa Bell (Hall of Fame)
- Mickey Mantle (Hall of Fame)
- Richie Ashburn (Hall of Fame)
- Ty Cobb (Hall of Fame)
- Larry Doby

Leader of the outfield?

It is standard to make a big deal about the center fielder being the leader of the outfield. I disagree.

Leadership is a point of contention I have in many sports discussions. The only need for leadership is on balls that split the seam. Someone needs to say, "I got it."

True, the center fielder is in those situations more often than the right and left fielders, but I see no need to seek out a leader for the position or to try to turn someone into a leader.

Leaders are born, not made. You can improve anyone's leadership with instruction. But you generally cannot change a non-leader into a leader no matter how hard you try. In my experience, the leaders in right-center and left-center seam situations will emerge. It may be that the leader in the right-center seam turns out to be the right fielder, but the leader in the left-center seam turns out to be the center fielder. It's a function of the kids involved.

For example, when I played right, if the center fielder that day was **inexperienced**, **I** would lead. On other occasions, the center fielder had more experience than I, so **he** led.

Just let the leaders emerge. Do not put anyone "in charge." This is especially important with youngsters where any authority can quickly go to their head.

Hit runners in the back

One problem the center and left fielders have that the right fielder generally does not have is the danger of his throw hitting a runner in the back. Accordingly, he may want to deliberately throw off line in order to get the ball around the runner. Runners will sometimes round their path outward deliberately to get in the way of the throw from center. Don't teach that to kids. Remember that a ball hitting a child sometimes kills the kid so you cannot advocate anything that increases the chances of a child being hit.

Back up steal throw at second

One of the center fielder's most important jobs is to back up the catcher's throw to second on a steal. One of the middle infielders is doing this also, but the more the merrier. The center fielder needs to stay at least 15 to 20 feet behind the base or other backer upper if there is one.

Also, the center fielder is probably going to have to throw to third, whereas if the middle infielder catches the passed ball the runner probably will not try to go to third.

This play needs to be practiced with a base runner to make sure the center fielder does not get into the habit of throwing through the area where the runner will be. This practice also helps the third baseman. I once threw a ball to third on a steal overthrow when I was playing center in semi-pro. My throw was accurate, arriving over the right shoulder of the runner. But the third baseman missed it, saying later he didn't expect it to get past the runner and was mentally unprepared when it did.

Back up pick-off throw at second

Pick-off throws can come from the pitcher or catcher. At the teenage level, the pitcher can throw to second from the rubber. Below the teenage level, he can still do it, but the runner is not allowed to take a pre-pitch lead so there is rarely any point. At all levels the pitcher may make a pick-off throw to second at any time. The center fielder must be alert to it.

The catcher can also make a pick-off throw to second. I have not seen much of that in youth baseball. It takes a catcher with a lot of self-confidence. It also takes some practice and communication to make sure the middle infielders are not surprised by it. You should know whether your catcher is inclined to make pickoff throws to second before you take the field.

May have the longest throw

It is well established that the strongest outfield arm goes to right because of the throw to third. But the **longest** throw in baseball is the center fielder's throw from deep center to home plate. The reason is the fence is farther from home in center. Little league Baseball recommends the same 200-foot distance to the fence for all fields, but it is traditional to make the center field fence farther from home plate.

You should practice the throw from deep center to home because it may need a relay. Whether it does will vary according to the fence distance, if any, and the strength of the player's arms.

You may also decide to forget about trying to throw home from deep center because of a too-low probability of success given the accuracy and strength of your kids' arms. If that's the case, the center fielder should probably throw to second or third. Again you need to experiment to see what's feasible with your field and personnel.

See the strike zone

You can never play a true straightaway in center, because you cannot see the plate through the pitcher. You have to shade to one side or the other so you can see the bat hit the ball. If the umpire blocks your view of the plate, you can ask him to move and he usually will.

Know your neighbor

One of the great benefits of assigning each player to one position and keeping him there all season is getting to know your neighbor. When I played center or right with a **new** guy next door it was difficult. But when I was playing next to the same guy for months, we would learn to work together.

You learn each other's strengths and weaknesses. One of us was usually faster than the other. So the boundary or seam would move in the direction of the slower guy and the faster guy would start calling for a wider range of balls on his side of the new seam location.

Similarly, on deep balls, we knew which one of us had the stronger arm. On a ball that got to the wall in the gap, if I had the stronger arm, I would quietly say, "I got it" as the two of us approached the wall. If he was a **new** neighbor, he might aggressively go after the ball at the same time as I did, which can cause collisions and delays in throwing the ball in. He would not know that I called for grounders and might not defer to me if I did.

On a fly to the seam, the weaker fielder defers to the stronger fielder. I was usually the weaker fielder. But, again, with a new neighbor, I wouldn't know.

In general, baseball is not much of a team sport. It's mostly individual. But when a ball is hit into the seam between outfielders or between an outfielder and an infielder, coordination of their efforts is most certainly a team sport and it takes time for those teammate pairs to learn to work together.

To an extent, rotating players around the different positions increase the safety risk of the players. There are more collisions between neighbors who are not used to working together. Collisions between players kill a youth player or two each season.

Give the players a chance to discover stuff for themselves

Coaches tend to think their players know nothing except what the coach teaches them. Give the players more credit than that—even kids. If you assign them to one position, and leave them there all season, they will learn all sorts of useful stuff that you would never think of.

For example, they might discover that they always have to shade to right field because when they shade to left, the background behind the batter is a baseball-colored house that makes it hard for them to pick up the ball. They may learn that their outfield neighbor is timid about shallow line drives.

Not all good things that happen on the baseball field stem from coach teaching. The players themselves will figure out a whole bunch of stuff if you give them the opportunity.

Sneaking a peak at the third-base coach

In general, an outfielder should throw a base hit two bases ahead of the lead runner. But there is as time when that is not correct—and it happens far more often in youth baseball than in the Majors where I got this trick.

I mentioned Duane Anderson, a former Major League ball player. His son and mine were on the same Little League team one season and we became friends. He told me of a company softball game where he used this trick and made a big impression on his boss.

Anderson was playing short and acting as the relay man on a deep hit to left with a runner on second. Normally, he would relay the throw to home. But as a wise old pro, he knew to sneak a peek at the third base coach as the runner approached the base. The coach gave the stop sign, probably not wanting to test the arm of a former Major League baseball player.

Out at second

Anderson saw the stop sign and, upon receiving the throw from left, instantly wheeled around and threw to **second** where the batter was loafing in. He was tagged out.

Outfielders can also sneak a peek at the third-base coach after they catch the ball. Or a fellow outfielder who is deferring to the other on the catch can sneak a peek at the third-base coach and quietly say to the nearby outfielder who is making the catch, "Stop sign. Go three." Or "Two."

Anderson went to second to get the batter. But you can also go to the base where the lead runner is being stopped. Often, when he gets the stop sign from the third-base coach, the runner will round the base in a big, lazy arc making him vulnerable to being picked off.

I have said repeatedly in this book that youth baseball base coaches are notoriously chicken about sending runners. So the admonition to throw the ball two bases ahead of the runner, while smart at levels where base runners know what they are doing, is often out of sync with the actual behavior of the opponents at the youth level.

You need to practice this if you are going to do it. Otherwise, neither the runner nor the baseman will be expecting it.

Playing shallow in center

In researching this chapter, I often came across references to great center fielders who played very shallow, most notably Tris Speaker. It must be noted that Speaker's career started in the **dead-ball era**. When the live ball came in, he had to move back, but he still played shallow by today's standards.

The theory behind the shallow approach is that most hits are shallow and that it is better to take away those hits by catching them in the air than to worry about the more rare extra-base hit. I do not know that I can argue with that, although clearly certain game situations make preventing the extra-base hit more important.

It is also true that once a player gets on base, he is more likely to advance in youth baseball than at the higher levels so it is more important to keep youth play-ers off base to begin with. In other words, if everybody who gets a single is going to get to second and/or third in a couple of pitches anyway by way of a passed ball or steal, why place a premium on preventing extra-base hits?

This will vary according to the age and skill level of your team. I recommend that you chart the impact point of each hit against you and move your outfielders to the alignment that is most likely to keep runners off base.

Of course, playing shallow increases the need to learn how to go back on a fly ball. That is very difficult to achieve with the limited experience and practice time of youth baseball.

Afraid to catch line drives

Also, many youth baseball players are **afraid** to catch line drives. They will **not** catch the ball and take away the base hit if you move them in, they will simply turn singles into doubles and triples by stepping aside and letting the ball go by. Actually, they usually camouflage their shying away by taking a circuitous route to the ball and throwing themselves on the ground as if to say, "See, I really tried. Nothing more I could have done."

At least when they are deep, the shying away takes the form of waiting until the ball one or two hops to them.

My main point here is do **not** tell your players to play like Tris Speaker or Willie Mays or any of the other greats who played shallow center field. Rather experiment and observe. See where the balls go and ask yourself, where should our center fielder have been on that play for optimum success. Make a dot on your chart at that location. Over time, your chart will probably show a pattern. You want to position the center fielder where he is closest to the largest number of dots in his area.

Also, observe your players' performance. If they shy away from catching line drives, try to find extra time to do the 85% drill using a soft ball and line-drive trajectories. Using a pitching machine to shoot line drives at outfielders would probably be a good idea. They could get a zillion reps. A tennis-ball shooting machine would also probably do a good job for this purpose. You might want to put goggles on even reluctant-to-wear-goggles players for this drill.

Fungoes OK in center

I have said emphatically that I do not like right or left fielders to practice by catching fungoes. Fungoes go straight and balls hit to right and left curve toward the line. But in center, fungoes are close enough to what the ball does. (It actually curves a little toward the foul lines if it's not hit to absolute straightaway center.)

The key to judging fly balls is experience, experience, experience. Give your center fielders a million fungoes. Have the back-up center fielders or left or right fielders yelling "Back!" or "In!" as appropriate. All outfielders need to learn how to judge flies, but the center fielder needs to know more because he covers more ground and his area is generally busier.

Cover second on the wheel play

If there are runners at first or second, you may want to run the **wheel play** in case of a bunt. In that play, the middle infielders head for the foul lines and cover the corners while the corner infielders and pitcher charge the bunt. That leaves no infielder to cover second so the center fielder must. You need to practice this play.

Position clinics (age 6 to 9)
Clinic #1

6:30	One step play catch
6:35	Yell "Back!" and "In!" to teammates
6:37	Catch grounders on asphalt using one knee technique
6:42	Throw ball to second base
6:47	Back up throw to second base
6:52	Catch fly and throw behind runner who did not tag up
6:57	Calling for shallow pop
7:00	End

Clinic #2

6:30	Sliding catch (on cardboard)
6:35	Sun techniques
6:38	One-step play catch
6:45	Back up throw to second from catcher
6:48	Catch grounder regular technique
6:53	Ready position before pitch and step toward plate on pitch
6:57	Backhand catches of grounders and flies
7:00	End

Position clinics (10 and up)
Clinic #1

6:30	Chalk talk:
	curve toward foul line
	ground ball bounce toward line
	need to run smoothly
	ball hit right at you
	wet and dry grass
	gambling on various catches
	where align before pitch
6:35	Yell "Back!" and "In!" to teammates
6:37	Drop step first on deep ball
6:38	Watch ball over your head with one eye
6:40	Lateral move (crossover step)
6:41	Going back on ball hit to right- or left-center seams
6:45	Calling for shallow pop
6:47	One-knee grounder technique
6:48	Regular grounder technique
6:49	Do-or-die grounder technique
6:50	Do-or-die fly technique
6:53	Throw two bases ahead of the runner
7:00	End

Clinic #2

6:30	Sliding catch (on cardboard)
6:35	Back up throw to second by
	catcher
	pitcher
6:41	Back up shortstop and second baseman fielding (deliberately let ball go through)
6:45	Back up throw to second from shortstop
6:48	Line up fielding for throw
	grounder
	fly
6:53	Fly-catching steps
6:57	Sun techniques
7:00	End

14 Left field

Left field is known as the good-glove, weak-arm outfield position at the higher levels of baseball. At the youth level, it is known as the **busy** outfield position, although I think examination of where balls are actually hit in youth games may well reveal that more are hit to right.

People assume left is busier because they think most hitters are **pull hitters**. But in my observation, youth hitters almost always use a bat that is too heavy and they are, consequently, **behind** the pitch when they hit. Also, many youth baseball players are not really baseball players. They are unathletic kids who are trying the sport because it is the thing to do. They, too, tend to be behind the pitch and hit to the opposite field if they hit at all.

Two shortest throws

Outfielders have three throws to make:

• second
• third
• home

In general, they never throw to first. The only exception would be a right fielder throwing behind a runner when there was a chance to get an out. All three outfielders have **one** long throw to make—to home. Only the right fielder has **two** long throws to make. His throw to third is also long. The center fielder has a short throw to second and a medium throw to third. Only the left fielder has two short throws—to second and third.

So there is a rational basis for saying that left field is the place for the weakest-armed outfielder. This is more true in youth baseball than at the higher levels because many youth outfielders have such weak arms that they should never throw try to home.

Glove more important

At the youth level, there are extremely few outfield assists. But there are many outfield put-outs (catching fly balls). So it is the **glove** hand that matters most in the selection of youth baseball outfielders.

Put your best glove in the busiest outfield, as determined by charting where the batters in your league actually hit the ball. Only put your best **arm** in **right** after you have put your best **glove** in the **busiest** field.

Hits curve toward the foul line

As with right field, balls hit to left curve toward the foul line, regardless of which side of the plate the batter swings from. Accordingly, left fielders need much practice shagging **live** hit balls as opposed to **fungoed** balls.

Relay and cut man

The left fielder may have occasion to throw to a relay man on an extra-base hit. You should give your left fielders and relay men (shortstop in this case) practice doing that. If he has a strong enough arm to throw home, he should practice throwing through the cut man to home.

Hitting the runner going home in the back

Left fielders who have strong enough arms to throw home need to practice dealing with the problem of hitting a runner who is going home in the back. Generally, the runner will be **out**side the baseline and the fielder will be **in**side the baseline, but not always. The runner may be on the baseline in some circumstances. Also, the left fielder may be outside the baseline when the ball is hit near the line then bounces outside it.

Practice this with live runners and with the catcher, pitcher, third baseman, and shortstop. In some cases, the left fielder just needs to move a little bit to the side to get a clear shot. In others, he will need to make use of a cut man to change the path of the ball around the runner. This requires fast, good judgment which comes only from practice.

Deeper to pull

As I said earlier, I do not believe that youth batters pull more than they hit straight away or opposite field. However, it is true that all hitters are stronger when they pull. So wherever your left fielder plays in terms of closeness to, he should play deeper when right-handed hitters are up because if they do manage to pull the ball, they will probably hit it deeper. And he should play more shallow when left-handed hitters are up.

As stated elsewhere in the book, you should, after each hit that falls in, ask yourself where should the left fielder have been to prevent that? Mark the spot on a field diagram, then position your left fielder in the center of those dots. If you have a scout report on a particular hitter, typically from his previous at bats against your team, that trumps the general positioning indicator chart which is based on **all** opposing batters.

Read the center and right field chapters

I already covered most of what left fielders need to know in the chapters on right and center. If you are only reading a few chapters of the book, make sure you read all the outfield chapters because only that way can you get the whole picture for left field.

Position clinics (age 6 to 9)
Clinic #1
6:30	One step play catch
6:35	Yell "Back!" and "In!" to teammates
6:37	Catch grounders on asphalt using one-knee technique
6:42	Throw ball to second base
6:47	Back up throw to third base
6:52	Catch fly and throw behind runner who did not tag up
6:57	Calling for shallow pop
7:00	End

Clinic #2
6:30	Sliding catch (on cardboard)
6:35	Sun techniques
6:38	One-step play catch
6:45	Back up hit to third
6:48	Catch grounder regular technique
6:53	Ready position before pitch and step toward plate on pitch
6:57	Backhand catches of grounders and flies
7:00	End

Position clinics (10 and up)
Clinic #1
6:30	Chalk talk: curve toward foul line ground ball bounce toward line need to run smoothly ball hit right at you wet and dry grass gambling on various catches where align before pitch
6:35	Yell "Back!" and "In!" to teammates
6:37	Drop step first on deep ball
6:38	Watch ball over your head with one eye
6:40	Lateral move (crossover step)
6:41	Cutting off ball hit to right- or left-center seams
6:45	Calling for shallow pop
6:47	One-knee grounder technique
6:48	Regular grounder technique
6:49	Do-or-die grounder technique
6:50	Do-or-die fly technique
6:53	Throw two bases ahead of the runner
7:00	End

Clinic #2
6:30	Sliding catch (on cardboard)
6:35	Back up throw to second by catcher pitcher
6:41	Back up shortstop and third baseman fielding (deliberately let ball go through)
6:45	Back up throw to third from catcher
6:48	Line up fielding for throw grounder fly
6:53	Fly-catching steps
6:57	Sun techniques
7:00	End

• walk
• hit
• reach on an error
• dropped third strike (at the teenage level)
• hit by pitch

At the adult level, any of those are sufficient. But at the youth level, you must **not** encourage players to "take one for the team."

'Take one for the team'

Adult baseball players are often encouraged to "take one for the team." That is, deliberately get hit by a pitch in order to get on base. That is unethical. The rules say you must try to get out of the way. I played in an adult game once where an opposing batter let a ball hit him. The umpire called it a ball and would not let the guy go to first because he made no effort to get out of the way.

When I was a kid living in the Philadelphia area, my dad told me a Phillies player named Solly Hemus was a genius at getting on base by being hit by a pitch or whatever. Hemus was a middle infielder with the Cardinals and Phillies in the fifties and a manager from 1959 to 1961. Working backwards from *Total Baseball* figures, it appears Hemus was hit a total of 60 times in his career.

The career leader in getting hit by a pitch is Don Baylor (267). Your kids should instead follow the example of Sandy Alomar, Sr. who, in 1971, had a league-leading 689 official at bats plus 41 walks without **ever** being hit by a pitch.

Risk of death

At the youth level, you must never encourage batters to let the ball hit them because youth players are uniquely vulnerable to being killed by a pitch.

I interviewed by phone the mother and father of Ryan Wojick, a Tampa ten-year old who got hit by a pitch and died. His father Jeffrey, who was in the stands, told me the pitch was unremarkable, traveling only about 40 miles per hour after being thrown by a fellow ten-year old who was not known for his fast ball.

It hit Ryan halfway between his left arm pit and left nipple. He immediately collapsed and died even though he was near a fire house and they immediately gave him aid. How would you feel if you had been his coach and had urged Ryan to "take one for the team?"

Is a walk as good as a hit?

You often hear coaches say that a walk is as good as a hit. Actually, that's **not** true in many circumstances. Runners often advance **more than one base** on a hit. They rarely do on a walk. There are more chances for errors on a hit than a walk.

But I do agree that a batter ought to have the attitude that a walk is as good as a hit in terms of setting **goals** for what he wants to accomplish in the batter's

15 Batting

The **primary goal** of batting is to **get on base. The secondary goal** is, if you cannot get on base, at least make an out by **putting the ball in play**. But these goals are too complex for the child to keep in mind when he is in the batter's box and the pitch is on the way. So the coach must reduce the batter's task down to a very narrow, within-the-batter's-control chore. That is, **swing only at hitter's pitches on the first two strikes and make sure you put the ball in play on the third strike**.

A youth baseball players will get about 30 to 75 plate appearances per season depending upon the level, the coach's playing-time policies, and the skill of the player. This chapter is about how to make the most of those appearances.

Extra-base hits

Hitting an extra-base hit would be better than just getting on first, but since you cannot control whether you get an extra-base hit, it is inappropriate to make getting extra-base hits a **goal**.

Look the part?

Unfortunately, most youth baseball players and coaches act as if the batter's goal were to look as much like a Major Leaguer as possible.

Proper attitude

I do not say this to kids, but the proper coaching thought when a batter leaves the dugout to go to the plate is, "Don't come back here until you have scored a run. And if you must make an out, at least force the defense to handle the ball. Don't strike out!"

When I played in the adult leagues, my attitude about batting was that my job in the batter's box was to find a way to get on base or at least give the defense a chance to screw up my batted ball. In my last year, 1994, I batted lead off for much of the season.

Walk, hit, reach on an error,

How do you get on base?

box. In other words, a batter ought to take a walk if he is offered one. He should hit if he sees a good pitch.

No bat

If a youth baseball player goes to the plate **without a bat**, he will get on base by walking about 30% to 40% of the time. (A pro without a bat would almost never get walked.)

The purpose of this chapter is to make sure each of your batters gets on **at least** that often and to tell you when and how to use the bat to increase your on-base average **above** that level or to at least avoid striking outs.

Get a walk

Taking a walk in youth baseball is a controversial subject. So let me start by talking about taking a walk in **semi-pro** baseball.

Semi-pro baseball players are mostly current or former high school and college players, with a smattering of former professional minor leaguers. In 1992, I was the player manager of the San Ramon Orioles in the Stan Musial semi-pro league. I wrote a team newsletter and once put an item in there which resulted in an instantaneous, dramatic rise in our team on-base average starting with our very next game. Here is the item.

In general, we Orioles have not drawn enough walks. Dave Russo has 11 for 44 plate appearances or a .250 walks-per-appearance average. I am second in total walks with 7 for 32 or a .220 average. Overall, the team is 65 for 449 or .140 in walks per plate appearance.

*There is no reason why **everyone** on the team should not have a .250 walks-per-plate-appearance average. All you have to do is take the darned pitch. Hitting takes talent. Not everybody has talent. Taking pitches does **not** take talent. All it takes is restraint. And everybody can learn that. In the majors, some players have higher walks-per-plate-appearance averages because the opposing pitchers fear their bats. I doubt there's any of that in our games. Dave Russo has the most walks because of what **he** does, not because of what the opposing **pitchers** do. [Note from author of this book: There was no scouting in our semi-pro league.]*

I would like our team walks-per-plate-appearance average to be over .200 from now on. So please swing only at the choicest of pitches. If you don't see that pitch, take it. Unlike many managers, I do not get upset about called third strikes.

*I am **not** saying you should go to the plate looking for a walk. Rather I am saying that you should go to the plate looking for **your** pitch. If you see it, whack it! Bounce it off the pitcher's forehead [inappropriate for youth baseball]. If you **don't** see it, take the pitch.*

The wallks-per-appearance stat column in that newsletter showed that some players were as low as .000 and .080.

Really dumb

In youth baseball, the player with the highest walks-per-plate-appearance average will generally be **higher** than the .250 described above. That's because youth pitchers are not as accurate as semi-pro pitchers.

You should calculate the walks-per-plate-appearance averages of your players and chew out all but the top two or three. If **any**one can draw walks at the rate of the highest two or three, **every**one can. It is unbelievably dumb for any youth baseball player to have a walks-per-plate-appearance average that is lower than the best players in that category. Jeez! All you have to do is stand there!

Elsewhere in the book I told you about a player I had who had the **best batting average**, but the **worst on-base percentage**, on my team. I benched him for that when he did not respond to my admonitions to take more walks. He had zero walks for the season. When he and his father complained bitterly and disrespectfully, I asked him to request a transfer to another team, which he did.

Everyone on your team should have roughly the same walks-per-plate-appearance average and it should be .300 or higher in youth baseball. Failure to make that happen is coaching malpractice.

Max Bishop and Gene Tenace

My Major League heroes in this category are Max Bishop and Gene Tenace.

Bishop was a second baseman with the Philadelphia Athletics and Boston Red Sox from '24 to '35. No pitchers were pitching around him. He had a career batting average of .271 and a slugging average of .366. But he is second all-time on the walks-per-appearance average at .204.

Tenace was a catcher with Oakland, San Diego, St. Louis, and Pittsburgh from 1969 through 1983. He was a lifetime .241 hitter with a .429 slugging average. He made the All-Star team once in 1976, but he is not in the Hall of Fame. Nobody was pitching around Gene Tenace, but he still ended up seventh on the all-time walks-per-appearance average at .183. He led the league twice.

Good eyes

How did Bishop and Tenace achieve this? By doing nothing more often than almost anyone else. OK, they might have better eyes than other players. Bishop's nickname was "Camera Eye." You can't increase your walks percentage in the Major Leagues by just **randomly** not swinging.

It seems to me that if Max Bishop and Gene Tenace can achieve a .183 to .204 walks-per-appearance average, then **every** Major League position player can do the same.

Higher at the lower levels

At every lower level of baseball, there is a corresponding walks-per-appearance average that can be achieved by anyone who wants to use his head in the batters box. As I said, in my semi-pro league, the achievable walks-per-appearance average seemed to be about .250. In youth baseball, I would expect to it be in the .300 to .400 range.

Emphasize only swinging at hitters' pitches on first and second strike, and see how high your best-walks-player's average goes. That, then, is the walks-per-appearance average that **everyone** on your team can achieve if they are appropriately selective in the batter's box.

Umpire backlash

I have occasionally encountered umpire backlash on this issue. Many people believe that the percentage of walks in youth baseball should be the same as in Major League baseball. I do not disagree with that **goal**, but I say the only proper ways to achieve it are to use **machine pitch** or **coach pitch** when the player pitchers cannot throw enough strikes.

They expand the strike zone

The more common way to achieve it is to expand the strike zone. I am outraged by that because it is simply **cheating on behalf of the pitcher** and **ruins the hitters** by forcing them to behave in a way which we all know is extremely poor hitting technique, i.e., chasing bad pitches.

It is all the more outrageous when you consider that the youth baseball plate is the same width as the Major League plate, but the youth baseball player's arms and bat length are much smaller than the adults' arms. If anything, an argument could be made that the strike zone should be **narrower** for youth players than for adults.

Occasionally in my career, umpires have punished my team with expanded strike zones because they thought we were getting too many walks. I just tell my kids to behave as we normally did until we get two strikes then to swat at the expanded-strike-zone pitches, fouling them off *ad infinitum* or finally drawing a walk when the ump finally calls a ball on a pitch in the dirt or outside the catcher's reach or behind the batter.

I **never** teach my kids to swing at pitchers' pitches with less than two strikes and I **never** teach my players to swing at balls outside the strike zone. Any coach who **does** should be horsewhipped. The same is true of any league or ump who tries to force batters to destroy their ability to hit in that manner.

Using the bat to LOWER on-base average

When you think about it, it is absurd for any batter to have an on-base average that is lower than what he would have if he went to the plate without a bat. But the fact is that the majority of youth batters do exactly that. I started this book by saying that 98% of youth baseball coaches are incompetent. On-base averages that are below the no-bat level are "Exhibit A" in my case to prove that.

All-time walks champion

Who was the best **hitter** of all time? Many people would say Ted Williams. But do you know who the best **walker** of all time is? Also Ted Williams. Hmmmm. Maybe there's a correlation there. Williams walked .208 of the time. Babe Ruth is third at .197 and Mickey Mantle is seventh at .176.

Those guys drew a lot of intentional walks (although none of the three is on the top twenty list of those intentionally walked), but the top walkers list also includes light hitters like #2 Max Bishop who walked .204 of the time and # 4 Eddie Stanky who walked .188 of the time.

Why take a bat?

I originally called this chapter "Hitting." Then I realized that's a misnomer. At all levels of baseball, batters only rarely hit. More often they make an out. Often, they walk. Sometimes they get hit by a pitch. On rare occasions, their at bat is prematurely terminated by a runner making the third out on base.

The vast majority of youth baseball players and coaches think the reason you take a bat to the plate is to swing at about half the pitches thrown to you. They may not **say** that. But if you watch their behavior, that is what they **do**.

Youth coaches complain when their batters do **not** swing at half the pitches. Youth coaches get especially incensed at batters who take a called third strike.

3/4 of a good pitch per at bat

This is wrong. In 1992, I analyzed my youth baseball team's games and found that there is only about 3/4 of a good pitch per at bat. In other words, in our league, which was 11-12 minors, a batter should only swing his bat about three times total in four at bats. That is, he would typically swing once per at bat for three at bats and not swing at all once every four at bats.

That stat surprised me. It probably surprises you. If you doubt it, chart the pitches in your league and see what your local ratio is. It may well be **lower** than ours.

What's a 'good' pitch?

A **pitcher's pitch** is one around the edges of the strike zone. From the **batter's** perspective, those are

bad pitches. A **hitter's pitch** or **good** pitch is one in the heart of the strike zone. (Individual batters have different good pitch zones. Mine is low and a bit away from me. But the generic hitter's pitch is down the pipe.) Here's a diagram:

Strike zone

pitchers' pitches

hitters' pitches

pitchers' pitches

The typical at bat offers a mix of balls, pitchers' pitches, and an **occasional** hitter's pitch. In youth baseball, the mix is skewed toward the ball out of the strike zone. In Major League professional ball, it is skewed toward the pitcher's pitch.

Which more important than how

Which pitch you swing at is far more important than **how** you swing.

The way Ted Williams put it in his book, *The Science of Hitting* was,

> There were, as far as I'm concerned, two great pieces of advice given me early in my career. One was from Rogers Hornsby... He told me the single most important thing for a hitter was "to get a good ball to hit."

(Rogers Hornsby was a Hall of Fame middle infielder and manager. His career batting average of .358 is the second highest in history behind Ty Cobb's .367. His career slugging average of .577 is seventh all-time.)

All baseball players and coaches should read Ted Williams book *The Science of Hitting*. In it, he has a diagram of the strike zone and the batting averages he would get swing at pitches in all the various possible locations.

Williams personal hitter's pitch zone was waist high

and more inside. He was a dead pull hitter. But most of his "happy zone," as he called it, was where my generic hitter's pitch zone is in the above diagram.

Whether you define the hitter's pitch generically or customize it for each hitter (which is better), you will still find that the hitter's pitch zone is sufficiently small that the pitcher only hits it about 3/4 of a pitch per at bat.

Major breakthrough

Discovering this and proving it to my players was a major breakthrough for me in coaching youth batters. Until they met me, my players thought they were supposed to swing at all strikes. No one had ever taught them about pitcher's pitches.

Pitchers' pitches are strikes, but you should **not** swing at them on the first or second strike. Why? Because they are very hard to hit well.

In general, if you swing at a pitcher's pitch at the **top of the strike zone**, you will **foul it straight back or pop it up**. If you swing at pitcher's pitches on the **inside or outside of the strike zone**, you will **foul them down the line**. And if you swing at a pitcher's pitch at the **bottom of the strike zone**, you will hit a **weak grounder** or a worm-killing smash into the dirt in front of the plate.

Sometimes they are hits

One of the longest hits I ever got was on a chest-high pitch that I should not have swung at. It was caught on the fly at the warning track at California High School.

Same thing happens with my Little Leaguers. They occasionally swing at a high pitcher's pitch and get an extra-base hit. That causes them to doubt my teaching. Then I have to explain that, yes, swinging at high pitcher's pitches occasionally pays off big. But **percentagewise**, it usually does **not**, so you should not swing at them.

I did not do it in the past, but if I coached again I would keep track of what happened to high pitcher's pitches that were swung at so I could show the kids that although it is **occasionally** a long hit, it **usually** is a pop up or foul back.

'That's a strike!'

Often, when an opposing batter poleaxes a foul, I wait until the oohs and ahs from his crowd subside then point out to my pitcher, "That's a strike!"

Same is true of my batters. If a particular pitch is going to be a strike, better it be a **called** strike than a **foul** strike, except on strike three. Why? Because foul strikes are sometimes caught on the fly for outs. Foul strikes that are not caught by the catcher often nullify stolen bases. (Believe it or not, a caught foul tip is a live ball on all three strikes at all levels of baseball. You can steal on a caught foul tip on all three strikes, not just the third.) A called first or second strike is just a strike.

What is a hit?

The vast majority of youth coaches believe the goal of batting is to get a hit and that settling for a walk is sometimes necessary, but borderline dishonorable. That's nuts.

Think about what a hit is. When I was in the army, I received some artillery training. Where an artillery shell lands is a function mainly of three things:

- azimuth
- elevation
- charge

The same is true of where a batted ball goes, although they use different terminology in baseball:

- direction
- angle up or down
- how hard you hit it

A batter has little control over these three factors. You **try** to hit the ball in fair territory. You **try** to hit line drives rather than pop-ups or grounders. And you **try** to hit it hard. But even the greatest hitters in history only succeeded at doing these things about 40% of the time.

Then there is the placement and range of the **fielders**. You may hit a hard, fair, line drive, only to see it turned into an out, not a hit, by a well-placed and/or wide-ranging fielder catching it on the fly or throwing to get a force.

So a hit in baseball is not just a combination of the correct direction, elevation, and strength, it also requires **luck**.

If there was no such thing as a strike, you'd never swing

If there was no such thing in the rule book as a strike, you should never swing the bat. Why? Because so many well-hit balls turn into outs, as do most not-so-well hit balls. If a ball was a ball, but a strike was nothing, you would just stand there until you accumulated four balls. You would not risk a swing that would most likely result in an out if you made contact.

You swing to avoid striking out

So you do not swing at hitter's pitches because you want to hit a fair line drive, you swing at hitter's pitches because if you fail to do so, they will call a strike and your chances of making an out will be thereby increased. You swing at a hitter's pitch because the probability of getting on base by doing so is lousy—only about 30% to 50% in youth baseball—but it's better than the 0% chance of getting on base if you strike out.

(At the teenage level, the probability of getting on base if you strike out is a bit above zero because of dropped third strikes.)

Dumb and dumber

Swinging at hitters' pitches is dumb. **Not** swinging at hitters' pitches on the first and second strike, and at **any** strike on the third strike, is even dumber, but only because it's "three strikes and you're out at the old ball game," not because there is something good about hitting the ball.

Most contact between the bat and ball produces a **bad** result for the batter, even if he is the greatest hitter of all time.

Ty Cobb

The player with the highest career batting average and most career runs scored in history was Ty Cobb. Here's what he did in his plate appearances

At bats	11,429	
Hit by pitch	92	
Walks	1,249	
Appearances	12,770	
Hits	4,190	32.81%
Walks	1,249	9.78%
Strikeouts	357	2.8%
Hit by pitch	92	.72%
Sacrifice bunts	296	2.32%
Batted ball out or reached on an error	6,586	51.57%

Cobb's career on-base average was .423. So what Ty Cobb, arguably the greatest hitter ever, did **most of the time**, was hit the ball into an out.

Looking at those numbers, it appears that the great Cobb did not walk enough. Cobb is not in the top 35 on the all-time walk-percentage list. But he is third on the all-time stolen base list. There are no stats on it, but I suspect he was one of the all-time best at taking extra bases as a result of his teammates' hits. He was one of the all-time best at taking extra bases on his **own** hits. He is second all time in triples and fourth all-time in doubles. So it would have been nice to have him on base more often.

Bat like Ted Williams

Actually, your batters should be like Babe Ruth. He was the best guy in history in the batters box. But he was gifted with power that most players simply do not have and cannot get. Williams is a bit more human. Success in the batter's box could crudely be measured by slugging average plus on-base averages.

Player	SA	OBA	Total
Babe Ruth	.690	.469	1.159
Ted Williams	.634	.481	1.115
Lou Gehrig	.632	.442	1.074

Since slugging is a desirable **result**, but not a proper **goal**, the best stat to focus on is **on-base average**. The highest career on-base average in history was Ted Williams' .481 (.483 if you count being hit by a pitch). Here are the components of how he did that.

	#	% of appearances
Hits	2,654	27.2%
Walks	2,019	20.8%
Hit by pitch	24	.2%
Sacrifice hits*	2	.02%
Sacrifice flies	23	.2%
At bats	7,706	78.8%
Strikeouts	709	7.3%
Batted outs	4,343	44.4%
Appearances	9,774	100.0%

* *The Boston Globe* once ran as its front-page headline, "Ted bunts."

The thing that Ted Williams did most when he went to the plate was hit the ball into an out. The hits, for which he is so famous, were a distant second to his batted outs. And he walked almost as many times as he hit. Only about 1/7 of his walks were intentional.

Little Leaguers' numbers

Here are my son's numbers as a nine-year old (league-age ten). He was our best offensive guy and this team made it to the league semi-finals.

	#	% of appearances
Hits	15	32.6%
Walks	10	21.7%
Hit by pitch	3	6.5%
At bats	33	71.7%
Outs	18	39.1%
Appearances	46	100.0%

As you can see, his ratios were quite similar to Ted Williams' numbers. These are the kinds of ratios a good batsman should have regardless of the level at which he plays.

Here are Karel Exner's numbers for the following year when my son ended up the number two offensive player on the team. Karel was number one. This is the year I first taught waiting for a good pitch on the first two strikes.

	#	% of appearances
Hits	23	37.1%
Walks	23	37.1%
Hit by pitch	0	.0%
At bats	39	62.95%
Appearances	62	100.0%

Here you see the benefit of being selective on the first two strikes. The walks percentage of .371 is much higher than Williams' career .208. That's because of the poorer quality of the pitching in youth baseball. Also, look at the batting average when you only swing at **your** pitch on the first two strikes: 23 hits in 39 at bats or 23/39 = .590!

Dan had 23 hits in 52 at bats for an average of 23/52 = .442.

Our **team** batting average the year I made a big deal out of waiting for a hitter's pitch on the first two strikes was **.320**. Our team **on-base average** was **.590**! Ted Williams, eat your heart out. And our team slugging average swinging only at good pitches on the first two strikes was .463.

To those who might criticize me for accepting a lot of walks as not teaching the kids hitting, I point to our team batting and slugging averages. They were probably the highest in our league and were likely higher than most youth teams in the U.S.

It should be noted that a rare few batters have a rather large zone which can be considered "their pitch." Hall of Famers Yogi Berra, Joe Medwick, and Ed Delahanty were known as a "bad ball hitters." Do not try this at home. Don't even tell your Little Leaguers bad ball hitters exist or they will all use it as an excuse to swing at everything.

Machine or coach pitch

Every time I advocate swinging only at hitters's pitches on the first two strikes, critics complain that will turn the game into a walk fest. Once again, I give my same response.

The rules should allow the defensive manager to demand **machine pitch** or **batting-team-coach pitch** any time he wants. During times when a machine or coach is pitching, balls and walks will be eliminated, called and swinging strikes will count, and there will be a limit to the total number of pitches a batter can see. That will solve the problem without screwing up the batters.

Pitching machines

Pitching machines give the best ball to hit of all. That's why former American League president Dr. Bobby Brown said,

A significant benefit of the pitching machine concept is that it promotes a feeling of self accomplishment within each player when they hit with consistency which ultimately leads to building self confidence. Unfortunately, accomplishment and confidence are conspicuously lacking for the majority of youngsters playing in youth baseball programs today.

A program that allows for a high degree of success generally tends to be more fun and interesting for the young participant.

In other words, Dr. Brown is saying that if you want your players to have confidence in their hitting, give them Rogers Hornsby pitches to hit. Use a pitching machine that will put it right down the pipe. Pitches like that make almost every player a hitter.

Day after day in the summer, youth batters walk dejectedly back to the bench after striking out. They are bummed out because they think their failure was caused by lousy hitting ability. In fact, the problem almost certainly lies with what pitches they chose to swing at.

Bat discipline

Remember that I stopped all batting practice starting with the 1992 season. All I did for batting was to **talk** about waiting for hitters' pitches on the first two strikes. (We had each kid hit a few line drives of polyball soft toss before each game.)

How to take a pitch

If you want kids to take pitches, you need to **teach them how**. You stride the same as if you were going to hit. But if you decide the pitch is **not** in your hitting zone, you just watch it into the catcher's mitt. Your head turns to follow it.

This is a distinct movement which I demonstrated, then had each kid practice. Taking a pitch is generally considered a bit wimpy. But if you do it correctly, it is a very definite, confident movement.

My kids looked a bit like Pete Rose when they took pitches. That is, they had a little attitude that seemed to say, "My momma didn't pay no $125 for me to swing at a crap pitch like that. If you want to see me swing, put it down the pipe. Otherwise, I'm gonna just stand here and watch you tire yourself out."

I pounded into the kids' heads that only stupid batters swing at pitchers' pitches. Smart batters take any non-hitters' pitch on the first two strikes.

The contrast in games was distinct. When one of our **opposing** players took a pitch for a strike. He would look ashamed and downcast. When one of **our** guys would take a pitcher's pitch for a strike, he would look proud of himself and confident, as he should. All game long, I would be saying "Good take!" from the coaching box, reinforcing the good decisions.

Correct/incorrect decisions

There are two correct decisions on the **first two strikes**:

• swing at a hitter's pitch

• take a ball or pitcher's pitch

There are two correct decisions on **third-strike** pitches:

• swing at strikes
• take balls

We charted the location of every pitch, whether the batter swung at it, and what the result of the at bat was. Then we calculated a **percent-good-decisions ratio**.

'All I want are good decisions'

What I wanted my batters to do in the batters box was **not** to get hits or walks or even to get on base. All I wanted them to do was **make good decisions** about when to swing. I figured the walks, hits, and getting on base would take care of themselves if we made good decisions. And they did.

This also took the normal batter's box pressure **off** the kids. I told them again and again, "All you have to worry about is making good decisions about which pitches to swing at and which to take. Let the hits and all that fall where they may. *Que sera, sera.*"

Give the pitcher some credit

On everybody else's team, kids who strike out feel bad. On my team, I tried very hard to say the kid was only responsible for the swing decisions. If a kid struck out, I would often go over to him and show him the pitch chart.

"Scott. Look at where your pitches were. The pitcher threw you **three** pitcher's pitches. You took the first two as I taught you. And you swung at and missed the third. That's to be expected.

"Pitcher's pitches are hard to hit. That's why they **call** them pitchers' pitches. So don't feel bad. Sometimes the pitcher deserves credit for having a great at bat against the batter.

"That's what happened in your case. **You** did not do **badly**. The **pitcher** did **great**. Actually, he has not had a better at bat today. You are the only batter on our team who got three pitchers' pitches in one at bat.

"So what he really did was get lucky when you were at the plate. He's not that good. Except for missing the third strike, you had a great at bat. It's just that the pitcher had an even better at bat. He most likely won't be able to do it again next time you come up."

Charting pitch locations

To chart pitch location, you need to make a form like a score-book page, but instead of little baseball diamonds, it has a strike zone for each at bat. Here it is.

124

Name	1	2	3	4	5	6	7	8	

You fill the pitch-location chart out with a felt-tipped pen. Write the batting order down the left side. Substitutes who go in during later innings are added to the name box under the player they replace along with the inning when they went in, just like a regular score book.

Mark the location of each pitch as a black ball. If the batter swings at that pitch, draw a horizontal line through it. If he swings and hits it into fair territory, put a plus sign over the black ball in question. Write the result of the at bat, e.g., K, 6-3, 2B, or whatever in the strike-zone box for that inning. Here's an example:

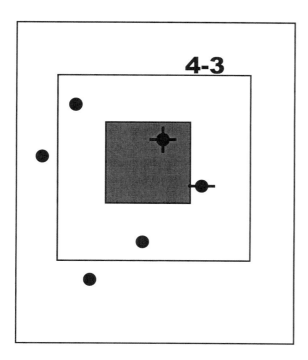

This would be an unusually **long** at bat. I did that to show each different type of pitch. In this at bat, you have a ball inside (to a right-handed hitter; this is the catcher's perspective) and a ball low. You also have three pitcher's pitches—a very rare occurrence.

The batter swung (horizontal line through the outside pitcher's pitch) at one, probably the third strike, and must have fouled it off to stay alive. He finally got a hitter's pitch when the count was 2-2. The batter swung at it and hit it in fair territory (plus sign on the pitch in the upper outside of the hitter's pitch zone). The second baseman fielded the grounder and threw the batter out at first base (4-3).

Perfect at bat

This is a **perfect at bat** by my standards. The batter made no bad decisions. The fact that he made an out is irrelevant. I would compliment this kid when he came back to the dugout. "Perfect at bat, Joey. Sometimes they are lucky enough to have a guy where you hit it.

Keep up the good decisions and you'll get your share of hits and walks. The pitcher had a near perfect at bat against you. He threw **three** pitcher's pitches. Too bad we didn't have more luck on his one hitter's pitch."

Poor at bat

Here's a poor at bat. On April 12, 1994, my son struck out in this at bat.

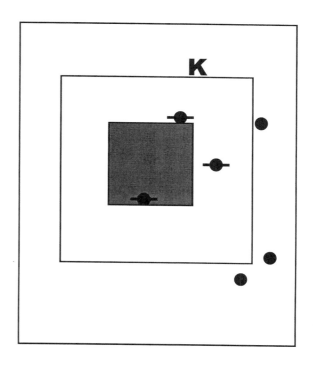

He did a nice job taking the three pitches which were balls. But he swung at two pitcher's pitches. It could be that he had to swing at one because he already had two strikes on him. To tell the sequence, you would use numbers rather than black balls to indicate pitch location.

He made at least one and maybe two bad decisions in this at bat. In both cases, assuming it was not yet the third strike, he was too aggressive, swinging at pitcher's pitches.

He did swing at a hitter's pitch, which is correct. But he apparently fouled it off if it was one of the first two strikes, or he completely missed it or tipped it into the catcher's mitt if it was the third strike.

In general, to succeed at the plate, you must make **no mistakes**. You can sometimes get away with **one** bad decision, but you rarely get away with **two**. In this at bat, my son made one or two bad decisions and one poor swing.

We can**not** control the quality of the swing in youth baseball. But we **can** control the decision making. I would not have criticized my son for failing to hit the hitter's pitch into fair territory. But I would have pointed out that he was too aggressive on at least one of the pitcher's pitches.

Most likely, it was in a location he has trouble laying off. Laying off that pitcher's pitch would not have changed the strikeout result in this at bat. It would have been a called strike. But over the long run, laying off that pitch will increase my son's on-base, batting, and slugging averages.

Copy it, distribute it, talk about it

I would make a photocopy of the game stats and the pitch-location chart for each player. Circle the name of one player on each copy then give each player the sheet on which his name is circled. That way, you can tell who is absent, and give him his sheet next time he comes.

At the end of the next practice, when there was about ten minutes left, I would sit the team down in a circle on the grass or in the bleachers and hand each one a copy of the pitch-location chart from the last game. I would then go through it at bat by at bat. Each kid would have his sheet in his hand and be looking at it as I talked. Here's an actual game, 4/12/94, and the way I would have discussed it with the kids.

Coach: "OK. Let's look at Dan's first at bat. How many good pitches did he get?"

Players: "None."

Coach: "Right. He had one ball, which he took. Then he got hit by the next pitch. Perfect at bat. Next batter was Criss. How many good pitches did he get?"

Players: "Two."

Coach: "Did he swing at them?"

Players: "Yes."

Coach: "Good job Criss. Did he get any pitcher's pitches?"

Players: "Yes, one."

Coach: "Did he swing at it?"

Players: "No."

Coach: "Excellent job, Criss. He also got two pitches outside the strike zone, which he took. And what was the result of Criss's perfect at bat, guys?"

Players: "He got a hit."

Coach: "See. The stuff I told you about waiting for a hitter's pitch actually works. How many good pitches did the next batter get?"

Players "None."

Coach: "How many did he swing at?"

Players: "One."

Coach: "Uh oh. That's our first bad decision of the game. What mistake did Scott make?"

Players: "Swung at a pitcher's pitch."

Coach: "Correct. But I must say that it was right on the borderline of being a hitter's pitch. Can't complain too much about that decision. How many **good** decisions did Scott make?"

Players: "Three."

Coach: "Right. And how many bad ones.?"

Players: "One."

Coach: "Right. The pitcher's pitch he chased was at the top of the strike zone. What happens usually when you swing at a high pitcher's pitch?"

Players: "Pop up."

Coach: "Correct. And what was the result of Scott's swing at **this** high pitcher's pitch?"

Players: "Popped out to the third baseman."

Coach: "There's what the coach told you coming true again. Scott, everybody, lay off the high pitches. Almost all of you have a tendency to chase high pitcher's pitches. Go up to the plate looking 'Low. Low. Low.'"

Obviously, this would represent a session after at least a week or two because the kids in this example are very conversant with the correct approach. Your initial sessions would involve more teaching.

Remember, this is **all** I did to make these kids better batters. We never had batting practice all season. Charting and talking about pitch location and its relation to batting success are two of the best things you can do to improve your team batting success. I promise you it will have a dramatic effect in about two weeks if you emphasize pitch selection strongly and quit messing with your batters' swings.

Good pitches, not good swings

Line drives do not come from good **swings**. They come from swinging at good **pitches**. Outs do not come from poor **swings**. They come from poor **decisions** about what to swing at.

If you swing at, for example, a low pitcher's pitch—with **perfect** mechanics—you will almost certainly ground out. But if you swing at a hitter's pitch with **average** youth mechanics, you will almost certainly hit the ball hard. **Where** matters far more than **how**. A mechanically good swing at a bad pitch gets you nothing.

That's great news for coaches because **pitch selection is eminently coachable**. Batting mechanics, on the other hand, are very hard to improve.

What I strive for as a coach is not more hits or walks, but increasing the percentage of good decisions my batters make. In 1992, toward the end of the season, the top half of my batting order would make the right decision about 90% to 100% of the time. The bottom half ranged from 36% to 85% good decisions.

Try to push your team and each individual player's percentage of good batting decisions up as the season progresses. You do this by explaining the correct approach at he beginning of the season, then by coaxing, cajoling, reminding, nagging, etc. the rest of the season.

You will see a dramatic improvement at the beginning, because they never heard of this stuff before and they have been up there hacking away at every strike or near strike.

More pitches

One of the often overlooked benefits of taking pitchers' pitches is it makes the pitcher throw more pitches per batter. That tires him out and puts his fielders to sleep.

Track all categories

You should track all categories of both good and bad decisions:

- Good take
- Bad take
- Good swing
- Bad swing

We also counted hitters' pitches. We found about 15% to 30% of the pitches were hitters' pitches and there were about four total pitches per at bat.

The reason you track all categories is because batters vary as to the **nature** of their bad decisions. **Most** are too **aggressive**. A **few** are too **conservative**.

Once you establish which a particular batter is, you should remind of him of his error tendency as he heads for the batter's box. For example, most of my players made good decisions on their takes, but they were inclined to swing at bad pitches. Specifically, each player tended to have a zone where he would swing at pitches he should not swing at. As a player headed for the on-deck circle (now outlawed in Little League), I might say, "Jeff. Remember you have a tendency to chase high pitches. Look for low pitches." Of course, you need to prevent the opposing team from hearing this conversation.

Hitting success factors

Whether a batter hits the ball well or not are determined by the following:

- batter's eyesight
- contrast between the ball and the background
- skill of the pitcher
- appropriateness of bat weight and length
- location of the pitch
- self confidence of the batter

Bat weight

In Dr. Bobby Brown's Rookie League concept, batters use "...an ultra-light weight wood bat specifically designed for their physical attributes."

Brown's main concern is that youth baseball players have success and he believes batters will have more success with an "ultra-light weight bat." I generally agree.

Almost all the batters in the 1999 regional Little League championships appeared to me to use bats that were too heavy. They were also racking up strikeouts in the double digits. It appeared that the batters were not used to the speed or breaking pitches of the pitchers on the top teams, but that they did not make the obvious adjustment of switching to a lighter bat.

My bat

As I said elsewhere in the book, I used a 27-ounce bat in adult baseball. I was about 5'11", 190 at the time. Invariably, my teammates said it was too light. But after the printing showing the weight rubbed off, and I moved to a new team, I found many of my teammates asked if they could use my bat. They said they liked its "feel."

Macho B.S.

There is a lot of macho bull in baseball, but the main example of it is batters using bats that are too heavy. Why do they use bats that are too heavy? Because they are afraid someone will put them down or snicker at them or some such if they use a light bat. Even in the Major Leagues, Hall of Famer Willie McCovey found time to taunt Tim McCarver with "How do you hit with that little toy?" regarding McCarver's 31- to 33-ounce bats.

The ounces printed on the bat barrel are essentially regarded as a measure of your manhood at all levels of baseball down to and including tee ball. This use of overly-heavy bats to avoid ridicule is stupid and has robbed baseball players of untold millions of hits over the years at all levels.

But don't take my word for it. Here is a survey of what various experts have had to say about the appropriate bat weight.

My preference was a light bat. I see no percentage at all in using a heavy bat. You can get the same result by being quicker with a light bat. **Ted Williams** [Williams once borrowed a teammate's extremely light bat. "Pumpkinwood" Williams called it. "A toothpick!" With a three-and-two count, Williams choked up and "gave this bat a little flip." Result? A 410-foot grand slam to center.]

Most of today's hitters lean toward bats of around 31 to 33 ounces for greater bat speed. It's not the size of the club, it's the speed. **Johnny Bench**

Batters can't have a short , quick stroke if they use a heavy bat. If waiting and then using quick hands are the two elements of sound hitting, then why

128

would you use a heavy bat? If you have a heavy bat, you have to start sooner. Lighter bats make it easier for you to speed up the bat head so you can wait longer—and by waiting longer you pick up the ball better and then use your quick hands. There are too many arguments against a heavy bat, especially as more hard throwers come into the big leagues. That's why Barry Bonds, who is the best fastball hitter in baseball, uses a thirty-one ounce bat. A toy." **Tim McCarver**

The length and weight of your bat are so important. If it is too big for you, you're not going to have a controlled, fluid swing. I believe in using a light bat. I hit .301 my sophomore year at San Diego State [with a 32-ounce bat]. [With a 31-ounce bat later,] I hit .430. A lighter bat is better for most hitters. When I was in the minors, I found three Mike Ivie 016s, 32 inches and 31 ounces. I brought my new bats to the ball park the next day and everybody laughed at how tiny they were. But I started using the 32/31s right away, and from that point on I went on a tear. I hit home runs in five straight games. **Tony Gwynn**

It is better to have a bat too light than one that is too heavy. **Ron Polk**, Head Baseball Coach, Mississippi State University

Many young hitters influenced by peer pressure, think about bat size more than how to use a bat effectively. And often a young hitter, particularly one between the ages of 8-12, is judged by the size of the bat rather than how well he really performs with the bat. It is one of the first responsibilities of a coach of young players to assist them with proper bat selection. **Dusty Baker**

Joe Morgan, the career home run leader among second basemen, used a 30-ounce bat.

Al Kaline, a Hall of Fame slugger, used a 32-ounce bat.

Hitters of all ages, from Little Leaguers to Major Leaguers have a tendency to use too big a bat. Studies have shown that a hitter is more efficient with a lighter bat. The name of the game is bat control, and if you use a bat that is too heavy, you are kidding yourself. It becomes a 'macho' thing with some hitters…pick one that feels 'too light.' **Bob Cluck**, Author of *Hitting*

Every hitter needs to experiment with different size bats; but keep in mind that a very common error is to select a bat that is too heavy. **John W. White**

and **Charles T. Prevo**, authors of *Batting Basics, Science of the Perfect Swing*

Many home run hitters use light bats, not big war clubs. Harmon Killebrew (fifth all-time in home runs, third in home-run percentage)… used a bat that was…only 31 or 32 ounces. Kent Hrbeck [also used]…a 31- or 32-ounce bat. **Tony Oliva**

Often on youth league teams the only bats available are too heavy. **Bragg A. Stockton**, University of Houston Head Baseball Coach

But here you run into problems—ego problems and macho self image problems. Psychologists could argue for days over why many players feel they've got to swing a big club. All I know is that there are an awful lot of players at all levels of the game using basts that are too big for them. **Charley Lau**, Major League hitting coach

The bat you choose can make a big difference in how well you hit. Don't make the mistake of thinking the heaviest bat in the rack will produce the longest hits. If you can't swing it easily, that heavy bat will only produce strikeouts. **Bob Carroll**

A young hitter makes a big mistake when he uses a bat that is too big for him. Coaches and parents should pay close attention to bat length and weight. Most hitters begin at an early age trying to use bats that are too heavy. A heavy bat can cause you to make a variety of mechanical mistakes. Mechanical errors associated with using heavy bats can permanently scar a hitter. Defects may develop that are difficult if not impossible to correct at a later date. **Steve Garvey**

Weight is probably the most important factor. The most important point is to tell the youngster that a heavy, thick bat will not propel the ball any further than a lighter, thinner bat. Youngsters usually select a bat that is too heavy, feeling they can hit the ball further with it. **Skip Bertman**, LSU Head Baseball Coach

…at every level of play I've observed hitters using bats too heavy for them to control. Beginning players in particular have a tendency to choose too heavy or too long a bat, hoping this will improve their power. The result is loss of balance and control, slower wrist action, and impaired timing. One key to hitting is waiting as long as you can before you swing, learning as much as you can about the pitch before you commit yourself. Then you must swing quickly. The heavier the bat, the harder this is. **Dave Winfield**

Few Little League hitters show the symptoms of using too light a bat—e.g., swing early or consistently [pulling] the ball [foul]—but many show the symptoms of using a bat that is too heavy, such as swinging late or consistently fouling [to the opposite side]. **Ned McIntosh**, author of *Managing Little League Baseball*

Most young hitters use a bat that is too big and/or too heavy. **Jerry Kindall**, Head Baseball Coach, University of Arizona

Game symptoms of a too-heavy bat

There a few fairly obvious symptoms of a too-heavy bat. I will list them here so you have more ammunition to use with fathers and players who want to use a bat that's too heavy.

There should be **no pattern** to where a batter hits balls. If a batter hits **opposite field** most of the time, or worse, fouls it off toward the opposite field, the bat is almost certainly too heavy.

Does pulling mean your bat is **too light**? Not really. It's hard to **ever** say that a bat is too light. If you are pulling, you can simply wait longer. You're supposed to do that anyway so you can get a better look at the location of fast balls and the movement on breaking balls.

Pulling is easy to fix by just waiting or moving up in the batter's box. But inability to hit straight away or pull indicates the batter simply cannot use his bat the way he needs to.

Missing the ball completely is another indicator that the bat is too heavy. At the very least, you could point out to the recalcitrant player and/or father that if he is **not hitting the ball at all** with the heavy bat, it surely cannot be any **worse** using a lighter bat.

Step one is making contact. No one argues that a heavier bat has any advantage other that hitting the ball farther—a misconception, but that is the reason given for using a heavy bat. But if you are not even making contact, how far your bat will make the ball go is beside the point.

Dave Winfield says, "A light bat that hits the ball is infinitely better than a heavy bat that doesn't." Edd Roush swung the heaviest bat in the league when he played—48 ounces. He made the Hall of Fame, but not as a home run hitter. He was a singles hitter. So much for the theory that heavier bats make the ball go farther.

My 23-ounce bat

When I was playing adult baseball, I found a bat that was 32 inches long, but only weighed 23 ounces.

It was labeled "Little League." I bought it and tried it in adult baseball. My teammates made fun of it. But one of them was playing third base one day when I was taking batting practice with my 23-ounce bat.

I hit screaming line drive after screaming line drive to him. He started cursing and expressing serious concern about his safety. He backed up way behind third. The catcher felt compelled to remind him, "That's why they call it the hot corner."

The hot corner is a lot hotter if the batter is swinging a really light bat.

In a game, I flied out to deep opposite field once using that bat, to the amazement of my teammates.

Did I have any problems with the bat other than getting teased by my teammates? Yes. It **stung** like crazy. In later years, I wore a rubber thing around my thumb to prevent stinging, but by then my 23-ounce bat had become **cracked**.

Other than the stinging and the lack of durability, the 23-ounce bat was not a problem. In retrospect, I probably should have used a lighter bat, maybe 24 or 25 ounces, against the more difficult pitchers. By more difficult, I do not mean faster. Good pitchers, regardless of whether they are fast or have good breaking balls, require that you wait longer before committing to a swing.

Bat that feels right

One of the common comments you read in baseball hitting books is that you should pick the bat that feels right. I agree. Unfortunately, you cannot say that to players because they will **lie** and claim that a too-heavy bat "feels right."

If there were no one else on earth to make fun of them for using a light bat, the last Little Leaguer on earth would try different bats, pick the one that felt right, and use it in his solitary batting-cage sessions. But as long as there are others around who might possibly raise an eyebrow about how light a player's bat is, you cannot trust a player to really pick a bat that feels right.

Keep Your Eye on the Ball

The book *Keep Your Eye on the Ball* by Robert G. Watts and A. Terry Bahill has the most comprehensive scientific analysis of correct bat weight. Here are some of the things they say.

- Putting cork or rubber balls inside a wooden bat has no effect except to prevent a hollow sound. (Paper presented at the 10/87 meeting of the New England section of the American Physical Society by P. Brancazio)
- Fungo bats weigh only 23 or 24 ounces because the slower the pitch, the lighter the bat must be. [Author's note: youth pitches are quite slow]
- Based on scientific testing, they found the ideal bat

weight for a group of professional Major Leaguers to be 32 ounces and for a group of unspecified age "Little Leaguers" to be 20.1 ounces. (They mentioned one Little Leaguer was ten.)

- Switch hitters have different ideal bat weights for each side of the plate.
- For the Little Leaguer…the batted ball speed varies greatly with bat weight. This means it is very important for him to have the correct weight bat. However,…most professional baseball players…could use any bat in the range 33 to 40 ounces and there would be less than a 1 percent change in batted-ball speed.
- Fatigue affects bat speed greatly.
- Could not find any correlation between bat weight and body weight. [This sounds crazy to me if you're talking about youth players. Even the bat makers acknowledge differences.]

Eye-hand reaction time

Bahill and Watts found that there were two kinds of players—essentially quick and slow—at all levels. Quick players need precisely the right bat weight to do their best. For slow ones, a range of bat weights will do.

To measure quickness, they had a player poise his index finger and thumb on both sides of a meter stick at the 50-cm spot. Another person would hold the top of the meter stick. The player would watch the fingers of the other person. When he saw the other person drop the meter stick, he would grab it with his fingers. The distance it falls in the interim measures the player's quickness.

Bat manufacturers pander to machismo

One of the huge problems in getting players to use correct bat weights is the labeling of the bats by the manufacturers. They know what I am telling you in this chapter. That is, most players use bats that are too heavy. But they have made a conscious decision to join in the lie for marketing reasons.

Although Bahill and Watts found that the ideal Little League bat weight was 20.1 ounces, they could not find a single Little League-approved bat that weighed less than 21 ounces. Smaller bats are labelled "tee ball." So in sub-teen youth baseball, you need to rub off not only the printing that shows bat **weight**, but also the designation as to what **gender** or **level** the bat is for.

Rare is the ten to twelve-year old baseball player who will use a bat marked "tee ball." But 19- and 20-ounce "tee ball" bats are precisely what bats most ten to twelve-year olds **must** use to have the maximum success.

This is another of the outrages in youth baseball

where grown-ups deliberately screw up the kids because of a hidden agenda.

Little League Baseball, Inc. could fix this problem by coming out with a correct weight-level table and refusing to approve bats that are mislabeled. All the manufacturers want to have the words "Little League approved" on their bats.

(By the way, the same thing happens in adult soft ball. The **ideal bat weight for slow-pitch softball players is 19.4 ounces**, because the pitch is so slow, but **the lightest bats that are marked "softball" weigh 27 ounces**.)

The quivering-arm test

A number of experts say you can tell if a player's bat is the right weight by having him hold it parallel to the ground with his dominant hand. If he can hold it 25-35 seconds (Dusty Baker) without it quivering, it's an acceptable weight. *Little League's Official How-to Play Baseball Book* says the same thing, only their criterion is "a few seconds." In *Baseball, Play the Winning Way*, Arizona University head coach Jerry Kindall says it's **ten** seconds.

Well, which is it guys? There's a big difference between a few seconds and 25-35 seconds. Heck, there's a big difference between 25 and 35 seconds!

My humble opinion

I said at the outset of this book that I would not give much of my own opinions because, "Who cares?" Baseballwise, I'm nobody. But I must make an exception here.

In my opinion, this hold-a-bat test is absolute rubbish. The fact that various experts who advocate it cannot come close to agreeing on the time span is proof. Also, just think about it. The ability to hold a bat parallel to the ground depends on wrist and finger strength. Batting uses far more muscles and uses them in a different way.

The arch-the-back test

Here's **my** test. If you let someone swing a fly swatter, their upper body will show no effect of the swing. On the other hand, if you have a batter swing a 4"x4" fence post, he will arch his back like a track-and-field hammer thrower to compensate for the centrifugal force of swinging the too-heavy bat.

I watch batters swing the bat. If they **arch their back**, it's too heavy. But I am more inclined to use a **table** of what I have found to be the best bat weights for various size kids.

Corked bats

Those same macho Major Leaguers who make fun of light bats are often caught corking their own bats. Norm Cash said he used a corked bat when he won the

American League batting championship with a batting average of .361 in 1961.

Corking is illegal. It means cutting off the fat end of the bat, hollowing it, filling the hollow space with cork or super balls, then putting the end back on so that you cannot tell that it has been corked.

Why do they do this? TO MAKE IT **LIGHTER**! Corking takes about 1.5 ounces out of the bat.

Some might think that the cork gives it greater bounce. Nah. The sole purpose of the cork is to prevent the hollow sound. There is no bounce in cork.

There is a **legal** way to accomplish this to an extent. You are allowed to hollow out the fat end of the bat to a depth of an inch like the bottom of a wine bottle. Anyone using a wooden bat should take advantage of this rule.

Late season or fast pitchers

Many pros, like Rod Carew and Ted Williams, say that they switched to a lighter bat than normal **late in the season** when they are getting **tired**. Others say the same about when they face an exceptionally fast pitcher. Your youth baseball players, who are out-of-shape couch potatoes and non-athletes, are **always** in this situation.

Tony Oliva, who won three batting championships, said he used a 34-ounce bat against left-handed pitchers and a 33-ounce bat against right-handed pitchers.

Choking up

Each **inch** you choke up has an effect equivalent to taking an **ounce** of bat weight away. When I grew up in the fifties and sixties, we had only wooden bats. Those suckers are heavy. We **all** choked up.

Many of the great batsmen in Major League history choked up. Former Major Leaguer Al Rosen said Ted Williams and Mickey Mantle did not choke up if they had no strikes. They choked up a half inch with one strike and an inch with two strikes. Hall of Famer Nellie Fox choked up. He is third on the all-time list of fewest strikeouts.

Wee Willie Keeler choked up on his lightest-in-the-league bat. He always chopped down on the ball. He has the second highest single-season batting average of all time. (.424) and the 13th highest career batting average (.341). It was his record that Joe DiMaggio broke when he hit in 56 consecutive games. He is still second at 44 (tied with Pete Rose).

Legendary hitting instructor Charley Lau was a big advocate of choking up, but he said the Major Leaguers would not do it. One of his players, Dave Duncan, used to choke up one inch when he had two strikes on him. Lau kept track and found that of the 16 homers Duncan hit that season, twelve of them came when he had two strikes and was choking up.

So if you cannot get your players to use an appropriately light bat, get them to choke up. It's better to use a lighter bat though because choking up diminishes the reach of the batter and with child-length arms and child-length bats, they are already having trouble covering the width of the same-as-adult-rules-wide plate.

Rub out the weight and level

Get hold of all the bats your team uses and rub out the writing that says the weight and what level the bat is to be used at. Do this the first day or even at the parent meeting. This will reduce resistance to using lighter bats. This way you can say, "Jeff, use the red bat," rather than "Jeff, use the 19-ounce bat."

My bat-weight table

Here are the weights I think your players should use. You can deviate one ounce either direction based on your observations of the player in question, but no more. Furthermore, your deviations ought to be equally high and low. If all your deviations are upward, you are probably just succumbing to player and parent machismo pressure.

Age	Bat weight
12	21 ounces
11	20
10	19
9	18
8	17
7	15-16
6	14

At the **teenage** level, the correct bat weight will be around 23 to 28 ounces. Teenage boys, who are almost by definition terrified of anything that questions their manhood, will fight fiercely to use bats in the 30-ounce range. They would rather strike out, which they think they can finesse by throwing a tantrum on the way back to the dugout, than get a hit with a light bat. You, as coach, can either let them destroy your team batting average or you can order them to use a correct weight bat.

Lighter bats are hard to find. You will have to use **girls** bats for boys (softball bats are legal for hard ball, but hardball bats are not legal for softball), tee ball bats for Little Leaguers, and Little League bats for teenagers.

To **find** these bats, you may have to call a zillion sporting goods stores and/or to buy them on line or by direct mail. But do it. I cannot say for sure, but I would expect about a 50 to 100 point increase in team batting average when you go from kid/parent-chosen bats, which are typically about three or four ounces too heavy, to coach-chosen bats.

Making your players use appropriately light bats will cause an **instant** improvement in your team batting average.

132

In 1990, I coached my middle son's tee-ball team. A year or two later, I met one of the fathers from that team in Burger King. He was now coaching a farm team (8-9 year olds) and said his team wasn't hitting. I told him to tell them to wait for a pitch down the middle of the plate (this was coach pitched) and to insist that they use 17- or 18-ounce bats. His kids had been using 20- and 21-ounce bats.

Next time I saw him, he was extremely enthusiastic. "It worked! I did what you said and our team started hitting the crap out of the ball immediately!"

You gotta be hard-nosed

In order to succeed in management, you often have to be hard-nosed. You cannot be hard-nosed about **everything**. But neither can you lead any group to new heights pussyfooting around all the time. Bat weight is one of the few things you have to be extremely hard-nosed about when you coach a baseball team.

To an extent, the players secretly welcome this. They **know** their bat is too heavy. They **know** they would hit better with a lighter one. But they fear the "wimp" label and absolutely will not use the correct-weight bat unless you force them. However, when you **do** force them, they secretly welcome both the light bat and the opportunity to cover their manhood by blaming **you** for forcing them to use the "wimp" bat.

There is a lot of that in parenting. Kids publicly protest restrictions, but secretly welcome them as a way of deflecting peer pressure.

Summarizing thus far

Let me stop here and emphasize what I have said thus far about batting.

If you spend dozens of hours teaching and practicing batting mechanics, your players will probably hit **worse** as the season goes on. That's because it takes far more time than you have and far more time than almost all your players are willing to devote to change someone's mechanics. And changing mechanics, like switching from batting right-handed to batting left-handed, causes players to get **worse** before they get **better**. You **do not have time** even to begin that process.

You **do** have time to teach getting a good pitch to hit. It only takes about ten days to two weeks (two games and one practice a week) to see a dramatic improvement, then your team will get better more gradually as the season progresses. Teaching being selective on the first two strikes **works** in the context of a real-world youth baseball season. Teaching mechanics does **not**!

But there is something else you can do that will have an **even faster dramatic effect** on your team's batting: require that each batter use an appropriate weight bat.

Strikeouts

Your players should think of themselves as **hockey goalies** when they have two strikes. Their job then is to keep the ball from going past them in the strike zone. I sometimes played a practice game where we drew a strike zone on a wall in chalk then had pitchers try to hit that zone with a soft baseball while batters pretended they had two strikes and tried to protect the strike zone. If the pitcher hit the strike zone with no foul swing, the batter lost. If the batter bunted foul he lost. If the batter prevented the pitcher from hitting the strike zone with a non-foul, the batter won.

Joe Sewell has the lowest ratio of strikeouts to at bats in history. (He is also a bit famous for being the player who replaced Cleveland's Ray Chapman, the only Major Leaguer ever killed in a game.) Sewell had 7,132 official at bats and only struck out 114 times in his whole career—a 114/7,132 = 1.6% strikeout ratio! That shows what is possible.

One of my opponents mentioned that he had not struck out all season late in one of my adult baseball seasons. That intrigued me.

At the outset of my last adult season, I decided that **I** was not going to strike out that season. We played a long season of Sunday double headers. I generally played the whole game and was lead off for much of the season. I struck out a total of **three** times:

• caught foul tip
• bad call by the ump (chin high)
• swung and missed

Slash

How did I do that? I did not **learn** how to do it or **practice** doing it. I just **decided** to do it.

My method was that when I had two strikes on me, I would take a new stance with a slightly deeper crouch and move closer to the plate. I would choke way up on the bat like you do in the fake-bunt-and-slash play and hold the bat over the plate as I awaited the pitch. (In the fake-bunt-and-slash play, you hold the bat as if you were going to bunt. Then you leave your top hand where it is for a bunt and slide your bottom hand up to where your top hand is to execute the downward slash swing. In general, you are holding the bat near the top of the rubber or leather sleeve on the bat handle.)

As the pitcher released the ball, I would cock the bat back a little bit and slap down on the ball if it was a strike or near strike. What I really wanted to do was **bunt**, but because a bunt foul third strike is a strike out, I did the next closest thing to a bunt which is the fake bunt and slash.

That way my hands only moved forward about six inches in my "swing."

By putting the ball in play, I was able to **reach first on an error** a few times. I was able to **advance runners** when I made an out many times. And to my amazement, I even got **several clean base hits** with this swing—line drive grounders through the holes in the infield or bloops over the infielders' reach. I hit no extra-base hits with this little chop.

The bad news

That's the good news. The fake bunt and slash worked like a charm for **me** all season, with no practice whatsoever. The bad news is that I have had no success at all teaching this to my players, including my oldest son.

I did successfully teach our team the fake-bunt-and-slash play *per se* in 1990. That was not a third-strike tactic. We were using the fake-bunt-and-slash in its normal manner.

I think the reason we were successful then, but not in later years, is simply the number of repetitions. It seems to me that any idiot can execute the slash. But it does take some reps. I would guess at least 50 to 100 repetitions to master it.

Third-strike bunting

The high-bat-control alternative to the slash on third strike is bunting. Most people think you should not bunt on third strike because, unlike on the first two strikes, if you bunt foul on the third strike, you are out.

So don't bunt foul. Bunt fair.

How do you do that? Same way you get to Carnegie Hall. Practice. Practice.

Third-strike bunting is not just some kooky idea of mine. In his book *Art and Science of Hitting*, Rod Carew calls Steve Garvey "the premier two-strike bunter in the National League today." Carew also said, "the foul-ball-on-a-third-strike-and-you're-out rule intimidates most batters and coaches. But not Mantle and not Garvey." Carew himself was 12 for 12 on two-strike bunts one season.

By the way, bunting foul on the third strike was made an out because of Hall of Famers Luke Appling and Wee Willie Keeler. They could bunt third strikes foul by the hour until they got a walk. Appling had such great bat control that the *Wall Street Journal* called him the "William Tell of Fungo." He was so accurate with a bat that he could "pitch" batting practice from the mound using a fungo bat. He would ask the batter where he wanted the pitch, then hit it to that part of the strike zone! In 1984, at age 75, he made the news by hitting a home run in an old-timers game in Washington.

Everybody should bunt

All players on your team should learn to bunt and actually bunt in games. Even your power hitters will find that bunting is smart for them because fielders will move deeper when they come up. Bunting keeps those fielders honest. If a power hitter bunting causes them to move in, his normal hitting will become more effective.

Also, you need to prevent bunting from becoming a sort of performance ghetto to which only weak players are banished. By having **everyone** do it, you remove the stigma. Joe Morgan says, "There comes a time in every baseball season when anyone—even hulking sluggers like Cecil Fielder or Frank Thomas—should bunt."

On the other hand, some people can't bunt. If you encounter a bunt situation, but your batter is one of the few who cannot bunt, don't call the bunt. You need **both** the situation and a competent bunter at the plate to bunt, not just the situation.

Getting on base is more important in youth baseball

Grownups have tried to make youth baseball an imitation of Major League baseball. But the attempt breaks down in many areas. One is that it is easier to advance from first base in youth baseball than in the pros. Consequently, getting to first is much more valuable in youth baseball.

At some pre-teen levels, stealing second is almost automatic. When I played Little League in the late fifties almost anyone who got to first stole second on the next pitch. The only exception would be a very slow kid.

Stealing third is a bit harder because you cannot take a lead at the pre-teen level. But a youth runner at second generally will advance to third on a passed ball or almost any sort of putting the ball in play. To a lesser extent, the same is true of scoring from third.

So youth coaches should behave differently from pro coaches in their efforts to get batters to first. And the way you do that is be very selective on the first two strikes, then play "little ball" on the third strike.

'Little ball'

"Little ball," also called "the short game," is bunts, slashes, hit and run, run and hit, squeezes. I have never heard the expression "big ball." But "big ball" would be taking full swings.

"Big ball" is relatively uncoachable, especially within the limits of a youth baseball season. **"Little ball," however, is highly coachable**. If you practice full swings, you probably will see **no improvement** at all. If coaches and fathers **criticize** the players during the full swings, the players will probably hit **worse** as the season progresses.

However, with "little ball," you will see dramatic improvement in a short period of time. Youth players of all athletic ability can learn to bunt and/or slash within the short duration of a youth season.

Insist that everyone learn to bunt

Dusty Baker says, "Any hitter can pick up some percentage points on his batting average and be an asset to his team by knowing how to bunt the ball properly." The coach's corollary to that would then be, "All coaches **must** make sure their players know how to bunt properly in order to maximize the team's batting average."

You should all but eliminate strikeouts on your team. Remember, a strikeout is about as worthless an out as you can get. Runners rarely advance. The batter feels miserable.

The way to eliminate strikeouts is to be very selective on the first two pitches, which will increase walks and hits, then to play "little ball" on the third strike. This is what I personally did in adult baseball. Get your strikeouts down to 5% of appearances or lower.

No-strikeout practice game

One way to encourage this would be to play a practice game where anyone who strikes out must leave the game and go work on his third-strike batting. Kids do not like to be demoted, plus it shifts the time spent to where it is needed: upgrading the third-strike skills of players with poor third-strike skills. This practice game format also sends a message to the players that when the coach says there will be no strikeouts, he **means** it.

You could even tell the kids that striking out in a game will mean they are out of the game, although that substitution should be done unobtrusively so as not to embarrass the player. I once saw a coach angrily remove a sub-teenage player from a game **in the middle of an at bat**! Why? The kid had swung at a 3-0 pitch.

It was obvious that the player was not **deliberately** violating the coach's policy. Rather the coach had failed to make sure every player understood the policy. It was a very ugly scene that left the kid crying. And this was in the **summer** league where kids just got tee shirts and caps. The summer competition was supposed to be taken less seriously.

I watched the 1999 Little League World Series tournament on TV. I was appalled by the number of strikeouts. Yes, I know that the pitchers on those teams were excellent. But whatever happened to bunting? Better that than striking out. What about switching to ultralight bats? Do something! Don't just go up there and strike out one after another!

One-time Oakland A's manager Steve Boros said, "On the high school level especially, I would do more bunting because so often the defensive team does not execute. Young players do not handle the bunt as well. They will throw the ball away or somebody doesn't cover a position." What do you suppose his advice would be for the **youth** level?

Easy, but requires practice

There are two baseball skills which are easy in the sense that every player, regardless of ability, can learn them. They are bunting and sliding.

Unfortunately, most youth coaches assume that because these skills are within everyone's reach, they are so easy that you do not need to practice them. That is absolutely wrong.

Even your **best** athletes will **not** be able to bunt (or slide) unless you give them a lot of practice. On the other hand, even your **worst** athlete **will** be able to bunt (and slide) like a champ **if** you give them enough practice. Dusty Baker and his fellow authors of *You can teach hitting* say, "We cannot overemphasize that if you don't ask your players to bunt the ball on a daily basis, it's *extremely difficult* to expect them execute the bunt in a game." [emphasis in original]

I am dead set against **batting** practice in youth baseball. But that does not apply to **bunting** practice. Batting practice **harms** youth hitters. Bunting practice makes them **better fast**.

Bunt technique

I am opposed to teaching batting mechanics pertaining to the full swing in youth baseball. But I am **not** opposed to teaching bunting mechanics.

Stance

There are two schools of thought on stance:

• square around
• pivot

Here's the square-around:

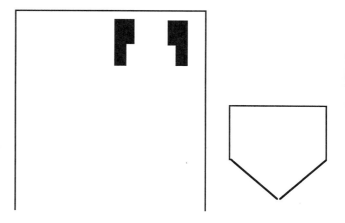

Here's the pivot:

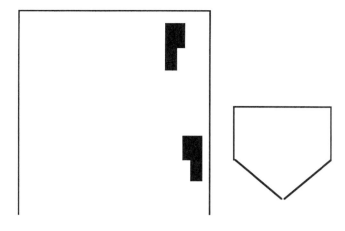

It is easier to succeed with the square-around style, but the batter is more likely to get hit by the pitch with that method. Because of the danger of hit-by-pitch cardiac arrest in youth players, I think the square-around method should be **outlawed**.

You should move as far forward in the batters box as legal to increase the probability that the ball will be hit into fair territory. If you make contact with the ball with either foot out of the batter's box, you are out, although I have never seen that rule enforced.

Hands

Your top hand slides up to about the middle of the bat—just before it gets fat. Your bottom hand stays where it started. In the case of both hands, you are mainly holding the bat with your thumb and forefinger. In the case of your top hand, your thumb and forefinger are on the backside of the bat so they do not get hit by the pitch.

Rod Carew, one of the greatest bunters in the modern era, says to extend the index finger of your top hand along the back side of the bat as if you were pointing toward the fat end of the bat for greater pinpoint control. In that case, you hold the bat between the thumb and middle finger of your top hand.

Bat position

While waiting for the pitch, the bat is parallel to the front edge of the plate. Its skinny end is below the fat end by about four to six inches. When you actually make contact, you will want the fat end or the skinny end more forward to direct the ball toward third or first. You must **not** keep the bat parallel to the front edge of the plate at contact because that will make the bunt go toward the **pitcher** which is the **last** place you want it to go.

Almost all other baseball books have perfectly adequate photos and drawings of the correct position for bunting so I will not waste any space with additional photos or drawings.

Bunt target area

The best place to put a bunt in youth baseball is probably **twenty feet from home toward third** base and about 12 to 18 inches from the edge of the grass rather than on the dirt base path. If you bunt on the dirt base path, the ball will likely roll foul. If the third baseman fields it, he is charging hard toward the plate and has to make an off-balance throw to first. Also, third base will probably not be covered so a runner from first can often advance easily all the way to third.

It is hard for the pitcher or catcher to field a bunt to this area because they are facing the wrong direction even more than the third baseman. They are also going away from first base.

Another trickier target area for the bunt is **past the pitcher toward the second baseman**. If the pitcher gets to it, you are toast. Better it should roll foul on the first two strikes than go to the pitcher. If the second baseman gets to it early, you are also toast. Bunting more toward the first baseman may work better in youth baseball because most coaches fail to give their players any practice at the pitcher cover first play. Or they give inadequate practice.

This target area works better against a **left-handed pitcher** because he ends up facing somewhat toward third base when he completes his pitch. You should experiment in practice to see which area works best for each batter.

If you are squeezing a runner home from third, you would probably do better to bunt toward first to make it easier for the scoring runner.

You can make a fun game of this by creating a target on the infield surface out of rope circles. Putting the ball in the bull's-eye get five points. In the next ring gets three, and keeping it fair gets one point. Dusty Baker says it is easier to bunt to the opposite field.

Coaching points

Coaching points are things that require extraordinary emphasis because kids tend to screw them up even after being instructed correctly. There are three coaching points in bunting:

- keep handle below head of bat
- if the pitch is a ball, take it
- let the ball hit the bat, don't swing at the ball

Keep handle lowest

The bat should be held at the top of the strike zone. Then, if the pitch is lower, the batter should **bend his knees** to get down to it, **not** rotate the bat head downward. Batting consultant Oscar Miller calls this "Elevator down." Practice this in **shadow** mode, that is, with no ball in the drill.

Kids have a tendency instead to pivot the bat around the bottom hand which they keep at the same altitude. This causes the bat head to get **under** the pitch and

136

causes bunt pop-ups which are usually easy outs and double plays in the case of a hit and run or squeeze. Rotating the bat around the original bottom-hand position also makes it more likely that you will foul the bunt off, which you cannot do when you have two strikes.

You want to get the bat head on **top** of the ball and to do that you must keep the handle lower than the bat head no matter how high the pitch is.

Take the pitch

Because of lack of practice taking balls when bunting, youth bunters tend to bunt at the ball no matter where the pitch is. Once they get it in their head that they are going to bunt, either because of a coach's signal or their own idea, they completely forget about the fact that the pitch may not be a strike. When bunting, youth batters chase pitches that even they would not chase if they were hitting in the normal fashion.

To fix this, you must give your players practice taking pitches while in a bunt mode. They must recognize the pitch is a ball and pull the bat back distinctly. It's not hard to do. But if you do not give your players some practice repetitions doing it, they will behave in games as if there is no such thing as a ball when they get into a bunt mindset.

No swing

Kids tend to swing or reach out toward the pitcher when they bunt. Remind them to wait for the ball to come into the bat. Let the ball hit the bat. Do not chase the pitch. Practice and a few reminders should take care of it.

Instill pride in bunting skill

Earlier in the book I urged you to teach outfield in such a way that the players at those positions will take pride in their knowledge and skill. You have to do the same with bunting. Bunting is to hitting what right field is to fielding. It is considered the realm of the weak.

There is some truth to that, but that does not mean that either playing right field or bunting are so easy that you can do either without practice and training.

One of the greatest hitters of all time, Rod Carew (career .328 average), took great pride in his bunting. Early in his career, he would get 20 to 30 base hits a year from bunts. In one game against the Oakland A's, he got three hits bunting down the third base line. By the third one, the A's Sal Bando was playing him half way down the baseline. Later in is career, Carew said he bunted less because third basemen would play in on him, but he figures he then got 15 to 20 more **regular** base hits a year because they were playing in.

Getting infielders to play in because they fear your bunt skills increases the probability that you will get a base hit if you take a full swing. Being able to both bunt and hit is like a football team being able to both pass and run. If you only do one or the other, the defense in football will arrange itself to handle the one you can do and ignore the other.

In baseball, if you can both hit and bunt, the defense will not know whether to play you up or back. Like a football coach, you can "take what the defense gives you." If they play in because you bunt well, swing away. If they play back, bunt.

Steve Garvey says, "I have bunted for many base hits in my career. I'll look down and see a third baseman playing so deep he's in another zip code, and I'll drop an average bunt down and beat it out." In 1910, Nap Lajoie was contending for the batting championship late in the season. To stop him, an opponent played their infielders deep so they could prevent more hits from getting to the outfield. He went 8 for 8 that day, including seven bunts.

Another indication that a bunt is in order is a catcher who kneels or sits down when there are no runners on base. He cannot move quickly to fiddle a bunt

Harmon Killebrew, who hit 573 home runs, never bunted. "I wish I had to keep the infield honest," he later said. Mississippi State Coach Ron Polk said, "The ability to drag bunt can surely add an additional ten or fifteen points on a hitter's batting average."

Take advantage of the fact that your opponents cannot execute the pitcher-cover-first play

Elsewhere in the book, I said my team was almost the only one in our league that could execute the pitcher-cover-first play. If that is also the case in your league, bunt the ball to the first baseman (away from the base) all day. His pitcher will stand on the mound while the first baseman moves away from the base to field the bunt. You can run through the base unmolested by anyone being there to catch the throw and force you out. If the opposing **coach** won't give his players practice with the pitcher-cover-first play, your **batters** should.

Almost all expert observers of baseball complain about the lack of bunting. They are discouraged that it seems to be becoming a lost art. Not if I have anything to do with it.

One way to instill pride in bunting while practicing it is to have a practice game where only bunts are allowed. (You still need an outfield because they need to practice backing up throws to the bases.) That will get everyone's competitive juices flowing. It's also fun. You could also do a practice game where only slashes are allowed.

Element of surprise

Since we are not doing sacrifice bunts, you generally want to disguise your intent to bunt as long as possible, so as to delay the corner infielders charging down the line. This is an advantage of the pivot bunt technique.

No sacrifices other than squeezes

I am a big advocate of bunting on the third strike if you cannot slash. I am also a big advocate of the squeeze bunt because it trades an out for a run, which is generally a bargain. But I oppose the sacrifice bunt in the Major Leagues and I am dead set against it in youth baseball.

Why? It's stupid. In professional baseball, you are slightly **worse off** if a sacrifice bunt **succeeds** than you were before you tried it. Furthermore, sometimes it **fails** in that you get a double play or the runner on first is unable to advance. Then you are **much** worse off.

The details on this are in the *Hidden Game of Baseball*. They studied tens of thousands of baseball games and found teams were slightly more likely to score a run with a runner at first and no outs than with a runner at second with one out. The same was true for runner at second with two outs versus runner at first with one out.

And that's the **pros**, where sacrifice bunts would come **closest** to making sense. At lower levels, it is easier to advance from first to second without any help from the batter. Plus the sacrifice is more likely to fail at the lower levels. So you absolutely do **not** use a sacrifice bunt to move a runner from first to second in youth baseball. He can probably get there on his own.

I am not saying you do not bunt with a man at first in youth baseball. If your batter has two strikes and cannot slash, he'd better bunt. But we are not trying to execute a sacrifice with the bunt. We are just trying to avoid a strikeout and get the youth baseball "pin ball machine" going so we might profit from a series of errors.

Safety squeeze

The safety squeeze is a bunt with a runner on third where the runner does not leave until the bunt is heading for the ground. At the sub-teen level, this is the only squeeze allowed because the runner must stay at the base until the ball gets to the plate.

The squeeze is a fabulous play. You ought to use it almost every time you have a runner at third and less than two outs unless you have a high likelihood of the runner scoring on a passed ball or some such. It is a great play that is easy to learn and that results in runs.

In general, you should trade an out for a run whenever the situation presents itself. Although there have been times in my youth coaching career when we were averaging more than three runs per inning so I told my players to **stop** trading outs for runs and just wait for the batter to move them around.

If you are not averaging more than three runs per inning, and few teams are, you trade an out for a run every time you can. In pre-teen youth league baseball, that would get you 18 runs a game; at the teen level, 21.

Suicide squeeze

At the teen level, you can choose either the suicide squeeze or the safety squeeze. In the teen version of the **safety** squeeze, the runner at third would take a primary and secondary lead, but he would not commit to home until he was sure where the ball was hit toward the ground.

The **suicide** squeeze is essentially a run-and-bunt play with a runner at third. The runner goes home as soon as the pitcher is committed to pitching to the strike zone, in other words, when the pitcher is about to release the ball. In *Baseball, Play the Winning Way*, Jerry Kindall says you break for home when the pitcher's stride foot hits the ground. If the runner goes too early, the pitcher can throw at the batter or throw high so the batter cannot get his bat on the ball.

The batter's job is to make sure the catcher does not catch the ball, throwing the bat at a hard-to-reach pitch if necessary. Preferably, the batter will bunt the ball on the ground in fair territory.

This play is impossible to stop if executed with a modicum of skill. My adult baseball team could do this one batter after another, and did on occasion, and we never practiced it. We were pretty good at it and understood it, but adult players generally do not practice.

If you are at the teenage level, by all means put it in and use it. The proper circumstance is

- runner at third
- less than two outs
- less than two strikes

I once called a suicide squeeze against Dublin when I coached teenagers. My son was the runner at third. He stole home in a cloud of dust. The batter put the bunt down beautifully, although straight back to the pitcher.

Unfortunately, the pitcher then fielded it and calmly threw the batter out at first for the third out, thus erasing the run. I wish I could say I thought there were less than two outs. The truth is I forgot to think about how many outs there were at all. Dumb!

Don't tip it off

The suicide squeeze is the most tipped-off play in baseball. The sign is given. The pitcher and catcher in the bull pen stop to watch. The players in the offensive dugout all stop talking and press up against the chain link on the front of the dugout.

It's like that western movie scene where the stranger walks into the saloon and asks if anyone knows Ben Carruthers. The piano player and all conversations stop as they turn to stare at the stranger.

The runner asks for the sign to be repeated. The coach yells at the batter and gives the sign a second time to make sure he doesn't do a full swing and possibly decapitate the runner.

If your team does all this tipping off, forget about it. The pitcher will throw a pitch-out. Step one, don't tell anyone but the runner and batter. Better yet, let the runner call the play in a signal to the batter, not the coach, then even fewer people will have the knowledge to tip it off. Step two, don't be stupid. You have to act nonchalant or the other team will recognize this play, especially if you are known for it, which you should be. You have to discuss and practice this nonchalance.

Psyches pitchers out

Showing bunt early psyches many youth pitchers out. It is an unexpected movement as they are concentrating on their pitch. It often, maybe usually, distracts him and causes the pitcher to lose concentration and throw a bad pitch.

Fattest bat

When it comes to bunting, I do not care about bat weight. In fact, the best bat is probably the one with the biggest diameter and the longest length. You might want to have such a maximum size bat in the dugout for your team's bunting.

Would that telegraph that you were going to bunt? I suppose, although you could run the fake bunt and slash with a big bat.

Experiment. If the bigger bat helps your players bunt better, don't worry about the tip-off disadvantage.

The fake bunt and slash or slug bunt

Previously, I discussed the fake bunt and slash as a way to get much batter bat control for thirds strike hitting, while avoiding making an out because of a foul ball. But the fake bunt and slash is actually a batting trick you should teach and use.

In the fake bunt and slash, you show bunt early. Then, when the first and third basemen come charging down the line (assuming they have a wheel play on), you suddenly slide your bottom hand up the bat, cock it back, and slap down on the ball. The idea is you will hit it past the charging infielders into the outfield.

I actually did it once in a semi-pro game. It worked like a charm. One of my players was coaching third when I batted. For some reason, third base coaches cannot keep themselves from giving signs. He gave a bunt sign. I was the manager and did not want to bunt, but neither did I want players arguing with me on the rare occasion when I gave the bunt sign, so I followed orders.

I showed bunt. The pitch was a ball, which I took. The bunt was now off.

Next time I came up, I thought, "Hey, we accidentally set up the fake bunt and slash. I wear the only face-mask batting helmet in the league. I showed bunt once in my previous at bat. The other team may think I'm some kind of wimp who can only bunt."

To add to the deception, I went to the third-base coach and told him to put on the steal sign. I also yelled down to the runner on first, "Make sure you get the sign."

As the pitcher started his windup, I showed an early bunt, the third baseman charged down the line toward me. Then I slid my bottom hand up the bat, slapped down on the pitch, and hit it right past the third baseman into left field.

You should teach this to your players and practice it. It helps persuade them that they need to learn how to bunt, too.

This play is so good it is outlawed in some youth leagues. The stated reason is safety. I don't buy that. The corner infielders are not likely to get as close as the pitcher always is. Plus they have a big glove to protect themselves. Unlike the pitcher in his vulnerable end-of-follow-through position, the fielders are **ready** for the hit. Finally, the batter slaps **down** on the ball to try to make sure the hit is a grounder. I have studied a lot of baseball safety stuff and I have never seen any indication of injuries from this play.

Bunt left-handed

An argument can be made that every youth player should learn to bunt left-handed. Bunting is so easy that you can do that. Why bother?

With a runner on first, a left-handed batter obstructs the vision of the catcher and the throw of a right-handed catcher. If there is a danger of the runner being throw out, this is a good tactic, even if your batter has no hope of hitting from that side. The worst that can happen is a strike.

Left-handed bunters also can execute the drag bunt. That's a bunt for a base hit that you execute as you start running toward first.

If you can't hit, bunt

Sometimes, you cannot hit. It may be that you are a weaker player. Or it may be that you are a strong player in a slump. Or it may be that your whole team is, today, facing a really tough pitcher. You can always bunt. Sometimes you can hit and sometimes you can't. But you can always bunt.

Whenever your **bunt** batting average is higher than your **full-swing** batting average, bunt. Isn't that obvious? That may be an everyday situation with a bottom-of-the-order player. It may be a once-in-a-while situation with a leadoff man. In his manual on how to manage, Billy Martin said, "One basic rule for any manager is to manage according to his personnel…a good manager changes his style of managing to suit his personnel." If Major League managers were suddenly forced to coach youth baseball players, they would be bunting and stealing like crazy.

But when you encounter that situation, bunt. Don't just flail away and strike out again and again. That's dumb. One of the most widely heard admonitions in sports is "Stay within yourself." In this context, it means that if you cannot hit, you must bunt.

Pete Rose

Pete Rose was one of the best baseball players ever. He was a winner—helping Cincinnati to four pennants, then going to the hapless Phillies and leading them to two pennants. It is especially noteworthy that he did it without talent relative to the rest of the Major Leaguers he played against.

A lack of talent also characterizes youth baseball players. Pete Rose should be their model in many ways. (I do not endorse all of Pete Rose's on-field behavior and I condemn his notorious off-field behavior.) Rose was called "Charlie Hustle." There is an old saying in coaching: "You don't need talent to hustle." The corollary is also true: "If you do not have talent, you'd better hustle."

The *Official Major League Baseball Book Hitting* says, "Against a pitcher you have trouble hitting, knowing how to bunt can mean the difference between 0 for 3 and 1 for 3 for the day."

Dave Winfield says, "In youth leagues, where mechanics are not highly developed, bunting should be used more often." Winfield goes on to say that a youth bunter may even end up on second. Darned tootin' I have seen **many** bunt "doubles" in youth baseball, and a few bunt "triples."

Bragg Stockton, head baseball coach at the University of Houston, says, "The weaker a player's hitting is, the stronger his bunting must be. This concept is just as true about weak-hitting teams." He's a college coach. By his standards, **every** member of a youth team is weak and had better be strong at bunting.

Transition to hitting

Elsewhere in the book I told how I once was forced to use a high-speed batting cage I had previously tried, but could not hit. All the other cages were busy. So I figured I would at least get some work on my bunting and fake bunt and slash.

As expected, I was able to bunt successfully and slash successfully in that cage, where I never previously could hit. But to my surprise, I tried taking a couple of full swings and was amazed to find that I was suddenly hitting. Bunting is an excellent bridge between hitting failure and success.

Major Leaguers like Ty Cobb have said that they often used bunting to overcome slumps or difficulty with a particular pitcher. Don't ask me why it works, but it does. An argument could be made that you should bunt first time through your lineup in games at the lower, less-skilled levels. It would be a nice confidence builder for your team and prevent the opponent from the psy-

chological uplift of getting off to a strong start on the mound with multiple strikeouts.

Hit and run

The hit and run does not apply to sub-teenage youth baseball because the runners cannot take a pre-pitch lead or steal before the pitch reaches home plate. At the teenage level, I suspect it could only be mastered at the elite level. Minor league teenage teams are old dogs who have trouble learning now tricks and have lousy practice attendance records. Accordingly, it would be hard to get your players to practice it and it probably should not be run without practice.

On one of my semi-pro teams, one player seemed to feel that he had to give live signals whenever he was in the coach's box. He was constantly putting on hit and runs and bunts. He got me thrown out twice on hit and runs. The batter missed the sign in each case.

It was probably my fault for creating such a sign to begin with, but then I rarely called the darned thing. I only called a hit and run when I was confident that the batter could perform it and that the runner had a good chance of stealing the base anyway. And I would take pains to make sure everybody got the sign and understood it. I only called two squeeze plays that season, winning games by one run in each case.

If you can get the kids to practice it, the hit and run is a good play for the teenage level. The batter MUST hit the ball, even if he has to throw his bat at a pitch-out to do it. The prime hit-and-run situation is runner at first and less than two outs and less than two strikes. The batter should be more careful than usual about getting picked off. Ideally, the runner will advance two bases and the batter will be safe at first.

Tin roof

When I was eleven, I did something that may have helped my hitting a lot. We had an old garage with a tin roof. Tin roofs have a one-inch-high ridge every 18 inches. The ridge is the part you drive the nails through. The ridge is elevated so the rain will not go through the nail hole and it is 18 inches apart because 18 inches "on center" is a standard spacing between roof joists (the wood to which the tin sheets are nailed). There was probably about 17 inches of flat space between the ridges.

Coincidentally, home plate is 17 inches wide.

To get ready for the 1958 season, I got into the habit of tossing a rubber baseball up on the roof and batting it when it rolled back down.

At my eleven-year-old height, I could not **see** the ball when it was up on the roof. But I could **hear** it rolling down. I would not know which side of the 18-inch wide between-the-ridges area it would come off of. It would come off at the last instant with some speed and I would have to react to where it was and hit it.

Also, this was in the alley behind my house. If I hit it straight up the middle, it would just bounce around where I was batting. But if I hit to right or left "field," it would ricochet down the alley and I would have to go chase it. To avoid chasing the ball, I got into the habit of hitting the ball straight up the middle.

I cannot say for sure whether this helped my hitting. But the previous season I batted **last**. After working out at my tin roof "batting cage," I moved up to **third** in the batting order, hit safely in every game, batted over .400, and made the county all-star team on the strength of my hitting and in spite of my fielding. I think it helped my hand-eye coordination and gave me some good muscle memory.

The only change I would recommend is that the hitter should wear protective goggles. I could have knocked my eye out hitting line drives into a wall that was about five feet in front of me.

Does this contradict my feelings on team batting practice here? No. I am not opposed to **individual** batting practice outside of **team** practice.

Batting cages

Do **not** hold any of your team practices at a batting cage. It's a waste of time and money. The kids will almost all go play with the video games.

In order to hit the machine, you must spend a number of sessions learning to time the machine. This is a waste of time and money because knowing how to time the machine is of no use in games. During this learn-the-machine period, you will **diminish** the confidence of your players.

The fact that you paid 25¢ or so for each pitch tends to make you want to swing at each pitch. That is a bad habit.

The only thing you could practice in a cage is bunting and fake bunt and slash, but even then, you cannot tell where the ball would have rolled on a bunt so it is a lousy place to practice even that.

If your league has its own batting cages, as our San Ramon Valley Little League does, and assigns each team a cage time slot each week, skip it. It is a waste of your time, if not your money.

When I was playing adult and semi-pro baseball, I went to a local cage daily. Then I bought my own Granada pitching machine for my back yard. I logged thousands of hours in the cages and against my backyard machine. My conclusion: It had little or no effect. I did experiment with little things and adopted a few of them permanently. But if I had it to do over, I would not have bothered.

My own batting average went up far more when I adopted a selective approach on the first two strikes and when I went to a slash technique for all two-strike pitches. Those were simply **decisions** I made, not things I practiced.

Batting order

Batting order is important and I think most youth coaches do it wrong. There are two schools of thought:

- traditional
- best first

In the traditional batting order, the leadoff guy is good at getting on and stealing. Second is a little bit better hitter. Third is your best hitter. Fourth is your best slugger. And so on.

In the best-first system, you just put your best offensive player first, then your second best offensive player, and so forth.

Numerous studies have been done at the Major League level on which is best. They keep finding that you get about the same results with either.

I favor the best-first system because hitting performance is less distinct at the youth level. The hitting performance differences between Mark McGwire and Rickey Henderson are clear. But the differences between Scott and Jason on the typical youth team are quite blurred. Youth coaches are really not in a position to use the traditional batting order because they do not have the data to pigeonhole hitters like the pros.

Best first

The theory behind the best-first approach is that the players closest to the beginning of the batting order get the most at bats over the course of a season. Your players only get the same number of at bats in games where the number nine hitter gets the last at bat of the game. In all other games, the guys at the beginning of the order get one more at bat than the guys behind the player who makes your team's last out of the game. Your team performance is maximized by having your best offensive performers come to the plate the most times.

Don't block good base runners

However, there is one modification that needs to be made at the youth level. Baserunning is the main thing that goes on offensively in youth baseball, not hitting. Your batting order is also your baserunning order (to the extent that a batter gets on base), so you must try to avoid clogging up the base paths with non-runners.

I used to do strictly a best-first batting order. My son was usually the best offensive player (as determined by his Bill James Runs Created Score—see below). He was also the best youth base runner I have ever seen.

After the first inning, before I learned to take baserunning into account in making the batting order, my son would often get on first with the weakest player on the team, the number nine offensive player, on second. My son could usually steal around to home in two or three pitches, but not if there was a non-runner ahead of him.

So I learned to make a best-first offensive player order and a best-base runner order. The batting order would compromise between putting the best offensive players up first, and avoiding having the worst base runners batting just ahead of the best base runners.

Worst base runners bat 5th and 6th, not 8th and 9th

To do this, I would do a best-first batting order. Then see what kind of baserunning distribution I had. If the seventh, eighth, and ninth batters were decent base runners, I would leave the order alone. But if one or two of the last three batters was a lousy base runner, I would move them up to fifth and sixth in the batting order. Our team accomplished more with our legs than our bats, so we were willing to give up a few at bats a season for better batsmen in order to clear the base paths for our best runners.

In the Major Leagues, they often walk good hitters if first base is open. At that level, you take that into consideration and try to protect good hitters by putting other good hitters behind them. But in youth baseball, I think I have only seen one intentional walk in all my years of coaching and playing. There probably should be a few more, but the ease of advancing once you get on base should discourage intentional walks.

In his book *Billy Ball*, Billy Martin says you manage around your offensive leader. If he is a hitter, like Harmon Killebrew on Martin's Twins, you protect him and avoid making outs on base or leaving first open when he comes up. But if your offensive leader is a runner like Rickey Henderson on Martin's A's teams, you manage around **him,** making him leadoff, putting on the hit-and-run or steal of home. In youth baseball, your offensive leader is more likely to be a runner than a hitter. Even if you have a hitter, you are likely to have more runners than hitters on the team.

Left-handed second

Tim McCarver says it's good to have a left-handed batter batting behind a good base stealer. The left-handed batter blocks the vision and throwing arm (if the catcher is right-handed) of the catcher. If he pulls the ball (at the teen level), has a hole to hit through when the first baseman is holding a runner on. Also, a runner on first is more likely to get to third on a pulled single to right field.

Bill James Runs Created

Bill James is a baseball book author with a heavy statistical bent. He devised a way to measure overall offensive performance, that is performance both at home plate and on the base paths. I modified his formula a bit for youth baseball. Here is the formula I called Bill James Runs Created:

$$[(H+W+ROE-CS)(TB+[.55SB])]/(AB+W)$$

where:
H = hits
W = walks
ROE = reached on an error
CS = caught stealing
TB = total bases
SB = stolen bases
AB = at bats

This is not hard to calculate once you create a computer spreadsheet for it. Because some kids missed some games or sat the bench, I found it necessary to divide the Bill James Runs Created score by the number of innings played to come up with a runs-created-per-inning-played score.

In 1997, when I was in a league that prohibited stealing, I used a simpler, self-explanatory, bases-per-plate-appearance to rank my offensive performance.

Earlier, when I said my son was usually my best offensive player, you may have suspected me of nepotism or favoritism toward my son. Nope. I used the runs-created formula, which I explained to all parents in the team newsletter and/or weekly stat sheets I handed out to everyone. At the end of the 1992 season, my son fell to number two behind Karel Exner, and thereby lost his leadoff position in the batting order.

I told parents and players that I did not make the batting order, the **players** did with their performance. By doing detailed stats after every game and either handing out a copy to each player or posting them on the team Web site, I all but eliminated the usual complaining about playing time, positions, and batting order.

One parent did not like stats

Elsewhere in the book, I told the unusual story of a player who had the best batting average on the team, but whom I benched. His Bill James Runs Created score was the reason.

The kid was the slowest runner, relative to his peers, I have ever seen in youth sports. He hit the ball hard, which got it to the fielders sooner when he hit it **at** someone. And he **never walked.** He rarely, if ever, reached on an error. Consequently, in spite of his high batting average, he had the lowest on-base average on the team and was a one-man traffic jam once he got on base. There were no two-throw, double plays in the league, except when he was the batter. He was thrown out at first by right fielders twice.

He and his father got angry at me because the kid had been a star on every team he had previously played on. I explained that was because his previous coaches were not smart enough to use runs created instead of batting average. They were not pleased with this explanation and, at my request, successfully requested a transfer to another team. This "player personnel action"

142

significantly increased the on-base percentage and all-around offensive performance of my team.

I had similar experiences in youth football and high school volleyball. In general, coaches should understand and use statistics. But when you do at the teenage levels, you sometimes uncover an imposter who has been erroneously regarded as a star his whole life. Such people do not take kindly to being exposed.

Mechanics

I have said repeatedly in this book that you should NOT coach batting mechanics. It will make your hitters **worse**, not better. However, that applies only to what the batter does when the pitch is **in the air**. There are some mechanics you can and should coach **before** the pitcher releases the pitch.

Stance

Once a youth player is experienced, you probably should not mess with his stance. It is likely suboptimal, but it's close enough for government work or a youth season. Leave him alone or you will make him self-conscious.

But rookie player, like tee ballers, **do** need some help with their stance. Find a pavement adjacent to your practice area. Use chalk to draw a home plate on the ground then draw the batter's feet position.

I recommend that all players start batting left-handed, but you may not choose to do that. If not, draw a pair of feet on each side of the plate. Then have the players stand in the foot prints to bat initially. Otherwise, they will be all over the place and it will be difficult to either verbally describe what you want or even to physically move their feet to the correct positions.

Hand position

Also, rookie or second-year players need help with their hand position. They often put the **wrong hand on top**. No baseball expert in history has ever advocated that.

I would not mess with the **spacing between their hands**, however. Most batters have no space between the hands. But my youngest son, on his own initiative, adopted a several-inches separation. Once, an opposing coach stopped our game so I could correct that. "What's the matter?" I asked. "His hands are apart," said the opposing coach. My response was, "Yeah, him and Ty Cobb. Batter up."

Indeed, the great Ty Cobb had a several inches separation between his top and bottom hand when he swung the bat. Reportedly, he slid the bottom hand up or the top hand down according to the pitch. I wouldn't recommend teaching **that** to kids.

Honus Wagner also had his hands apart in his grip. Hall of Famer Wagner won eight batting championships and six slugging championships. He is third all-time in triples, seventh in hits, and eighth in doubles.

So did a few other Major League batters over the years. Leave the kids alone on that score.

Measure off

Batters generally measure off their distance to the plate by tapping the far side of the plate with the end of the bat while holding on with their bottom hand. However, I have seen a million Little Leaguers do that, then take a step back away from the plate. In the 1999 Little League World Series tournament on TV they had center field cameras for each pitch. It was obvious that many of the batters were standing so far away from the plate that they either could not cover the plate or, in some cases, could not even reach it. Why? Apparently because they were terrified of the fastballs of the pitchers.

Unfortunately for the defense, the hard-throwing pitchers did not have enough control to throw to the outside part of the plate, which is where their catchers were wisely setting up. Placement of the pitches seemed to be random.

I used to get on batters about that. But they would do the exact same thing every time no matter what I said. I finally concluded they were simply afraid and there was absolutely nothing I could do about it. Same with stepping in the bucket (stepping away from the plate while swinging). It stems from **fear**, not lack of knowledge, and it is absolutely **uncorrectable**. All you will accomplish by trying is to make the kid miserable.

'Bucketfoot' Simmons

There is at least one step-in-the-bucket hitter in the Hall of Fame: Al "Bucketfoot" Simmons. He is fifth all-time in slugging average, eighth all-time in home-run percentage. He won two batting championships, led the league in hits twice and in runs and RBIs once each.

Here's what *Total Baseball* said about Simmons's stride: "He had a classic foot-in-the-bucket batting stance with his left foot pointing toward third base, just the way kids are taught not to do it from the time they pick up a bat. Critics said he'd better change or he'd be back in Milwaukee pretty quick."

In view of Bucketfoot Al's batting performance, and the fact that "correcting" stepping in the bucket is absolutely impossible, you should never even mention it.

Rest

Almost all youth baseball batters get set too soon. I taught my players what Oscar Miller taught me: rest, ready, relax. That is, measure off, put your feet in the correct places, then place the bat on your shoulders parallel to the ground with your legs locked and look at the pitcher. Only when he begins his windup do you get into a crouch with your bat off your shoulder.

I instructed my pitchers to let a batter stand there

for a while if the batter got ready too soon. Don't overdo this or the opponent will figure out what you are doing, call timeout, then wait longer before getting set. You want to keep secret that you are doing this. But just wait about as long as you can get away with before pitching. It makes the batter's body vibrate from tension and fatigue, especially when their bat is too heavy, which it almost always is.

I have seen many a youth batter get set when the catcher was still standing up putting on his helmet.

Dumb as it sounds, you must explain, demonstrate, and practice the rest position a little. This is even true above the rookie level.

Grip

The batter should not grip the bat too tightly. His grip will naturally tighten when he swings. There is no consensus about how deep in the hand the bat should be held or knuckle alignment. I hold the bat in my fingers, not palm, and I align my door-knocking knuckles, but what do I know?

So leave the kids alone as long as they are not white knuckling it before the pitch.

Movement

Some batters stand still while waiting for the pitch (Joe DiMaggio and Stan Musial), others have motion in their waiting (Willie Stargell). There is no consensus. Both types are in the Hall of Fame. Do not bother your kids about this.

Bat position

Major Leaguers have all sorts of pre-pitch stances and habits from Willie Stargell's vigorous waving the bat over his head to Carl Yastremski's holding it real high and so forth. But as the pitch approaches, they all move their hands to the same position: around the top of the strike zone and about six inches from their body. The bat angle at that time is generally near vertical.

I wouldn't mess with a kid about bat position unless he was trying to do something way out of whack. Many people mistakenly think Major League star batters are still in those varied pre-pitch contortions as the pitch is delivered. Look at some still photos of batters and you will see that they all have the same ready position just before they swing.

Your kids will probably do the same naturally, but be on the lookout for a kid who is artificially forcing himself something he imagines his hero is doing.

Hitch

Many baseball batters have a hitch in their swing. Many a youth coach has spent much time trying to get rid of his batters' hitches. Leave them alone. There are a number of guys in the Hall of Fame who had hitches throughout their careers, like Frank Robinson and Hank Aaron. Kevin Mitchell and Jose Canseco had hitches.

Crouch

Generally, leave the kids alone on this. But be on the lookout for exaggerated crouches or a standing-straight-up, waiting-for-a-bus nonchalance. Neither will work. I won't go into the perfect crouch. It's generally what you see on TV and what you and your fellow coaches would do. Close enough for government work. Leave the kids alone if they are not way out of whack.

Head

Your head faces the pitcher squarely or as close to squarely as possible. You generally have trouble getting your back eye a clear line of sight. Opening your stance can help some players.

Stride

Leave it alone. This takes place when the pitch is about to be in the air. I don't care whether he has no stride (like the Doyle Baseball School teaches) or a high-kick stride (like Hall of Famer Mel Ott). Leave it alone. This is one of the things you do not have time to take apart and put back together in a youth baseball season. Plus, there is no consensus among **experts** on the correct stride, so who are **you** to be changing a kid's stride?

If you insist

Many of your are going to teach pitch-in-the-air mechanics in spite of all my warnings not to. So I am now going to tell you the "correct" mechanics so at least you will be giving your kids the right stuff.

When you swing, your back foot pivots on its ball as if you were squashing something. Some coaches call it, "squashing the bug." When you hit the ball and follow through, your back foot is pointing at the pitcher and your back heel is off the ground.

Some hitters, like Ted Williams, recommend cocking your front hip and shoulder in as you start your swing. I found that gives me more power, but makes it harder to keep my back eye on the ball.

Your hands and bat go back and up slightly before they go forward, same as if your were going to punch someone in the stomach. It's called cocking or coiling. This cocking of our hands going back happens simultaneously with your stride going forward, if you stride. Your weight is almost entirely on your back foot during the cock and stride. Oscar Miller describes what you do with your stride big toe as if you were tentatively testing thin ice before putting your weight on it.

As you swing, your back foot pivots to point at the pitcher, your front heel slams down on the ground (as if you were crushing an aluminum can), and your hips pivot to face the pitcher.

At the moment of impact with the ball, your back foot, belly button, and breast bone all face the pitcher squarely. Your head is down so that your nose points straight at the ball at the moment of impact. Having the head down makes you much stronger.

Your top hand is palm up and your top arm is bent at a 100-degree angle as if you were punching someone who was standing very close to you in the stomach. Your top forearm is almost touching your hip. You do NOT "extend your arms" as so many baseball announcers say. That happens only in the follow-through. Look at any photo of a batter at the moment of impact and you will see that his top arm is bent 100 degrees and close to his body.

Watch ice skaters. When they want to spin really fast, as a baseball batter wants to do when he swings the bat, they bring their arms in **close** to their bodies. When ice skaters want to slow down a spin, which is exactly what you do NOT want to do in a baseball swing, they extend their arms outward. You want the "compact swing," not "extended arms."

The bottom palm faces down. The bottom arm is only slightly bent at a 170-degree angle at impact. Oscar Miller says your bottom arm and hand move as if you were "karate chopping a midget in the throat."

Your front leg is locked at the knee at the moment of impact and your front foot points to the opposite base (e.g., first base for a right-handed batter). At the moment of impact, the bat and shoulders are parallel.

After impact, your arms continue around in the follow through. If they do not, it means you were slowing them down before impact. Your nose remains pointed at the impact spot throughout the follow through.

Swing level'

Do **not** tell your kids to "swing level." The only logic to it is that if you swing on the same plane as the ball, you have a longer opportunity to hit it. But the pitch is falling so you would have to swing **upward** to be on the same plane. If you hold your hands at the top of the strike zone, which almost everyone does, you would have to loop your swing down, then up, to get on the same plane as the falling ball.

Kids often take the "swing level" instruction literally. You see them drop their bat straight down to pitch level then swing completely flat or horizontally at the pitch. If you programed a robot to hit baseball, that is probably the way you would do it. But human anatomy does not work like that. The correct path of the swing is **downward**, not because I say so, but because if you start with your hands at the top of the strike zone, almost all pitches will be lower and your hands will have to go down to the pitch. No one in the Major Leagues does the drop-the-bat-straight-down-then-swing-flat routine you see done by youth players whose coaches told them to "swing level."

That's it, babe. Now if you try to teach that stuff to your players, they will hit **worse** than they did before they met you, because they will be thinking about all that junk in the batter's box as the ball is approaching.

That is very bad because all they really have time to think about is whether to swing.

Sybervision video

One of my favorite batting videos is by Sybervision. It shows Rod Carew hitting line drives over and over. Not a word is spoken on the tape. Some hits are at regular speed. Some are in slow motion. Some are in the dark with Carew wearing a special suit with luminous lines on it.

Carew crushes screaming line drive after screaming line drive. It made me think there should be a country-western song called, "Mommas, don't let your babies grow up to be shortstops." I have always wished I could have that tape running in the dugout and have my players stare at it when they are on deck.

One problem I had with the tape was that Carew batted **left-handed**. I do not think my subconscious could relate to that because I bat right-handed. I think you need a similar tape of right-handed batters. You could easily make one by taping games on TV and making a highlight film of right-handed line drives.

How to get a TV-VCR in the dugout and power it are another matter. It may also violate some rules. If it seems to be working, you can be sure your opposing coaches will get out the rule book. This, to me, is one of the only permissible ways to teach batting mechanics. Just silently show them the right mechanics over and over.

Leave the top hand on

Since Charlie Lau taught George Brett to do it in the early seventies, taking your top hand off in the follow-through has become fashionable. *The Official Little League How-To-Play-Baseball Handbook* even advocates that. I take **my** top hand off when I swing.

However, I found it is too hard for youth players to remember to keep the top hand on **until after the ball has been hit**. They tend to take the hand off **before impact** and end up doing a sort of tennis backhand to hit a baseball, which is awful.

The trick to doing it right is you must end up like Dracula when he throws his cape over his shoulder. That is, the bicep of your top arm ends up against your chin and your top hand is over your shoulder behind your front-side ear. When kids do it, their top hand ends up in front of their belt buckle. Don't even start down that road. You'll spend the rest of the season trying to undo the mess you made.

Hit a basketball

There is one simple way to impart all the "correct" mechanics without risking messing up your kids. It's fun, too.

Put a toilet plunger upside down in a batting tee stem. Place a large, heavy ball like a basketball, volleyball, or soccer ball on the toilet plunger tee. Then have your players hit the ball off the tee with a bat.

I had the kids hit five balls per turn. Other kids would collect the balls for the next batter. You need a large area because the balls will rocket out about 150 feet. The kids love this drill. I do not know if it helps them hit better in games, but it is harmless and fun. It only takes time.

One of my coaches misunderstood me once on this drill and **pitched** the basketballs to the kids. Two were hurt from the bat bouncing off the balls. Hitting off a tee works. Soft toss from behind or the side might work, but **not** pitching.

Beginners should bat left-handed

I and my two oldest sons bat right handed. My youngest son, however, bats left-handed. The reason is I got over being stupid by the time he started playing baseball.

Before you decide this is nutty, let me point out that I submitted an article on this to *American Baseball Coaching Digest*. Not only did they print it, but *Collegiate Baseball Newspaper* **re**printed it. Those are the two top baseball periodicals in the world.

I got **zero criticism** and a few attaboys. No less an expert than St. Louis Cardinals manager Tony LaRussa told me he agreed with everything I said in the article, except that he liked switch hitting better than I do. If I coached in the **pros**, I might like switch hitting, too. But in youth baseball, switch hitting is a grotesque waste of time.

Why left-handed is better

Baseball is a unique sport. It is played on a diamond, not a rectangle, and there is a prescribed traffic-flow direction: counterclockwise. This makes "handedness" important.

The release point and movement on pitches varies from right- to left-handed pitchers. Batters can stand on either side of the plate. Humans also have one dominant eye, which is different from handedness. In all, there are ten technical reasons why it is usually better to bat left-handed.

1. Closer to the bases

The left-handed batter's box is closer to first base than the right-handed batter's box. Getting a hit is a race between the batter and the fielder. It is idiotic to choose to start that race two and a half to three feet farther from first base than you are required to.

Starting closer to first base will increase the number of hits and reached-on-an-errors you get. In the left-handed batter's box, you are also closer to second, third, and home, so there will also be an increase in the number of **extra**-base hits you get.

Right-hander Billy Martin says he ran to first base in 3.6 seconds when he was a player with the Yankees.

He says Rickey Henderson was slower. And he says his Yankee teammate, the extremely fast Mickey Mantle, was timed at 3.1 seconds from the left-handed batter's box and 3.2 seconds from the right-handed batter's box.

In the book *High Percentage Baserunning*, author Howard Southworth says it takes the average high school baseball player 4.1 seconds to get to first if he bats right-handed and 3.9 seconds if he bats left-handed. In sports, two-tenths of a second is an eternity.

2. Finish swing facing first base

Left-handed batters finish their swing with their chest facing the direction they need to run. Right-handed batters finish their swing with their **back** facing first base.

Imagine similar behavior in the Olympic 100-meter dash. If world-class sprinters approached their sport the way most professional baseball batters approach the race to first, most Oylmpic sprinters would choose to set their starting blocks up two and a half to three feet **behind** their competitors. And they would face **away** from the finish line to start the race!

I can only conclude that there were some really stupid people involved in the early stages of baseball. There should not even **be** a right-handed batter's box marked on the field.

3. See pitch better if opposite the pitcher

Because the batter is turned sideways, it is a little bit hard for him to see the release point of the pitch. It is **harder** to see the release point from a **same-handed** pitcher. It is **easier** to see the release point from an **opposite-handed** pitcher. For example, a left-handed batter has to turn his head less far to see the release point of a pitch from a right-handed pitcher.

Since 90% of youth pitchers are right-handed, you are better off 90% of the time batting left-handed in youth baseball.

Right-handed batters are at a disadvantage in this category and in Number 7 because opposing managers can **platoon** pitchers more easily against them. That is, opposing managers can substitute a right-handed pitcher to throw against a right-handed batter more often than they can substitute a left-handed pitcher against a left-handed batter because there are more right-handed pitchers available.

4. Home plate is not an obstacle to left-handed batters

Batters occasionally trip over home plate, especially on poorly maintained youth fields. Or their cleats slip if they step on it. If you bat right-handed, there is a plate between you and the end of your race to first. If you bat left-handed, there is nothing but dirt between you and first base.

5. Left-handed batters can drag bunt

A drag bunt is one in which you start running before you bunt. This can only be done by left-handed batters because they need not run through the strike zone.

6. Left-handed is better for pull hitters

If you tend to pull the ball, as most people do when they are not using an overly heavy bat, it is better to bat left-handed when there is a runner on first.

 a. Nearly all second basemen and most first basemen are right-handed which makes it **harder for them to throw to second to start a double play**.
 b. When there is only one runner and he is at first, first basemen at the teenage level generally play on the bag to **hold the runner near the base**. This opens up a hole for the pull hitter to hit through and thereby increase his chances of getting a base hit.
 c. A runner on first is more likely to **advance two bases** on a hit to right field than on a hit to left field because the **right fielder has a longer throw to third**.

7. Opposite-handed hitters have easier time hitting breaking balls

Curveballs and sliders thrown by a same-handed pitcher as the batter start out coming at the batter, then break away from him. They are harder to hit than curves and sliders that break **into** him.

8. Left-handed batters block catcher's line of sight to first-base runner

This delays a catcher's realizing a runner at first is stealing or taking an overly large secondary lead.

9. Left-handed batter are in the way of right-handed catcher's throwing arm

If a runner steals second, the left-handed batter makes it harder for a right-handed catcher to throw to second base. I have no qualms about using a left-handed catcher, but most baseball coaches **do** have such qualms. As a result, far more than 90% of catcher's throw right-handed.

10. Most batters are right-eye dominant and therefore hit better left-handed

Everyone has a dominant **side** and a dominant **eye**. They are not necessarily the same. For example, I am right-handed, but left-eye dominant. When I tested my players one year, I found 11 of 16 or 69% were right-**eye** dominant as opposed to 90% having right-**side** dominance.

You hit better when you have **cross dominance**, that is, when your eye dominance is opposite your batting side. A better way to put it is that you hit better when your dominant eye is closest to the pitcher. Since most people are right-eye dominant, if eye dominance were the only thing that mattered, those people should bat **left**-handed. Others, like me, who are left-eye dominant would bat right-handed, again, if eye dominance were all that mattered. It's not.

A 1988 article in the *New England Journal of Medicine* by J.M. Portal and P.E. Romano said cross-dominant batters have higher batting averages. Optometrist Don Teig of the Institute for Sports Vision studied seven Major League teams in 1980. He, too, found that cross-dominant teams had higher batting averages.

In that year, the Royals had by far the highest team batting average in the Majors: .286. That was the highest team batting average since the 1950 Red Sox batted .302. According to Tieg, the 1980 Royals also had "...incredible 80% cross-dominance, which is almost four times that of the general population." (It must be noted also that the Royals home field favors hitters.)

Traditional switch hitting makes less sense when you realize that a switch hitter is fighting **against** the benefits of cross dominance when he is on one side of the plate. You would have to calculate which gave you the greater advantage, having your dominant eye closest to the pitcher or hitting opposite the pitcher's arm.

Opposite-handed batters averages are higher

It is well documented that opposite-handed batters' batting averages are higher than same-handed batters. That is the entire rationale for switch hitting.

Why is this? It stems to one extent or another from reasons 1, 2, 3, 4, 5, 6, 7, and 10 above. The main reason switch hitters are more successful is that they bat left handed 2/3 of the time in the Major Leagues (where only 2/3 of the pitchers throw right-handed).

The opposite-handed advantage

In the *Physics of Baseball*, Professor Robert K. Adair gives the statistics on the advantage of batting opposite-handed. Left-handed batters hit .0287 better against right-handed pitchers than they do against left-handed pitchers. But right-handed batters only hit .0164 better against left-handed batters compared to how they do against right-handed pitchers. That suggests that the left-handed batter's box has a .0287 - .0164 = .0123 advantage that stems from factors other than the ability to hit curves and sliders better.

Does switch hitting make sense at ANY level?

Switch hitting in **youth** baseball is silly because you would only get to use the right-handed hitting about 10% of the time when you were facing the rare left-handed pitcher.

The only reason to switch hit in youth baseball would be to prepare for a career in the Major Leagues.

But does switch hitting make sense even there? I wonder. When a switch hitter bats right-handed, he gets advantages #3 and #7 above. But he gives up all the others with the possible exception of #10.

If he is left-eye dominant, he is better off on that score batting right-handed. But most people are right-eye dominant and therefore most switch hitters are probably right-eye dominant. So a right-eye-dominant switch hitter batting right-handed loses #10 as well.

The bottom line is the old notion that you have to hit equally well from each side to be a switch hitter is wrong. You have to hit **better** right-handed because you are fighting against seven or eight technical advantages that you have when you bat **left**-handed.

The very idea of a switch hitter batting right-handed implies that batting opposite the pitcher is such an overwhelming advantage that it compensates for the seven or eight disadvantages of the right-handed batter's box. Not likely.

Throw right, bat left

Which side you **throw** with is generally predetermined by your dominant side. It is difficult to learn how to throw well from your non-dominant side, although I read about a Latin player, Dennis Reyes, who did just that. He spoke to a pro scout who jokingly said he only looked at left-handed pitchers. Reyes, who was a right-handed pitcher, immediately became a left-handed pitcher because he did not know the scout was joking. He later pitched in the Major Leagues.

Unless you are a pitcher, it is best to throw right-handed. Left-handed pitchers are more valuable because they are harder to find and managers like to use them against the many left-handed batters in Major League baseball.

About 90% of people throw right-handed. Also, roughly 90% of the general public bats right-handed, because they erroneously believe that's what you're supposed to do if you throw right. But the breakdown of right-handed throwers and batters in the Major Leagues is starkly different.

In all my years of playing baseball and coaching baseball, I only saw **one** player who threw right and batted left on one of my teams—a twelve-year-old teammate of my oldest son's.

But in the Major Leagues, **fully 17% of all position players throw right and bat left**. That is an amazing statistic.

If you went to 50 different Little League games and saw 100 different teams, you would be lucky to find **one** kid who throws right and bats left. But in the Majors, almost one in five does. That means your chances of making the Major Leagues as a position player are about .17/.0008 = 212 times greater if you throw right and bat left. It is by far the most successful baseball throwing-batting combination.

Thirty-two percent (16) of the top fifty career-batting-average guys of all time threw right and batted left. I put the Hall of Famers in **bold**.

Ty Cobb	.367
Shoeless Joe Jackson*	.356
Billy Hamilton	.345
Ted Williams	.344
Eddie Collins	.333
Rod Carew	.328
Earle Combs	.325
Sam Rice	.322
Ross Youngs	.322
Charlie Gehringer	.320
Chuck Klein	.320
Mickey Cochrane	.320
Ken Williams	.319
Earl Averill	.318
Arky Vaughan	.318
Zack Wheat	.317

* Shoeless Joe would be in the Hall if he had not been part of the Black Sox gambling scandal.

The sixteen guys I just named are not all the left-handed batters in the top fifty; only the ones who batted left and threw right. How many of them batted **and** threw left, batted and threw **right**, or were switch hitters?

BLTL	15
BRTR	19
Switch	0

None of the top fifty batting-average guys of all time were switch hitters. If switch hitting is so great, how could that be? Counting both kinds of left-handed hitters, 31 out of the top 50 batted left. That's 62% compared to just 10% left-handed batters in the general population.

Many other famous baseball position players threw right and batted left, including:

Yogi Berra	George Brett	Kent Hrbeck
Wade Boggs	Joe Garagiola	Roger Maris
Joe Morgan	Tony Oliva	**Mel Ott**
Dave Parker	Boog Powell	**Duke Snider**
Andy Van Slyke		**Carl Yastrzemski**
Richie Ashburn		**Bill Dickey**
Larry Doby	Darrell Evans	Nellie Fox

Jay Johnstone	Tony Kubek	Charley Lau
Bob Lemon	**Eddie Mathews**	Tim McCarver
Bobby Murcer	Craig Nettles	Don Newcome
Eddie Robinson		Mike Sciosia
Joe Sewell	**Enos Slaughter**	Rusty Staub
B.J. Surhoff	Vic Wertz	**Billy Williams**

Switch hitters bat **left**-handed about two thirds of the time in the Major Leagues so they are really predominantly left-handed hitters. Switch hitters are not quite so rare in Little League as those who throw right and bat left, but I have only played with a few of them and never coached one.

The six combinations

There are six possible combinations of hitting and throwing. To calculate the approximate percentage of each among Major League position players (non-pitchers), I counted how many of each are in the book *Total Baseball* from pages 1,000 to 1,099. Here are the results along with my guess as to the incidence of such people in the general population.

Combo	Major Leagues	General pop.
BR/TR	61%	89%
BL/TL	13%	10%
BL/TR	17%	0.001%
BB/TR	7%	1%
BB/TL	0.2%	0.1%
BR/TL	1%	0.1%

"BB" is "bats both" or switch hits.

It should be noted that **left-handed throwers** are **discriminated against** as position players. They are only allowed to play **first base** and **outfield** in the pros. First base and outfield are primarily hitting positions so it is harder for a left-handed **thrower** to become a Major League position player than it is for a right-handed thrower.

But it is easier for a left-handed **batter** to become a Major League position player. In the general population, left-handed batters comprise about 10% of all batters. But in the Major Leagues, they are 37.2% of the position players.

People who bat right and throw left are quite rare. The two most famous are Rickey Henderson and former President George Bush who played baseball at Yale. Regarding why he bats right-handed, the left-handed Henderson said in his autobiography *Confessions of a Thief*, "When I was a little kid, all my friends were right-handed and swung from the right side, so I thought that's the way it was supposed to be done." I wonder how many more hits and stolen bases he would have if he had batted left-handed.

Left-handed switch hitters

Note the incidence of switch hitters who throw left-handed. Only two guys (Joe Mack and Otto McIvor) out of 1,080 players were left-handed switch hitters. Why would that be? Most laymen would probably figure that the breakdown between right-handed switch hitters and left-handed switch hitters would be about 90-10. No way.

In youth baseball, where the vast majority of switch hitters start, 90% of pitchers are right-handed. Accordingly, right-handed batters who know about the advantages of opposite-handed hitting are feeling bad about their side of the plate about 90% of the time. To them, it seems worthwhile to learn how to hit left-handed.

But a batter who is **already** left-handed only feels bad about the opposite-handed hitting advantages about 10% of the time. So he figures, "Why should I bother with switch hitting when I would only use it one in ten at bats?"

When it comes to switch hitting, left-handed batters are like the lady from Boston who said, "Why should I travel? I already live here."

Curveballs and sliders

Basically, the idea behind switch hitting is that it will help you hit curves and sliders. Or, as Charley Lau put it, "This is also the main reason for switch hitting. Batters are scared to death of having a ball come at them and then go away."

If you are at a level where you see a lot of curves and sliders, and you are having trouble with them, you might want to consider switch hitting more seriously than other players.

On the other hand, not every pitcher has a good curve and slider. So right-handed hitting against a left-handed pitcher who does not have a good curve or slider only gets you the improved ability to see his release point. That's not much, especially if you are right-eye dominant.

Also, there is thoretically such a thing as a "**switch pitcher**." A pitcher who has both a curve and a **screwball** can simply throw curves to same-handed batters and screwballs to opposite-handed batters, thereby canceling out the breaking-ball advantage of the batter being opposite the pitcher. A screwball is the mirror image of a curve. It breaks away from an opposite-handed batter.

Too late to switch to left-handed batting?

I say that all beginning batters should bat left-handed. Organized baseball should phase out the right-handed batter's box year by year starting with tee ball. Left-handed batting should be the only kind allowed.

What about older kids? I do not think they should be **forced** to change. Although one of the responses I got from my article on left-handed batting was a call from the Peoria (IL) High School baseball coach. He said he makes all his players switch to left-handed batting during their freshman year. He said it takes about two years for them to become proficient left-handed. Actually it's not years, but repetitions, that matter. I am sure you could become proficient faster by increasing your effort.

The notion that you can only choose your batting side when you are five or six years old is incorrect. True, Pete Rose started batting left-handed when he was ten. Mickey Mantle, Jim Lefebvre, and Wes Parker also started young. But there are a number of stories of Major League right-handed batters deciding to become switch hitters in their twenties.

Harold Reynolds did not start switch hitting until he was 20. Maury Wills did not start switch hitting until he was 27. Tris Speaker switched to throwing and batting left handed while his broken right arm was healing as a kid.

Coaches stop my son from batting left-handed

When my oldest son was eight (league-age nine), he decided to become a switch hitter on his own initiative. He got the idea at a Christmas hitting camp at a local batting cage.

By the time Little League season started, he was almost as good left-handed as right-handed. He got picked as one of the two nine-year olds on a 9-10 minors team, the highest a nine-year old could go. But when he told the coaches he was a switch hitter, they observed him hit from both sides of the plate.

He was still slightly weaker from the left side, although he was better left-handed than most of the kids on the team were batting on their chosen side. The coaches said no way would they allow him to bat left-handed until he was exactly the same on both sides, My son was so discouraged that he totally abandoned batting left-handed.

That incident epitomized the bad Little League coach to me. They placed their own win-loss record and egos above the development of my son. Given a choice between what was in my son's best interest and the remote possibility that they **might** lose a game because of my son missing one hit left-handed that he would have gotten right-handed, they instantly chose to place their own short-term interests above the child's long-term interests.

Helping promising players

Discouraging a youth or freshman high school player from learning how to bat left-handed ought to be prohibited by all coaching codes of ethics. If your son or another player on your team has an interest in playing baseball at the high school or higher level, you have a **duty** to him to encourage him switch to batting left-handed. This will hurt your win-loss record, but youth baseball is for the youths, not for you.

Failure to switch a right-handed batter to batting left-handed will almost always cause him to **end his career one level below the level he would have attained had he batted left-handed**. Yes, I know that a lot of right-handed batters have achieved great success in the Major Leagues. But they would have achieved even **more** success had they batted left-handed.

If you let your kid or other promising position player continue to bat right-handed, I hope you will, in future years, repeatedly hear my voice in the back of your head saying, "It wouldn't have happened if he had switched to batting left handed." I hope you hear it whenever any of the following occur:

- thrown out at first on a close play
- thrown out at second, third, or home on an extra-base hit
- strikes out against a same-handed pitcher
- pulls a ground-out to the third baseman with a runner at first
- does not get picked for the next higher level
- does not start
- does not get picked for the all-star team
- comes in second for team MVP
- gets cut from his freshman high school team
- just misses getting drafted by a Major League team
- never gets called up to the Majors if he plays minor-league professional baseball

Eventually, your child is going to bump into a ceiling in his baseball career. That ceiling is set by his talent **and which side of the plate he bats from**. It will cause you great pain when it happens. And if you let your son continue to bat right-handed after reading this book, it will cause you even more pain when it happens, because you'll know it didn't need to happen—at least not this soon.

Well-known switch hitters

Switch hitting is a waste of time for amateur players and dubious even for Major Leaguers. It requires an extreme work ethic. There **have** been a few famous switch hitters.

Mickey Mantle
Pete Rose
Maury Wills
Eddie Murray
Ozzie Smith
Harold Reynolds

But it must be noted that there is **only one switch**

hitter in the top 100 career batting-average guys. Hall of Famer Frankie Frisch, who played from 1919 to 1934 ranks 56th all time.

Only 1% of the top 100 career batting-average guys are switch hitters; but 7% of all position players are switch hitters. My conclusion: switch hitters are wasting their time batting right handed.

In theory, the switch hitters ought to **dominate** the career-batting-average stats. They **always** bat opposite-handed. They are **never** platooned. The fact that switch hitters have had disproportionately **less** success than their numbers would suggest proves that opposite-handed hitting is not enough of an advantage to overcome the handicaps of being in the right-handed batter's box one third of the time or of having to take twice as much batting practice.

'Your natural side'

I asked three former Major Leaguers (other than Tony LaRussa) what they thought of my idea that everyone should bat left-handed. They all thought each player should bat from his "natural side."

And just how do we determine that? The kid must be free of any outside influences. No seeing baseball on TV. No parents, friends, siblings, or other relatives teaching him how to bat. What do we do, put each three-year old on a desert island with a bat and a continuously running pitching machine, then come back in a year or two to see which side they chose to bat from?

In the real world, kids do not choose which side to bat from. Somebody chooses for them—generally some highly-qualified baseball "expert" like a fellow five-year old or an older kid or relative.

That person usually teaches the kid to bat the same way **they** do, with no effort whatsoever being made to ascertain what the new player's "natural side" is. In most cases, the new player is asked whether he is right- or left-handed, then led to that side of the plate.

I do not believe there **is** a "natural side." If there were, switch hitting would be **impossible**. But even if there is a "natural side," and its advantages outweigh all the advantages of batting left-handed, it does not matter, because there is **no way to find out what a player's natural side is**. Choosing a side to bat from happens at the pre-school level far from the eyes of anyone who knows what he is doing. By the time most players first meet a competent coach, they have long since become addicted to batting right-handed.

Who named it?

The main culprit in the left-handed-batting drama is the idiot who said that you were batting "right"-handed if you are in the **left** batter's box with your **left** eye and **left** side closest to the pitcher and striding with your **left** foot and spinning your upper body to your **left**. What's right-handed about that?

The only thing right-handed about right-handed batting is your right hand is the top hand. So what? If you take your top hand off the bat in your follow through, your **left** hand is on the bat the longest—if you bat "right"-handed. That makes perfect sense.

Let's look at it in segments. What happens from the waist down is that you shift your weight from your back foot to your front foot. That would be the same as walking or ice skating. Do you walk right-handed? Do you ice skate right-handed?

How about the upper body? Ever hear a figure-skating commentator talk about a right-handed spin by a skater? I know of no advantage of being right-side dominant when rotating your upper body counterclockwise.

Moving to the arms, right-handed tennis players do indeed swing like right-handed batters when they hit a forehand stroke. But they only use **one** hand! In baseball, you hit with **two** hands. So how can there be such a thing as right-handed or left-handed batting? You bat **both**-handed.

(There have been two one-armed baseball players in Major League history: outfielder Pete Gray in 1945 and pitcher Jim Abbott from 1989 to 1995. Both had only one good arm—their left arm. Both batted left-handed. I agree with their batting that way because they were essentially doing a tennis forehand stroke and everyone knows you are stronger with a forehand stroke in tennis.)

Why name a batting side after the **top** hand in the grip? Why not name it after the **bottom** hand? Or the stride foot? Or the side of the plate you stand on?

The Peoria High School coach who called me about my left-handed-batting article said in ice hockey, **right**-handed players' strongest slap shot is when they swing the stick in the manner known as **left**-handed batting in baseball.

The closest non-baseball movement I know of to baseball hitting is chopping wood with an axe. In wood chopping, you "switch hit." You take a couple of whacks with your right hand on top, then you take a couple with your left hand on top. No one chops wood "right-handed."

Many switch hitters; hardly any switch pitchers

People believe that you have to **bat** right-handed if you are right-side dominant because you have to **throw** with your dominant side. Throwing is another **one**-handed activity, that's why you always use your dominant side arm to throw.

There are darned few pitchers who can throw equally well with both arms.

If you had to bat with your dominant hand on top to be successful, switch hitting would be as hard to do as switch pitching. The same is true of throwing right and batting left. But there are thousands of players who have done exactly that.

As far as I can tell, the incremental difficulty of a right-handed boy **starting out** batting left-handed compared to his starting out batting right-handed is zero. I started my youngest son out batting left-handed, even though he is right-side dominant. It was effortless. (He is not athletically oriented and stopped playing youth sports at age 11, so I cannot report any great success.)

If a four-, five-, or six-year old is told to bat left-handed when he or she takes those crucial first swings, he or she will have much more success as a hitter.

Selling left-handed batting

At the parent meeting of my 1993 tee-ball team, I thought I sold the parents on the idea of our whole team batting left-handed. I spent 15 minutes or so explaining it. They all said OK.

I did not sell it to the kids. I figured they were only five to seven, they'll do what I tell them. That was a **mistake**. I should have sold it to the kids as well.

Everything went fine until about half way through the season when one father said his kid wanted to go back to batting right-handed. The kids were hitting about as well as the other teams, but not every kid hit a home run every at bat and all non-home runs were blamed on left-handed hitting.

Once **one** kid got permission to bat right-handed, batting left-handed became spinach and batting right-handed was ice cream in the minds of some kids. By the end of the season, I believe about three were back to batting right-handed. The following season, when the players were on all different teams, I got the impression that all but one or two went back to batting right-handed. Apparently the parents were not convinced by my parent meeting pitch. Rather they were just playing office politics, going along because I was the boss.

In later years parent meetings, I just told parents their kid ought to bat left-handed, gave them a copy of my article on the subject, and moved on. My own youngest son continued to bat left-handed for his whole baseball career.

Pre-game soft toss

I noticed that when I batted in a cage against a pitching machine, it always took me five or six pitches to start hitting. Bunting the first two helped speed that up a little. Projecting that slow start to my game play and that of my players, I concluded that it was a very bad idea for my players not to see a pitch to swing at until the actual game. So I always had every player hit soft toss before every game.

Lots of coaches do this—with a real **hard ball** against a chain-link fence—often a fence that sports a sign saying, "No soft toss." This is insane.

It is **extremely dangerous** to both the soft tosser and the batter as well as others in the vicinity. Else-

where in the book I related how I got hit right on the bridge of the nose by a hard ball that I had hit off a tee into a soft net. Unfortunately, the spot I hit had an electric junction box behind it and the ball ricocheted into my face. I was wearing safety goggles at the time, but I was still bleeding both externally and internally from the impact.

Chain link fences have a steel pipe rectangle framing the spot into which you hit. If the ball hits the pipe on any of the four sides, the ball will ricochet off hard and could seriously injure or kill whomever it hits.

There is also the possibility of completely missing the fence or screen into which you are hitting. I once attended an San Ramon Valley Little League clinic.

When the professional minor leaguers who were giving the clinic started to do soft toss into a screen with a hard ball, I quietly offered them a poly ball. They said they were "professionals" and did not need to worry about inaccurate hits. I did not believe them and went behind another chain link fence where I was safe from ricochets. There were no ricochets. But one of them did hit a ball that completely missed the screen and went into a neighbor's yard.

When my oldest son was in Pony League, his coaches insisted on doing **hard ball** soft toss into a chain link screen before every game. I insisted that my son wear his face-mask batting helmet to do that soft toss.

There is also the issue of destroying the fence. Fences at youth baseball fields all over America are curled up at the bottom in a manner that is dangerous to players during games because adults ignore signs saying "No soft toss."

Pre-game soft toss is great and absolutely necessary in my opinion, but **only with poly balls**. These are like Wiffle balls only the holes are round and uniformly distributed around the entire ball. I have each kid hit until he gets about three line drives.

Dumbo's magic feather

In the Disney movie *Dumbo*, a mouse discovers a baby elephant can fly by flapping its ears. The elephant won't believe it can fly, so the mouse gives him a "magic feather." It's **not** a magic feather. The mouse is lying. But the elephant believes it and proceeds to fly successfully—until he drops the feather. Then, as the two plummet to earth, the mouse confesses that the feather was not magic and Dumbo regains his confidence in time to pull up just before impact.

I have noticed a magic-feather effect in my own hitting and in the hitting of my players. As I was trying to make myself a better hitter, I often found some little tip that I would try, like fluting (rapidly opening and closing once) your hands just before you swing. Rod Carew fluted one hand. I tried fluting both. I saw an immediate improvement and kept that in my swing.

'Placebo effect'

More importantly, I found immediate improvement from **almost everything** I ever tried. In general, the improvement seemed to go away over time. Based on what I read, it sounded like such and such chance might help my hitting. I suspect that my hitting immediately improved because, like Dumbo, I **believed** it would. In medicine, this is called the "placebo effect."

When they test medicine, they set up three groups of patients: controls, those who get the medicine being tested, and those who receive a placebo. The controls get nothing. They are just a similar group of people who are watched during the trial period. The placebo group gets a sugar pill, but they are not told whether it is a sugar pill or the medicine being tested. In almost all cases, the group receiving the sugar pill improves somewhat. This is because they **believe** the pill might help and want it to help and mind often triumphs over matter.

Because of the ultra-subtle difference between one mental state in a successful at bat versus an unsuccessful, baseball players are among the most superstitious athletes. Religion also seems to be more popular among baseball players.

Whether you rely on a "magic feather," lucky penny, sugar pill, God, or the notion that fluting your hands might help, you can temporarily improve performance with any of these tricks.

It would be unethical for you to encourage your players to be superstitious or to lie to them about any sort of "magic feather." It would be improper for you to try to make any religious converts. However, I think it **is** proper to offer an occasional suggestion, especially before a big game, as to a minor change that has been recommended by one batting expert or another.

I once suggested to my players that they try to be unready for the pitch until the last second because I had seen that work on occasion. A number of players tried it and it seemed to work for them, at least for several games. Other minor adjustments I have seen work on me or my players or teammates include:

• turning the front shoulder and hip in as you cock
• opening your stance a little
• looking at the top of the ball
• choking up

It almost doesn't matter **what** tips you adopt. The various baseball books are full of such things. Since what is really happening is probably the **placebo effect**, it doesn't matter which one you choose. The only limits I would set would be no superstition, religion, or dishonesty. All tips used in this fashion should be truthful and have an authoritative source. For example, the turn-your-hips-and-shoulder-in tip is from Ted Williams.

The human magic feather

A few years back, batting coach Walt Hriniak went to a new team. *Sports Illustrated* did an article about how much that team's batting average went up. The way I read the article, Hriniak was the most valuable man in baseball. But since that year, I have read nothing about Hriniak. One of the unfortunate things about placebos is that they wear off. I suspect that Hriniak had a placebo effect on his team. They **believed** he would help their hitting. It became a self-fulfilling prophecy.

Three balls

When a batter gets ahead of the pitcher 3-0 or 3-1, his coach often yells out from the dugout, "He's got to throw you a strike now." Well, the pitcher may **have to** throw a strike with three balls, but that doesn't mean he **can** throw a strike. At higher levels, a 3-0 or 3-1 pitch is usually a good pitch to hit. But in youth baseball, it's just another pitch. Do **not** encourage your batters to be more aggressive with those counts. They should approach a 3-0 or 3-1 count the same as any other count where there are less than two strikes.

Summary on improving your team's batting

• Your batter's only goal on the first two strikes is to make good decisions.
• Your batter's goal on the third strike is to put the ball in play in fair territory or draw a walk.
• Players should take a full swing during the first two strikes unless they personally are more successful bunting.
• Players should slash when they swing at a third strike, or bunt if they cannot slash.
• Prohibit the square-around bunt stance for safety.
• Track the location of each game pitch, whether your batter swung, and the result of the at bat. Distribute this chart to your players and discuss it with them.
• Do not hold full-swing batting practice.
• Practice bunting and slashing.
• Do not make any attempt to change a batter's mechanics when the pitch is in the air.
• Coach pre-ball-in-the-air mechanics.
• Practice taking a pitch in both a full-swing mode and a bunt mode.
• Always do pre-game soft-toss with poly balls.
• Make your players use a bat whose weight matches my bat-weight chart. If they still struggle, make them choke up or use an even lighter bat or switch to bunting.
• Do not tolerate strikeouts or a walk percentage that is significantly below the best on the

team. Take action like insisting on a lighter bat, bunting on third strike, more bunting or slashing practice.

- Do not use sacrifice bunts to advance runners to any base but home. Practice the squeeze play and use it in games.
- Urge beginning players and those who hope to play in high school to bat left-handed.
- Make your batting order so that your best offensive players bat the most times over a season, but avoid putting lousy base runners right in front of good base runners.
- Evaluate your offensive performance using the Bill James Runs Created score per inning.
- Discourage switch hitting at the parent meeting and on the first day of practice, but do not stand in the way of a player who wants to switch hit regardless of his performing less well on one side (which is almost always the case even in the Major Leagues).

I want to make one more pitch for not messing with the pitch-in-the-air mechanics of your players. I did it for years. I have seen other coaches do it every year. It **does** make your hitters look **prettier** when they swing.

In the movie *Dirty Dozen*, an ex-convict soldier is pretending to be a general. He is forced to perform a dress inspection of an army unit that does not know his true identity. As he concludes his inspection, the private says to the colonel in charge of the inspected unit, "Very pretty, colonel. But can they fight?"

I would have the same question for any baseball coach who has emphasized batting mechanics and created a team of picture-perfect swingers. The question is not how they look, but where they go when they leave the batter's box. The correct answer is first base, not the dugout.

In 1991, I emphasized batting mechanics with my team. One day, when we were batting, I was standing next to the opposing bleachers. In that bleachers was a wizened old baseball guy who had a deep tan from his countless hours of coaching. He commented out loud on what a great swing one of my pylayers had, unaware thhat I was a coach from the opposing team.

I later told the batter about the compliment and asked if he had attended a batting camp. He said he learned all he knew about how to swing from me.

So how did he hit? Poorly. He was in the bottom of our batting order and that was the year I found that we had five hits per game fewer than our less pretty opponents.

Your job as a coach is to increase your team's on-base percentage. You must have an attitude about it. Scrap, fight, claw, whatever to get on base. Your players are not actors in a training film on the correct swing. Get them on base. Do not accept poor decisions on the first two swings and do not accept strikeouts on the third swing. The vast majority of coaches are too accepting.

Too many people are **process**-oriented rather than **results**-oriented. They figure if the kid did his best to swing at the ball and hit it, that's the breaks. I agree, but the batter needs to be more than a one-trick pony who can only take full swings. A results-oriented coach say, after his player strikes out, "Gee, that didn't work. We'd better try something else next time for that batter."

You can do better. Your players can do better. Making them better is your job.

almost always successful since a high percentage of pitches are bounced or thrown far enough off to either side of the plate. Bulky, improper-fitting of catcher's protective equipment and slow physical reaction make it almost impossible for any young catcher to throw anyone out. A close look at most youth league games shows the batter reaching first base via a walk; stealing second base on the next pitch; stealing third base on the following pitch; and scoring shortly thereafter on a wild pitch. The pitching machine eliminates that type of play and will equalize the bigger and smaller players.

16 Baserunning

If you talk to coaches who know me, they will probably tell you my strength is coaching baserunning.

I think my strength in this area has two dimensions:

• study of and experience with baserunning
• willingness

Baserunning is the most coachable area of baseball. You can coach a kid to hit all day, and he will still usually miss when he swings. You can coach kids to field by the hour, and they will still muff the ball or make inaccurate throws.

But if you coach a kid to run to second, he will run to second. His **throw** to second may miss, but his run to second never will. There are hitting slumps. The typical Little Leaguer is in one that lasts the whole season. But there are **no slumps in baserunning**.

I do not understand hitting, pitching, or fielding. No one fully does. We have all seen great stars strikeout, walk or hit a batter, or muff a routine defensive play. But none of us has ever seen a base runner muff. When a base runner fails, the cause is clear. In general, he either should not have gone or should have gotten a better jump or should have used better sliding technique.

We all wonder why Mark McGwire sometimes hit home runs and other times strikes out. McGwire himself wonders. But we never wonder why Rickey Henderson gets tagged out. Hall of Famer Frank Robinson says, "Speed comes to the park every day. The three-run home run doesn't. Speed is the most consistent thing you have."

The predictability of running *per se* is aided in youth baseball by the high incidence of fielding, throwing, and catching errors.

The brochure for Babe Ruth Baseball, Inc.'s Bambino Rookie Division has an intelligent discussion of youth baserunning. It says,

Generally, base stealing at the younger level is

I think they overstate the case, but they have the general idea right. I like the pitching-machine idea as a way to stop this type of baseball game from happening. But there is great resistance to this approach from what I call the "aluminum bat traditionalists." (Coaches who invoke "tradition" to stop any improvement that they do not like. They like aluminum bats, so they ignore tradition when it comes to bats.)

The way I would describe the situation is that when children are nine or ten, they generally have long experience with running, but relatively little experience with throwing or catching. Consequently, if you tell a sub-teen player on first to **run** to second, he will almost always make it. But if you tell a sub-teen player to **throw** to second, the ball often does not make it there accurately, or if it does, the fielder at second misses it.

At the sub-teen level, baserunning generally starts out superior to baserunning defense, that is, throwing and catching, regardless of coaching. If you coach all three competently, your baserunning will improve dramatically and your baserunning defense will improve somewhat.

My teams were generally the best in the league at baserunning and baserunning defense. But we were better at baserunning because it's much harder to get good at throwing and catching in the span of a youth baseball season.

Deliberate incompetence again

Some coaches have lousy baserunning because they are incompetent at coaching baserunning. But a fair number of coaches have lousy baserunning because they deliberately decide not to teach good baserunning. Why? Because if they do teach good baserunning, their team will do well, but it will do well in a way that angers opposing coaches and parents. They want to be popular, so they deliberately refrain from teaching good baserunning.

Not just being aggressive

There is a school of thought in youth baseball that since the fielders are so bad, you can just run as if they do not exist and they will screw up so often that you will go all the way home on the play.

In fact, although I agree that aggressive baserunning can cause errors—at all levels—I do not subscribe to this approach. I probably commented once a season to my players that being aggressive often causes defenders to screw up. But I spent far more time telling my runners to be **less** aggressive.

More to it

We had a game once where we were having our usual baserunning success. The opposing coach was getting really frustrated. Suddenly, as his team was about to bat, he called a huddle.

I could not hear what he was saying, but from the context and his body language, I knew what it was. He told them that all we were doing was running blindly and that they were now going to do the same and give us a taste of our own medicine. In other words, he told his runners to keep running until they scored.

'Let's get two'

Later in the inning, he had a runner at second and one out. The batter reached first base on an error and the runner from second went to third. The ball was in the vicinity of first base when the play was over.

However, the opposing coach had told his players not to stop, so the runner at third went home and the runner at first took off for second. Our amazed players threw home, where the catcher, my son, easily tagged the runner out.

Then, we looked up to find the batter now heading for third. My son threw to third and the third baseman easily tagged the runner out there. End of inning.

Suicide

There were two things wrong with the opposing coach's approach:

1. Just being blindly aggressive is generally suicidal above the tee-ball or farm level.
2. In the process of our becoming the best base-**running** team in the league, we also became the best baserunning **defense** team in the league.

We were the best baserunning **defense** team in the league for two reasons:

1. We spent a lot of **time** on baserunning and had players playing the role of defenders during those practices.
2. We were very **conscious** of baserunning which helps on **both** offense and defense.

There is an old saying which is especially pertinent:

"It takes a thief to catch a thief." My teams were almost always the biggest thieves in the league. We were also the best at catching thieves, although we were not as dominant in that role.

I wish I had a video tape of that play to show to all the coaches who think our successful youth baserunning was nothing but mindless aggressiveness.

Keys to success

My base runners were the best because:

- I taught good pop-up sliding technique
- I drilled sliding incessantly
- I gave all but the slowest runners a season-long green light to go whenever they thought they should
- I gave a thorough "tour of the bases"
- I taught and drilled specific stealing techniques
- My oldest son set a heck of a good example
- During games, I constantly exhorted them to be intelligently aggressive

'Billy Ball'

In 1979, the Oakland Athletics lost 108 games and finished in **last place** in the Western Division of the American League. Jim Marshall was their manager.

In 1980, Billy Martin became the Oakland manager and he inaugurated what *Oakland Tribune* sports writer Ralph Wiley called "Billy Ball." To most laymen, "Billy Ball" means kicking dirt on an umpire's shoes. That's incorrect.

Martin found that there was a **reason** why his team lost 108 games the previous year. They had little talent.

Last to first

The following season, with **only one new player**, Dave McKay, new manager Martin took his team to second place in the division. In 1981, Oakland **won** the division. *Newsweek* said Martin "…had taken baseball's most scorned team and led them clawing to the top of the American League West. After more than a year of goading, cajoling, screaming, scheming and teaching every trick in the book, Martin has turned Charlie Finley's rejects into a polished team of hustlers." How did he do that? "Billy Ball."

Martin figured he could not rely on big bats to move runners. He had to become very aggressive and unpredictable on the base paths. He even had third-baseman Wayne Gross, who is 6'2" 210, steal home successfully twice in one season. Gross celebrated the first one by throwing his hat in the air. Talk about the element of surprise.

Baserunning

"Billy Ball" involved much stealing, bunting,

squeezing, hit and run, run and hit, and the runner at first deliberately falling down on the way to second to draw a throw so the runner at third could score.

Martin had weak players, but his weakest player was about ten times better than the best player you will ever coach in youth baseball. So if Martin needed "Billy Ball" at the A's, you need "Billy Ball" times ten.

In his 1987 book, *Billy Ball*, Martin said his style consisted of "…good, hard, aggressive baseball; forcing the other team into making mistakes; steal, hit-and-run, take the extra base." He also said this, which I and most youth coaches and players can identify with:

Nothing ever came easy to me as a player. I had limited ability and I had to do the little things to make myself a more valuable player: those little things that make the difference between winning and losing.

The best coaches in all sports tend to be those who had limited success as players. When they were players, they had to learn to get the best out of little talent. That's also what coaches do, especially in youth sports.

Here are some more phrases from Martin's book as he explains what Billy Ball is:

• Smart aggressive. Not overhustle.
• Take the extra base.
• Bunt when they're expecting hit and run.
• Squeeze with your best power hitter.
• Hit away with your best bunter or in a prime squeeze situation.

In *Men at Work*, George Will says, "Aggressive managing means making moves that will fail if the other team executes its response perfectly. Over the course of a season, the best teams will, more often than not, force failure—which is anything less than perfection—from opponents."

Taking an extra base

Coaches do not encourage runners to take an extra base often enough. I think there ought to be a statistic which I call "bases beyond batter." That is, the number of bases a runner advances above and beyond the number the batter got. So if the batter hits a single and the runner on first goes to third, the runner would get **one** base beyond batter. On the other hand, if the runner went from first to third on a double, he would get **zero** bases beyond batter.

Taking an extra base is especially likely to succeed in youth baseball when the batter sent the ball to the outfield. Youth outfielders generally cannot throw accurately to a base that is not adjacent to their territory. Accordingly, timidity in advancing is unwarranted.

Bunt-and-run from first to third

You have to practice this to put it in the kids' heads

and to show them that it works. Billy Martin practiced using a bunt toward third to advance Rickey Henderson from first to third. This was a run-and-bunt play with Henderson stealing on the pitch.

Martin says the catcher usually forgets to cover third. I do not recommend having the catcher cover third in youth baseball and I have never seen a youth coach teach that. But I think it's just as likely that the shortstop will forget to cover third.

Element of surprise

One of the main aspects of *Billy Ball* was the element of surprise. Having a slugger bunt or a slow runner steal home. By definition, element-of-surprise tactics cannot be used very often.

Steal home

In 1969, when Billy Martin was manager of the Twins, Rod Carew stole home seven times, tying Pete Reiser's all-time season record.

When he managed in the minor leagues, Billy Martin told his first baseman, one of the slowest players on the team that he was going to steal home. The player couldn't believe it. But he ended up stealing home twice that season. Marin says,

You don't have to have great speed to seal home. You steal home by learning the habits of the pitcher, by getting the proper lead, by having the instincts to go at the right moment, and by employing the element of surprise.

My son Dan stole home a number of times. But once was special. He did it **standing up**. He ran right through the plate as the pitch was arriving. He got there so early that the catcher was not in possession of the ball, therefore the rules did not require a slide. The catcher ended up getting so discombobulated by the whole situation that he missed the ball, but it didn't matter. Here's how it happened.

First off, when I say steal home I mean there was **no passed ball**. A steal of home occurs when the batter slides into home plate and the catcher catches the pitch and attempts to tag the runner out. Or in this extreme case, when the batter arrives at the plate before the pitch arrives at the catcher's mitt.

Dan had stolen home a couple of times that season. And he had been called out twice trying to steal home, although the consensus was that one out was a bad call. It was more that the umpire **did not believe his eyes**. The other was a failure of the umpire to call a **balk** on the pitcher who broke his full windup motion and jump pivoted after Dan started to run. That season, one umpire in that league told me it was **impossible** to steal home.

Batter should show bunt

One of the problems Dan and I noticed when he stole home was that our batter would run away, that is, scurry out of the batter's box. That made it much easier for the catcher to catch the ball and tag Dan out. So I gathered the players and said, "Guys, Dan likes to steal home. But when he does, our batters are running away. That's wrong. It helps the other team. **Stay there**. Dan won't hurt you.

"If you bat right-handed, he will either slide between your legs or in front of or behind you. It depends on where you are in the batter's box. Stand still so he can see where to go.

"Furthermore, we would like you to **show bunt**. Pull the bat back at the last instant. The bat in front of the catcher's eyes may make it hard for him to catch the pitch. Whatever you do, do not let the ball touch your bat. If you foul it off, Dan has to go back to third and we probably cannot try another steal of home during that game."

'Mr. Cool'

In the game in question, a guy who thought he was Mr. Cool was pitching for the other team. One of the ways his self image manifested itself was that when he threw from a full windup, he did so **excruciatingly slowly**, as if he liked being the center of attention and wanted it to last as long as possible.

My son's reputation as a master base stealer had preceded him. The pitcher pitched from the stretch when Dan was on first and second. Nonetheless, Dan stole second and third.

Coming into third, Dan slid and hurt his knee drawing blood and causing much pain. This in spite of wearing a knee pad. The darned things slide up your leg. Because of the injury, he was not planning on being so aggressive going home on a passed ball.

Stopwatch

But Dan and I had a standard routine. I wear a cheap watch. I think it cost me $17.95. But it is a sports watch and has a stopwatch capability. Whenever Dan got on base, using my wrist stopwatch, I would time the pitcher's delivery from the time his body started to move until the pitch hit the catcher's mitt. Dan and I had discussed fast and slow delivery times on many occasions.

When Dan arrived at third, the pitcher stopped pitching from the stretch and went to a full windup. I couldn't believe our good luck. Plus, when there were no runners on earlier, we had noticed he had the world's slowest full windup. I timed him. **4.0 seconds!** That is extremely slow and easily long enough for my son to steal home.

Also, the third baseman did not make any effort to hold Dan close to third. As was our habit, I whispered from behind the dugout, "Dan!" When he looked at me, I showed him four fingers, then a zero (OK sign). His

eyes widened in amazement. We had been doing this for years and neither of us had ever seen a 4.0.

Because he had hurt his knee, he wasn't planning on going anywhere for a while. But with a 4.0 delivery on the mound, he figured this was the chance of a lifetime, which it was.

Billy Martin says when a pitcher or other fielder makes a mistake relating to a runner, you must **immediately** take advantage. If you do not, he may realize his mistake, or have a coach say something to him, and you won't get the chance again.

Teen time of throws to home and second

In his book *Hit and Run Baseball*, Tennessee coach Rod Delmonico says high school and college pitchers are taught to deliver their fast ball to the catcher's mitt within 1.3 to 1.5 seconds of their body starting to move. Breaking balls are supposed to get there within 1.5 to 1.8 seconds. Catchers are urged to get their throw to second base within 1.9 to 2.3 seconds. That means the total time from the start of the pitcher's body moving until the ball arrives at second should be between 3.2 and 4.1 seconds.

Big walking lead

Dan took a bigger-than-normal primary lead. This was when he was 14. As he and I had discussed, it was a **walking lead**. Pitchers are supposed to make the runner stop walking before they pitch. But "Mr. Cool" was in a full-windup stance and totally ignoring my son. As a result, he got a huge walking lead.

Break on first movement of glove-side heel

At that time, my son and I erroneously believed that he should break for home on the first movement of the pitcher's glove-side heel. We have since learned that's a bit early.

Our thinking was that once the pitcher moved his glove-side heel backward, he was committed to throw a full-windup pitch to home. If he started that heel back, then did anything else, it was a balk.

We had practiced stealing home. As Dan walked into his lead, he focused his eyes intently on the right-handed pitcher's left heel. As soon as it made the slightest movement backward, Dan exploded toward the plate. This pitcher either knew he was not allowed to jump pivot out of a full windup, or he was so focused on his "Mr. Cool" act that he did not figure out what was going on until too late.

As Dan ran down the third-base line, the batter heard him coming and remembered to stay put and fake a bunt. He did so perfectly, yanking the bat at the last instant. Dan went across the plate at full speed much as one might run through first on an infield hit. The pitch just barely missed hitting Dan. Dan and I had discussed that, too, and he knew that he had no obligation to avoid being hit by the pitch.

No warning

We did not signal to the batter that Dan was coming. For one thing, I was not the manager of that team. For another, the element of surprise is crucial and it is hard to communicate to the batter with one runner on at third without arousing suspicion that a squeeze or steal is on. On the other hand, the batter, especially a right-handed one, must **not** take a full swing or he could literally kill the runner.

Element of surprise

My son was well known for his base stealing. So his stealing home was not exactly the element of surprise, although it certainly was a surprise to "Mr. Cool." The better situation would have been a less famous base stealer at third when "Mr. Cool" did his 4.0 delivery. We would have been successful with almost anyone on the team if we had practiced it.

For the rest of the game, "Mr. Cool" threw from the stretch when there was a runner on third.

Again the following season

The following season, my son was on the A-level Big League team. At one game, our pitcher was an 18-year old who had just won regional high school Athlete of the Year. I was talking to the pitcher's father by the backstop. The top runner for the other team advanced to third base.

The Athlete of the Year then threw a full-windup pitch. I said to his father, "Whoa! If my son had been the runner at third, he would have stolen home on that pitch...or the next one. I don't think it's a good idea for him to be throwing from a full windup with that guy at third." On the next pitch, the opposing runner took a much bigger primary lead and secondary lead. I again expressed my fear that the runner was going to steal. On the next pitch, he did—successfully. "Well, you sure called that one," was the father's comment.

Do **not** pitch from a full windup with a runner at third.

Do not steal home with two strikes

You should generally not steal home with two strikes because the batter must not swing during a steal of home, but if the pitch is a strike, he will be **out** if he does not swing.

Robinson's 1955 steal of home

Jackie Robinson is famous for stealing home in Game One of the 1955 World Series against the Yankees. Tim McCarver says that was a "truly foolish play" because the Dodgers were down by two runs at the time.

First-and-third double steal

When he had runners at first and third, Billy Martin liked to have the runner at first steal badly, maybe even falling down, and get himself caught in a rundown, even with two outs. The rule is that the run counts if the runner crosses home plate before the stealer from first is tagged out.

I call this the "**Staying alive**" play, a name which always inspired my comedian youngest son to break into a rendition of John Travolta disco dancing.

With two out, we taught the runner at first to get caught in a rundown. The runner at third would then take off for home. The runner at first was to "stay alive" until the run crossed the plate. Once it did, we would yell out "Run scored!" and the runner at first understood that we would still like him to get a base safely, but that he had done his job and it would be OK if he were tagged out now.

Stealing second on a walk

I was notorious for having my youth players steal second on a walk. We did this occasionally if the opponent was sleeping. But we **always** did it if there was a runner at third, regardless of the number out.

Ty Cobb used to work this play when he was on third and his teammate, Sam Crawford, drew a walk. In their version, Crawford would jog toward first then break toward second late, when the opponents least expected it. Cobb was sneaking down the third-base line and broke for home on the throw to second.

I told my semi-pro team about this play, but we never practiced it. Once, in a game, we had two outs and a runner at third. I drew a walk and rounded first and tore off for second. Predictably, I got into a rundown. But as I was running, at age 46, being chased by 20-year olds, I glimpsed my 22-year old third-base runner and my 21-year old third-base coach standing at third watching me!

"Go home, you idiot!" I screamed at him. He did and managed to score just before I was tagged out.

The opposing players then taunted me for being so stupid as to make an out on a walk and thereby ending the inning. I said nothing, hoping to run the play again later in the game. But one of my players stupidly pointed out to the opponents that we had traded an out for a run and that it was **they** who got outfoxed.

Managing smart has **two** components: being smart and keeping the opponent from knowing how smart you are. If you just do the first, then brag about it, you aren't so smart.

If you came to one of my late-season Little League games in, say, 1992, every time one of my players drew a walk you would hear the opposing players, coaches, and parents start yelling, "Watch him! Watch him!" before my guy got out of the batter's box. This was because we had stolen second so many times on walks in the past against them. I never told the opponents we were trading outs for runs, but we did it so many times that they figured it out on their own.

First-base coach

The only live-ball duty of a first-base coach is to tell a runner approaching first what to do on a ball hit down the line in left. That's because it would slow the runner down to try to look that way.

Third-base coach

Billy Martin says a good third-base coach can win you several games a year in the Major Leagues. Youth-baseball teams play far fewer games per season, but I think the same statement applies. A competent youth third-base coach can win one or two games a year.

The main thing is to send runners home aggressively, especially with two out. Once or twice a year, I would send a runner home and he would be thrown out. Had I run myself out of the inning, the great fear base coaches have? Absolutely. But you have to play the percentages. I had done the same thing ten or twenty other times in the season and it worked.

Also, whenever I sent a runner home and he got tagged out, I would always announced loudly to the entire crowd that it was totally **my** fault and that the runner had done an excellent job of following my instructions.

Many times in this book I have told you to shut up. As a base coach however, when the ball has not yet been pitched, you have to talk a lot. As Martin says, "Remind. Remind. Remind." I am constantly reminding runners of the situation and cajoling them into taking the next base. Here is an example of what I might say:

"Billy. Congratulations on getting to first, but there's no prize for that. You need to score. Find a way to get to second as soon as you can."

Ultra timid runners

Many times, the runner at first or second was timid. Sometimes, I would give him a steal sign, and he would stay. They I would say, "Billy!" and give him the steal sign again, and he would still stay. Then I would say, "Billy, get the sign!" and again he would stay. Then I would say, "Hey, Billy! Steal on this pitch. Do you understand, Billy?"

Yes, I would say this in front of everybody, often from the dugout or third-base coaching box. I don't like to do that, but enough is enough!

One of the disadvantages of using signs is that players can use "I didn't get the sign" as a B.S. excuse for not doing what they are afraid to do. You cannot tolerate that.

Manager Eddie Stanky once made his timid base runners take turns playing catcher in spring training so they could see how hard it is to throw out a runner going to second on straight steals or passed balls.

Avoid controlling runners

In the 1997 season, when I was not the head coach and our team had relatively lousy base runners by my standards as a result, I still had an opposing coach admit to the head of the league that he was so impressed with our baserunning that he deliberately played catch with his son near our practice one day to learn how I taught baserunning and how I talked to the players about it. I remember seeing him and wondering why the guy was so close to our practice when there were vast areas of grass no being used elsewhere. I did not recognize the guy as an opposing coach.

One of the main things I do that other coaches screw up is I refrain from controlling the runners. I teach the heck out of baserunning in practice, then give as many players as possible the green light in games. Other coaches constantly yell "Go!" or "Stay there!" at their players. I rarely use those words. Baserunning takes split-second decisions. By the time your player hears the words "Go" or "Stay," it is too late.

I tend to try to control runners too much when it comes to judging whether a fly will fall in for a base hit. In view of the fact that I often get it wrong, I ought to shut up. Let the kids make that decision, too. They have a better angle to see.

This reminds me of the difference between the American and German armies in World War II. American soldiers would follow orders, but they would not wait for them. If they had a situation and could not contact higher headquarters quickly, they would make their own decisions on the spot and take initiative.

German soldiers would never do anything until higher headquarters told them to. That was frequently, or even most of the time, too slow. You are coaching American players in an American sport. Forget the "Go" and "Stay" nonsense, unless you join the Wehrmacht.

Have to control them sometimes

I **do** control a runner when he has shown he consistently makes poor baserunning decisions, either being too timid or being too aggressive for his speed. But I much prefer players who make their own baserunning decisions.

At the end of the 1997 season, I am told that all the coaches were complaining at the league meeting about our baserunning. They thought it was dominating the game.

That's an exaggeration. Pitchers always dominate. But we were constantly taking advantage of little mistakes by the defense and taking another base. We accomplished this not by things **I** was doing **during the game**. Rather it was all the tricks I taught in practice. During the games, the kids themselves were in charge.

Sometimes a coach would complain to us during a game and we would say, "It's not us. It's the kids."

Sometimes, when we had a big lead, the players would still be running bases like they were down by one in the last game of the World Series. That embarrassed us coaches and we would yell out to our base runners to stop using all their tricks because we had a big lead. It took a lot of effort to get them to stop, though. Once they learned the tricks, they wanted to use them to the fullest.

Hustle to first on every hit

I am trying not to bore readers with the obvious in this book. A few years back, I would have thought that telling players to run full speed to first on every hit was too obvious to mention. Not any more.

Now we have Major Leaguers routinely engaging in the bush-league habit of admiring their hits as they leave the batter's box. They don't break into a home-run trot when the ball leaves the park. They break into a home-run trot when the ball leaves the bat!

In some cases, they are embarrassed, but not much apparently, to later learn that their hit did **not** leave the park after all, and they reached one or two bases fewer than they should have because they were not hustling. Barry Bonds once trotted toward first on a ball that hit the outfield wall.

In youth baseball, the more common problem is players not running out close fouls or fly balls. Your policy ought to be that everyone will run full speed on every possible fair ball. That policy ought to be clearly explained and strictly enforced. Violators should be punished by making them do it right twenty or thirty times, or more, for every time they do it wrong. The punishment should be whatever it takes to either get them to clean up their act or to quit the team.

The Little League Pledge ends with the words, "I will always do my best." Lou Holtz says, "Discipline is not something you do **to** someone. It's something you do **for** someone." Parents do not sign their kids up for youth baseball to learn how to become baseball players. They sign them up for youth baseball to learn how to become good citizens. It is your duty to the kid to insist that he always does his best.

Run to first on a walk

Running to first on a walk is generally considered taking hustle to ridiculous extremes.

Excuse me.

A walk is a live-ball play. The reason you run to first on a walk is because something might happen that will allow you to get to second on the play. This is especially true at the youth level.

My guys are trained to go to **second** on a walk if the defense lets their guard down. For example, walks are unhappy occasions. Sometimes the catcher, pitcher, and middle infielders mope. At least one of the middle infielders is supposed to cover second.

Other times, the middle infielders may go to the mound to console the pitcher and boost his spirits. If you think you can make it all the way to second because of such a lapse in concentration, go.

Of course, in youth baseball, you also have the ever-present possibility of an error. If an error occurs, you want to be near first at full speed when it occurs, not dawdling out of the batter box.

The name "walk" is a misnomer. When the ump says, "Ball four," you haul butt. That's not to show the grandstand what a great hustler you are. It's because it is stupid not to get to first as soon as possible whenever the ball is live.

Can't call time after a walk

In his book *Managing Little League Baseball*, Ned McIntosh says,

> *We so frustrated one team with this aggressive baserunning that the opposing manager ordered his catcher to call timeout every time one of our boys got a walk, only to be more frustrated by the umpire who would not grant timeout until the play was completed, i.e., when the runner showed no inclination to go beyond first base.*

Same thing happened to me many times. The Little League timeout rule [5.10(h)] says,

> …no umpire shall call "Time" while a play is in progress

The first item in a supplementary case book, which is also published by Little League Baseball, is called *The Right Call, Knotty Problems in Little League Baseball* and says on page 3,

> A base on balls is a live ball and time is not granted until the batter-runner shows no inclination to advance beyond first base. Rules 2.00 and 7.05(i) NOTE.

Had to carry rule sheet

For this and other reasons, I found it necessary to carry a plastic covered sheet which I called "Often-misunderstood rules." Coaches initially would say I didn't know what I was talking about when I said they could not call time on a walk until the runner was done.

It took too long at a game to find the rule in the rule book, and the opposing parents would raise hell while you were looking. So I typed the 22 rules that everybody kept screwing up onto a single sheet of paper, along with their rule numbers. (I'll give you those rules later in the book.)

One coach even demanded, "Who typed that? You?"

implying that I had multiple such sheets with false rules in my pocket and that I whipped out just the right false sheet for each situation. That caused me to consider using a photocopy of each rule, but I decided he was a nutcake and, indeed, he appeared to have been the only coach I ever saw who was banned from coaching again. (He also shoved and cursed at my co-coach at that game.)

Coach screaming 'timeout!'

One opposing coach knew he could not call time after a walk, but he did it anyway. In fact, he would scream it at the top of his lungs.

Our umpires were teenage boys who were intimidated by this. I then started talking to them before each game with that coach, showing them the rule, telling them what that coach did, and getting their promise to not fall for that trick. Then, during the game, he would scream, and they would instantly call time. When I complained, the teenage umps would look at their shoes.

That opposing coach would scream, "Tough!" at me when I said that was illegal. Of course, deliberately cheating and screaming at the teenage umpire and opposing coaches violates the rules, the Little League Pledge, the article "Little League's Greatest Challenge" in the front of every Little League Rule Book, the National Youth Sports Coaches Association Code of Ethics, the Golden Rule, and other rules and ethics too numerous to mention. Such coaches should be banned. That coach was promoted to a higher level the following year.

I actually had to run a drill in which I would say "Ball four," then, as my batter was running around first base, scream, "Timeout!" like that coach to get my kids to ignore him and keep running. They, too, were intimidated.

Throwing to first after a walk

One coach temporarily stopped us from executing our double-steal of second and home on a walk by always throwing the ball to first as soon as the ump said, "Ball four."

That league had an odd rule. It was called the Chuck Moore Rule. Actually, that's the phony name I gave a real coach at the beginning of the book. The rule used his real name.

His teams stole home a million times. So the next year, they outlawed stealing home unless an attempt was made to throw out a runner.

One of my players, Joe Swec, pointed out to me during the game, that we should send the runner at third as soon as the ball left the catcher's hand on its way to first. I checked the local rule, thought he was right, and consulted with the umpire between innings. The umpire agreed that the runner on third would be allowed to advance if the ball was thrown to any base by the

catcher. In other words, the act of throwing the ball to first nullified the Chuck Moore Rule.

Unfortunately for us, the situation never came up the rest of the game. But if one of your opponents tries to prevent you from stealing second on a walk by throwing to first, have your runner at third take a long secondary lead on the base line after the walk then break for home on the catcher's throw to first.

I was impressed with this tactic and tried it with one of my teams. Our second-string catcher threw the ball into right field, the runner at third scored, and the batter ended up at third. Know your personnel.

Tour of the bases

You need to give your team what is called a tour of the bases. Do not try to do it all in one day. The kids will get bored. Do five or ten minutes of it each day.

Normally, the tour starts with instruction on how to leave the batter's box. Other than teaching your players not to throw the bat, don't do that. You want their brain clear when they are swinging. You do **not** want them thinking about how to leave the batter's box. Besides, how hard is it to leave the batter's box? Teaching players how to leave the batter's box is overcoaching at the youth level.

Dropped third strike

At the teen level, batters can run to first if the catcher drops the third strike. Thirteen-year olds especially need a bunch of repetitions of running to first on dropped third strikes to get them in the habit. All their career, they have been walking back to the dugout after the third strike. I takes some practice to shift mental gears.

At the older teen levels, you sometimes get kids who do not want to be bothered because they think it's uncool. Give them a warning or two and some practice reps. If they **refuse** to hustle to first on dropped third strikes, throw them off the team.

With a runner at third, the batter should take off for second after he touches first, same as on a walk.

Approaching first base

There are two ways to approach first:

- run through
- round the base

Stay outside baseline last half

You are required by the rules to stay on the outside of the base line for the last half of the way to first. That's why you see a long skinny rectangle between first and the halfway point to home on thoroughly-marked baseball fields. If your hit is fielded by the catcher, and his throw hits you when you are inside the baseline, you are out. I saw this happen in a Major League baseball game once.

Run through first

After he leaves the batter's box, the batter needs to sneak a peek at his hit to see where it is. If it is stopped by an infielder, he has to run through first. He must then fix his eyes on the near edge of first base.

He should step on the bag on that **near edge**, not in the middle of the base and certainly not on the far edge. Here's a diagram:

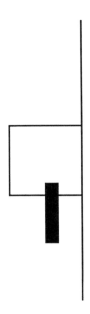

I deliberately made a block rectangle of a foot rather than draw a normal footprint. One reason is it's hard to draw feet with my computer. But the main reason is I do not want you to get the wrong impression about which foot you use to step on the bag. You use **whichever foot comes up**.

There are two reasons to step on the near edge:

- it is closer so you get there sooner
- if the base is hard plastic, as most are nowadays, stepping on the middle may cause you to slip

If they are not trained in the proper way to step on first, the players will tend to step on the middle.

You step on the near edge of the base with the **ball** of the foot, not the instep or heel. Put the group of players you are teaching around the first-base coach's box. Explain it, then demonstrate it at a walk. Then have each player execute it starting from about 20 feet away to save time. Mark the starting point with a cone or something. Have each player run through first twice, once with each foot. You accomplish this by having them start with the right foot at the cone the first time then with the left foot the second time. If you find anyone always stepping on the bag with the same foot, make him do it correctly at a walk, then jog, then run.

No big final step

Another common mistake players make is taking a giant final step as they reach the base. You get there fastest by just running normally.

You can only increase speed or maintain speed when one of your foot is in contact with planet Earth. When you are up in the air with neither foot touching the ground, you are slowing down because of gravity and air resistance. You cannot see this unless you use high-speed photography, but isn't it logical?

Also, taking that big giant final step makes it look to the umpire as if you think you may be out if you do not do that. You should never make a play look worse than it is. By running confidently through first, you increase the probability that you will get the call on a close play.

Stretch your chest forward

You should do what sprinters do as they cross the finish line: extend your chest forward as if you were breaking the tape. A properly trained umpire will not see this. He should be looking at the base and listening to the ball hit the mitt. But we're talking youth baseball here. Many youth umps will mistakenly watch the mitt and thereby see your upper body, not your foot.

Kids tend to decelerate into first

You really have to work hard to get kids to run **through** first rather than **to** first. As you would expect, rookies tend to decelerate into first so they do not overrun it. What is maddening is that this behavior continues all the way up to the teenage level. You must brainwash your kid about this.

When they do it wrong, it is **your** fault. Don't tell me how many times you told them. My response will simply be that it wasn't enough times. If it had been enough, they would not have made the mistake in the game. Punish a kid who does not run through first.

The first time he fails to run through first, make him do it over twenty times. Have him start about twenty feet from first and run through then turn around and start twenty feet from the outfield side of first and run through it toward home. Just keep increasing the number of punishment runs until the kid stops doing it wrong.

There is no excuse for a kid not running through first base. But it happens all the time at many levels of youth baseball. The reason is that the coach did not give the kid in question enough repetitions of doing it right. He may have given him dozens of reps, and you might think that ought to be enough. But I am not interested in what **ought** to be enough. You have given the kid enough reps when he stops doing it wrong, period.

Peek right after crossing first

Immediately after you cross first base, peek to the right to see if the ball got by the first baseman. If it did, make a judgment as to whether you can advance to second. This is often a function of the fencing along the first base line. If it's close to first base, you may not be able to advance even on a passed ball at first.

Turn after crossing first

Many people mistakenly think that the runner must turn toward the foul line (right) or he is liable to be tagged out. That is not true. The rule actually says,

A batter-runner cannot be tagged out after overrunning or oversliding first base if said batter-runner returns immediately to the base. 7.08(c)

However, the vast majority of youth baseball coaches and parents, and many teenage umpires, think you are not allowed to turn left, so teach your kids to turn right.

Beware the catcher covering first

In the fielding chapters, I told you of a play in which the first baseman goes out toward the outfield on a base hit to right. This causes the runner to think he can take a big turn. But if the catcher follows him up the base path and covers first, the outfielder can throw behind the runner and pick him off. If you practice this from both perspectives: defense and offense, you should not fall victim to this play.

Sliding into first

Do you ever slide into first? Generally, no, for the same reason you do not take a giant final step. Doing anything other than running slows you down.

But there is **one exception**. If the throw to first draws the first baseman off the base toward home plate, he will have to tag you out. In that case, you will increase your chances of being safe by getting under the tag.

You need to practice this to put it in the minds of the players. One caveat, at the less competitive levels, the opposing coaches probably have not taught their first basemen to sweep tag the runner when they are pulled off first. In such leagues, your batter is better off running through the base.

You can **run** past first, but can you **slide** past first, too? Yep. See the rule above.

Rounding first base

You round first base when there will not be a play at first on the hit. That could be a base hit or a fly ball. But there is a question about whether rounding is actually the fastest way to get to second. One book I read said it's actually faster to run straight to first then hang a 90-degree right turn toward second.

Having to decelerate to make a right turn costs you some speed, but so does taking a circular path, which make you have to run father. I suggest that you run some races each way to figure out which is actually faster, and to **prove** which is better.

People who do shuttle runs against a clock do not round their turns. Competitive swimmers do not round their turns.

When you round first or any other base, be careful that you **do not pass the runner ahead of you**. If you do, you're out. Tim McCarver's first Major League home run appeared to be a grand slam. Unfortunately, it went into the score books as a three-run single because, in his excitement, he passed the runner at first who was waiting to see if the ball went over the fence.

How to step on a base when you are going to the next base

When you are going to the next base, you step on the corner of the base closest to the pitcher's mound. It looks like this:

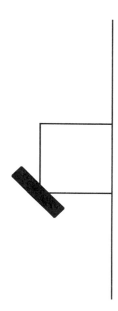

Which foot do you use? **Whichever one comes up**, same as running through first. If you try to use your **favorite** foot or your **dominant-side** foot or your **inside** foot, you will often find that it is not the one coming up and you have to stutter step to get that particular foot on the base. Stutter stepping slows you down. Do not do it.

This is not only how you run through **first** toward second, it is **also** how you run through **second** and **third**. Again, you have to explain this, demonstrate it, and have your players practice it until they successfully step on the base with each foot during the drill. Make them do it over at a walk and a jog if you catch one stutter stepping to use the same foot every time.

Path approaching first base

All baserunning books have a little diagram that shows the batter to loop out as he approaches first. I really do not have any strong feelings about the "right" loop trajectory. Furthermore, I oppose coaching when the kids are doing it "close enough for government work" to begin with. The path you take rounding first strikes me as pretty much instinctive. I do not recall ever being unhappy about a runner's loop at first. Don't worry about it.

Think two

Good base runners are constantly thinking about going to the next base. Indications that you might make it to second on a single include:

• outfielder running away from second to field hit
• muff by outfielder
• combination of weak outfielder arm and deep hit
• a lead runner who is approaching third or home

Force the outfielder to stop you. Don't stop yourself. You can be really aggressive at first if the ball is hit to **left** because the left fielder will never throw **behind** you.

Draw a throw

How far past first do you go on a base hit? It's a judgment call. First and foremost, you want to stay close enough that you do not get thrown out. But on the other hand, you want to get far enough out that you draw throws.

How far is that? Practice with the ball being hit to each of the three outfields. Start the batter about thirty feet from first to save time and energy, not at the plate. Just throw the ball to the outfield and order the outfielder to always throw behind the runner for this drill. This will show the runners how far away from the base they can get and still make it back.

But you must encourage your runners to draw throws whenever they are on base. A certain percentage of such plays will be errors and the runners will be able to advance on the error. It is bad baserunning and bad base coaching to never draw throws.

Advance on the throw to the wrong base

I drilled my runners to be on the lookout for a throw from the outfield to the **wrong base**. When the fielder made such a throw, my guys were trained to explode to the next base.

We drilled this with a runner rounding first and the outfielder throwing the ball to the pitcher or to third or home. The batter would round first watching the outfielder. If he throws other than to second, the runner would explode toward second.

This is a subtle point, but it won't happen if it's not coached. This is the kind of thing that drove my opponents nuts and was great fun for my kids.

This is also an example of why we were the best baserunning **defense** in the league. When our base runners were playing in the field, they knew that if they did not throw to second, the runner at first might advance.

Advancing on other errors

A throw to the wrong base is not the only opportunity to stretch a single into a "double." Train your runners to be alert for other opportunities like:

• inaccurate throw to the correct base
• uncovered base in front of you
• muff by fielder at the base ahead of you

Lead at first

Sometimes, you get to first and cannot advance on the play that got you there. In that case, you will be taking a lead on the pitch.

At the sub-teen level, you cannot take a primary (before the pitch) lead. But I do teach two primary **stances** at that level. If there are **no outs** or **one out**, I have the runner put his left foot beside the near edge of the base and face the plate. Except for the foot touching the base, this looks like the pro lead. Here's a diagram:

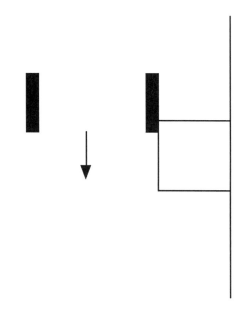

The arrow shows that the runner is facing home plate. Note that you take the lead at the back or outfield corner of the base. Why? Because you want to be as far as possible from the ball, which is now at the mound and will probably be at the catcher position after the pitch.

If you steal, you steal from the **back** of first base to the **back** of second base to be as far as possible from a throw from the pitcher or catcher. If the ball were hit to, say, right field, while you were stealing, you would slide into the **in**side corner of second to be as far as possible from the outfield throw.

At the teen level, if the first baseman moves in toward home in anticipation of a bunt, the runner at first should take a huge lead and steal when the pitcher's body starts to move.

Two-out stance

When there are two outs, I have my sub-teen players get into a sprinter's stance with their hands on the ground. They face the next base with their head turned to see the result of the pitch. They use the base as a starting block for their back foot, usually their dominant-side foot. Here's a diagram:

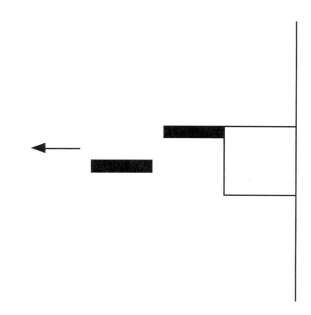

Logically, they could and should do this for **all** out situations. But I have found it hard to get the kids to differentiate between two-out and non-two-out situations. So I used these two stances as a way of making sure the kids did not wait to see if a fly was caught with two outs. As with failure to run through first, you should give additional reps to any kid who forgets to take off on a two-out fly ball.

Tag up

At the rookie level, you have to teach the whole idea of tagging up on a catchable fly with zero or one out. Kids at that level tend to treat **all** situations as if they were two outs. Then, when they get older, they go to the other extreme.

With tee-ball kids, explain the that you can be doubled off the base if you fail to tag up after a fly is touched. You also have to explain that they are forced to run if they are at first and there is a base hit.

The tee-ball drill is to put a kid at each of the three bases. Then throw balls from home plate—some grounders and some flies. Make sure some of the flies are **fouls** so that the kids learn you can tag up and advance on them also.

Have a fielder available, preferably a father, to catch some of the flies. This is like a "Simon Says" game. They lose if they fail to tag up on a fly or fail to run on a grounder. Losing means you stay for another rep. Those who do it right move on to the next drill.

This is a difficult concept for rookies. I have gotten many double and triple plays at the lowest levels because opposing runners did not tag up.

Touch, not catch

A tagging up runner takes off when the ball is **touched**, not when it is caught. You often see runners freeze when they are tagging up on a fly and the fielder muffs the ball. They were going to take off as soon as he caught the ball. But he unexpectedly **didn't** catch it. Now what?

Obviously, the answer is you run, but the surprise nature of the situation sometimes flummoxes the runner. To prevent this, I have a fielder deliberately muff flies while runners tagging at each base go when it touches his glove, regardless of whether he catches it or not.

Tag up BEFORE it comes down

For some reason unknown to me, runners, even at the teenage and semi-pro levels, seem to think all they have to do on a fewer-than-two-outs fly is being heading back toward the base they came from when it arrives at the fielder's glove. That is dead wrong.

They need to be "in the blocks" at the base ready to explode full speed toward the next base when the ball hits the fielder's glove. To make this happen, you need to practice it.

Put all your runners at first in a line. Throw a ball to the outfield. On the "hit," they all take a secondary lead. Then, when they see it is a fly, they go back and get their foot on the base ready to explode toward second when the ball is touched. The key point here is making sure they are "in the blocks" before the ball hits the fielder's glove.

'Half way'

Actually, at first you frequently do **not** tag up *per se* on a catchable fly. Rather you go "half way" to use the phrase so many coaches yell out. The more accurate phrase is "part way."

The basic idea is that second base is a close and therefore easy base to throw to from all three outfields so you generally cannot tag up on a catchable fly and still make it to second. Accordingly, you **assume** that it will **not** be caught and get as close to second as you can without risking being doubled off first if it is caught or tagged out going back if it is not.

The actual distance you should go is not "half way" literally. Rather it varies according to where the ball is hit. If it is hit to shallow right field, you'd better **not** go half way to second because you will get doubled off. The farther the ball is hit from first base, the farther off the base you can get when waiting to see if it is caught. It might be half way on a ball hit to center and two-thirds of the way on a ball hit to left.

But on the other hand, there **is** a distance where you could make it to second even if the ball was caught and you tagged up. That would be the **deep right and left field corners**. Maybe a deep hit to **any** field if your outfield has no fences or they are deep compared to the arms of the outfielders. If the ball is hit so far from second base that you think you could tag up and be safe there, you should tag up, **not** go "half way."

If runner on second, tag up

If there is a runner on second base, he will tag up, so the runner at first should also tag up. He cannot advance any farther than the runner ahead of him so he should mimic that runner.

If runner on third, tag up

If second base is open and there is a runner at third, tag up at first. The outfielder should try to stop the runner at **third** from scoring. While they are doing that, you **can** advance to second. Take off when the ball leaves the outfielder's hand.

Note that in many cases, especially at the lower levels of youth baseball, the outfielders are taught to always throw to second. In that case, you obviously should not go to second after your tag up. But you should try to draw a throw behind you by taking a big post-tag-up lead.

Walk off first after the fly is caught then explode toward second on the ball leaving the outfielder's hand in a first-and-third situation, but keep your eye on the ball and be ready to stop if he throws to second.

Always tag up on a foul fly

You always tag up on a **foul** fly at all bases. Why? Because a caught foul fly is the **only** kind of foul hit you can advance on. Always try to draw a throw if you do not try to get to the next base.

Never run into a tag

Even though you are forced at first when the batter puts the ball in play, you do not have to run all the way to second. You do not have to run anywhere. Normally, you go full speed to second. But if the ball is hit to the second baseman, and he is standing in the base path, stop. Make him chase you or throw to second for the force. Do not let him tag you where he caught the hit, then throw to first for a one-throw double play.

You have to give your kids one session practicing this.

Infield-fly rule

You need to learn the infield-fly rule and teach it to your base runners. The rule is much easier to remember if you understand why it exists. The purpose of the infield fly rule is to prevent cheap double plays.

On an infield fly, runners tag up to avoid being doubled off their bases. But if the fly ball hits the ground, runners that are forced suddenly have to get to the next base which is far away.

With runners on first and second, it would make sense for the infielder to pretend to catch the fly, then, at the last instant, deliberately let it drop. Then he would pick it up and throw it to the third baseman, who would then step on third and throw to second, thereby getting an easy double play. If the infielder catches the fly in the **air**, he only gets **one** out.

Force at third and less than two outs

To prevent this cheap double play, the infield-fly rule says the batter is automatically out if he hits an infield fly when there is a force at third and less than two outs. The hit must be fair and not a line drive.

Actually, the rule requires that the umpire yell out "Infield fly!" I have been told that the infield-fly rule does not apply unless the ump yell this, although I am skeptical because in the Major Leagues you often cannot hear the umpire.

Aside from the fact that most youth coaches don't have a clue what the infield-fly rule says, there a number of common misunderstandings about the infield-fly rule.

The **ball is not dead**. Many coaches think the ball is dead when the batter hits an infield fly in an infield-fly situation. Bull! The ball is **live**. Runners may advance if they wish, but they are not forced to because the batter is out. If your runners see a chance to advance, they should.

Advancing runners must be **tagged** out. If the defense wants to get your advancing runners out, they must tag them. In most cases, your opponents will not know the rule and will think they can get a force out. So it might be wise to run. When they do their force play, keep going and stay at the base after you arrive.

After a few minutes of arguing—hopefully there will be a competent ump—the other side will realize that the ball is live and that their failure to tag you means you are safe.

If the fly is **caught**, the runners must **tag up** before they advance. If they do not, they can be doubled off.

Against a team that knows the infield-fly rule—if

such a team exists in youth baseball—your runners should simply **stay put**. I used to tell my runners, "On an infield fly, you're a stay-put guy."

You have to give your guys a little practice recognizing infield-fly-rule situations and reacting correctly to them.

'Too advanced'

At times, I have been told in pre-game preliminaries that "We are not using the infield-fly rule in this game because it's too advanced." That always makes me smile. I then tell my fielders never to catch an infield fly in that game when there is force at third and try to get the cheap double play.

The infield-fly rule protects runners. Not having it leaves the runners unprotected. The notion that it is "advanced" just reveals that the speaker does not understand baseball.

If two outs, go on contact

Of course if there are two out, you go on contact without worrying whether it is caught. In other words, this business of what you do as a runner at first is a bit complicated. Here is a matrix that explains it.

Runner at 1st behavior on fly ball		
	less than 2 out	2 out
no runner at 2nd	part way	go on contact
runner at 2nd	tag up	

Two outs is a base runner's dream situation. I once scored from first on a base hit in a semi-pro game. How so? It was two outs and a full count. I took off on the pitch thinking scoring all the way. As I approached third, the coach waved me home. There was not even a play there.

In another game, I scored from second on an infield hit. The ball was hit to the third baseman. He moved toward the plate to field it while I was running behind him. I assumed that he would throw the runner out at first, but I knew I was supposed to go full speed toward home. The first baseman dropped the ball. I almost ran over the runner coming in from third. When I crossed the plate inches behind the third-base runner, my manager said, "Where'd you come from?"

I love being a runner with two outs.

The problem is that too many youth players are asleep and not aware of the outs. Even when they are aware, they do not understand what a great opportunity two outs is for a base runner. Make sure you teach your runners that two outs is heaven for a base runner so they will take full advantage of the situation.

Two outs, two strikes

If there are two outs and two strikes, the runner at first should go on the **swing**. Tim McCarver says to go in this situation when you see the ball will be in the strike zone, which would apply only at the teen level. It will either be a hit, a foul, or a strikeout, so there is no reason to wait and see when you are forced. This **always** applies to runners at first, but it also applies to runners at second and third when they are forced.

Two outs, full count

If there are two outs and a full count, all **forced** runners should go on the pitch. At the sub-teen level, you must wait until the ball gets to the plate, but you need not wait to see the result of the at bat. You must practice this because your kids will not believe or understand you if you just tell them to "go on the pitch."

I have been amused on a couple of occasions to see my opposing managers tell their **un**forced runners at second or third to go on the pitch with two outs and a full count. That's incorrect. With two outs, you do not want a runner at second or third to run into a tag. Make the fielder throw to first. This is more important at the youth level because of the increased incidence of errors. Again, you need to practice this so the kids understand. You only need one five-minute session.

At the teen level, the runners **must not leave too early**. It is common in a full-count, two-out situation for the pitcher to draw his leg up as if to pitch then continue to turn and throw a pick-off to second or throw to the corner base he is facing. The runner at third may be able to score on this pick-off play. The runners at first and second, if they get caught in this situation, should get into a pickle and stay alive until the runner at third crosses the plate. The best thing would be for everyone to dive back beating the pick-off throw.

If the pitch goes to the plate, no runner can get into trouble going on the pitch—because the result of a pitch must be a foul, base hit, walk, or the third out. But going "on the pitch" with two out and a 3-2 count is a very bad idea if what you thought was a pitch turned out **not** to be a pitch. "Go on the pitch" does **not** mean go on the pick-off.

Lead at first, teen level

At the teen level, you can take a pre-pitch lead.

When do you take that lead? **Not until the pitcher is on the rubber**. Why? Because that immunizes you from the **hidden-ball trick**. If the pitcher steps on or astride the rubber with**out** the ball, it is a **balk**. [Little League Rule 8.05(i)]

How long after he steps on the rubber do you wait to take your lead? You take it **immediately**. The pitcher may throw quickly, so you must take the lead immediately. You want to be at your maximum lead when he gets his sign from the catcher.

How do you leave the base? You leave the base taking **slide steps**. That is, you move your right foot out, then slide your left foot over next to the right foot. Then you do it again. Throughout, you are intently watching the pitcher for an early pick-off move. Your legs are bent in a good athletic ready position. Keep your hands off your doggone knees.

Some kids **hop** off the base. That is **wrong**. If the pitcher wheels around to throw a pickoff, you have to wait until you fall back to planet Earth before you can dive back to first. My pitchers watch for hopping leads and throw over early to take advantage of them. If you see a hopping lead, say to your pitcher, "Ehhh. What's up, Doc?"—Bugs Bunny's signature line.

Some kids **cross their legs** when taking a lead. You can get away with that on the **first** step, although I see no point. But if you do a crossover step on the second or third leadoff step, the pitcher should pick you off. Coaches should have a code word to alert their pitcher to that. It should be something seemingly unrelated like the idiotic "Throw strikes, Todd."

Peeking back at the base

Many players keep shooting looks back at the base as they take their lead and after they get to their maximum lead. This drives me nuts. I keep asking, "What are you afraid of? The base moving? It's attached to a concrete peg. It'll be right where you left it if you have to dive back. **STOP** doing that!"

Really, sports fans. If you take three slides steps to your **right** from a base, the location of the base from your max lead position is and will always be three slide steps to your **left**.

I teach my pitchers to throw a **pick-off** throw to a base if the runner shoots peek back at it as he takes his lead. We try to time it so we catch him in mid peek. The runner peeks, we throw to his base, as he brings his eyes back to the pitcher he sees the ball already on its way and hears his teammates yelling at him to get back. Too late.

Where do you take your lead? You take your lead off the **back** of the base on a straight line toward the back of second base. Again, you want to be as far away from the pick-off throw as possible.

Watch the right heel of a right-handed pitcher

As you take your lead, you watch the right heel of a right-handed pitcher. If it **lifts up**, you **dive back** to first. If the pitcher's body begins to move and the right heel stays down, take your secondary lead or steal.

Some people say to watch other parts of the pitcher's body. They never worked for me, but the right heel always did.

Left-handed pitcher pick-off

I am not sure what to watch on a left-handed pitcher.

The various baseball books all seem to say something different. In theory, if the pitcher's glove-side knee breaks the plane of the rubber, he must throw home or it's a balk. But when we tried to rely on that, we found the umpires saying they did not see the knee break the plane because they did not have the correct angle. In youth games, there are typically only two umpires and neither is on the plane of the rubber.

The glove-side knee may still work. In general, you can treat the glove-side knee as pointing at where you should go. If it points toward second, you can take your secondary lead or steal. If it points toward first, dive back. But I cannot guarantee that rule.

It is definitely harder to steal second against a left-handed pitcher because there is no way you can take off on first body movement the way you can with a right-handed pitcher. You have to leave later.

Help from the batter

The batter has the best angle to see a pickoff move. He should help runners at first against left-handed pitchers and runners at third against right-handed pitchers. He simply yells "Back!" if he sees a move toward the base instead of a pitch.

If I were coaching a teen team, I would try to **scout** opposing left-handed pitchers with a **video** camera, then identify the earliest indicator of a pickoff or pitch to home and show it to my players.

Drill this by putting one of your pitchers on the mound, a catcher at home, a first baseman at first, a middle infielder at second, and a runner at first. Have the runner take his lead. He has to steal on each pitch and dive back on each pickoff move. The pitcher should execute every trick in the book including early pick-offs, stepping off, regular pick-offs, and throwing home. Also have your catcher throwing pick-offs to first. This is a competitive drill and helps both offense and defense.

How far out?

We had a contest to see who could get the farthest away from first and still dive back. Each player would take his lead and we would mark his outer foot on the ground. If he got back safely, we would make another mark a little farther out and make him try from there. We kept pushing the mark out farther until he got picked off. It was a competition with yourself to establish a new personal best. It was also a competition with your teammates to see who could take the biggest lead.

My son Dan, won. It was those huge leads, not his speed, that made him look so fast to parents in the crowd. When he subsequently played for other coaches, they would see him take his lead and start screaming, "Get back! Get back!" We tried to explain to them that they should leave Dan alone. But most coaches are ignorant of good baserunning and very timid. A chain is only as strong as its weakest link. The weak link in baserunning on the vast majority of youth teams is the ignorant, chicken coach.

Average players can get to about ten or twelve feet. But most players only take a five to eight-foot lead. This is an outrage. Roger Clemens could not pick off a guy with a five- to eight-foot lead. If a baseball player (and/or his coach) is that big of a coward he ought to find another sport. In his book *The Game According to Syd*, Syd Thrift says a professional pickoff throw to first takes one second and that the average runner can get back from a 12-foot lead in one second.

Many of my players "graduated" from my teams as super base runners, only to move up in subsequent seasons to new coaches who would never give them the green light. What a waste!

Many pitchers afraid to throw to first

Many youth pitchers lack confidence in their pick-off move—with good reason. With those guys, take an extra long lead and if they do try to pick-off, go to second. They are also likely to throw the ball away. That's why they lack confidence in their pick-off move.

How to dive back

You dive back by taking one crossover step with your right foot then laying out and diving. Your right hand lands on **top** of the **near** edge of the **back** of the base. Do **not slide** into the **side** of the base. You'll jamb your fingers. Rather you fall down on **top** of it. Here's a diagram:

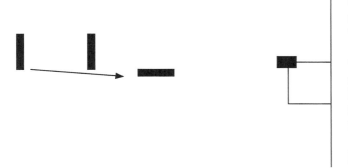

On TV, you frequently see the runner at first go back to first **standing up**. I have no idea what that's about. If he was that close, the pitcher should not have thrown over. Also, if he was that close, he did not have a big enough lead.

'Up by seven'

Taking a huge lead can have other repercussions. In a 1993 semi-pro game, I took my usual huge lead off first in the second inning of a game. Because of my huge lead, the pitcher threw over a couple of times. About the third time he threw over, I made it back safely, but the umpire shocked everyone by calling me out, ending the inning. My teammates went nuts. I was the player-manager and quietly told them to cool it.

Later, when I walking out to my position at the end of a half-inning, I stopped by that ump and quietly asked, "Why'd you call me out on that pick-off?"

"You were up by seven. Wasn't that enough?"

He saw my huge lead as an attempt to run up the score and he thought I needed to be taught a lesson. Our team had lost plenty of games where we had big leads. To me, I was just doing the same thing I always did, playing good baseball.

I laughed and said, "If you think a seven-run lead is safe, you haven't seen my team play."

Full windup is automatic steal at teenage level

Once, in adult baseball, one of my teammates stole second and made it look extremely easy. There was no throw or slide. When he got back to the dugout, I asked, "How did you do that?"

"Pitcher did a full windup," was his answer. He explained that it was automatic that you stole second or third if the pitcher forgot that there was a runner on base and pitched from a full windup. In those two cases, you **do** go on the pitcher's glove-side heel starting to move backwards.

Also, the batter in such a case **must not swing** unless he has two strikes and the pitch is near the strike zone.

We had a code word for this: "Patient." If we saw a pitcher get on the mound in a full windup with a runner on and an open base in front of the runner, we would say to the **batter**, not the runner, "Be patient, Todd," or whatever the batter's name was.

We did **not** speak to the **runner**, because we did not want the pitcher to be reminded that there **was** a runner. We found that this situation came up a lot in youth baseball, but the runners were as asleep as the pitchers. So we needed a code word to wake up our runner and batter, but not the pitcher.

Be ready to go to second on a pick-off error

After you dive back into first, you cannot relax. You must immediately see if the throw got past the first baseman. Make sure you see the actual ball. Sometimes the first baseman will tear off into foul territory as if he missed the ball when he actually caught it, trying to decoy you into leaving the base.

You need to practice this at least once to get your players into the habit of immediately getting ready to run if the ball gets past the first baseman.

Straight steal of second

It is almost standard to steal second base on the first pitch after you get to first in sub-teen youth baseball.

Still, too many players and coaches are too timid. If the catcher is really good, and the runner is slow, it may be better to wait for a passed ball. But in general, players and coaches wait far too long to steal second.

Every pitch you delay increases the risk that you will be forced at second or fail to score on a double because you were still on first when it was hit. On one team, we had two adult base coaches. When there was only a runner at first and no runners on, we had an adult base coach at first and a kid coach at third. When the lead runner got to second, the adult base coach at first would step back behind the first-base dugout and a kid would replace him.

In my experience, many kids are reluctant to steal even though they are quite fast enough to succeed. Kid base coaches cannot get them to go. Adult base coaches can. You almost need a cattle prod to get some kids out of there.

Count your steps

Tony Gwynn, who is great at getting the most out of a relatively untalented body, counts his steps to second like a long jumper. He says he takes a 4 1/2-step lead, then runs 10 1/2 steps before he starts his slide. The number of steps you take vary according to your height and speed.

Easier on an off-speed pitch

It is easier to steal any base on an off-speed pitch, like a curve, than it is to steal a base on a fastball, for the obvious reason that the flight time of the pitch is a factor in how fast the ball can get to the base you are stealing.

Alert to a passed ball

If the kid cannot steal because of his speed and the catcher's arm, he should be hyper alert for a passed ball and advance then. Some kids are so timid that they won't even go on a passed ball. You have got to get those kids moving.

At the sub-teen level, you cannot leave until the ball gets to the plate. But you can anticipate leaving if you see that the pitch is heading for the dirt. Rare is the sub-teen catcher who can throw a runner out at second after digging a ball out of the dirt.

Two bases on a passed ball four

If the passed ball occurs on a ball-four pitch, you are guaranteed the next base if you are forced. But thhe batter may be able to take a **second** base as well. Remember a walk is a live ball. Not everyone knows that. The defense team may suffer a momentary loss of concentration after a passed ball four. Your runners should be alert to take advantage.

First step of a steal

You do the first step of a steal a certain way. Make a **crossover** step with your left foot. Stepping first with your right foot is too slow because you can only step about six to twelve inches. A crossover step covers more ground.

Fake steal

In the fake steal, you do the same thing, but sort of run in place just traveling about ten or twenty feet. You should take a shorter primary lead at the teen level so you can run farther in your fake mode. I put this in one week before we had a practice game with a higher level team.

We were called 11-12 minors. They were AAA. In theory, the **worst** player on their **team** was better than the **best** player in our **league**, let alone on my team. That's because our league was made up of the kids left over after the AAA teams picked their teams.

Actually, my team was pretty good. There must have been some politics involved in a number of my players not being in the higher league.

We ended up beating the AAA team, to the enormous embarrassment of the AAA coach, who ended the game early claiming he had promised the field to another team. I stayed afterward at the nearby snack bar. No other team ever arrived.

Drove them nuts

One of the things that drove the AAA team nuts was our newly-learned fake steals. We had to use fake steals against them because their catchers could throw to second much better than the ones in our league.

The first time we did a fake steal, the catcher threw to second. Since the runner had not stolen, the catcher looked foolish. Same thing happened the second time we did the fake steal. Now the catcher looked even more foolish.

Advance on throw behind

The third time we tried it, the catcher threw to **first**. I had taught my players that if the catcher throws **behind** you, go to second. The runner went to second without even a throw there because kids that age cannot throw fast enough to get the ball to first, then second in the time it takes a kid with a big secondary lead to get to second.

Whether to go to second on a fake steal where the catcher throws behind you is a function of the level at which you are coaching. At teenage levels, this would be less likely to work.

By now, the catcher has decided he ain't throwing **anywhere**. The manager has stopped yelling, "He's going!" because he, too, has been made the fool.

Boy who cried wolf

What do you do now? A straight steal of course. It's like the boy who cried wolf. You faked a steal three times. Now when you actually go, the catcher will hesitate to **make sure** you are really stealing. He who hesitates is lost. This way, a kid who is too slow to steal against a strong-armed catcher can succeed in stealing. Furthermore, even the faster runners on the team will be helped by their teammates' fake steals earlier in the game.

Also, sometimes the catcher's throw to second on the fake steal will end up in the outfield. You can also get to second on many of those overthrows. The fake steal also sets up the **delayed** steal on the catcher's throw back to the pitcher because they start ignoring your large secondary lead. You explode toward second on a fake steal, then, when the catcher throws back to the pitcher, and you are still going toward second albeit almost jogging in place, you explode to second as soon as the ball leaves the catcher's hand.

In the 11-12 minors league, we generally did not **need** the fake steal. We could do a straight steal. But about half-way through the season, one of the opposing catchers got the range and started throwing us out at second. So, thereafter, when we played him, we made much use of the fake steal. The fake steal may get the offense a ball call on a pitch that was really a strike if the catcher responds to the fake steal by standing up prematurely to throw to a base and blocking the plate umpire's view of the pitch.

The fake steal is a legitimate tactic. Just because you don't see it on TV doesn't change that. I did not invent it. I got it out of baseball books. Other than runner fatigue, there is no reason not to do a fake steal on **every** play which is not a real steal. The more fake steals the better.

Secondary lead at first

A secondary lead is one you take after your primary lead. The primary lead is pre-pitch.

At the sub-teen level, you take your secondary lead after the pitch reaches the plate. The runner should assume a base hit initially and start toward second. As he is doing that, he must read the actual result of the pitch. If a hit leaves the bat at a downward angle in fair territory, the runner at first must take off full speed toward second. The same is true of **any** two-out hit, toward the ground or not.

On a less-than-two-out fly ball, he must react according to where it is hit and whether there is a runner at second as described earlier in the chapter. On a line drive, you freeze. If it goes through the infield, you take off for second full speed. If it is caught, you dive back to first.

You must **practice** the secondary lead at first and the runners reaction to various results. Have a coach at the plate **throw** the ball instead of a batter hitting it in order to get all the situations you want.

Going back to first after the pitch

Many times, you will want to go back to first after the pitch. First, don't get picked off by the catcher. Second, try to get the catcher to **try** to pick you off. You do that by being far away from first and/or by seeming not to be paying attention.

Don't go back on your own initiative. Make the catcher **force** you back. At the sub-teen level, the pitcher can force you back by throwing the next pitch because the rules say you have to be touching first when the pitch reaches the plate.

At the teen level, you **never** have to go back, although the base is a good place to be when your attention is directed away from the ball, like to get your signs. Remember that you are vulnerable to the hidden-ball trick as long as the pitcher is not on the mound.

Sliding

Sliding is crucial to good baserunning. Time and again every season my kids would be safe even though they arrived after the throw did. They slid **under the tag**.

As I said elsewhere in the book, I trained my fielders to put the tag on the ground. Most coaches do not. So if you combine that bad habit of tagging high with sliding low, you get a lot of bases you did not deserve.

More importantly, your runners arrive earlier at the base if they know how to slide properly. Players who do not know how to slide, which is almost all of them, slow way down as they approach a base.

Figure-four, pop-up slide

I teach the figure-four, pop-up slide. The head-first slide is so dangerous that it ought to be outlawed at all levels, certainly in youth baseball. In the figure-four slide, the runners **sits** down on **both** butt cheeks. The leg that touches the base first is bent slightly (about 160 degrees) at the knee. The first thing to come into contact with the base is the **heel** of this foot. The other leg is bent at a right angle at the knee. The ankle of the right-angle-bent leg is directly under the other knee. Here's an **aerial** view showing the moment of contact with the base.

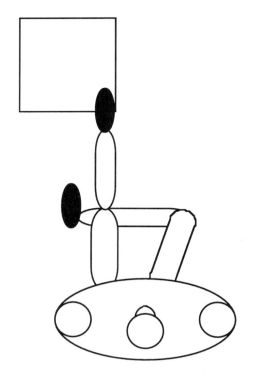

You can see the figure-four position of the legs in the aerial view. Here's a **side** view:

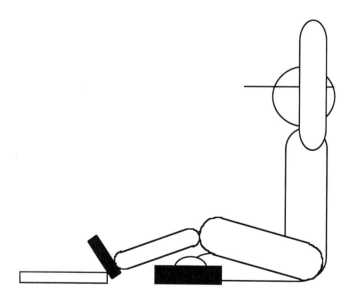

Note:

• The player is sitting **straight up**, not leaning back. This is crucial to being able to pop-up after you reach the base. Lying on your back is a common mistake.

• **Arms are raised up** as if a robber said, "Hands up!" This is to prevent injury to the hands. Major Leaguers often carry a batting glove or grass in each hand to remind themselves to keep their hands off the ground.

• **Left heel is slightly above ground** so it does not drag.

• The outside of the right leg and foot are dragging on the ground. This and the butt cheeks are what bring the runner to a quick stop.

It does not matter which leg you tuck under and which leg you contact the base with. Just pick the one that's most comfortable.

Tuck leg is last to step

Your last step is with your tuck leg. After your last step, you tuck that leg under the other. You reach out toward the base with your non-tuck leg.

Sit, don't jump

The most common mistake is a painful, dangerous one. Players think they are supposed to jump **up** in the air with their last step. No way. That hurts, It slows you down prematurely. And it makes you more susceptible to a high tag.

Just **sit**. Your hips are at a certain level as you run. When you slide, they just go straight down, never up.

Pop-up

After your heel makes contact with the base, and you are safe, you continue to slide. When the shin of your tuck leg hits the base, your momentum and movement propels you up to a standing position.

You want to do this at second and third because there is often an error at the base and you can advance to the next base as well. You cannot advance quickly if you are lying on your back. The pop-up is especially important in youth baseball because of the high incidence of errors.

Sit straight up

In addition to lying on their back, players tend to lean to one side. There is some logic to leaning away from the direction of the throw, but that increases the chances of injury from not spreading the contact out over the widest possible body area.

One of my helper fathers once said, after I taught this slide, that he saw Mark McGwire slide into a base exactly this way. I did not make this slide up either. It's standard stuff.

Step one: figure-four position

Start by having each player sit in the figure-four position. You can do this *en masse*.

Then have the player sit in the figure-four position

and push the base at him until his top leg collapses back and his tuck shin hits the base.

Then have them stand on one leg—the one they plan to extend toward the base—put the tuck leg in the figure-four position, and sit down.

Cardboard

You finish teaching sliding with a large piece of cardboard. I brought such a piece of cardboard to almost every game and practice. Have the kids take their shoes off. If they keep their shoes on, the cleats get caught in the cardboard which injures the players and shreds the cardboard too quickly.

But a loose, soft base or baseball glove at one end to represent the base. They run at it from about 30 feet away. Focus on technique. Insist on perfect execution.

If a player does it right, he is excused to move onto the next station. If a player does it wrong, he goes back in line and does it again.

Some of the times, have the players pop-up and sprint to their left as if go to the next base. You do not want them to get in the habit of behaving as if the slide is the end of the play.

Wet grass?

Many people think you teach sliding by wetting the grass and sliding on it. Maybe at a college where you have a locker room, showers, and a change of clothes. You can't do that in youth baseball where the kids will be picked up by the parents at the end of practice.

Every practice and pre-game

One of the big differences between competent and incompetent coaches is that competent ones know **how long** it takes to get players to learn each skill. My base runners had better sliding technique than any others I have ever seen in youth baseball, year in and year out. But I am not the only coach who knows proper sliding technique. The difference is that I figured out over the years that it takes almost the whole season to get the kids to slide correctly.

My players practice sliding at **every practice and at every pre-game**. That means we had about thirty sessions of practicing sliding.

Teaching versus parenting

A lot of people say coaching is teaching. I say teaching is only part of it. I think parenting is the better analogy.

Parents **teach** their kids to eat with the right fork. They **teach** their kids how to buckle a seat belt. They **teach** their kids how to button their shirt. But if all a parent ever did was teach, they would have some rotten kids.

Parents earn their money not with their teaching, but with their **disciplining** and **motivating**. There is

an article about this at my football Web site www.johntreed.com/parenting.html.

They don't want to

I have a news flash for you: kids do not **want** to slide. It hurts.

Another news flash: That's tough. They **must** learn to slide, if only for their own safety.

You need to **teach** them how to slide. But that's only the beginning. Then you have to **insist** that they **do** slide.

As I said elsewhere in the book, you must urge the players to pad up. They need to wear a knee pad on their tuck knee and they need to wear some sort of sliding pants under their uniform.

Then you have to run the slide drill over and over insisting on perfect execution before the particular player is allowed to move on.

My 11-12 team started to complain about the slide drill about three-quarters of the way through the season. By then, they really had it and were quite good at it. If and when you reach that point, you can and probably should have only the few players who are still refusing to slide in games do the drill.

Approaching second

You go into second in one of two ways:

• slide
• round the base

You slide when you think there might be a play there. If there is not a play there, you need to either look at your third-base coach or make your own decision about whether you are going to third.

You cannot consult the third-base coach if there is a runner ahead of you. The coach will be directing that runner. Although if he is sending that runner home, you certainly have an open base at third. On the other hand, if the third-base coach stops the lead runner, the runner approaching second also must stop because he has nowhere to go.

In general, the trailing runner should mimic the lead runner. If he goes, you go, because the fielders will generally go after the lead runner. There are exceptions, of course, like when a fielder is standing between you and the next base holding the ball. You never run into a tag.

If there is **no runner ahead** of you, and the ball was hit **behind** you to right field, the runner approaching second base needs to rely on the third-base coach regarding whether to advance to third.

If the ball is hit in front of you to center or left field, you do **not need** to consult the third-base coach on whether you should advance and you should not. Your own decisions are quicker than decisions made by others then communicated to you.

Breaking up a double play

Do not teach youth baseball players to deliberately slide into middle infielders to break up double pays. I know it's standard baseball. It's also unethical. The rules say the runner has the right to slide into the **base**. But they also say he has no right to go off elsewhere chasing the fielder so he can ram him.

True, the umps are scandalously resistant to enforcing this rule. But umpire timidity does not excuse deliberate unethical behavior by a coach.

Injury risk

At the youth level, there is an important safety issue. Collisions between unprotected kids kill a couple of children per year in youth baseball, soccer, and other sports. The body of a child is uniquely vulnerable to cardiac arrest from upper-body trauma.

What double play?

At the youth level, there is also an ability issue. Youth baseball players do not have the ability to execute a two-throw, double-force play successfully. Unfortunately, their coaches are too dumb to know that so they teach and practice two-throw, double-force plays, and youth players try to execute them in games, thereby setting up this situation where Neanderthals think the right thing to do is for the runner to ram his unprotected body into the fielder's unprotected body.

Youth players can hardly ever complete a two-throw, double-force play, but if you teach your players to ram the opposing middle infielder, they will execute that dangerous ram every time.

In other words, you do not **need** to break up the double play at youth levels other than the elite teenage level. They cannot execute the play fast enough or accurately enough. So if you teach your runners to break up double plays, they will unnecessarily risk injury and penalty to themselves as well as risking injury to their opponent. As an adult coach, you have a responsibility to protect both your own players and those of your opponents.

No one covering third base

Especially in youth baseball, third base is often uncovered. In that case, assuming third is also unoccupied, the runner approaching second must continue on to third regardless of where the ball was hit or whether the fielder can throw it to third before the runner gets there.

Practice approaching second

You need to practice approaching second base. The practice should include a middle infielder, third base-man, third-base coach, and outfielders as well as a runner approaching second and, sometimes, one approaching third. The practice script should include the above scenarios:

	Runners	
Situation	1	1 & 2
hit to right		
hit to left		
hit to center		
3rd uncovered		
error at 2nd		

Approaching second base with a mind toward going to third if at all possible is an extremely important aspect of baserunning. Aggressive baserunning is not just something you do **after** a pitch. It is also something you do after a hit and **during** a play.

If you put a telephoto camera on the faces of base runners in my games, I suspect you would see a distinct difference between my players and the other team's. The **opponent's** players would have their eyes focused on the base they were approaching and they would have a look of relief that they were arriving safely. My guys, on the other hand, would come into a base with their eyes darting between the ball, their base coach, the lead runner (if any), and the next base looking for an opening to exploit.

Attack! Attack! Attack! Always alert to opponent mistakes.

Taking a lead at second base

At the sub-teen level, you take a lead at second the same as at first. The rules preclude anything else. You can generally take a bigger **secondary** lead at second because it is a longer pick-off throw for the catcher.

At the teen level, the lead at second is complicated. There are three situations:

• runner at 2nd is forced
• runner at second is not forced less than two outs
• runner at second is not forced two outs

Lead when runner is forced

If the runner at second is **forced**, he takes his lead the same as at first. That is, off the outfield side of the base and on a straight line to the outfield side of third base. The one difference between taking a lead at second when you are forced and taking a lead at first, where you are always forced, is the responsibility of the **base coach**.

At first base, you generally assume that the first baseman is holding you if there is no runner on second. Also, he positions himself in front of the base so the runner can **see** him. If the first baseman does not hold the runner at first because of another runner on second, the runner at first may be able to take a bigger lead depending upon how far away the first baseman gets from the base. In this case, the first baseman is **behind** the runner so he relies on the first-base coach.

The first-base coach controls the runner in that situation by saying "Out" or "Back." In response, the runner takes **one step and only one step**. If the coach wants the runner to move another step in the same direction he repeats the word. One word, one step. Two words, two steps; and so forth.

At second, the **runner** is generally responsible for watching the **second baseman** and the **third-base coach** is responsible for the **shortstop**. That's because the runner can see the second baseman, but he cannot see the shortstop. If there is no runner at first, the first-base coach watches the second baseman.

Both base coaches say "Back" as necessary. Only the third-base coach can say "Out." I wonder if those base-coach roles should not be reversed. Instead of having the base coach watch the **closest** middle infielder, maybe he should watch the farthest because he has a **better angle**. Runners at third generally do not need base-coach help.

Lead with less than two outs, no force

With less than two outs, you take your lead at second **three feet behind the base line**. Why? Because with no force, you will not be in a great hurry to get to third. If you were in a great hurry, you could just not go.

Since you are not in a great hurry, you will only go to third when there will be no chance of a play there so you can round third base thinking about scoring. By lining up behind the base line, you give yourself a better angle to round third and go home.

Lead with two outs no force

With two outs and no force, you take your lead **ten** feet behind the base line. Why? You are going on contact with the bat, unless the ball is fielded by the third baseman or shortstop in front of you. You do **not want to run into a tag**. Force the fielder to throw all the way to first to get the third out.

You also do not want to get caught in a pickle at the teenage level. At the sub-teen level, getting caught in a pickle is less of a problem.

If the ball is **not** hit to the third baseman or shortstop, you take off full speed rounding third and watching the third-base coach to see if you should go home.

In the discussion about approaching second, I said you were always looking for an opportunity to go to the next base. Going into third that is even more true because taking another base when approaching third means scoring a run. Runners and base coaches should be much more aggressive about trying to score from second base, especially with two outs.

Competitive take-two-bases drill

One of the competitive drills I run involves a runner at first trying to get to third on a base hit or a runner at second trying to score on a base hit. I throw the ball to an outfielder and the runner **has to** try to go two bases. This gives the outfielders great practice at throwing the ball in on a line-drive trajectory without hesitation, and it gives the runners a strong sense of how often they can advance two bases on a hit. At the lower levels of youth baseball, you should almost always go two bases except for a hit to shallow left when you are at first. This drill is so much fun my pitcher-infielders often ask if they can play outfield to try their hand at throwing people out at third or home.

Get a decent lead

For some reason, teen runners at second are scared to death of being held on. At first, with the first baseman holding them, they take a ten- or twelve-foot lead. Then the same runner gets to second, the shortstop momentarily darts over to second base, and the runner panics and decides he has to be within three feet of the base. What's that about?

If you can take a twelve-foot lead at first with the first baseman standing on the bag waiting for a throw, why can't you take at least the same lead at second with the baseman running toward the base?

You need to practice this so your players relax and understand that middle infielders darting it and out toward the base are **less** of a threat than a first baseman in the normal hold-the-runner position.

Do not tolerate this nonsense. Give your players however many practice reps they need to relax and get a proper lead.

Straight steal of third

Youth baseball players are generally more reluctant to steal third than second. That is correct at the sub-teen level. They cannot take a lead and the catcher is much closer to third than second.

However, at the teen level, it is another story. Major League base stealers like Rickey Henderson say it's easier to steal third because you can get a bigger lead at second base.

Walking lead

You can sometimes get a walking lead at second. Normally, that is not a good idea. But many youth teams are so poorly trained that you could get away with it.

Against a well-trained team, you start your steal the same as you do at first base. Your third-base coach will tell you whether to stay up or slide. Be ready to pop-up and go home in the case of an error.

Delayed steal

This is one of my specialties. We usually do it at second, although it can be done from any base. In one type of delayed steal, you break for the next base when the ball leaves the catcher's hand on his throw back to the pitcher.

Ideally, the runner at second should take a longer and longer secondary lead after successive pitches. He must be careful to do so nonchalantly and unobtrusively.

He must **not** attract any attention. I have had some kids who dance off the base very aggressively attracting all kinds of attention to themselves when they are getting ready to do the delayed steal.

Timeout. "What the heck are you doing.? You want to make them **forget** that you exist, not get them thinking you are going to steal. Stop that doggone dancing."

Indications and contra indications

This play works best when the catcher **lobs** the ball back to the pitcher. It is also good if the catcher **stays in the catcher's box** and the pitcher **stays on the mound** for the throw back to the pitcher. Also, some pitchers help the delayed steal by getting into the ritual of **strolling toward first after each throw** back from the catcher. Some catchers get into the bad habit of **dropping to their knees** after they catch the pitch and conclude that the runner is not going, but before they throw back to the pitcher. Your runner could take off as the catcher initiates his drop to his knees. It's hard to put yourself in a fall then stop in mid fall and throw to a base.

The delayed steal works less well when the **catcher zips the ball back** to the pitcher or when the pitcher and catcher **walk toward each other** after every pitch. I have protested that this is a delay of the game with some success. I do not allow my battery to do that. You can also do a delayed steal on a **pick-off throw** to your base or any other base either from the catcher or the pitcher.

The third baseman should go to third after each pitch when there is a runner at second. The play is more likely to work when the opposing third baseman does not know he should be going to third. This happens frequently, especially with teams where the coach believes in rotating his fielders through all the positions.

A delayed steal from **first** works a little better if the batter is **left**-handed. Ditto a delayed steal from **third** or **home** if the batter is **right**-handed.

Walking secondary lead

Ideally, you will get a walking secondary lead. That is you will be slowly walking toward third when the catcher throws back to the pitcher.

Break on daylight

When the runner sees daylight between the hand of the catcher and the ball, he explodes toward third base. After a second, the defense usually explodes in shouts. The pitcher usually has his back to the runner and won-

ders what the heck everybody is yelling about. By the time he turns to see, it is too late.

The third baseman sees what is happening, but he is not mentally prepared for it and it takes him a second or two to realize he needs to go cover third base. Often, there is not even a throw to third. We were hardly ever thrown out at third on this play. When we were, it was the second or third time we executed the play against the team in question.

Georgie

In 1993, my **oldest** son was on a AAA team for 11- and 12-year olds. I was managing my **youngest** son's tee ball team that year so I only helped out with the AAA team.

In one game, a kid I coached the year before was on the opposing team and reached second base. Let's call him Georgie. Georgie was chunky—maybe more than chunky. He was also slow. But he was smart.

When he got to second in the 1993 AAA game against my son's team, it appeared to me that he was fixing to do a delayed steal. I walked over to the chain link fence "dugout" and said to the manager, "See that runner on second? That's Georgie. He is a graduate of the Jack Reed School of Baserunning. He was on my team last year. I think he's getting ready to do a delayed steal. You'd better warn your pitcher and catcher."

The manager looked at the very chunky kid on second and figured, "Yeah, right." He gave no warning.

On the next pitch, Georgie executed a perfect delayed steal of third, so perfect there was not even a throw. The manager turned to look at me and I gave him an "I told you so" shrug.

My son usually played catcher when he was not pitching. But on that AAA team, they usually put another kid at catcher. If my son had been the catcher, Georgie probably would not have tried it.

If he had tried to do a delayed steal against my son, Dan would have called a timeout and explained what was happening to the pitcher, third baseman and shortstop. Then he would have taken countermeasures like pump faking a throw to the pitcher, throwing to the shortstop away from the bag, asking the pitcher to come toward home to get the ball. The delayed steal is not a hard play to stop, but it will work great if the runner can use the element of surprise.

Three delayed steals in a row

One of my youth football players came over to my house with his dad when baseball season started. I taught him how to do a delayed steal. His dad later told me that at the next game, his son did a delayed steal of second, then third, then home on three successive pitches. I guess you don't always need the element of surprise.

Always tag on a less than two-out fly at second and third

You always tag up on a catchable fly when there are less than two outs at second and third base. Actually, if you want to get technical, you tag up whenever you are not sure you would not be able to advance to the next base on the tag up. For example, if the fly is hit to shallow left field, you probably cannot go to the next base on a tag up. In that case, get off the base to improve your chances of advancing after the muff, but not so far that you cannot get back in case the ball is caught in the air. As always, draw throws.

Fake advance after a tag up

A fake advance after a tag up is like a fake steal. It is a way to draw throws, which may result in errors that would allow a runner to advance. To do a fake advance after a tag up, tag up, then explode toward the next base when the ball is touched. But take baby steps after the first few steps so you do not get too far from the previous base.

Passed balls

Passed balls are extremely common in youth baseball. If there are a lot of them at your level, you should probably not take too many risks stealing. Just wait for a passed ball.

I am not saying don't steal when there are a lot of passed balls. I am saying be less aggressive about **risking** getting thrown out. If the catcher who cannot keep the ball in front of him cannot throw to second either, you are a fool to wait for a passed ball.

You should **practice** advancing on passed balls. For one thing, your extremely timid runners need it. Also, it is important to practice advancing on passed balls at third because your runners need experience to tell how good of a passed ball they need to make it home.

This is a good time to run a **competitive** drill so your pitchers and catchers can practice stopping a steal of home on a passed ball. I think runners and coaches at third are too timid about going home on a passed ball where the catcher will have to throw to the pitcher. If the catcher can make the tag on his own, you should not go. But in youth baseball, it is very hard for the pitcher and catcher to make the connection quickly and without error.

Making the first or third out at third

There is an old saying in baseball that you should never make the first or third out at third. I can see some logic to that. If there are no outs and you are at second, there is a decent chance you will be able to advance to third on a passed ball, walk, or hit. But, sometimes, if you fail to take an opportunity to advance to third, you may find that you never score. I don't think you can say **never** make the first out at third. But I agree that

you should be a little more conservative that early in an inning.

Unforced walk to third

My oldest son always wanted to try this, but it never came up. He wanted to walk to third from second after a base on balls was given up to the batter—when there was no runner on first. He figured the defense would not notice that he was unforced. I suspect that if you did it, the defensive coach would think you had to go back. Nope. A walk is a live ball. Unforced runners may advance at their own risk.

Walk on ball three

I got this from Cliff Petrak, the author of The Art and Science of Aggressive Baserunning. With a runner at first, your batter works the count to two balls and a strike or two. You give an innocuous verbal signal to the batter and runner. It means, if you get ball three, both of you pretend you thought it was ball four. The runner at first trots over to second and the batter drops his bat and trots to first base.

Petrak, who is a high school coach with over thirty years of experience, has done this play three times in high school games. It worked all three times. The first time, no one said anything and the umpire, after consulting his ball-strike-out counter several times, shrugged his shoulders, cleared it back to an 0-0 count and called for the next batter! In the more normal situation, the opposing team says, "Hey! That was only ball three!" The batter then comes back to the plate. When they say the runner at second has to go back to first, you ask, "Why?" Time was not requested by either team or granted by the umpire. There was no foul ball. The ball was live at all times. The runner at first simply stole second, albeit at a trot.

Advancing from second to third on a grounder to the shortstop or third baseman

As a general rule, an unforced runner at second can advance to third when the shortstop or third baseman throws to first. Be careful on a ball hit to the pitcher. The runner should take a small secondary lead, not enough to get picked off. Although I have never seen a runner get picked off second on a grounder to short or third. Often in this situation, no one covers second base. As soon as the ball leaves the hand of the infielder, explode to third.

You should practice this a bit. It would be a **competitive** drill in which the defense either tries to pick the runner off second or they try to hold him and still get the runner at first. The defense loses if they get no outs or if they get the batter out, but the runner at second advances to third.

You must put it into the minds of the runners that

they can advance on this play. And you must put it into the minds of the fielders that they should not ignore the runner at second.

In the Northeastern region of the 1999 Little League championships, a Toms River, NJ base runner went from second to third on a cleanly-fielded 6-3 play then scored on a cleanly-fielded 2-3 bunt out. Nicely done.

Advancing to third on a grounder to right side

In general, if the ball is hit past the pitcher to the first baseman or second baseman and they have to throw to first for the out, you can make it to third on the hit. I would not, however, try to go to third if the ball is hit close to first and the first baseman can step on the base himself early. Try this in practice so the runners can learn their limitations.

Advancing to third when the third-base runner is caught in a rundown

If your teen third-base runner gets caught in a rundown with less than two outs, the runner at second should advance to third. With two outs, you need to leave third base open so the runner caught in the rundown has the most options to avoid making the last out of the inning.

Taking a lead at third

You take your lead at third **in foul territory**. This is the only base where you can do this and you should to take advantage of the rule that says you are not out if you are hit by a batted ball in foul territory. Here's a diagram for the pre-pitch, sub-teen lead at third:

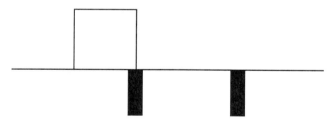

At the teen level, you want to get a foot or two farther out into foul territory to make sure the umpire does not think you were in fair territory when you were hit by a batted ball. Plus, you want to take a big pre-pitch lead at the teen level. In general, you can take your biggest lead at third because the third baseman rarely holds you. On the other hand, a right-handed pitcher can make a deceptive move to third.

You rarely see pick-offs to third, but my kids take such enormous leads that we do draw those throws. (Remember that runners should always be trying draw throws—both pre-pitch and during plays.) A certain percentage of those throws get by the third baseman and then we score.

Try to get a **walking lead** at third. The pitcher should make you stop, but in youth baseball, he may not be trained well enough to do that. If the third baseman move is real close to be ready for a **bunt**, the runner at third should **follow him** because there is no one to throw to back at third base. The coach can watch the shortstop and left fielder.

If you cannot make it home safely on a tag play, don't run into the tag. Get into a pickle and make them take a lot of time to get you so your trailing runners can advance behind you. If you run into a tag, the defense may be able to go after the other runners so quickly that they cannot advance.

Runner hit by batted ball

Almost all youth coaches think a runner hit by a batted ball is out. That's not true. What the rule says is that a runner who is hit by a batted ball is out **only if the ball has not passed the nearest non-pitcher infielder** when it hits the runner.

For example, if the first baseman is holding the runner on first and playing **in front of** the runner, a ball that is hit to the first baseman, but gets through him does not make the runner out if it then hits him. Same is true of a ball that hits a runner after being **deflected** by an infielder.

Understanding the **purpose** of the rule helps you remember it. The purpose of the rule is to discourage runners from deliberately getting hit by the ball to help themselves and the batter get to the next base safely.

So if a runner gets hit **before** the infielder has a chance to field the ball, he is out and the ball is dead. But once the batted ball gets by the infielder, the runner would have no incentive to get hit by it and thereby keep it in the infield. So a runner getting hit by a ball **after** an infielder has had his chance to catch it is meaningless. The ball remains **live** and the runner is **not** out.

Secondary lead at third

The secondary lead at third should be a foot outside the foul line.

You need to be alert for a catcher pick-off. Third is close to home and a runner at third is far more of a scoring threat than one at first. You can take a longer secondary lead at third if the batter is right-handed than you can if he is left-handed.

Going back to third

You go back to third base **on** the base line. That way if the catcher throws to third, he has to throw **around** you. Don't let him get a straight view of the base. Do not take your eyes off the ball. Do not go back on your own initiative. Make the catcher **force** you back. Try to draw a catcher pick-off throw.

Some of my players and those of other teams have done a dare-you-to-get-me dance complete with heckling the other team. I tell my kids to knock that off.

Yes, they should draw throws, but not that way. Just by distance from the base and seeming inattention.

Delayed steal of home

The normal delayed steal of home is usually not a good idea because the catcher is covering the plate and the pitcher will see what you are doing, as opposed to a delayed steal of second or third where the action is behind the pitcher's back.

But as I said earlier in the book, the way to do a delayed steal of home is the "Dayo" play. That is where you explode for home on the catcher's throw back to the pitcher, but only when neither the catcher nor the pitcher are at home plate. This typically happens after a passed ball or caught foul pop.

You can often make it happen artificially by taking a really big secondary lead at third. Often, the catcher will respond by walking menacingly toward third. Then, when the runner relaxes, the catcher will stop half way up the base line and throw to the pitcher on the mound. If the catcher throws back to the mound from somewhere other than home plate, and no one else is covering home, the runner should go home. He will score easily.

Advancing from third on a ground ball when not forced

Going home on a ground ball from third when you are not forced is tricky. I generally told my runners to go if the ball got past the pitcher.

I did that once myself in a semi-pro game and got thrown out by a mile. In that case, the ball was hit sharply to the third baseman who was playing in. I sort of had no choice. I had a big secondary lead and might have also been tagged out if I had tried to go back to third.

None of my youth players has ever been tagged out trying to go home on a ground ball hit past the pitcher.

Tag up at third

If a fly ball is hit so deep that there will be no attempt to throw home, the runner at third should tag up and delay leaving until about one second **after** the catch in order to remove any doubt that he left early.

Suicide squeeze departure time

For the suicide squeeze against a right-handed pitcher, you take a walking lead then explode toward the plate when the pitcher's stride foot hits the ground. With a left-handed pitcher, you can leave earlier because he has his back to you. With a left-handed pitcher, you depart when he lifts his stride leg.

On-deck batter is home plate base coach

The on-deck batter is the home-plate base coach.

When a play is underway, he should position himself near the backstop on line with home and third base. You need to practice at least once this so the kids do not forget. Have each kid on your team give a slide and stay-up sign as a runner approaches home.

'Your run doesn't matter'

My son once ran us out of an inning in the last inning of a playoff game, ending our season. The problem was he kept being aggressive on the base paths out of habit, but was ignoring the game situation.

We were down by two runs. It was the bottom of the last inning. When he got to first with two outs, I said from the third-base coaching box, "Dan. Don't be aggressive. Your run does not matter unless the batter scores, too. Wait for the batter to move you around to second."

He wouldn't listen. He promptly stole second. This was against a playoff team with a strong-armed catcher at the teenage level. Again I yelled, "Dan. You should not have done that. We have two outs and we need to score **two** runs to tie the game. Wait for the batter to advance you because if **he** does not score, **your** run won't matter." Again, he did not listen. He tried to steal third and was thrown out, ending our season.

Later, he figured out what I was trying to tell him and agreed he was wrong. I may have been hoist on my own petard in that instance. He had been aggressive for so long that he did not understand there were times when it was not appropriate.

Trading an out for a run

My teams were very big on trading an out for a run. That is, whenever we could score a run if we let you tag out one of our guys, we would take that deal.

Double steal

Trading an out for a run comes up most often in the double-steal play. Typically, you do that with runners on first and third. You try to get the defense to go after the runner from first to second so the runner at third can go home.

I have found in youth baseball that teams will generally let the runner at first go to second and make no effort to stop him if there is also a runner at third. Accordingly, I have a batter who gets a walk when there is a runner at third take off for second as part of the walk.

Teams are more likely to go after him in that situation, which is what we want. I have no idea why teams are more likely to go after a guy who steals on a walk than a guy who waits until after the next pitch. I guess they are just not used to it and they get more angry about a guy going from home to second than a guy going from first to second.

I **want** them to go after the runner going to **second**. I do not want them to just let him go there. So I try to find situations where the other team does not perceive it as a first-and-third.

Tim McCarver says when there is also a runner at first, but none at second, the runner at third should take his lead **on** the base line. That makes it harder for the catcher to tell how far off the base the runner at third is.

Opposing coaches often complained that my stealing second on a walk when there was a runner at third was "taking advantage of the weak arms of kids that age." But those same coaches would invariably have **their** players who walked with a runner at third steal second on the first pitch after the walk.

I never understood how **I** was taking advantage of weak arms, but **they** weren't. The only difference I could see was that no one was dumb enough to go after the runner going to second if you waited one pitch, but most teams **were** that dumb if you combined the steal with the walk.

In one league I coached in, they outlawed stealing on a walk the following season because of me. Having a rule changed because of you is sort of the Nobel Prize of coaching.

You have to stay set for one second in football now because of the effectiveness of Knute Rockne's Notre Dame shift. I already told you about the Chuck Moore Rule in our league that preventing stealing home. Many rules in sports came about because some coach in the past came up with a tactic that no one could stop.

At the teen level, on a dropped third strike, the runner at third should get a good secondary lead on the base line and go home on the catcher's throw to first.

Runners at the other corners

The phrase "runners at the corners" refers to runners at first and third. "Runners at the other corners" refers to runners at second and home.

If you have a runner at second and the batter hits a base hit, having the batter stupidly try to stretch the hit into a double when he has no chance will enable the runner who started at second to advance to home as the defense tries to make a play at second.

The key to the double steal, especially in youth baseball, is that you must do it **when the other team is not expecting it**. They are expecting it on the first pitch after they offense gets runners at first and third. It is standard to have the runner at first steal second in that situation. If the defense makes a throw to second, the runner at third goes home. It is also almost standard for the defense to say, "Let him go," when the runner at first steals second in that situation.

You cannot trade a run for an out if the defense makes no effort to stop the runner at first from going to second.

When the double steal is a surprise

The double steal is a surprise:

- as part of a play that did not start out with runners at first and third, but **now** has runners at first and third
- when the previous play has ended, but the pitcher has not yet stepped on the rubber
- when the pitcher has stepped on the rubber, but not yet come set
- when the pitcher is in the stretch, but has not yet begun to move his body for a pitch or pickoff
- when the runner at first takes off in response to a pitcher pick-off throw to first and the runner at third takes off in response to the initial move of the pitcher's body in the pick-off throw
- runner at first deliberately falling down during his steal attempt

Plays that delay the steal at first until **after** the normal time—on the pitch— have a far lesser chance of working. One would be for the runner at first to do a **delayed steal** on the catcher's throw back to the pitcher. The runner at third would go if the pitcher made a move toward the runner going to second.

Another would be for the runner at third to **draw a catcher pick-off throw** and explode toward home as soon as the ball leaves the catcher's hand. This could be accomplished just by taking a big secondary lead or by the runner at first stealing and the catcher executing the first-and-third defense play which calls for a pick-off throw to third instead of to second.

Runner at first dives back toward invisible base

Here's a trick Cliff Petrak learned from a California coach who attended one of his baserunning clinics. You have runners at first and third, less than two outs, at the teen level. The runner at first takes an enormous and several-feet-behind-the-base-path lead that forces the pitcher to throw a pick-off to first. Instead of diving back to first base, the runner at first dives toward an invisible first base about eight feet farther out toward right field on the foul line.

The runner at third takes a walking lead, but does not break for home until the first baseman turns his back on the runner at third to chase the runner at first. By rule, the first baseman need **not** chase the runner at first. That runner is already out because he went more the three feet away from the base line to avoid a tag, although the ump may not realize this or may not realize it immediately.

I would have thought that the runner on third was waiting too long to break for home, but Petrak says this is how long you must wait. They tried going sooner and the first baseman saw them and threw home. And they found that once the first baseman has turned his back on home plate, he cannot reorient himself fast enough when his teammates start shouting about the runner at third going home. Petrak says the first baseman always takes two steps toward the diving runner before he realizes he needs to throw home.

Steal toward an occupied third base

Here's yet another Cliff Petrak trick. You have runners at second and third. On the pitch, the runner at second takes off full speed toward third, as if he forgot it was occupied. When that runner gets two-thirds of the way to third, and the pitch has arrived at the plate, the third-base coach and everyone else on the offfensive team starts screaming, "Go back! There's a guy at third already!" The runner, acting for an Academy Award, says, "Oh, @#$%!" in body language and throws himself into reverse.

The catcher sees this and figures he's got the runner who has now reversed direction back toward second. Forgetting the runner at third, the catcher throws to second and the runner at third, who has a bit of a secondary lead, breaks for home when he sees daylight between the catcher's hand and the ball. One of Petrak's former players played in the Major Leagues and later managed a professional team in the AAA minors. In pro AAA he executed this play 18 times one season—fifteen of them were successful in trading an out for a run. If there are two outs, the runner at second must "stay alive" long enough for the runner at third to score before he gets tagged out.

Balk rule

The purpose of the balk rule is to protect **runners**. Accordingly, I teach the balk rule to both my pitchers **and** my base runners at the teen level.

The balk rule is confusing. I believe you need a **video** to teach it. The one I use comes from the National Federation of State High School Associations (816-464-5400).

To a runner, the balk rule tells him when he can steal or take a secondary lead without fear of being picked off by the pitcher, or at least that's the theory. The main thing that happened to me as a result of my learning the balk rule well was that I was ejected for the only time in my career by a teenage ump who did **not** know the balk rule when I complained about his enforcing the rule only against my team.

In the case of the double steal on the pitcher's pick-off move to first, the balk rule says the pitcher cannot fake a pick-off to first from the rubber. So if the pitcher's body starts a pick-off throw move, he must complete it with a throw to first or he has committed a balk. Indeed, one of the things you are trying to do with this double steal is get the pitcher to balk. A balk is a very successful double steal because both runners are safe. You did not have to trade an out for the run.

Make sure you are out before you leave the base

If you are in baseball long enough, you will see a runner slide into a base on a close play, get called **safe** by the ump, but assume he is out and walk away, at which time he is tagged out. I do a one-time drill to prevent this. The runner slides into a base and is tagged out on a close play. But he stays on the base and asks the ump "Was I out?" before he walks away.

Wandering runners who are safe

I also do a drill where the runner is safe and knows it, but wanders off base after the play. This is a common mistake at the lower levels of youth baseball. By having my fielders hold the ball a few seconds longer looking for a wanderer to tag, I teach both my fielders and my base runners to do the right thing in this situation.

Keep your eye on the ball

A general comment on youth baserunning: youth players tend to take their eye off the ball. They must keep their eye on the ball at all times except when getting signs. If they take their eye off the ball for an instant, they may either be tagged out or lose an opportunity to advance.

One common cause of players taking their eye off the ball is **chatting** with their base coach or the opposing baseman. Teach your base runners and base coaches not to chat while the ball is live.

Overthrow rule

As a general rule, your runners all get to take **two** bases, not one, if the defense throws the ball out of play—like into a dugout or off the playing field. The vast majority of youth coaches and parents and too many youth umpires think the runners get only one base. You need to know this rule so you can argue for the second base. Here's the actual Little League Rule 7.05(g):

Each runner including the batter-runner may, without liability to be put out, advance—

(g) two bases when…a thrown ball goes [out of play]. The ball is dead. When such wild throw is the first play by an infielder, the umpire in awarding such bases, shall be governed by the position of the runners at the time the… wild throw was made.

Note those last words. It's two bases from where the runners were **at the time the throw left the thrower's hand**. In the typical overthrow at first, where is the batter at the moment the throw leaves the thrower's hand? He is on his way to first.

So he is awarded two bases: first and second. To the average idiot, that looks like an award of just one base.

The misconception may also stem from a special

rule [7.05(h)] which says you only get **one** base if a pitch or pick-off throw from the rubber goes out of play.

Awarded third base

I once got awarded **third** base on an odd overthrow at first in a Men's Senior Baseball League game at the University of San Francisco. All my life, I had worn **rubber** cleats. I decided to try **steel** cleats.

In my first at bat with the new cleats, I hit a base hit to shallow right-center field, but as I left the batter's box with the unaccustomed longer cleats, I tripped and did a full somersault. I actually did not lose much speed from the trip because I did a running forward roll and popped right back up. I lost more speed because I was laughing so hard.

Anyway, the center fielder saw me fall and figured he could throw me out at first. He threw the ball into the first-base dugout instead. But to make matters worse for him, I had actually crossed first base by the time he let loose of the throw. He made his decision to throw to first when he saw me fall. He was no longer paying attention to me when I popped right back up and made it to first quickly.

We had professional umpires in the MSBL. The two umps in that game directed me to **third** base, which is two bases from where I was at the moment of the center fielder's throw.

'What's the rule?'

In a San Ramon Valley Little League game, our opponent once threw a ball into the weeds behind third base. People started yelling "One base." I quietly said, "Actually, it's two."

Everyone started screaming at me, but the opposing manager had coached against me for years and knew I knew the rules. He said, "What's the rule, Jack?" I explained it, reading from the plastic-covered sheet I always carried. The opposing manager then said, "If Jack says that's the rule, that's the rule." My runners got two bases **that** time.

But on most other occasions, the entire adult population of the game site laughed at me as if I was some kind of idiot. Many times my runners only got one base because the incompetent teenage umpires in the San Ramon Valley Little League resolve almost all disputes by Gallup Poll of the most vociferous adults present.

Sliding rules

Almost all adults males involved in youth baseball believe that you always have to slide at home in youthh baseball. Furthermore, they believe it's up to the runner whether to slide at the other bases.

Wrong on both counts.

What the rule says is that you have to slide at **any** base other than first if the fielder there is in **possession** of the ball. Here's the actual Little League Rule 7.08

Any runner is out when—(a)(3) the runner does not slide or attempt to get around a fielder who has the ball and is waiting to make the tag.

The purpose of the rule is to discourage collisions intended to knock the ball loose. Note there is no mention of home plate. This rule applies to **all** bases.

Must have possession

Note also that it says the fielder must have the ball in his **possession**. My runners have been called out at home because they did not slide on plays where the ball was not caught by the catcher or had not arrived yet.

In one case, I showed the ump and opposing coaches the rule and they backed down. In all other cases they said I was misinterpreting the rule or they won the argument by saying, "It's a local rule." In the San Ramon Valley Little League, you can win almost any rules dispute by uttering those words. Of course, the SRVLL rarely puts the local rules in writing. So when you ask to see the local rule in question, they always say, "It's a **verbal** local rule."

Called out over 'local rule'

Once, an opposing manager called me out when I said, "If we are supposed to follow the 'local rules,' the league ought to give us a copy of them." We were immediately surrounded by adults and teenagers. The adults kept saying, "It's not worth it, Jack." The teenagers silently wanted a fight.

I thought the whole thing was silly. The guy in question was a financial executive who was about a half a head shorter than I. Plus he came toward me, but stopped about fifteen feet away and then ran his mouth continuously.

I have not been in many fights, but I know that they are not conducted from fifteen feet away and they are nonverbal. It appeared certain to me that the guy was bluffing, posturing like some male baboon or something in a *National Geographic Special*. He finally cursed at me in front of the assembled teenagers and parents and walked away.

My son said, "Why didn't you punch the guy out? He started it."

"Dan, if I had touched that guy, the story in the media would have been 'Two Little League coaches get into a fist fight.' There would be no discussion of who started it. The story line would simply be, 'What a couple of jerks!'"

I am not dumb enough to fall for the "local rule" nonsense. But most SRVLL teenage umps are.

So at SRVLL, runners are encouraged to slide into empty home plates, thereby increasing the risk of injury unnecessarily. And they are **not** discouraged from running into basemen to try to knock the ball loose, also unnecessarily risking injury.

I suspect this is going on in other leagues as well. It is a prime subject for a pre-season discussion and written guidance on the issue. The guidance ought to say that there are **no** local rules pertaining to the issue, that only the Little League rule (or whatever league) applies.

Caught foul tip is a live ball

Hardly anybody knows this rule: a caught foul tip is a **live** ball. You can steal on a caught foul tip.

Around 1994, I was playing in a semi-pro baseball game at California High School in San Ramon. The opponents had a runner at first who stole on the pitch. The batter foul tipped the pitch and the catcher caught it. The ump signalled foul tip by brushing one hand against the other.

We told the runner to go back to first, which he started to do. But then the guys in his dugout yelled for him to stay at second. We complained "Foul ball! Doggone it! He has to go back."

When the runner stopped going anywhere and just stayed put at second, the ump let us call time. He then explained that a caught foul tip is a live ball. We said, "But it wasn't strike three." "Doesn't matter," he said.

When I got home after the game, I looked it up. He was right. In Little League, it's rule 2.00 under the definition of a foul tip.

A FOUL TIP is a batted ball that goes sharp and direct from the bat to the catcher's hands and is legally caught. It is not a foul tip unless caught and any foul tip that is caught is a strike, and the ball is in play.

Interference

Runners cannot "obstruct, impede, hinder, or confuse" a fielder who is attempting to make a play. The penalty is a runner is declared out. For example, if a batter interferes with a catcher trying to throw out a guy stealing third, the runner trying to steal third would be declared out because of the batter's behavior. Interference by a runner rarely occurs.

Obstruction

Obstruction is a fielder who is not in possession of the ball or fielding a ball getting in the way of a runner. This happens in virtually every youth baseball game, but I have only seen it called once in my whole career.

The penalty for obstruction is that the ump puts all the runners where he thinks they would have gotten had there been no obstruction. "The obstructed runner shall be awarded at least one base beyond the base last legally touched by the obstructed runner, before the obstruction." [Rule 7.06(a)]

Once, in 1992, one of my runners was obstructed

from getting back to first by the first baseman at the end of a double-steal play. The runner had gotten caught in a run-down between first and second while the runner at third scored when there were two outs. Ultimately, the runner in the pickle made it safely to first.

I asked the teenage home plate umpire if there was obstruction. He gave a vague response with his body that seemed to motion the runner to second. Because it was vague, I asked again to make sure. The opposing manager bellowed, "WHAT DIFFERENCE DOES IT MAKE? HE WAS SAFE!"

The difference it makes is that whether he was safe at first is irrelevant. If it was obstruction, my runner gets to go to **second**. The ump then settled the matter with those words which are the inexplicable yet ubiquitous "mating call" of the SRVLL teenage ump, "I didn't see it."

Funny, he was looking right at it. What he really means is he didn't see it in the rule book during the twelve seconds he spent studying it before the season. What he also meant was that he didn't enforce rule-book rules. He only enforced "rules" which were common knowledge among middle-aged men.

When a play is being made **on the obstructed runner**, the ball is **dead**. If **no play is being made on the obstructed runner**, the play **proceeds** until over. Then the ump calls time and puts the runners where they would have gotten to had there been no obstruction. [Rule 7.06(b)]

Throw accidentally hits ump or coach

If a thrown ball accidentally hits an ump or coach, it means nothing. The ball is live and in play. If a coach **deliberately** touches a live ball, usually to helpfully field it and throw it back in, that is interference and the runner is out. [Rule 5.08]

Base coaching

I am inclined to base coach with a light touch in some respects. Your fundamental job as a base coach is to act as the eyes in the back of the runner's head when he needs to know what's going on behind him.

I reluctantly have had to take on a second role that should not have to be done by a base coach: to give courage and focus.

When my oldest son was on base, we communicated almost in silent code. I would yell his name and give a wink or a nod or call his attention to something with a gesture. He would nod and I would then watch him take advantage of what we had seen.

That's the way it should **always** be between a base coach and his runners. But in the vast majority of cases, I found I had to constantly urge runners to be more aggressive and to be more aware of the game situation.

"Johnny. One out. Base ahead of you is occupied. If

he goes, you go. Tag on a fly. Bobby. Congratulations on getting to second. Now get the heck out of there. Find a way to get to third. Look for a passed ball. Draw throws. Get to third. Get to third. Get to third."

Of course, I'm saying all this from the third-base coaches box so everyone at the game can hear me.

Code words

I would also typically be saying some **code words**. For example, I might have noticed that the catcher was **lobbing** the ball back to the pitcher. We might have designated the word "intelligent" to mean the catcher is lobbing. So I might add into all the other stuff I was saying, "Be intelligent, Bobby. Don't do anything stupid."

What that really meant was, "Bobby, notice that the catcher is lobbing the ball back to the pitcher. Time for a delayed steal."

The best decisionmaker in baserunning is the base runner himself. True, runners are often too timid. But the time to take care of that is in **practice** and **between pitches**. Once the pitch has been thrown, the base coach is generally best off remaining silent.

Don't get me wrong. I would always yell "Tag up" on a catchable fly with less than two outs. I would yell, "Go! Go! Go!" to all runners when there were two outs and the ball was hit or to a runner approaching third if I wanted him to go home. I would yell "Slide!" to runners when appropriate.

What I object to, for example, is yelling, "Go! in response to a passed ball to get a player who is standing still to advance. I have chewed out many a player **afterwards** for not going on a passed ball. But during the event itself, I generally say nothing because I do not want him waiting for me to tell him what to do the **next time**.

I used to use fathers to coach bases. But they screwed it up, generally being too timid. I tried making up a 3 x 5 card of instructions. One father looked at it, scowled, crumpled it up, and threw it on the ground. Thereafter, I acted as my own base coach, used my assistant coach, or sent a player, who after all was trained in my methods and did not crumple them up.

Fathers are generally useless for such purposes because of the male ego.

Signs

I do not like signs. They are missed too often. Indeed, players who do not want to do what you ask, use the fact that signs are often missed to claim, falsely, they did not see the sign. Hand signals are also usually relatively easy to steal.

Giving signs takes time. I like to keep things moving when we are doing well.

Another reason I do not like to give signs is that I like for my players to take the initiative as much as possible in baserunning.

Because I was also a football coach, I was used to using **verbal numbers** to send signals. So I adopted a simple three-digit verbal code for my base runners. The first digit was for the lead runner. The second digit was for the second runner, if any. The third digit was for the batter.

If your digit was an **odd** number, you were supposed to do the "odd" thing which meant **steal** for a runner or **bunt** for a batter. If your digit was an **even** number, you were supposed to do the normal thing which meant **stay** for a runner and **swing away** for a batter.

For example, if you wanted the runner at first to steal and the batter to swing away, you could say, "742." The 7 tells the lead runner to steal. The 2 tells the batter swing away. The 4 means nothing because there is only one runner. To call a squeeze play with a runner at third only, you could say, "157." And so on.

This worked great. No one ever missed a sign. In one game, I wanted to have the lone runner at first steal and the batter hit. Before I could say a number, the opposing first baseman yelled out, "594!" Since that happened to be the play that I wanted, I said, "OK, Good idea. Let's do 594." And we did.

The opposing player then said, "594 means steal." I said, "You're right. Now you only have 999 more to figure out."

You could use other numbers like, for example, steal or bunt on numbers divisible by three (3, 6, 9) or only on numbers with no round strokes (1, 4, 7). There are other ways you could set up the code to prevent, say, readers of this book from stealing your signs.

Base coach signs during a play

When a play is under way, a base coach gives arm signals to tell the runner what to do as he approaches the next base. There are fairly straightforward. A wind-the-clock arm motion like a football referee uses to start the game clock means **go full speed to the next base**. Pointing both arms at the ground means **slide**.

A **stop sign**, both palms facing the runner, means **round this base and come to a stop** looking back at the ball to see if you can advance on an error. In response to this sign, the runner steps on the base then comes to a stop several steps later.

A **one-hand stop sign** accompanied by pointing at the base with the other hand means you do not need to slide, but the ball is right behind you, so do not overrun the base. In that case, the runner decelerates as he comes into the base and keeps one foot on it all the time after he arrives.

These arm signals should be accompanied by appropriate verbal commands like, "Go," "Slide," "Stop." I give my players one practice session a year of coming into third and responding to the various possible base coach arm signals.

Also, when I do my daily sliding practice, I or my assistant stands behind the base and gives the normal slide arm signal as well as the verbal "Slide" command. We want the response to the slide command to be Pavlovian, although I have never quite achieved that.

Catchers who take their masks off

In youth baseball, you often see catchers who remove their masks before they throw to a base to stop a steal. If you are in a game against a catcher who takes off his mask before making a steal throw, **steal**. Even your slowest runners can probably steal against a kid who does that.

Baserunning mentally

You have get into baserunning mentally at the beginning of each season. I noticed this when I played adult and semi-pro baseball. At the beginning of each season, I would get picked off. I was not sufficiently mentally alert. You have to get your brain in shape for baserunning. The way you do that is to get picked off or thrown out. That tends to refocus you. Make this happen in pre-season practice rather than in games.

Always touch the base

Many players, especially very young players, are slobs about actually touching the bases. They figure close is good enough. Many older players have this attitude about first base if they figure they will probably be out anyway. You must discipline your players to focus their eyes on each base as they approach it so they make sure to touch it.

When to be aggressive

I have talked a little bit about the fact that you should not be so aggressive on the base paths when you are averaging more than three runs per inning or when you are trailing in the last inning and you are not the tying or go-ahead run. Only the tying or winning run can be aggressive.

Winning run can be aggressive

One of my great moments in adult baseball was when I was the winning run in the bottom of an extra inning. I was at second. There was a runner at third. There was one out. The batter hit the ball to the infield and was thrown out at first. I tore around third hard and slid home in a cloud of dust. The catcher was unable to hang onto (or maybe find) the ball in the cloud.

My thinking at the time was that if I was out, we'd still have a tie game. But if I'm safe, we win. We had little to lose and a victory to gain by aggressiveness.

Refer back to the run-value table in the pitcher-fielding chapter. In general, when there is only one out. The value of moving the runner up one base is worth far less than the value lost if he makes an out on base. For example, moving a runner from 1st to 2nd with 0 outs

increases the run value by 1.068 - .783 = .285. But if you make an out in the process, you **lose** .783 - .249 = .534. You would have to have more than a 67% success probability to make it worthwhile.

Going from having a runner on 2nd to one on 3rd when you have two outs is worth .382 - .348 = .034. Making an out while trying to do that takes you to a run value of .000 which is a loss of .348 - .000 = .348. Thus the old saying, never make the third out at third.

How about making the **first** out at third? Going from 2nd to 3rd with no outs raises your run value by 1.277 - 1.068 = .209. But making an out in the process reduces your run value by 1.068 - .249 = .819. That's a relatively small benefit for a big risk.

And how about making the **second** out at third, which is supposed to be an OK thing? Successfully getting to 3rd from 2nd raises your run value by .897 - .699 = .198. Making at out in the process reduces your run value by .699 - .095 = .604.

True, making the second out at third has a better risk-reward ratio than making the first or third out there. But the risk-reward ratio for all three outs stinks. Seems to me that the old saying ought to be, "Never make **any** out at third." Or better this way:

• It's dumb to make the **second** out at third.
• It's even dumber to make the **first** out at third.
• It's unbelievably dumb to make the **third** out at third.

With two outs you want to gamble at third going home. Why? The run value of successfully going home is 1.000. Plus you still have the run value of having two outs and no one on base, which is .095. That's an improvement of 1.000 + .095 - .348 = .747. Whereas if you make an out in the process, you lose only .348. So you only need to be successful a little more than one third of the time to make the gamble worthwhile.

In contrast, going home with only **one** out gets you 1.000 + .249 - .897 = .352 increase in run value. However, making an out in the process costs you .897 - .095 = .802 in lost run value.

In general, it makes sense to gamble when the amount you gain far exceeds what you lose. The only one-base move where that happens is going from **third to home with two outs**. In all other cases, the loss of both the runner and the out is more costly than the benefit of succeeding.

Probability may be high enough

Remember, however, that all steals and attempts to take an extra base are not equal gambles. In many cases, there is little or no gamble. For example, stealing second on a passed ball is almost no gamble at all in Little League. When you can go to the next base with a 90% to 95% probability of success, you should do so. Remember also that these run-value numbers are based on Major League results. Youth baseball has much more advancing on errors and stealing.

Pitch count

The pitch count is somewhat relevant when it comes to base stealing. You generally do **not** want to steal when there are **two strikes** because the batter has to swing if the ball is a strike. A swing can result in a **foul** which sends the runner back. This is especially harmful if the steal in question relied on the element of surprise, like a delayed steal or a squeeze. It's hard to surprise the defense a second time with the same play.

Of course, the rule that forced runners go on the **pitch** when there is a **full count** and two outs always applies. As does the rule that a forced runner goes on the **swing** when there are two strikes and two outs.

With two outs and two strikes on a good hitter in an inning other than the last, it is OK to be aggressive on the base paths because making an out on base lets that good hitter come back and lead off the next inning. Of course the opposite is also true. That is, don't risk making the third out in an inning other than the last one with a weak batter up because if you do, it extends his time at the plate into the next inning.

Do not attempt to steal third when there are two outs, there is no runner at first, and the count is three balls. You could be **thrown out ending the inning on ball four**. The Mets' Carl Everett did that in a 1997 game.

Emphasize baserunning

Good youth coaches know that baserunning is the most coachable aspect of baseball. As a result, they emphasize it. If you spend fifteen minutes teaching a baserunning skill like the delayed steal, it is almost certain that your players will use it successfully in your **next game**. But if you spend fifteen **hours** on hitting, pitching, or fielding, it is likely that you will see little or no improvement and you may even see a decline in performance in those areas as a result of your practice.

A youth team that emphasizes baserunning will have much success, at least on a play-by-play basis, against opposing teams. This will anger opponents.

In his book *A Parent's Guide to Coaching Baseball*, John P. McCarthy, Jr. says,

> *There are so many passed balls and wild pitches that runners pretty much advance at will. Occasionally, you get a decent catcher who will hold it down, but stealing on passed balls dominates the game. I don't like it, but that's the way it is.*
>
> *So I keep my players running. Some leagues prohibit stealing, or at least stealing home. I agree with that—make them hit the ball. But until they change the rules, I will keep them running.*

Mixed feelings about baserunning

These mixed feelings about baserunning are typical among competent youth coaches.

My take on the issue is that youth baseball is unavoidably different from Major League baseball. The adults involved need to stop thinking that any difference between youth baseball and TV baseball is bad.

I, too, would support rules changes, especially at the lowest, least skilled youth baseball levels. But I have coached close to 30 teams and I would approach changing rules experimentally, rather than making wholesale changes. Base runners should not become mere chess pieces marking a spot with all advancement based on hitting. If you took the baserunning out of the Little League World Series, their scores would sound like soccer games and most games would be 0-0 ties until their pitchers were exhausted.

Until such rules changes are made, all youth coaches should evaluate the strengths and weakness of their players and the opposing players in their league and come up with a strategy that will maximize both individual and team success within the current rules.

Also, I always felt my opponents were too quick to demand rules changes and too unwilling to work on their baserunning defense. In general, **my** teams could stop most of the baserunning tricks we used. And we usually did when opposing teams tried to give us a dose of our own medicine.

Step one, at any league that is concerned about baserunning, should be to hold a baserunning defense clinic. When I was in Vietnam, *chieu hoi's* used to give us lectures about how they had penetrated our defenses. *Chieu hoi* is Vietnamese for "open arms" and it was the name of a program to encourage North Vietnamese and Viet Cong soldiers to defect to our side.

The San Ramon Valley Little League, instead of changing rules to stop me and Chuck Moore, should first have had the two of us give a clinic to all the coaches on how to stop what we were doing. That would improve the coaches and the players in the league.

The action they took instead, dumbing down the rules, made the "Home of Champions" a weaker organization. It was especially bad considering that those dumbed-down rules would **not** apply in post-season all-star play or when our players got to high school.

But youth baseball coaches are almost all men and you know how most men are about asking for directions, including directions on how to stop good baserunning. They would rather outlaw it or sour-grapes it than admit they needed help.

Turns out I finally did that clinic, after all. You are holding it in your hand.

17 Pitching

I do not know much about how to get youth baseball players to pitch better. That is an acknowledgment of ignorance, but I do not mean to set myself apart from other youth coaches in that respect. As far as I can tell, few, if any, coaches know how to get youth baseball players to pitch better.

Pitching is extremely important in youth baseball. The number of wins you get probably correlates better with pitching performance than with any other variable. The 1999 Little League World Series teams all seemed to have great pitching.

In *Baseball for Dummies*, Joe Morgan notes that the 1972 Phillies were so bad they only had a .358 winning percentage. But when Steve Carlton was on the mound, they had a .750 winning percentage, .110 better than the top team in the league. And the best youth pitchers dominate youth hitters far more than Steve Carlton dominated Major League hitters.

Unfortunately, pitching appears to be largely uncoachable, at least within the context of the mere 40.5 hours you get in a youth season. But I do know some things that I think will help you do better in that department.

Three factors

It appears to me that youth pitching success depends on three things:

- talent
- self-confidence
- fatigue

Mechanics are only a small factor, but that's what the vast majority of youth coaches focus on. Coaches who emphasize mechanics have more professional **looking** pitching. But my response to that is, "Very pretty, coach, but can they get batters out?"

It seems **logical** that the better a pitcher's mechanics, the better he will pitch, but in youth baseball, I have not seen a correlation between coaches who em-phasize mechanics and year-in-and-year-out team pitching success. In other words, I have seen a lot of good **pitchers** in youth baseball, but I have never seen a good pitching **coach** as measured by score-book success.

I am not saying that good mechanics are bad for pitchers. Rather I am saying that the process of teaching good mechanics takes too long for a youth baseball coach to begin it, especially when you consider that the first step is to tell the pitcher what's wrong with his mechanics. That hurts confidence.

If you had time to identify and correct each mechanical flaw, like high school and higher level coaches have, you should fix mechanics. But in a youth baseball season, about all you have time for mechanicswise is to hurt the pitcher's self confidence and make them think about too many things while they are trying to throw a pitch.

Definition of a good youth pitching coach

A good youth pitching coach is one whose team, year in and year out, is better than average in his league at:

- percentage of walks
- percentage of strikeouts
- percentage of hit batsmen
- bases given up to batter

I suspect there is no such youth pitching coach in the world. I also suspect there are about a hundred thousand youth baseball coaches who **think** they are good in these categories, but who have never run the numbers and will be very disappointed when they do. If I am wrong, I would like to hear from that coach. (Notice I am not including pitcher **fielding** in this chapter. Pitcher fielding is quite coachable.)

Talent is the ability to throw fast and accurately as well as the smarts to use good tactics like changing speeds against good hitters. Pitching talent is mostly genetic. For the most part, good pitchers are born, not made. To the extent that they are made, like strengthening their arms, it takes **years**, not 40.5 hours, to achieve significant results.

There are some kids who can pitch, but who lack the **self-confidence** to do so. If you ask who the pitchers are at your first practice, there will probably be one or two good pitchers among those who do **not** raise their hands. I once had a good pitcher who, part way through the season, asked to be removed from the pitching rotation. He was good and successful, but he simply could not stand the pressure of the job. In *Sports Illustrated's Pitching*, Pat Jordan says, pitchers must have "monumental egos" to withstand the pressure.

If you think you can't, you won't. That self-fulfilling prophesy prevents many a youth pitcher from achieving his potential or even having any success.

Youthful energy

If you go to Disneyland or any other theme park, you will see small children zonked out in strollers in the afternoon. Grown-ups are always saying about children, "I wish I had their energy." In fact, Grown-ups have far more energy than children. Children simply have not yet learned how to pace themselves so they expend energy at a high rate. But if you make a group of adults and children expend energy at the same rate, as in walking around Disneyland all day, the kids will poop out long before the adults.

Pitching is hard work. Because they lack stamina, kids get tired much faster than adults. When pitchers get tired, they lose their effectiveness. There comes a point when your number-one pitcher who can throw 55 mph when fresh, tires and throws slower than your number-two pitcher. Part of your job is to recognize that point quickly.

Recruiting or drafting, not coaching

The main way to have an excellent youth pitching staff is to recruit or draft talented pitchers. Do **not** rely on taking average material and turning it into excellent pitching with your great coaching.

Evaluating pitchers

You cannot evaluate a pitcher in the bull pen. Nolan Ryan says, "Never put much stock in how you throw in the bull pen…" He was referring to your pre-game warm-ups, but the lack of correlation between bull pen pitching and game pitching applies to both warm-up and evaluation. The only way you can evaluate pitchers is to put them on the mound in game conditions.

At Little League tryouts I have heard coaches discussing the mechanics of various candidates. Sounded to me like they were trying to impress each other with their knowledge of baseball. I don't give a rat's rump about mechanics (as long as the kid is not going to hurt himself). All I care about is, "Does he get people out?"

Bull pen pitchers

I have seen many a pitcher who looked great in the bull pen, but who could not get batters out. And I have seen many a pitcher who had nothing in the bull pen, but could get batters out. I put the second group on the mound when I coach.

One of my Men's Senior Baseball League teammates was an aging pitcher. He apparently had been a great athlete in his youth—option quarterback of his high school football team, letterman on the basketball and baseball teams. But when I played with him, he was graying.

He did not seem to have much. In fact, an opposing player once yelled out to his teammate batter, "That pitcher's got nothing'" when we were in the field. One of my teammates responded with, "We'd come to your aid, Dave, but he's right."

That aging pitcher could only do one thing: get people out. I still don't know how, but he was our most effective pitcher in spite of being our least impressive in the bull pen or by any measure other than results.

As a semi-pro player-manager, I once played pre-game catch with a new player. I was astounded. His ball had both speed and the most movement I had ever seen. And he would alternate throwing arms every pitch!

I put him on the mound in that game. My catcher had as much trouble catching his pitches during the game as I did in the pre-game warm-up.

Great pitcher? Nope. He got shelled by the batters he didn't walk. Once, I came in from my center field position to say, "Your pitch consistently moves way out to the left for a ball. Why not throw it right at the right-handed batter and it will then move left into the strike zone?" He agreed to try that and beaned the next batter.

Also in semi-pro, I had a catcher who was amazing. When a guy was stealing second, he would come up out of his crouch in what seemed like an overly slow move. You'd be thinking, "Doggone it, Ed! Get rid of the darned ball!" Then suddenly, he would flick his wrist and a perfect dart would rocket to the perfect spot at second. "Out!"

I asked if he could pitch. He said he could. On the mound he threw with great speed and accuracy. No walks, but lots of extra-base hits. He, too, got shelled.

In Little League one year, I drafted the only girl in the league. I insist that all players try out for pitcher and I ignore bull-pen performance. So I put her on the mound in practice games. Her only pitch was an Eephus pitch—a sort of slow-pitch softball pitch, only thrown overhanded. What's more, she couldn't throw it for strikes!

If I had made my decisions based on bull-pen performance, no way would she ever have been on the mound. But I had stated my policy and now I had to stick with it.

I put her on the mound in a pre-season practice game. To our amazement, she was effective. Although her pitches were generally not strikes, they looked so fat that the opposing players were swinging at them. Because they were swinging at balls and pitcher's pitches, they were striking out, grounding out, and popping out like crazy.

I kept her in the rotation during the season. Unfortunately, it was a small league and we had to play everybody twice. Second time around, they had figured out that she was not throwing strikes and began to take walks. I had to stop using her.

I previously mentioned Michael Ramos who had great control, but was relatively slow. He was our best pitcher, as long as we pitched him second after a fireballer. But his subsequent coaches rejected his as a pitcher based on bull-pen performance.

At the end of one later season, he managed to get on

the mound and was excellent. His coach said, "Why didn't you tell me you were such a good pitcher?" Actually, his dad had **tried** to tell him, but the manager wouldn't listen.

I repeat, DO NOT TRY TO TELL WHO CAN PITCH IN THE BULL PEN! Put each of your players on the mound in game conditions and keep a score book. The ones who get the best **results** are your pitchers, **regardless of how they look doing it or whether they fit the Hollywood central casting image of a pitcher**.

When you are scouting pitchers for next-season's draft, ignore everything but their **results**.

My tryout

In between my first and second years of Little League, I decided I might be a pitcher. Come spring, one of my Little League coaches gave me a two-minute look in the bull pen. He rejected me and I never pursued it again. That was probably a mistake on both our parts.

My oldest son was a good pitcher. As an outfielder, I got many compliments about my arm. Many years later, when I was starting with a new adult baseball team, the coach said he wanted to try everyone out for pitcher. The experienced catcher who caught the tryout said I had a good fastball and curve and that I was one of the top three or four pitchers on the team. But we got a couple of new pitchers and I never pitched in a game.

I doubt that I would have been a great pitcher, but I probably would have been a decent one and I have been in many game situations where the manager would have been very grateful to replace the guy on the mound with a decent pitcher.

Changes as you get older

Also, even if a kid is truly not a pitcher at one age, he may be one at a later age. So every kid should try out for pitcher every year. The classic story on that is Tom Seaver. He was elected to the Hall of Fame with the highest percentage of votes in history.

But he got cut from his high school baseball team every year except his senior year, when he had a .500 win-loss percentage and no interest from either colleges or the pros. After one year playing in junior college, he got a baseball scholarship to USC. The rest, as they say, is history.

Nolan Ryan Says, "I was a good player, not a great player, although I did pitch a no-hitter in Little League and was on the All-Star team as an eleven- and twelve-year old. I didn't develop great pitching velocity until my sophomore year in high school."

Orel Hershiser was cut from his high school varsity team his freshman and sophomore years. The same thing happened on his college team.

I wonder how many Tom Seavers, Nolan Ryans, and Orel Hershisers were permanently convinced that they were not pitchers by some yahoo youth baseball coach when they were nine.

Lower body strength

It is widely believed that pitchers need strong legs. I do not dispute that, although I wish someone would do a scientific study rather than rely on opinions of experienced pitchers and coaches. But either way, you cannot influence leg strength much as a youth coach.

My oldest son has been involved in a couple of professionally designed and supervised conditioning programs: one at Ather Acceleration in Castro Valley, CA and the Columbia University football team strength-and-conditioning program. Ather Acceleration is owned and run by Donald Chu, the author of several books on plyometrics.

These programs are long-term: Ather runs all summer and Columbia football is year round. They also require at least three sessions per week. They are also brutally strenuous. My son's shirt would be completely soaked with sweat after I picked him up at Ather. At Columbia, he has almost thrown up after some of the workouts.

You cannot get youth baseball players to do this stuff, and you should not try. If you have a gung ho kid who wants to pitch in high school, you should refer him to a batting-cage instructor, a program like Ather, or some such. If he has the work ethic, he can do three or four sessions a week, year round of strengthening and conditioning himself to pitch better.

Do not torment your players with conditioning in the context of a youth baseball practice season. You do not have enough time to do that stuff in the 40.5 hours of practice in your season. You do not meet frequently enough to condition. Most, if not all, of your players hate conditioning and did not sign up for youth baseball to go through hard conditioning.

Finally, and maybe most importantly, conditioning is a dangerous activity, especially with children because they have growth plates at the end of each bone. Improper conditioning of a child can result in permanent damage. You should point out the value of conditioning, but it must be done by the individual parent and child outside of your practices under professional supervision.

Pitching stats

In the Major Leagues, they focus on earned run average in evaluating pitchers. Forget that. When one of my player fathers mentions "ERA," I usually say something like, "You know I read that there was an earned run in a Little League game in Waterloo, Iowa in 1957."

Actually, earned runs happen more often than that in youth baseball, but not much more often. The reason ERA is important in the pros is errors are **unusual**. The reason ERA is **not** important in youth baseball is because errors in youth baseball are **common**.

Just look at the unarguable stats:

- walks
- strikeouts
- hit batsmen
- batters who get on base by a hit or error
- over-the-fence home runs

Actually, I wouldn't even cut it that fine. I look mainly at **runs**. If the batters score few runs against pitcher A and they score more runs against pitcher B, pitcher A is probably the better pitcher.

Multiple outings

You need to look at multiple outings. In 1991, I went strictly by the numbers. My oldest son had a terrible first outing as a pitcher. Based on his numbers, he went to the bottom of our pitcher list and never got another chance to pitch that season as a result. Turns out, he is a good pitcher who pitched virtually every season thereafter.

I had drawn a broad conclusion based on a mere one inning performance. You need multiple innings and multiple games to get an accurate reading. Pitchers run hot and cold. Some days your best pitcher is unhittable. Others, he stinks. This happens at all levels of baseball. No one knows why.

Go easy on the mechanics

What I said about batting mechanics applies, to an extent, about pitching as well.

You have an obligation from a safety standpoint to teach some of the gross mechanics, like stepping straight at the plate and bending the back low in the follow-through. But you should avoid getting into fine points of pitching mechanics.

Local instructors

If you have a kid who wants to improve his mechanics, tell him to take pitching lessons in the off-season. Local batting cages usually have a pitching instructor affiliated with them. They usually are former pros and charge $20 to $40 an hour. The typical youth baseball coach knows little or nothing about correct pitching mechanics and has no business getting involved in it.

As with batting, it may be helpful to make a highlight or training video of Major League pitchers throwing from the set position. Just show it without comment in the dugout or at practice or post-game pizza parties.

Pre-pitch mechanics

As with batting, it's OK to teach **pre**-pitch mechanics. Those are things like how you stand on the rubber and how you grip the ball. During-the-pitch mechanics refers to what happens after you come set and start to lift your stride leg.

Keep eyes on the target throughout

Many youth pitchers take their eyes off the target during their pitching motion, then find it again later. I assume they are trying to imitate something they have seen on TV. Get them to knock that off. They must keep their eyes on the target throughout the pitching motion. I have seen youth pitchers who were taking their eyes off the target and having control problems instantly erase their control problems in the middle of a game by keeping their eyes on the target.

Which arm?

If you have pro aspirations, you should pitch with your **left** arm if at all possible. There is far greater demand for left-handed pitchers at the pro level. At the youth level, there is more need for right-handed pitchers because 90% of the batters bat right-handed. Although left-handed pitchers sometimes get an advantage just from being different from what youth batters are used to.

Normally, you should throw with your dominant side arm. In fact, I did not think it was possible to do otherwise. But I have heard of at least two ambidextrous pitchers: the one who played for me in semi-pro and a kid on the Mexico Little League World Champs in the fifties.

There is also Dennis Reyes of the Dodgers. He is right-side dominant and threw that way until a Major League scout jokingly told him he only scouted left-handers when Reyes was a kid. Reyes thought he was serious and immediately switched to throwing left-handed. Throwing from his non-dominant side did not prevent him from pitching in the Major Leagues at age 20.

Consider, also, Mickey Lolich. He was born right-side dominant. But he was a left-handed pitcher in the Major Leagues from 1963 to 1978. How'd that happen? He broke his right arm when he was a kid and did not want to wait until it healed to start playing baseball again. So he learned to throw left-handed while the broken right arm was healing. He led the league in wins, innings pitched, fewest hits, and most strikeouts in 1971. He made the all-star team in 1969, 1971, and 1972. (His batting was a bit odd, too. *The Baseball Encyclopedia* lists him as a switch hitter, but say he batted right-handed in 1976, 1978, and 1979.)

Still, for youth purposes, just throw with your dominant-side arm.

Set position only

As I said elsewhere in the book, a former pitching coach from the University of California gave a clinic to the San Ramon Valley Little League. He said to teach only the set, not the full windup. Made sense to me. I have always done it that way since. (This is also called the "stretch" position although many pitchers no longer stretch before pitching.)

Some Major League pitchers only throw from the set. I have heard that some college coaches only use the set. In the greatest pitching performance in history, the perfect 1956 World Series game, Don Larsen threw only from the set even though there was never a runner.

I actually suspect that the full windup will disappear. When I was a kid, pitchers used to double pump. The right to do that is still in the rules. But you hardly ever see players single pump any more, let alone double pump.

Pitching coaches say your body comes to a complete stop at the balance point (top of the stride leg lift). If that's the case, how can it matter what you did before that point? I can see lifting the leg higher when there is no one on base, But I see no point to the choreography of the full windup. Furthermore, I have seen many a youth baseball player lose his balance when trying to execute a pro full windup.

The main reason you should not let your pitchers throw from a full windup is that it's more complicated, you don't need it, and learning how to do it right is time-consuming. Many authors say you have better control, but less velocity pitching from the set position. In youth baseball, the pitching characteristic that is most often lacking is control, so anything that will help control should be adopted.

Position on the rubber

Your pitchers should stand **in front of** the rubber, not **on** it. I have seen many youth pitchers stand up on **top** of the highest level of the rubber to pitch. That's crazy.

The rubber is often like two stair steps. You do not stand on the top step. You do not stand on the bottom step. The rules require you to be in contact with the top step, but I have never seen it enforced in youth baseball. You stand with the outside of your throwing side foot touching the front of the bottom step.

The reasons are that you want to be as close to the batter as possible, you want to grip the soil with your cleats, and you want to push off the rubber when you pitch. When you are standing on top of the highest step, you get no grip and you have nothing to push off. Standing on the bottom step lets you push off, but you cannot grip the rubber with your cleats so you may slip.

Here's a diagram:

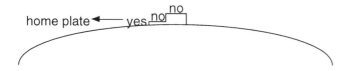

In some cases, there is just one step on the rubber. In that case, stand in front of it, not on top. Here's that diagram:

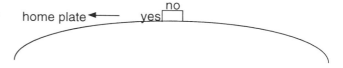

In many cases, pitchers dig a hole with their cleats where they want to stand. Dumb move. When Major League Baseball became convinced that pitchers were too dominant in 1968, one of the rules changes they made was to lower the mound. By digging a hole in the top of the mound, you further reduce the advantage given to you by the raised mound to begin with.

If your pitcher finds a hole there, have him fill it in. You may have dueling excavations every half inning, but you should not pitch from a hole.

I have seen some youth pitchers pitch from about six inches in front of the front edge of the rubber. That's illegal. I complained to the ump, but was told to forget about it.

Letting pitchers pitch while standing on the very top of the rubber is *prima facie* evidence that the coach is a baseball ignoramus. It's not a matter of opinion. It is just wrong—and surprisingly common.

Right, center, or left side of the rubber?

The rules say that when you pitch from the stretch, your entire foot must be in front of the rubber. But since the rubber is 24 inches long, that means you can put your foot at various places including **toe** even with the end of the rubber, **heel** even with the end of the rubber, and several other places in between.

Some pitchers need to pick one spot and stick with it in order to throw strikes. Others may be able to vary their position along the rubber on different pitches as a way of disconcerting the batters.

Be sure you **do not tip off** the type of pitch, like always moving to one side to throw a curve. Babe Ruth struggled as a pitcher until a teammate pointed out that he was sticking his tongue out every time he prepared to throw a curve.

Here are some diagrams of the legal and illegal set pitching positions.

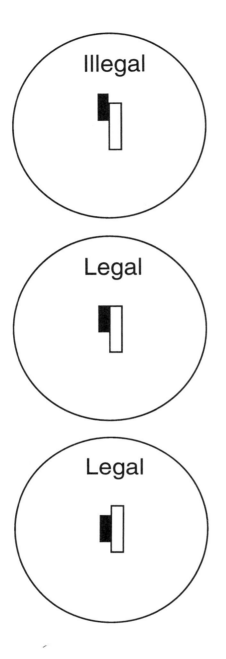

I have also complained about violations of this rule and was told not to worry about it by the umps.

Step off

The only way to step off without balking is to pick your throwing-side foot up and put it back down on the back side of the rubber. At the teen level, you need to have your pitchers practice this, in conjunction with your base runners, who must go back to their bases when this happens.

Stride

Just lift your stride-leg knee. Do **not** kick your stride-leg foot when you do so. When you stride, your stride foot should land just to the glove side of the center line drawn from where you stood against the rubber to the plate. Here's a diagram for a right handed pitcher:

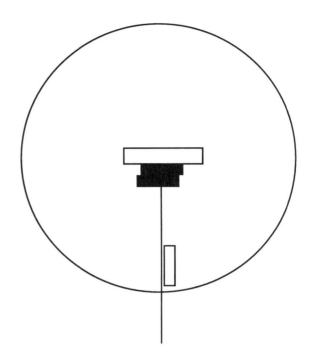

The black rectangles represent the starting point of the two feet. The white rectangle represents the landing point of the left (stride) foot. For a left-handed pitcher, everything would be the mirror image of this diagram.

You work on this by drawing a line in the dirt or otherwise marking the line. If the pitcher's stride foot lands on the other (throwing-arm) side of the line, he will be throwing across his body which diminishes speed and accuracy.

Hide the pitch

Try to use the glove to hide the pitch as long as possible as you stride. That is, have your glove follow a path that takes it in front of the release point as you open your body during the stride. Point your glove-side elbow at the plate as you start your delivery.

In the stride, you land on the ball of the foot, not the heel. Also, the knee is **bent**. I once had a youth pitcher whose stride leg was locked straight at the knee, like a batter's stride leg, when he pitched. I took him and his father aside and told them that was totally unacceptable, dangerous, and that he must correct it. He did not during the season, but I saw him in subsequent years and he had learned to land on a bent leg.

Bend your back

A common drill involves putting a coin on the ground just to the outside of the stride-foot landing. **Outside** is important. After a pitch, the pitcher's throwing hand should be outside his stride foot.

After the pitch, the pitcher picks the coin up off the ground. The purpose is to get the pitcher to bend way over when he finishes the pitch. Another way to put it is that the pitcher's chest should be almost on your glove-side thigh when he has completed the pitch.

I do not like to mess with mechanics during a game, but on occasion, when one of my pitchers has consistently been throwing high, I would tell him to bend his back more and it would generally correct the high-pitch problem.

Bending your back all the way in the follow through also helps with speed and accuracy. The pitcher must use his whole body to pitch, not just his arm. Coaches must remember to model this when they throw, or else the kids will unconsciously pick up the short-arm habit of the coaches.

Pitching coach Tom House says your pitcher should think "tall and fall," not "dip and drive" as they pitch. That is, get tall at the balance point (top of knee lift), then do a controlled fall toward the batter as you throw. Do not drive off the rubber as if you had to get under a low doorway. (I tend to commit the dip-and-drive mistake when I pitch adult batting practice or become the game pitcher at the sub-nine-year-old level.) On the other hand, Tommy John says dip and drive is good and cites Tom Seaver as a practitioner of that style.

Elbow height

The throwing elbow should be shoulder high as the ball passes your head in the pitching motion. From the front, the pitcher's arm is L-shaped at that moment. The bicep is horizontal and the forearm is vertical. Dropping the elbow is a sign of fatigue if the pitcher normally has it up where it belongs. But if the pitcher is still effective, I would not jump to any big conclusion about him dropping his elbow.

There have been effective pitchers with sidearm or submarine delivery, but those are dangerous to a youth player's arm and should not be taught.

One drill to correct this is to have a player throw while lying on his back. Do not throw **to** him when he is lying on his back. It's hard to catch while lying down, so it's dangerous.

Building self-confidence

How do you build a pitcher's self-confidence? All I know is to compliment successful pitches and shut up about unsuccessful ones. Do NOT pay your pitcher's cheap or insincere compliments. Just because they're kids doesn't mean they're stupid.

Also do not coach the pitcher continuously during the game. And do not let his relatives coach him during the game, if you can stop them.

Grip

The starting grip is the **four-seam** fastball I described earlier in the book. That is the inaccurately-named "**rising fastball**." (It is physically impossible for a ball to rise unless it is thrown in an upward direction.)

The **two-seam** fastball should give you a **sinker** ball. I recommend that you teach both the four-seam and two-seam fastballs to your pitchers. At the youth level, I doubt the ball is moving fast enough or rotating fast enough to generate movement "up" (the so-called "rising" fast ball actually just falls slower than normal) or down. But like Dumbo's feather, varying their grip between two- and four-seams may make your pitchers **think** they are doing something that will help.

Both grips are easy to master and neither poses any danger of injuring the player's arm. Teenage and older players almost always put just **two** fingers on the top of the ball. Because of their smaller hands, youth pitchers may find it helpful to put **three** fingers on the top of the ball.

Almost all baseball books say the fastball is the best pitch in baseball and that youth pitchers spend too little time on it. I agree. Nolan Ryan threw nothing but fastballs until he was 23. He was also throwing in the 90's when he was 43, a time when less that 7% of Major League pitchers could throw over 90. In the foreword to Ryan's *Pitcher's Bible*, Dr. Eugene Coleman said Major League pitching velocity was declining 2 mph per decade, apparently the result of young pitchers not throwing enough fastballs, enough pitches per workout, and enough pitches per week.

The pitch I had the most trouble hitting was the well-located, very fast fastball. Because it's so fast, you have to make a decision on whether to swing quickly—before you know whether it's a pitcher's pitch or a hitter's pitch.

Hall of Fame pitcher Robin Roberts said the only pitch he had was a fastball. In Roberts era, the fifties, about 80% of the pitches thrown by all pitchers were fastballs. Nowadays, old-timers say, pitchers are trying to be too "cute" with all their breaking balls. The last place you want to be being "cute" is on a youth team. Ray Miller says the recent decline of Major League pitching is partially a result of "overcoaching" at the Little League level, specifically, kids being taught to throw curveballs, knuckleballs, and split-fingered fastballs.

Fastball location

In the big leagues, you are supposed to put a fastball low and away or high and inside. I do not think sub-teen pitchers have enough control to teach them such things. At the teen level, they may be able to do it.

In the 1999 Little League World Series, I often saw the catcher set up on one side of the plate and the pitch go to the other. You generally do not see that in a Major League game. If your pitcher cannot hit the side of the plate that the catcher sets up on, forget this sort of fine control.

Changeup

Good **fastball** pitchers are **born, not made**, although practice improves the pitch. On the other hand, good **off-speed** pitchers are **made, not born**. All youth pitchers should have a changeup. When Scott McGregor was in the Major Leagues, he threw his changeup about 80% of the time. The ideal location for a change is low, but don't worry about that if your pitchers have trouble with control. Tommy John said,

> The changeup is the greatest pitch in baseball. I wish someone had taught me to change speeds when I was younger.

> The secret of pitching is to make the hitter think you're throwing a little harder than you are or a little slower than you are.

Only throw a changeup to a batter who can hit your fastball. In youth baseball, the batters often have no hope of hitting the pitcher's fastball, but they **can** hit his changeup. Save the change for the best hitters in the opposing lineup, and then only if they can hit the fastball.

My son simply threw slower when he wanted to throw a changeup. The real changeup is supposed to be thrown with the same arm speed as the fastball, only you do not whip your wrist. My son's slowing his arm did not seem to diminish the effectiveness of the pitch, but I suspect it would at the older age levels.

Many pitchers make the opposite mistake—they move their body faster when they throw a change to try to fool the batter. It ends up being a tip-off.

There are different changeup grips. One is the **palm ball** where you just grip the ball with your palm and the entire surface of your fingers. Normally, there should be daylight between your palm and the ball. Having your whole hand in contact with the ball slows it down. That's all a changeup is—just a slow pitch.

There is also the **circle change** where you make an "OK" sign with your hand (thumb and index finger form a circle) then grip the ball with the "OK" sign intact. This pitch goes slower because you are not using one of your strongest fingers, the index finger.

If you normally throw with a two-finger grip, switching to **three fingers** can produce a changeup lowering of velocity.

In his book, *Pitching from the Ground Up*, Bob Bennett says you can also throw a changeup, not with a different grip, but by keeping your back foot touching the rubber longer during the follow-through, then letting it drag off the rubber at the end of the follow-through. This is called the **dead-leg** changeup. He says that's the easiest changeup to learn, which should perk up the ears of any youth coach.

USC coach Rod Dedeaux says, "A changeup thrown at the knees is 100% effective; a changeup thrown below the knees is 50% effective."

Pitching books

There are several books with excellent discussions of these pitches as well as photographs of the grips. It would add nothing to the world's knowledge of those pitches if I took grip photos and put them in this book. Get the other books.

Nolan Ryan's Pitcher's Bible shows the four-seam fastball, circle change, and curveball grips.

In his book, *The Art of Pitching*, Tom Seaver has whole chapter on the fast ball, including both the "rising" fast ball and the sinker. He also shows not only his own grip, but also those of other pitchers like Nolan Ryan and Steve Carlton. He has another chapter on breaking pitches (curve and slider) and a chapter on the changeup. All three chapters have numerous photos of the grips from various angles.

Pat Jordan's *Sports Illustrated Pitching* has drawings showing proper and improper grips for the four-seam fastball. He also discusses varying the release point to 3/4 and sidearm to change the movement of the ball, as well as the best location in the strike zone to throw the fastball.

Jordan also shows drawings for the curveball, slider, changeup, screwball, forkball, and knuckleball. I do not believe it is possible for a child to throw a forkball. Their hands are not big enough. Also, throwing curveballs without expert training is ill advised at the preteen level.

Throwing any other kind of breaking ball is so dangerous it is often outlawed by team policy in the professional minor leagues. The only baseball players who should throw sliders are adults with a legitimate shot at the Major Leagues, but whose fastball and curveball are not good enough by themselves. Youth coaches must resist the temptation to show off to their youth pitchers by teaching them how to throw sliders and such.

If you can coach players to throw a knuckleball, God bless you. It's an impossible pitch to hit. Some say it's also impossible to catch. It may be the best pitch in baseball, but learning how to throw it seems to be a mysterious art. I had a knuckleball serve when I played volleyball, but I never learned how to throw the baseball equivalent. Some experts say that a pitcher cannot both throw a good fastball **and** master the knuckleball.

In his book *Pitching*, Dan Schlossberg shows two changeup grips. One is a palm ball with the five fingers avoiding touching any seams. In another, he has three fingers crossing the seams and the little finger off to the side.

I have no preference for any of the various changeup grips. Teach any or all to your pitchers and let them experiment. Again, they might benefit psychologically from using them all, thinking they are confounding the batters with a wide array of different pitches.

Curveball

Even when their mechanics are perfect, youth pitchers still should rarely throw it because it takes practice repetitions away from the fastball, which strengthens the arm. You can only throw a precious few times in each practice session or game. Young pitchers need to throw as many fastballs as possible to make their arms stronger.

Dan Schlossberg's book *Pitching* has a chapter called "Pitches you can throw now" and one called "Pitches you can throw later." The "Now" chapter only covers the fastball and changeup. He says,

> …coaches and trainers insist that young pitchers throw only fastballs and changeups until their growing arms have matured. *We cannot emphasize this strongly enough.* [emphasis in original]

In their book *The First Pitching Book*, the IBI instructors say,

> *Don't throw breaking pitches until your body has reached maturity (age 15, 16, 17?); and then, do so only under the supervision of a knowledgeable pitching coach.*

At the college and pro levels, pitchers generally need at least three pitches: typically the fastball, changeup, and curve. But at lower levels, the fastball and changeup are enough. They are difficult enough to master. A youth pitcher with a great fastball and changeup will outperform a youth pitcher with more pitches that he has not mastered, especially if the breaking-ball-throwing youth pitcher has injured his arm trying to learn to throw those pitches.

When I played **semi-pro** baseball, the vast majority of pitchers I faced threw fastballs and curves. But few of them could throw the curve for strikes. So if you had less than two strikes, you would generally just ignore the pitch when you saw the curve release.

If the semi-pros have not yet mastered their curve, it's a bit silly for eleven-year olds to be working on it.

Spit ball

The spit ball is illegal. It would be unethical to teach it to your players. However, you can have some fun and maybe increase your pitchers' success by starting **rumors** that they throw the spit ball. I never did this, but I read about it in Billy Martin's book *Billy Ball*.

You can teach the "dry spit ball," which is legal. According to Martin, you grip it only on bare leather, no seams. You throw it like a fastball, except that you open your hand when you release it. He says it sails, dips, and darts like a wet spit ball. It does not sound like there is any danger it would injure a youth pitcher. Plus, if you teach your pitchers the dry spit ball you can yell out to the mound during the game, "Throw him the dry spit ball, Mike."

Use of the phrase "spit ball," even when prefaced with the word "dry," psyches out the opposing team—both coaches and batters. As Martin says, if the opposing team **thinks** your pitcher is throwing a spit ball, that's almost as good as actually throwing it.

Major League legend Gaylord Perry wrote the book, *The Spitter and Me*. In 1974, Perry had a 21-13 record. Dave Duncan was his catcher. Duncan says Perry only threw one spitball all season. But he also says Perry adopted odd, furtive mannerisms on the mound to make batters wary and angry. Teach your pitchers and catchers to give the ball to the ump in the event of a challenge by a suspicious opposing manager. If you give it to the **opposing manager**, he may **put** some foreign substance on it to frame you.

Take care to make sure your players don't think you are winking at throwing a real (wet) spit ball.

Warm up before pitching

As a grown-up, I have to warm up my arm before I throw full speed. At the beginning of each season, I must also gradually get my arm into baseball shape. In fact, I made a point of playing semi-pro during the winter so I would not have to go through the pain and effort of getting my arm back into shape for the adult spring and summer season.

All the youth baseball books say youth players, especially pitchers, must also warm up their arms like grown-ups. I am not sure I believe that. I am a former kid. We played a ton of baseball in the fifties, but I do not remember any of us warming up our arms. Nor do I remember anyone hurting his arm because he didn't warm up. So I suspect this warm-up stuff is adults asking kids to do adult stuff because adults need to do it, not because kids need to do it. Like an overweight mom making her trim kids eat cottage cheese because **she** is on a diet.

However, I do not have the money to research this scientifically, so you had better have your kids warm up their arms before throwing hard. Although the fact that you are allowed eight pitches before each inning does not mean you have to take all eight. My pitchers generally did not take all eight because I counted them toward their total. They would take two or three to see if they felt OK then stop. Especially on a hot day, I would urge my pitchers **not** to use all eight pre-inning pitches.

The Individual Baseball Instruction School says your game-day pitching should be limited to 30-40 pre-game warm-up pitches, eight pre-inning warm-up pitches and 50 game pitches at the 9-10-year-old level and 70 game pitches at the 11-12-year-old level. A warm-up pitch is not thrown at maximum velocity. A game pitch **is** near max velocity. Tom Seaver says to finish your pre-game warm-up pitches about five minutes before the game starts.

Do not pitch from flat ground

Your pitchers should always pitch from a mound. Pitching from flat ground will screw them up because their stride foot will land sooner. Kids who want to work on their pitching at home should build a mound in their back yard. Youth baseball leagues should build extra mounds near game and practice fields so pitchers never have to warm-up or practice on flat ground.

Time until pitch

Much of sports is getting into a rhythm or preventing your opponent from getting into one. Accordingly, pitchers should vary the number of seconds that elapse between when they come set and when they pitch. This is especially important at the teen level with a runner on base. One year, I gave my son a number before each pitch. It was the number of seconds he was to pause before throwing. I varied it randomly. That is disconcerting to both batters and teen base runners.

Arm pump

You are allowed to pump once or twice before you pitch. If you can do it without screwing up yourself, you might want to throw in an occasional pump or double pump to mess with the batter's mind. Do not do it at the teen level with a runner on base, however.

Glove flick

Another thing we learned from baseball books and tried was having the pitcher flick his glove. You can do it every time or just some of the time. Tom Seaver recommends this. Jim Palmer, another Hall of Fame pitcher, also did this. It distracts the batter.

These may work as "magic feathers" that increase the pitcher's confidence. These are simple tricks that anyone can master and which can be taught in the brief span of a youth season.

Head jerk

Tim McCarver says, "Pitchers without dominating stuff find ways to throw off a batter's timing…some pitchers try no enhance their pitches with some odd body and head movements that catch the batter's eye when he should be looking only for the ball leaving the hand." He cited Stu Miller who used a dramatic head jerk. Miller head jerked his way to a 16-year career in the fifties and sixties including several league-leading stats.

Underhand

You are even allowed to pitch underhand like a softball pitcher or like the old-time baseball players. I played in a number of games in Golden Gate Park in San Francisco. They have a statue of a baseball pitcher there—and old-time pitcher. He is throwing underhanded. My oldest son practiced this, but never had the guts to do it in a game. It would be a good two-out, two-strike pitch in the final inning of a close game. It will probably make the opponents angry, but it's legal and it will definitely screw up the batter's concentration.

Cannot be tense

Pitching is a high-pressure role, but the pitcher must be tension-free to do his best. Remember, you do not throw as hard as you can, or at least you only do it rarely. Strive for a strong, but very smooth delivery.

'Let 'er rip'

Youth pitchers often try to be too fine. They get concerned about control and start looking like they are throwing darts. You must convince your pitchers to, "**Let** it happen, don't **make** it happen."

I tell my pitchers their sole job is to focus their eyes on the target and let 'er rip. I tell them not to think about control. "Control will take care of itself if you focus your eyes on the target. The main thing is to whip the ball at the target in a relaxed, but strong, way. It goes where it goes. *Que sera, sera.* Don't worry about where it goes. **I** will take responsibility for that. You just worry about where your eyes are focused and let 'er rip."

Sophisticated tactics

Most pitching books have extensive discussions of pitching tactics—subtle variations in locations and speed as well as set-up pitches. The authors are proud of their knowledge. Those tactics are, indeed, crucial to adult pitchers. But at the youth level, they are probably much too much. Kids have trouble throwing strikes. Just get them relaxed and focused. Leave the subtle tactics to the grown-up pitchers.

Signs of fatigue

Tired pitchers droop. Their elbow stops getting as high as their shoulder as they throw. The thigh of their stride leg stops reaching a point where it is parallel to the ground. As a coach, you should watch for these signs. Fatigue does not necessarily mean you need to take the pitcher out. That decision is always a function of who else you have as well as whether the pitcher is losing effectiveness. Maybe he is still getting batters out in spite of his fatigue because of his reputation or because his fastball has inadvertently become an effective changeup.

Ice after the game

All pitchers should ice their arms (shoulder and elbow) after each game. In fact, pitching injures the arm the way strenuous weight lifting does. In repairing itself, the arm becomes stronger. But the injury is, indeed, one which warrants icing.

It is now common for parents to provide snacks after each game. This is typically a cold drink and a candy or fruit. The parent of the day should be required to bring crushed ice or ice cubes. The team should also have zip-loc bags or other means of attaching the ice to the shoulder and elbow after the player comes out of the game.

No sore-armed pitchers

Never allow a pitcher to pitch if his arm is sore. Many a youth coach has left his star pitcher on the mound after the pitcher told the coach that his arm was sore. One of my youth pitchers said he had trouble ever since the previous season when another manager made him stay on the mound after he complaiend his arm was sore. Those coaches should be horse whipped.

Players and parents must be told before the season that no one is ever to pitch with a sore arm.

Location

Remember that you do not have to throw strikes to get a batter out. A pitch outside the strike zone is a strike if the umpires says it is or if the batter swings at it. In youth baseball, those two things happen often.

Umpire's blind spots

Many, if not most, youth umpires have one or more blind spots. Pitches thrown to those blind spots are balls, but the ump calls them strikes. When you spot such an ump, you should have your pitcher throw to that ump's blind spots all day.

How do you ascertain the ump's blind spots? Scout umps at other games and pay close attention at your own games. When you see the blind spots, call time and inform your pitcher and catcher if your team is not at bat.

Batter's blind spots

Many, probably most, youth batters have spots in or near the strike zone where they make the wrong decision. There are spots where you can throw a pitch that is a ball, but the batter will generally swing at it. If that's the case, hit those spots.

Some batters are reluctant to swing at any pitch. They are hoping for a walk. Against those guys, you might as well throw it down the pipe.

Some batters will swing, but not at some strikes, for

whatever reason. Those are the locations to which you should throw your strike pitches. For example, against my batters, who will not swing at pitcher's pitches on the first two strikes, you should throw around the edges of the strike zone.

Holes in batter's swing

Then there are other times when a batter makes the right decision about whether to swing, but he has a hole in his swing. That is, he cannot hit a pitch in a particular location even when he swings at it. Or maybe he can hit it, but he cannot hit it fair or he cannot hit it hard.

Scouting increases confidence

In youth football, one of the unexpected benefits I got from scouting was that my players became much more confident. Youth players are easily intimidated, especially by "good" teams.

But its hard to be intimidated after your coach has run through a list of the opposing batter's weaknesses, especially when, as the game progresses, the players see that #12 chase high pitches just like the coach said he would.

The list should be used also during the game to set the catcher's target.

0-2 pitch

When the count is 0-2, you often hear coaches say, "Don't give him anything good to hit." That's good advice, but at the youth level, you can often throw a strike which, for that batter, is "not anything good to hit." Or, you could throw a ball to a spot where that batter tends to swing at pitches out of the strike zone.

3-0 pitch

Here, you obviously have to throw a strike, unless you want to intentionally walk the batter. For most youth pitchers, they should throw whatever pitch they have the most control over. Many, if not most, youth coaches give the take sign on this pitch. I do not. But I have extraordinary confidence in my batters' abilities to lay off ball four. If the opposing coach appears to have the take sign on whenever the count is 3-0, throw it down the pipe using your best control pitch.

3-1 pitch

The batter probably has the green light on this pitch and is expecting a fastball down the middle. You have to throw a strike, but it would be nice to throw a changeup for that strike, unless the batter cannot hit your fastball.

Control your pitchers

In the baserunning discussion, I said to leave the runners alone. Do not try to control them.

I recommend the exact **opposite** with pitchers. Either you or your catcher should tell the pitcher what pitch to throw, where to throw it, and how many seconds to wait before throwing it. What I am trying to do with all this control is take as much responsibility off the pitcher's shoulders as possible. Also, I am trying to eliminate the pitcher **thinking**, which usually messes him up at the youth level.

If there is a bad result, like a walk or a hit, I can then say, "Hey, don't feel bad. It was **my** idea to throw those pitches. It's **my** fault he walked [or got a hit]." I want the pitcher to see his role as similar to just pushing buttons. It's as if he were sitting in front of a panel with many buttons and I was telling him, "Hit number three. OK, now hit number nine." And so forth. That is a much easier chore than "We need to get this guy out, Evan."

In general, I think the **manager** should control the pitcher in youth baseball. If you have an exceptional **catcher** who wants to do it, let him try. Clearly, the catcher has a better vantage point. The problem in youth baseball is that the catcher is a kid. He may be too unsure of himself or too ignorant about pitching to impart confidence or give good direction to the pitcher.

In some cases, your **pitcher** may want to call his own game. If so, let him try. If he does well, that's the optimum, but the typical youth pitcher lacks that much self-confidence. Do **not** let the catcher or pitcher call the game because "that's the way it's supposed to be done."

In the 1999 Little League World Series, I noticed that one manager squatted down like a catcher with a mitt on and called each pitch from the dugout. I agree with that much control, but I would prefer to do it by just holding up a white board or MagnaDoodle with code numbers on it.

For example, you could use a four-digit code in which the upper left number was the number of seconds to wait, the upper right was the location, the lower left meant nothing, and lower right was the type of pitch. Don't just do 1 = fastball and 2 = changeup. Do something harder to decipher like an odd number means changeup and even means fastball.

Work fast

In general, you should have your pitchers and catchers work fast. Some batteries take forever, which slows down the game, puts fielders to sleep, gives the pitcher too much time to think, and often causes games to run over into subsequent games.

Working fast means the catcher throws the ball back to the pitcher promptly from the catcher's box. He does not walk half way to the mound after every pitch like some catchers do.

The pitcher needs to catch the ball thrown back from the catcher, take a breath, then get on the rubber. Occasionally, when the pitcher is struggling, he should take a moment to gather himself. Some pitchers pick a distant spot like a water tower, and focus on it to calm themselves own.

When the pitcher gets on the rubber, he and the catcher get their sign from the coach, the pitcher counts the designated number to himself, then throws.

Pick smaller target than you can hit

If you aim at the strike zone, there is a good chance you will miss. But if you aim at a small spot within the strike zone, like the catcher's Adam's apple, you may not hit the Adam's apple, but it is more likely that you will hit the strike zone. Teach your pitchers to always aim at a target smaller than a baseball on the catcher's or umpire's body. They focus their eyes on that target throughout the pitching motion and let 'er rip.

Forget the last pitch

Everybody in baseball must forget what happened on the last pitch and focus on the next pitch, but that is most true of pitchers. Like football defensive backs, they must cultivate amnesia. There should be nothing in the brain but target and let 'er rip every time they throw a pitch. In addition to **what will be, will be**, pitchers must also understand that **what's done is done**. Nolan Ryan says, "I think the ability to respond in a positive way to failure is what sets winners apart from losers." As everyone knows, anyone who plays baseball is going to experience multiple failures, so they'd better learn how to handle them.

It might be useful in a pre-season practice game to stand next to your pitcher during the game and admonish him in the proper mental attitude.

Let's say he walks a sub-teen batter.

"Forget about it. What's done is done. All you can do is focus on the next pitch. Get your sign. Get your grip. Count to your self. Focus on the target. Let 'er rip."

He throws a called strike.

"That's good, but you have to forget about that, too. You cannot be thinking about recent failures **or** successes. Always focus on the **next** pitch. Check the runner. Get your sign. Get your grip. Count to yourself. Focus on the target. Let 'er rip."

He throws a ball.

"Deep breath. Focus your eyes on your calming spot (e.g., a distant flag pole). Check the runner. Get your sign. Get your grip. Count. Focus on target. Let 'er rip."

And so on.

At the teen level, you would need to add more runner checks and pick-offs.

Bad umpire calls

Umpires making bad calls is a part of the game at every level. Bad calls are really common in youth baseball where the umpires are often unpaid, inexperienced, poorly motivated, and/or poorly trained. Your pitcher needs to ignore bad calls. Give him some practice. Play the role of umpire and call balls strikes and strikes balls. Your pitchers and batters must remain absolutely poker-faced throughout.

Vary the number of looks

In teen level baseball, the pitcher should usually check any runner before pitching. But many pitchers get into the habit of doing the same number of looks each time. That is wrong. You must vary the number of looks from zero to two or three. You could make one of the numbers on the code board cover this at the teen level. You might say that the number of looks is to be the lower left number on the board minus two. Then a three in that position would mean look at the runner once before this pitch.

Pick-off moves

You need to practice pick-off moves at any level at which you plan to use them. Many coaches think they only apply to the teen level, because you cannot take a pre-pitch lead below that level. In fact, they probably do only apply to the teen level, but if you can do pick-offs at the sub-teen level, you can get some outs.

The move to each base is different. You need to practice each. I do not think this is so much a teaching drilling thing as just a reps thing. That is, if you give your players a chance to do it over and over, they will figure out the right way. You should get a training video, or make one by taping college or pro games off TV. Your players ought to do the same thing as those guys, and probably will without any instruction. Use the tapes just to make sure your players are not doing their pick-off moves in some convoluted, inefficient or inaccurate way.

Most youth pitchers are not confident enough of their pick-off moves. Consequently, they should be easy pickings for well-trained base runners. Giving your players a lot of pick-off reps will either give them more confidence, or reveal that they simply cannot execute the moves safely enough.

Pick-off at first

For the **right**-handed pitcher, the pick-off move to first from the set position involves a 90-degree jump pivot. This is difficult and requires practice to get comfortable.

For the **left**-handed pitcher, the pickoff to first is a piece of cake. He can either just flick the ball to first from the straddle position, or he can pick his stride leg up as if to pitch then step toward first and throw a pick-off. It is a balk for the left-handed pitcher to swing his stride knee behind the front plane of the rubber, then not pitch to the plate.

It is illegal to fake a pick-off to first from the rubber. You **can** fake a pick-off to first if you step off (put

your throwing-side foot behind or on the second-base side of the rubber) the rubber first.

It is also a balk to throw to any base from the rubber without stepping toward that base. If they enforce the balk rule at your level, learn it and teach it to your pitchers. Show them each type of balk and have them do it. Then have them do the **correct** version of what they were doing when they balked.

Pick-off at second

At second, the pitcher must do either a 180-degree jump pivot or step toward the base at the height of the stride-leg lift. For a right-handed pitcher, the leg-lift spin would be clockwise; for a left-handed pitcher, counterclockwise.

Pick-offs to second also require coordination with a baseman because they do not hold the runner like at first. Essentially, you have to make an "appointment" with the baseman, secretly communicating to him that you are going to throw to the base in three seconds. Then you make your turn as the baseman is breaking toward the bag and throw the ball above the bag. If the baseman misses the "appointment," your throw becomes a grounder to the center fielder. Accordingly, it is good if the center fielder also knows of the "appointment" so he can break in on the play.

The sign must be acknowledged. That is, the baseman and center fielder must indicate that they got the sign. Most pitchers do this by subtle things like touching a cap. In youth baseball, I suspect that you would be better off doing **obvious** signs like having the pitcher call out a two-digit number which the middle infielders and center fielder repeat back to him.

Basically, that tells the runner at second that the four nearby players are aware of him and that they may have put on a pick-off play. The element of surprise may be the best way to go in the pros, but at the youth level, an ounce of warning is worth a pound of throws.

More conservative ways to hold a runner close

Simply **stepping off** the rubber should cause an aggressive base runner to dive back. Your pitcher can step off a million times, but the runner cannot dive back a million times. Diving back is very tiring.

You do not need to throw a **top-speed** fastball over to the base every time you make a pick-off move. You can throw the ball slowly sometimes. While in the Men's Senior Baseball League, I saw some former pros' pick-off moves. Scary.

One guy would throw over at about 75 miles an hour and chest high a couple times. Then the next one would be in the 80's and right at the first baseman's right knee. If you throw slowly to first, remember that you must step toward the base and it must be one continuous motion.

The tricky part of pick-off moves is the **turn**. But you can make a pick-off move with**out** the turn if you do it **before** you step on the rubber or **after** you step off. You can make a hard, empty-hand fake to any base if you are **not** on the rubber and you can make such a fake to second or third, if they are occupied, even if you **are** on the rubber.

At the teen level, you can take a **full-windup position** on the rubber. After which, you can step off (put your throwing-side foot behind the rubber) and throw to first faster than if you are in the set position. This move also requires less of a turn.

You can even throw to first from the rubber in the windup position, if you can do so without making "any natural movement associated with delivery of the ball to the batter. . ." If the opposing runner knows to automatically steal whenever the pitcher throws from a full windup, this conservative pick-off move is even more likely to succeed.

Balk rule not enforced

The balk rule is in the Little League Rule Book, but I have never seen it enforced at the sub-teen level. And it was enforced sometimes and not others at the teen level.

Fine. Start every game by asking the ump and opposing coach if the balk rule will be enforced. When they say, "No," tell your pitchers to balk their butts off. You can do the hidden-ball trick and have the pitcher get on the rubber and fake throwing a pitch. That's a double balk, but the ump told you before the game started that they were not going to enforce the balk rule, remember?

Announcing that we are not going to enforce rules like the infield-fly, balk, or correct strike zone annoys me greatly. Those rules were put in for a reason. Those who announce we are not going to enforce them are just demonstrating their ignorance of the reason.

No walking leads

Never let a batter take a walking lead. Always wait until he stops before you pitch. Give each pitcher one rep of doing this at each base.

Competitive practice

You should do competitive pick-off drills to give both your base runners and your pitchers practice. Remember competitive drills are more fun and can last longer than noncompetitive drills.

Quick delivery to the plate

Walter Alston says the pitch should get to the catcher within 1.3 second of the first move of the pitcher's body. Stopping base runners is not just a matter of holding the runner close. Eventually, you have to throw a pitch. If you cannot throw the pitch to the plate quickly, the runner will successfully steal regardless of your holding him close to the base. One way of speeding up the delivery is the glide step, which means not lifting your stride leg as high as normal.

Intentional walk

You have to practice the intentional walk just a little. The trick is to avoid a **catcher balk**. That is where the catcher has one foot out of the catcher's box before the pitch is thrown.

Most people think you only do an intentional walk when first base is open. Seems to me you do it whenever the opponent will probably get fewer runs with that batter at first than with him swinging at pitches. Diamondback manager Buck Showalter intentionally walked Barry Bonds with the base loaded in a 1998 game! Before the intentional walk, Arizona was ahead 8-6 with two outs in the ninth inning. The batter after Bonds lined out ending the game. Arizona won 8-7.

On July 23, 1944, New York Giants manager Mel Ott intentionally walked the Cubs' Bill Nicholson in the 8th inning with the bases loaded and the Giants up 10-7 in the second game of a double header. Nicholson had hit four home runs that day. The Cubs got three runs without a hit (four walks and a hit batsman) and tied the score in the inning when Nicholson was walked. The Giants came back and scored two runs in the bottom of the eighth inning, which led to their victory when the Cubs went scoreless in the ninth. (Neither of these moves were brilliant managing. In both cases they were lucky to survive with a win.)

In youth baseball, where the disparity between the worst hitter and the best is often night and day, walking a strong hitter to get to a weak one makes far more sense than it does in the pros. There is also often a great disparity between a pitcher and hitter in youth baseball. You do not want a weak pitcher throwing to a .750 hitter.

I never intentionally walked anyone in my coaching career—either in youth or adult/semi-pro baseball. Looking back, I probably should have. I only remember seeing one other manager intentionally walk one of my batters. I do not recall the situation or whether the move paid off for them.

Fake intentional walk

In the 1972 World Series, Johnny Bench was batting for Cincinnati. With a 2-2 count, Rollie Fingers threw a wild pitch and the runner on first advanced to second. A's manager Dick Williams excitedly called timeout and pointed to first base. Catcher Gene Tenace then stood up as if to receive a pitchout. Suddenly he crouched behind the plate and caught a pitch while Bench was starting to walk toward first. Strike three! Bench was outraged and called it a "bush-league" play.

Sour grapes. Actually, it **was** a bush-league play, by

Bench. When you are in the batter's box and the pitch is coming, you always have to be ready to hit, especially when you have two strikes.

Bench still was not ready to admit he screwed up 27 years later when he wrote *The Complete Idiot's Guide to Baseball*. That book does not mention that play, but it mentions all the other noteworthy events in his career. Seems like he could have jokingly cited that play as evidence of his qualification to author that particular title. Williams' trick was excellent managing and it was superbly executed by Fingers and Tenace. Gene Tenace won the World Series MVP award that year.

Unintentional intentional walk

This is a phrase I got from Storm Davis when he was an Oakland A's pitcher. He said he would sometimes walk a strong batter intentionally, but that it would look like he was trying to get him out. He would throw the guy nothing but balls that were near, but not in, the strike zone. If the batter was dumb enough to chase them, he would get the guy out. But if the batter took the pitches, he would walk. Another way to put it is if a batter is really good, you may not want to give him anything good to hit. It's an intentional walk, but one with the possibility that the batter will screw up and turn it into an out.

Pitchout

I have never seen a pitchout in youth baseball. I rarely saw them in semi-pro. It might make sense at the elite teen level.

I **did** do a thing I called a "pitch in." In a "pitch in," I simply told my catcher to throw to second on the next pitch regardless of whether the runner went. That eliminated the split second that would be lost while the catcher was figuring out that the runner had gone. I would call this when a sure-to-go base stealer got on first.

Never had any great success with it, but it gave the runners something else to worry about. I only did this when I was confident about my catcher and middle infielder. Otherwise, it violates the youth rule of avoiding ball handling whenever possible.

Quick return pitch

There is a widespread belief among youth baseball coaches that you can throw the pitch anytime the batter has both feet in the batter's box. I have seen many coaches who deliberately teach their pitchers to throw the ball the moment the batter gets both feet in the box, even though he is not ready.

This is **illegal**. Little League Rule 2.00. "A quick return pitch is a pitch made with obvious intent to catch the batter off balance."

It is also extremely **dangerous**. Once, my oldest son was playing in a game where I was just a helper. I was coaching my younger son's team that year.

The plate umpire was the father of the opposing pitcher. One of our guys stepped into the batter's box and looked to third for the sign. At that moment, the umpire silently signalled for his son to the throw the pitch with a "come here" hand motion.

The pitch turned out to be a ball inside. Our batter never saw it coming. Fortunately, it did not hit him.

I went ballistic. I did not curse or anything, but I complained to all present that the pitch was illegal because it was unfair and could injure a batter.

The umpire "threw me out of the game," except I was not in the game to begin with. I was a spectator in the bleachers behind the screen. He knew he was wrong. He just didn't think anybody saw what he did or knew that it was illegal.

The punishment for an illegal pitch is a **warning** and the pitch is to be called a **ball** regardless of its location. If any **play** occurs, the manager of the batting team gets to **take the play or the ball** call, whichever he wants, just like in football. If there are runners on base, an illegal pitch is a **balk**.

When to take a pitcher out

This is a key managerial decision, but neither I nor anyone else seems to know how to make it (that is, prior to the maximum pitch count for safety being exceeded). Clearly, who else you have available is a factor. So is your game schedule for the next week.

I have taken pitchers out too soon and left them in too long. It's a judgment thing. Pitchers rarely improve after they get tired. But they do often recalibrate their attitude and find a groove. Some should be taken out immediately because they simply are not having a good day. Others run hot and cold during an appearance in which they are more effective on average than their replacement would be.

'Work fast. Change speeds. Throw strikes.'

One of the most famous admonitions in professional baseball is pitching coach Ray Miller's, "Work fast. Change Speeds. Throw strikes."

Is that also good advice for youth pitchers?

No. The youth version is modified.

"Work fast. Change speeds if the batter can hit your fastball. Throw pitches that either the batter will swing at or the umpire will call strikes."

It is crazy to change speeds if the batter cannot hit your fastball, which is common, if not the rule, in youth baseball.

It is also crazy to throw a pitch into the strike zone if the batter and/or umpire are turning some balls into strikes by chasing or mislabeling them, which also is common.

Practice throwing to bunters

You need to give your pitcher practice throwing to a

batter who shows bunt. The reason is that unexpected movement by the batter often discombobulates an inexperienced pitcher.

Opinionated old men

When I was writing this chapter, I got a huge stack of baseball books and read what each had to say about pitching. By the end of the stack, I was pretty annoyed.

For example, some guys tell you how to **kick** in your pitching motion. Others say you should **never** kick. In view of the fact that Juan Marichal kicked and did well, I think it's OK to kick, although it is probably more difficult to maintain balance if you do. Marichal probably had unusually good balance.

Half the authors think "rising fastballs" literally rise; the other half know that they do not. (That has been tested with wind tunnels and high-speed photography.)

Frequently, the book authors prefaced their advice with remarks like, "We feel that…" I have considerable respect for experienced people, however, I also respect the scientific method, which says it's not enough to sit around forming opinions. You have to **test** them.

I wish the East Germans had competed in baseball. They would have tested the heck out of every theory.

My general impression is that the various pitching experts are guys who got drafted out of high school, pitched in the pros, and hung around baseball afterward. They have observed and formed opinions.

That's not good enough. If you think, for example, that pitchers must run two miles a day, you should **test** that theory by having a bunch of them run two miles a day and a bunch **not** run two miles a day. Then observe their pitching performance and compare the two groups. You can also have a group of pitchers run two miles a day one season and not the next and compare their performance in the two seasons.

True, there can be many other factors that would explain differences in such tests, but **not testing at all** is fraught with even more potential for erroneous conclusions. The fact is such a test would probably be inconclusive, in which case the opinionated old man who thought running two miles a day made you a great pitcher should admit that it really didn't seem to have much effect.

In this book, I have told you of coaching theories I had that, when tested, did **not** seem to work. For example, I taught the heck out of batting mechanics in my early years, only to find that it seemed to make the batters **worse**. But I have never read a single admission that another baseball author once had a theory that turned out to be wrong. Not one. Consequently, I generally only put in this chapter the advice where there was a **consensus** among the opinionated old men.

Separate pitching coach

It is common for a youth baseball team to have a separate coach for the pitchers. Typically, that coach pitched in college or at least high school.

That's probably a good idea, but everything I said in this chapter still applies. No matter how expert the coach, it is a very bad idea to start down the road of trying to change pitching mechanics during the brief course of a youth baseball season.

What I would have such a pitching coach do is **model** the correct mechanics. That is, just silently demonstrate what good pitching mechanics look like many times over the course of the season. I would also have him focus on the other stuff in this chapter—proper stance, grip, etc.

Size of the ball

The ball thrown by 6'10" Randy Johnson in the professional Major Leagues has a circumference of nine to nine-and-a-quarter inches and weighs between five and five-and-a-quarter ounces. The ball thrown by a 3'6" Little leaguer is the exact same size and weight.

Excuse me.

Little League **bats** are smaller than Major League bats. Youth **football** players use two smaller sizes of youth football than those used by the pros.

Who came up with the bright idea to make youth baseball players throw a Major-League-size ball?

In Dr. Bobby Brown's Rookie League concept, smaller kids use a smaller ball. Makes sense. You should agitate for that in your league if you do not already have it.

Good youth pitchers are found, not made

In 1997, when I coached in the Orinda Valley Pony League, we were supposed to have a draft. But when we got there, the two coaches in charge **assigned** us our players. We previously had to fax in our ratings of each player. They said the players had been rated by the coaches and each coach was getting the same number from each rating category.

In retrospect, it appears to me that the two guys who ran the draft took care of themselves and gave the rest of us lesser players. I believe that they generally did give us players who were rated high, middle, and low, but the two guys who were in charge were very experienced in that league and knew the kids. I and some of the other coaches were brand new. I suspect the two guys in charge took the **real** best players and gave us the ones we **mistakenly** rated best because we only had a brief tryout to go on.

The two coaches who made those assignments finished first and second in the league. One of them told me at the end of the season that my team was the **best coached** in the league.

So why didn't my team win the championship? Because in baseball, coaching matters far less than talent, especially pitching talent. All but one of the teams in the league had just one good pitcher. The team that won the championship had three.

Did those three get good over the season because of their great pitching coaches? Nope. They were excellent at the beginning of the season. In all my career, I do not recall a single pitcher on any team in the league getting significantly better as the season went on.

In youth **football**, it is typical to see rookies blossom and become excellent players after about one or two months. I have never seen that in baseball during the course of a season. (I have seen baseball players get better from year to year, but that is not coaching. They have a different coach every year. It is maturation and experience.)

I know some fathers who got their kid private pitching lessons. Did it work? In the earliest years, yes. The kid looked great on the mound compared to the other, untrained players. But, over time, the score book revealed who really had talent and who did not and heavy doses of private, expert pitching instruction could not mask lack of talent.

If you want to win youth baseball championships, get good pitching. You do that by studying last year's score books to see which pitchers got the best results and drafting them, if you can. Do **not** look at things like who started. You are looking for **results** only, not previous coach impressions.

Many a youth pitcher who is regarded as the best on the team by his manager is **not** the best on the team. Witness my story of what happened to one of my best pitchers, Michael Ramos, when he was on other teams with other managers. He did not wow the manager in the bull pen, so he did not pitch.

So look for the Michael Ramoses in your local draft pool of talent and on your team—talented kids who are overlooked because of their quiet personalities or unlikely appearance. And if you do succeed in drafting them, do not then mess them up with a bunch of coaching of their mechanics.

When it comes to youth pitching, drafting beats coaching every time. As the man said in *Indiana Jones and the Last Crusade*, "Choose wisely."

Pitching position clinics
Clinic #1 (all levels)
6:30   Two-seam fastball
6:33   Changeup
6:38   Set-position stance
6:40   Signs
6:45   Select target to throw at
6:47   Thigh lift and stride
6:50   Follow through
6:55   Practice working fast
6:58   Pitch to batter showing bunt
7:00   End practice

Clinic #2 (all levels)
6:30   Keep eyes on the target throughout motion
6:35   Throw from various positions on the rubber: left, middle, right
6:40   How to step off
6:42   Dry spit ball
6:45   Vary time until pitch
6:47   Arm pump
6:49   Glove flick
6:50   Head jerk
6:52   Practice ignoring bad umpire calls
6:57   Intentional walk
7:00   End practice

At the teen level, you would give both of the above clinics and clinic #3.

Clinic #3 (teen level)
6:30   Keep eyes on the target throughout motion
6:35   Throw from various positions on the rubber: left, middle, right
6:40   How to step off
6:42   Dry spit ball
6:45   Vary time until pitch
6:47   Arm pump
6:49   Glove flick
6:50   Head jerk
6:52   Practice ignoring bad umpire calls
6:57   Intentional walk
        Pickoff (teenage level)
7:00   End practice

Obviously, it would be a good idea to have a pitcher clinic after **every** practice so you could not only introduce these skills, but also get good at them.

18 Easy way to learn the rules

"I will learn the rules and teach them to my players."

That is part of the Coach's Code of Ethics of the National Youth Sports Coaches Association. But it's so obvious that I was doing it before I ever heard of the NYSCA. I also felt I should learn the rules as a player.

To that end, I read **six books** on the rules of baseball. Some were the Little League and Major League rule books. The others were **case** books that clarified various situations you might not understand just from reading the raw rules. I also got and studied the National Federation of State High School Associations balk video ("Baseball: Pitching by the rules").

Only twenty-two rules

I learned the rules the **hard** way—by studying six books on the subject. But as a result of my learning them the hard way, **you** will be able to learn them the **easy** way. That's because I discovered that there are only about twenty-two rules that the typical youth coach or umpire does not know.

Study these rules. Understanding the reasons for them makes it much easier to learn them.

Transcribe (copy) these rules and their reference numbers to your league rule book onto a single, two-sided sheet of paper or card, encase it in plastic by lamination or put it in a plastic sheet cover, and take it to every game. Transcribing the rules onto that sheet will greatly enhance your remembering them. Carrying that sheet to games will accomplish two additional purposes:

• Help you find the rule you need quickly
• Give the rule- or case-book rule number so any skeptic can quickly check the actual rule book or case book to confirm the rule

Carry the actual rule book and case book with you at all times at games.

This is not foolproof. Once, my opponent re-spected my rules knowledge and did not need to see the sheet. Sometimes, I won the argument because of the sheet. But on other occasions, the opposing coach and umpire simply looked at the wording of the rule, saw I was right, and suddenly claimed that they were going by some never-before-heard-of "local rule."

'Local' rules

The way I read the Little League Rule Book, local leagues are **not allowed** to adopt local rules, except in rare specified areas. Unfortunately, the world headquarters of the various leagues do not police the rules within local leagues and there is no constituency who will complain. The coaches generally are blissful in their ignorance and the parents are either more ignorant than the coaches or terrified of rocking the boat for fear that their kid won't make majors or all-stars.

I urge you to **eliminate all local rules in your organization**. If you cannot do that, at least insist that the local rules be put in writing and distributed to each coach and umpire.

'You know the rules too well.'

I got chewed out once by the administrator of the league in which I coached. My crime? His exact words were, "You know the rules too well." This guy held a prominent and responsible position in local government. He was telling me to stop complying with the NYSCA Code of Ethics.

This is yet another example of the deliberate incompetence that is widespread within youth baseball. By learning the rules in the generally-ignorant-of-the-rules San Ramon Valley Little League, I had become the SRVLL equivalent of what some union members call a "rate buster." That is someone who makes the other workers look bad by producing more work per hour than they do.

I think NYSCA had it right. You should learn the rules and teach them to your players whenever you coach any sport. SRVLL's efforts to dumb my rules knowledge down to the ignorant group norm were out of line and unbecoming a "Home of Champions."

In the San Ramon Valley Little League, and I suspect in many other leagues, the coaches have not studied the rule book. They have their male ego instead. They played ball when they were younger. They watch TV. Having done thhose two things, they are outraged if you suggest they do not know the rules.

They **do** know a lot of rules—like three strikes is an out and four balls is a walk. But they do **not** know the twenty-two "often-misunderstood rules."

In SRVLL, rules disputes at games were generally decided in favor of the guy who made the biggest scene. There would come a point where the teenage umpire and opposing manager would decide, "It's not worth it," and surrender.

Invariably, these guys would be arguing with**out** a rule book. They were each issued one at the pre-season coach's meeting, but at the time of the argument, they probably could not tell you where it was. Or, in the alternative, they had it in their equipment bag, but they could not search it fast enough. If one coach tried to refer to a rule book during a dispute, the opposing parents would start moaning and groaning loudly and complaining, "C'mon, let the kids play," a phrase which invariably translates to "Let my side cheat."

My approach was to make a quick glance at my "Often-misunderstood rules" sheet and quietly state the correct rule. If anyone disputed me, I had the rule number and could offer to show it to them in my official rule book or case book, which were in my team loose-leaf binder in the dugout.

I was not loud or obnoxious about it, just firm and confident. The problem was my louder brethren had just committed themselves to the **in**correct rule in front of a bunch of fellow adults and their players, and they simply could not accept the loss of face inherent in being proven wrong. Indeed, they had begun the argument confident it would be decided as almost all SRVLL rules disputes were, by decibel level.

Furthermore, in a normal SRVLL rules dispute, you do not end up with a winner and a loser. You end up with one winner and another guy who seemingly took the "high road" by magnanimously letting the other manager have his way. Both end up happy in their respective ways.

But when they got into a rules argument with me, there was one guy who was right and one guy who was going to be publicly embarrassed for not knowing what he was talking about—at least until he started saying, "It's a local rule."

Teach the twenty-two often misunderstood rules

SRVLL had an annual rules clinic. It was required for the parents who agreed to umpire, as well as the teenagers who got paid to ump. It was optional for managers. I attended many years. Unfortunately, the instructor, who was an ancient umpire, focused on the **new** rules for that year, not on the often-misunderstood rules.

All leagues should have such a clinic and it must be **mandatory** for all managers, coaches, and umpires. The clinic should emphasize the twenty-two often-misunderstood rules and safety, as well as new rules for the year.

Rules arguments are one of the main sources of the ugliness for which youth baseball is famous. Leagues that refuse to hire real umpires have an obligation to the kids to find othher means to end these ugly incidents. Since there are only twenty-two rules that are causing almost all these rule-dispute problems,

correcting it is a simple matter, if the league will make the effort.

The twenty-two often-misunderstood rules

I have already discussed most of the twenty-two rules. Here they are along with their Little League Rule numbers:

- Balk 8.05
- Quick return pitch 2.00, 8.02(a)
- Obstruction 2.00, 7.06(a) & (b)
- Infield fly rule 2.00, 6.05(e)
- Timeout 2.00, 5.10(h)
- Stealing second on a walk 2.00 and page 1 of *The Right Call, Knotty Problems in Little League Baseball*
- Ball touches an umpire or base coach 5.08
- Runner hit by batted ball 5.09(f)
- Batter turning left after overrunning first base 7.08(c) exception and page 26 of *The Right Call*
- Overthrow 7.05
- Not sliding at a base 7.08(a)(3)
- Run scoring during third-out play 4.09(a)
- Batter hit by bounced pitch 6.08(b) and page 26 of *The Right Call*
- All male players must wear jocks 1.17
- Spectator interference (typically a base coach, umpire, passerby, or on-deck batter trying to be helpful) 2.00, 3.16
- Caught foul tip is live ball on all three strikes 2.00
- 20-second limit on pitches 8.04
- Batter out if either foot outside batter's box when hit ball 2.00
- Only one adult base "coacher" at a time 2.00
- Batter out if infielder deliberately drops ball when runner on first 6.05(l)
- Runner who passes another runner is out 7.08(h)
- Batter hit by pitch does not go to first if he swung at pitch or it was in strike zone 2.00

Note that the amount of pine tar allowed on bat handles is **not** on this list. That was one aspect of Billy Ball which I did **not** admire.

I deliberately did **not** type these rules out for you so you could photocopy the page for a number of reasons. One is I have a **1998** Little League Rule book. I tried to buy a more current one, but they refuse to sell it to me because I am not a "Chartered Little League Program."

You may not be in Little League. The rules and rule numbers in other leagues may be different.

It is an important learning experience for you to type the rules yourself. Type out the whole text of each rule and put its number at the end. Here's an example of the way two rules were typed on my sheet.

Timeout: …no umpire shall call "Time" while a play is in progress 5.10(h)

Walk: A base on balls is a live ball and time is not granted until the batter-runner shows no inclination to advance beyond first base. 2.00, 7.05(i) Note, and page 1 of *The Right Call*.

As you can see, you need not only a copy of your league **rule** book, but also a copy of the pertinent **case book**.

Use to win bets

I do not frequent taverns, but I have heard that arguments frequently arise there resulting in bets. You could win a lot of such bets with this list of twenty-two rules.

You might also win a game or two.

19 Parent meeting

You **must** have a parent meeting. I skipped it twice in my career and it was a disaster both times. Schedule your parent meeting before you call the parents to inform them that you drafted their kid. I recommend 7:30 PM on a week night at your home or the home of another coach or parent.

Make it mandatory

In an article in *Coaches Quarterly* (the magazine of the National Federation of State High School Associations, the organization that governs high-school sports), twenty-year high-school coach Dan Dickel says you must make your parent meeting **mandatory**. The way he achieves that is he hands out the **equipment** to the parents at the parents meeting. If they cannot make the main parent meeting, they must come to he makeup meeting. If they cannot come to the makeup meeting, they must arrange a personal meeting with the coach. No meeting, no equipment for their kid. No equipment, no participation in team activities.

The reason you must hold a parent meeting is to minimize misunderstandings. The typical parent has had bad experiences with youth sports in the past. Many have a chip on their shoulder as a result. When they don't understand something, they often jump to erroneous, negative conclusions about why you are doing things.

Here are the points you should cover along with background and what I would say about them and why.

Purpose of the league

The league usually provides you with a statement of the purpose of the league. Summarize it to your parents. I usually modify it. For example, the purpose of the nine-ten minors league I coached during 1990 was "developing skills and knowledge of the game."

I think the purpose is to let the kids participate in an activity with their peers. That's what kids say is their main reason for playing youth sports in various studies. I further state that the effort to learn the sport and play it well as a team produces many desirable lessons about life, like the need to persist in the face of failure, the value of hard work, the value of focusing on an objective. Finally, I point out that the game is designed to produce a drama.

Drama

I am a writer by profession. Most people do not realize it, but all drama, from plays to movies to sit coms, follow the same tight format. In Act I, the heroes and villains are introduced, along with the hero's compulsion (e.g., avenging his brother, getting a date for the prom, etc.).

In Act II, the hero encounters seemingly insurmountable obstacles thrown up by the villains. In Act III, he surmounts the insurmountable obstacles and succeeds in achieving that which he was compelled to achieve.

Baseball games have heroes (us) and villains (the opponents). They have a compulsion: to score more runs than the opponent. When the game unfolds in dramatic fashion, it seems like our team may lose. But then they come from behind to win.

It doesn't always happen that way, of course, but every game has that potential at the outset.

You also have the *geteilte Freude* effect which I discussed earlier. The fact that the game unfolds in front of an audience amplifies the various agonies and ecstasies of failure and success.

In short, the game of baseball offers drama and thrills for the parents and their children, as well as beneficial life lessons for the kids.

How to get volunteers

Invent the same number of jobs as you have players. Put them on a sign-up list and pass it around at the parent meeting. Tell each pair of parents to sign up for one job. If you just ask for several volunteers, you may get too few. But if you make volunteering for at least one job mandatory, you will get the people you need.

Team mom

Team moms are pretty much necessary. I have never seen a team Dad, but anything is possible in this enlightened era.

The team mom organizes the post-season party and sometimes interim meetings or parties. She also organizes the **post-game snacks**. Just assign each game to the parents in some order and tell anyone who cannot do it on their assigned day to trade with another parent.

The team mom should communicate with all the parents on some administrative matters. To make that as easy as possible, she should get **email addresses** at best, fax numbers for those who have no email address, and phone numbers as a last resort.

Assistant coach

I ask the parent group for an assistant coach. I explicitly say that I do **not** want anyone with strong opinions as to how a youth baseball team should be coached because I have my own strong opinions and they are not likely to coincide with the assistant's opinions. Basically, what I am looking for in an assistant is someone who will have a perfect or near perfect attendance record at practices and games and who is willing to help me do what's in this book.

If I could avoid having an assistant, I would. But they are necessary to keep order in the dugout and to cover for me when I cannot be there.

Scorekeepers

In the San Ramon Valley Little League, each team is required to provide two volunteer scorekeepers. They must attend a class on score keeping. Moms are almost always the ones who do it. They do a pretty good job, although as stated earlier, they aren't very good when it comes to errors.

'Sports writer'

Local newspapers generally try to print a brief story about each local game. The stories are parent written. The main trick is to attend the game and makes some notes, although the score book can substitute, and to get it in by deadline. Meeting the deadline is the most difficult thing, although I have no idea why. The paper usually has a fax number to which the story can be sent. Nowadays, I expect they would also have an email address or Web page to which stories could be submitted.

Field umpire

In the San Ramon Valley Little League, we were required to supply one field umpire per game. We usually got a father or two to volunteer.

All umpires ought to be paid professionals. I do not know why an area as affluent as where I live uses teenage plate umpires and volunteer parent field umpires who are the fathers of players in that same game.

Real umpires

In 1990, I had to be in DeSoto, Texas on business when our team back in California was in the playoffs. To assuage my baseball withdrawal symptoms, I attended a local nine-ten year old game as a spectator. I was amazed. DeSoto is a working-class community south of Dallas. Yet they had a large, illuminated, gorgeous youth baseball complex with snack bar and rest rooms.

In my area, one or two baseball fields are tucked into each elementary school playground all over town. They have no lights. Only one field has a snack bar or bathroom.

More importantly, each DeSoto game had three adult umpires dressed in umpire uniforms. In the San Ramon Valley Little League, games are constantly interrupted by arguing parents and coaches as well as by parental psychological warfare against opposing children. In DeSoto, parents were extremely well behaved.

I saw just one problem after a close play at third. The runner was safe. A defensive coach in the third-base dugout expressed mild disagreement with the call. The adult umpire turned toward him and said quietly, but firmly, "Another word and you're gone." There was not another word from him or anyone else for the rest of the game.

No parent umps

There should be no parent volunteer umpires in game involving the child of that umpire. I do not know how the DeSoto youth baseball organization did it, but they surely have fewer resources than the San Ramon Valley Little League. Quality umpiring is important to the safety and enjoyment of all concerned. Quality umpires are paid, uniformed, and impartial. Most San Ramon Valley umpires are none of the above. You get what you pay for.

Mandatory field work day

We had this in San Ramon Valley. If you have it or something like it, cover it at your meeting.

Practice schedule

Tell the parents your practice schedule. In addition, it should be a handout as well as posted on the team Web site. Practice should be the **same day and time every week**. I make the schedule in the form of a calendar. It includes all practices, all games, and any other team or league events.

Varying practice days or times will cause poor attendance and may necessitate the total cancellation of all practices, in which case you become just the equipment manager, not the coach.

Stick to one schedule

My youngest son's 1996 farm (eight- and nine-year olds) manager was a graduate student—married and in his thirties, but still a graduate student. His class schedule was irregular and he tried to get the parents to conform to **his** schedule. As a result, he was constantly changing or cancelling practices. Ultimately, people stopped coming.

That team lost every single game—the only youth baseball team I ever saw do that. Late in the season, we even had trouble getting players to come to **games**—a phenomenon I have **never** seen before or since at that age level. The kids were being taunted at school for being on the team.

I have found the best format for practice is an hour

and a half for the whole **team** followed by a half hour of **position** instruction. In 1998, I practiced from 4 to 5:30, then had a position clinic for selected players until 6. Some kids liked the position clinics so much they asked to attend **all** of them. My position clinics were mandatory for kids assigned to that position and optional for everyone else.

On time

I tell the parents that the kids need to be on time and not miss any practices. With subteens, I add that I have never had a problem with attendance or lateness, but that if I did, I would probably take some action like making the player a bench warmer.

In general, I give equal playing time to all players during the regular season. When we get to the playoffs, which are typically single-elimination tournaments, I switch to playing the best. But I would bench a chronic tardy or absent player during the regular season if I had one.

Beware of teens

As far as teens are concerned, I simply would not take a job coaching teenagers unless I was assured that I had sufficient numbers of players and that they were sufficiently motivated that I would be able to take effective action against chronic late or absent players. By effective action, I mean that I tell the kid to knock of the lateness or absenteeism and if he does not, I throw him off the team. In order to be able to do that, there must be sufficient number of players, about eighteen, to avoid shutting the team down from expulsions.

Self-respecting coaches should not take most teenage youth baseball coaching jobs because the coach on those teams does not have sufficient power to cause all the players to behave in a reasonable fashion. On a teenage team, you will probably have to throw a couple of kids off the team at the start of the practice season.

Good or bad takes over

Some teenagers are hard-core bad guys and must be gotten rid of. Others are good kids who will not misbehave no matter what. Those good kids want you to get rid of the bad ones. In fact, if you don't, the good kids may quit the team.

Then there is the middle group. They will go either way according to what you let occur. If you get rid of the hard-core bad guys, good guys will stay and the could-go-either-way guys will behave.

If your parent meeting is for a teenage team, you must make a strong statement that lateness, absenteeism, and attitude will not be tolerated so that the parents will carry that message to their kids.

Rainy-day practices

I never cancel practice because of weather. Keep in mind that I am in California. It rains during the beginning of the season here. But our practice fields are all at local public schools. California school architecture utilizes outdoor, covered "hallways." So when it rains, we simply practice in the covered hallways. To be sure, you cannot practice **everything** that you can practice on a normal field, but you can work on a lot of little things like putting the tag on the ground, bunting, pitching, rules knowledge, backup assignments, fielding, etc.

In 1998, we did not have a single day of rain. But in the early nineties, we once had rain almost every day in March. My opposing coaches cancelled practice week after week because of the rain. I never canceled it. I must admit that toward the end of the month, I was running out of stuff that could be done in a limited space. Also, about that time, my opposing coaches started holding practice regardless of the rain because opening day was imminent and they had done nothing all month. They practiced out in the rain that I had enough sense to get in out of.

I do not know where you practice on rainy days outside of California, but I would look darned hard for a place before I agreed to cancel.

You can do a little bit of chalk talk, but no more than about five or ten minutes or the kids will get bored. You can show a little bit of video, but again, no more than about five or ten minutes. When they get bored, they misbehave.

In northern high schools and colleges, they practice a lot in field houses and gyms. Indeed, many an article in the baseball-coaching magazines tells how to hold indoor practices.

Teamwork

Teamwork to me means that no member of the team can put down any other member of the team. Furthermore, any feuds from the past are suspended for the duration of the season. There will be no cliques on the team. We are one big clique.

I was interested to read that the U.S. Woman's Soccer Team that won the World Cup in 1999 had a policy that everyone had to change roommates every night during road trips. The coach implemented that policy to discourage cliques.

No cliques

When I coached high school volleyball, I noticed that when we paired off for two-man drills, players would pair off with their best buddy and some players would get left out. I then randomly assigning the pairs. The clique-prone players hated that policy. It was important to their self image to put down some of their teammates by shunning them. But it was destructive to the team.

For the same reason, I also had to adopt a policy on that team of insisting that every substitute entering the court be touched by the players on the court—high five, low five, whatever. The clique members hated it when I replaced a clique member with a non-clique member and demonstrated their feelings with body language, which hurt the confidence and performance of the substitute.

To my surprise, the touch-welcome policy worked. It did not make me any more popular with the clique members, but it eliminated the psychological harm to the subs.

Keep it secret

I tell the parents and the players that it is OK for a player not to like another member of the team, but it is **NOT** OK to **show** that dislike.

I always threaten to hold three-legged races in which I tie players who dislike each other together. I figure that will either cause them to learn teamwork or one of them will quit the team. Either way, I'm happy.

My message is that you better keep any dislikes of other member of this team a deep secret because if I find out, I will start my three-legged races. The races will be against pairs of players who like each other. And the three-legged races will continue until the guys who dislike each other beat teams who like each other.

League officials

Tell the parents the name and phone number of the administrator of the division in which you are coaching.

Safety

As a youth baseball coach, you have a moral, ethical, and legal duty to warn parents and players of the dangers of baseball. The vast majority of coaches and parents are woefully uninformed. Rita Glassman of the National Youth Sports Foundation for the Prevention of Athletic Injuries said, "Baseball has the leading number of fatalities and the least amount of safety equipment."

On June 27, 1999, in Omaha, a five-year old boy named Andrew Cook was hit in the chest by a soft-core ball thrown by an adult at a tee-ball game. He staggered several steps and fell, dying a couple of breaths later in spite of the assistance of a doctor who came out of the stands to help.

There was nothing remarkable about the throw. But there **is** something remarkable about the way children die when they receive a sharp blow to the neck or upper body. The Consumer Product Safety Commission said that 40 children aged 5 to 14 died between 1973 and 1980—five per year—in youth baseball. From 1986 through 1990, the rate was 3.3 deaths per year.

The American Academy of Pediatrics says,

Deaths have occurred from impact to the head resulting in intracranial bleeding and from non-penetrating blunt chest impact probably causing ventricular fibrillation or asystole.

Direct contact by the ball is the most frequent cause of death and serious injury in baseball. Children 5 to 14 years of age seem to be uniquely vulnerable to blunt chest impact, because their thoraces may be more elastic and more easily compressed.

Hit them less

We do not know how to reduce deaths caused by getting hit in the chest with a ball, except by hitting kids in the chest fewer times. That suggests using pitching machines or coach pitchers at the lower levels for one thing.

The American Academy of Pediatrics recommends "eliminating the on-deck circle" I agree. In a 7/29/99 story in my local paper, I read that Little League recently abolished the on-deck circle for batters 12 and under. Good.

Matt Keough pitched for the Oakland Athletics in the late seventies and eighties. In 1992, he was making a comeback with the Giants when he was hit in the head by a spring-training line drive while sitting in the dugout. It knocked him unconscious, sent him to the hospital with a serious head injury, and ended his career.

Talking about the "good" seats behind the dugout at a baseball stadium, an Arizona Diamondbacks spokesperson said, "…anyone who has been around the game a long time—baseball people—they always put their families behind the home-plate screen."

As you would expect, a kid dies from being hit in the head with a bat about once a year. Kids also die from baseball collisions—base runner to fielder or two fielders running into each other while chasing a ball or one fielder running into a wall or tree.

Baseball is leading cause of youth eye and teeth injuries

There are also many serious nonfatal injuries. For example, baseball is the leading cause of childhood blindness. According to a 10/95 press release from the American Academy of Pediatric Dentistry (www.aapd.org), "Youth baseball and softball now lead all sports in the number of oral, facial, eye, and head injuries."

Unfortunately, we do not know how to prevent the deaths caused by ball impact on the neck and upper body. But we can prevent almost all of the other injuries with inexpensive equipment.

Batter/base runner helmets

All youth baseball leagues require batting helmets. They even did when I played Little League in the late fifties, although our "head gear" had no tops. Requiring helmets is a step in the right direction, but it's **only** a step.

The batting helmets used in most youth leagues are unsatisfactory. They are often in **poor condition**. They rarely **fit** properly. They are usually **worn over a soft cap** which is unsafe. And, except in Dixie Youth Baseball, they **lack face guards**.

Little League rules say,

> **1.16**—Each league shall provide in the dugout or bench of the offensive team seven (7) protective helmets which must meet NOCSAE specifications and standards. Use of helmet by the batter, all base runners and coaches is mandatory. Use of a helmet by adult base coach is optional. Each helmet shall have an exterior warning label.

> **NOTE:** The warning label cannot be embossed in the helmet, but must be placed on the exterior portion of the helmet and be visible and easy to read.

The helmets provided by each league must meet NOCSAE specifications and bear the NOCSAE stamp as well as an exterior warning label as noted above.

Is that rule satisfactory? No.

Personal helmet for each player

Requiring only seven helmets per dugout almost guarantees that one or more players will wear a helmet that does not fit correctly and therefore is not safe. In the worst case, when bases are loaded, the batter only has three helmets to choose from. (The youth base coach is wearing one.) On many occasions, the correct size for the batter will be unavailable because it will be on the head of a base runner. I have seen some cases where **none** of the seven helmets fit some of the players on the team.

That happened to me and my oldest son. In adult baseball, the largest helmet our team had fit me like a vise. I went to a sporting goods store and bought my own XXL helmet. My oldest son's head is so large that he can only wear the largest helmet made by one obscure manufacturer.

The typical mix of seven helmets issued to a youth team by the league would be two smalls, two larges, and three mediums. If your team is precisely average, you will have 13 players including:

- one extra small
- two smalls
- seven mediums
- two larges
- one extra large

So you have **two** guys whose heads fit **none** of your team helmets and **seven** guys to fight over the **three**

mediums. Your large- and small-head-size guys might as well monogram their helmets. They are in great shape.

But most teams probably will not follow exactly the normal distribution. You have two possible ways to fit team helmets better. You can replace your youth base coach if he is wearing a helmet needed by the batter. You may also be able to borrow a helmet from the opposing team.

'Inspector 12'

Hanes underwear used to run TV commercials showing a tough woman rejecting defective underwear. She was "Inspector 12" and her signature line was, "They don't say Hanes until **I** say they say Hanes."

NOCSAE stands for the National Operating Committee on Standards for Athletic Equipment (www.nocsae.org). I called them several years ago to become more informed on their standard. I got to talk to NOCSAE's "Inspector 12," at that time, a Wayne State University Professor named Dr. Voight Hodgson, who actually performed the tests in their Department of Neurology. Helmets didn't say NOCSAE until **he** said they say NOCSAE.

More than compliance with the rule

At one page on NOCSAE's Web site (http://www.nocsae.org/StanCert_2.htm), they say,

> However, to legislate precautions via the rules books and equipment standards, while often necessary, is seldom effective in and by itself. To rely on officials to enforce compliance with the rules book is as insufficient as to rely on warning labels to produce behavioral compliance with precautionary guidelines. Compliance means respect on everyone's part for the intent and purpose of the rule or guideline, not merely technical satisfaction through some of its phrasing.

It appears clear to me that virtually all adults involved with youth baseball have the attitude that **any** helmet, regardless of the finer points of its condition or fit, complies with the rule that a helmet must be worn and complying with the rule is all they need to worry about. This violates NOCSAE's admonition to "respect...the intent and purpose of the rule...not merely technical satisfaction..." In my observation, youth baseball adults nationwide **do** engage in mere technical satisfaction, if that, of the rule requiring a helmet. That is an outrage and a scandal.

NOCSAE's test

NOCSAE tests baseball and softball helmets by mounting them on an "instrumented headform" which is free to move. An air cannon is used to shoot a baseball from close range into the helmeted headform at 60 mph at six different locations on the helmet. Impact accelerations are measured and a Severity Index is calculated and compared with the NOCSAE standard to determine if the helmet meets the standard.

If the measuring device indicates a head injury Severity Index of 1200 or less, the helmet passes.

60 mph good enough?

Do youth baseballs ever travel faster than 60 mph? Yes. Teenage pitchers can throw faster than that and the ball goes faster coming off the bat than it was traveling when it hit the bat. Exceptional subteen pitchers can also throw faster than 60 mph.

Several manufacturers now offer helmets that meet the NOCSAE standard when the ball is fired at **90** mph. That is the helmet that I wore in adult and semi-pro baseball. It is the helmet I required my sons to wear when they played baseball. And it is the helmet I recommend that each parent buy for their kid at my parent meeting. Is that overkill at the sub-teenage level? No. Why risk it?

It is abnormal, but not unheard of, for a ball to travel faster than 60 mph in a subteen game. And we are talking about the safety of your child's or player's head here. How can anyone quibble over safety standards?

90 mph should be the standard

It seems to me that all youth baseball organizations or coaches or parents should have followed my example and instantly adopted the 90-mph standard as soon as those helmets became available. I think the key question to be asked of any baseball league, coach, or parent is, "Did you provide your player with the best protection available?"

The only satisfactory answer is, "Yes," and you can only answer "Yes" if you provide the state-of-the-art helmet, which is the 90-mph helmet. They cost about $30. Writing in *Clinical Ophthalmology* in 1985, Dr. Paul Vinger said regarding defending yourself in an eye-injury lawsuit that you must show that,

> …those involved have acted responsibly, using state-of-the-art protective equipment…to protect the athlete to an acceptable level of risk, considering the nature of the sport.

To paraphrase a motorcycle helmet ad I saw, "If your child has a $12 head, let him wear a $12 helmet."

Fit

I believe it is disingenuous for Little League and any other rule-making body to call for helmets that meet the NOCSAE standard, but to leave out of the rule the fit specifications that come with each helmet.

NOCSAE's "Inspector 12" told me that when the helmets are tested, they fit **snugly** on the "instrumented headform." He further said that a NOCSAE standard helmet does **not** meet NOCSAE standards if it does **not** fit snugly. Therefore, Little League and the other organizations MUST add fitting requirements to their rule or they are allowing unsafe situations.

Unsafe cover boys

The 7/12/99 *Time* magazine has a cover story titled "Sports Crazed Kids." The cover photo is of a seven-year-old Denver youth baseball batter who is wearing a helmet that is obviously much too large for him and, therefore, that particular helmet is an unsafe helmet which does **not** meet NOCSAE standards on that particular boy's head.

The cover photograph on the 1992 and 1993 "Minor League and Tee Ball Official Regulations and Playing Rules" of Little League Baseball shows a base runner whose helmet is so far back on his head that his entire forehead and about two or three inches of the top of his head are exposed.

I discussed that photo with a couple of safety experts and they said the helmet must be worn so that the bill is parallel to the ground when the player's head is level and the helmet is covering the forehead. The player in the rule book photo is actually looking **down** at the base he is approaching, while the bill of his helmet is pointing **upward** at about a 45-degree angle.

On 8/14/99, while watching the Big League World Series (a subsidiary of Little League Baseball, Inc.) I saw a commercial for RC Cola, the official cola of Little League Baseball. It featured a smiling kid, wearing a helmet over a soft cap.

The fact that the photo on the front of an official rule book, of all places, would show a helmet worn in an unsafe manner shows the lack of concern of baseball authorities regarding the "intent and purpose" of the helmet rules.

Instructions that come with helmets

Baseball helmets come with "Important illustrated fitting instructions," to quote the warning in the Schutt catalog. They call for a "snug fit." The best fit can probably be achieved with helmets that have detachable, interchangeable jaw pads. That's the way football helmets are made. At least one manufacturer, Athletic Helmets, Inc., made such a baseball helmet (Model 2688) last I heard. They offered jaw pads of 5/8, 3/4, and 7/8-inch thicknesses.

Because those instructions are followed by the NOCSAE testers and they do not test helmets other than while complying with those instructions, those fitting instructions are an implicit part of the rules of leagues that require meets-NOCSAE-standards helmets. Accordingly, and in view of the fact that the fitting instructions are almost universally ignored, clearly the leagues are remiss in not incorporating those instructions, or at least reference to them and their importance, into their rule books.

Incorporate fit standards into rules

The rules should not just say that batters and base runners must wear a helmet that meets NOCSAE standards, rather they must add that the helmet must also **fit** the player in accordance with the manufacturer's instructions.

You want to see how youth helmets should be fitted? Go to the first week of any youth **football** practice. In the two youth football organizations I was involved in, we had each player step forward to be fitted. We tried different helmets until we got one that fit properly.

We had to be able to see his ear holes through the ear holes in the helmet. There had to be no more than one inch of forehead visible above the eyebrows. When we moved the helmet from side to side or front to back, the head had to go with it. Once we got it fit right, it became solely that player's helmet for the rest of the season. Baseball leagues could easily do the same thing at the beginning of each season.

The fitting instructions for AIR helmets require: 1. measure the child's head with a tape measure then matching the circumference to the helmet size on a sizing chart 2. Make sure there are two fingers distance between the bridge of the nose and the bill of the cap 3. Center the ear holes of the helmet over the child's ear. They further state, "The helmet should sit squarely on the head with a tight and snug fit—to prevent its spinning on the head during a missed swing or falling off while running the bases."

A helmet for each baseball player

That is the only way to insure a proper fit. Each baseball player must have his own helmet. If youth football can do it, where helmets cost $120 each and must be recertified annually, youth baseball can surely do it with their $12 helmets.

If your league refuses to buy a custom-fitted helmet for each player, you should collect money from the parents to do so. If your team's parents do not want to do that as a group, you should urge them to individually get a custom-fitted batting helmet for their kid. I collected money from my parents some years and urged them to get their own helmets other years. My children never wore team helmets. They always wore custom-fitted, family-purchased helmets.

Head lice and other people's sweat

There are other reasons for each kid to get his own helmet. Some kids have **head lice**. Sharing helmets is a great way to spread lice.

All kids **sweat**. The main reason children commonly wear a soft baseball cap under an oversize helmet is to avoid touching the sweat left in the team helmets by other kids. In short, **team** helmets are **gross**. Each of your players should have his own helmet.

Helmet for base runners

Do base runners need a helmet, or is it really just for batters? Base runners **do** need a helmet, maybe even more so than batters. At least batters see the pitch coming. Base runners usually have their eyes focused on the base they are approaching. The ball may be coming toward the same base from almost any angle, including many directions which they cannot see.

Base runners need protection from collisions with fielders and sometimes even other base runners. They also need protection from balls thrown by fielders.

When I was on the phone with the Wayne State NOCSAE professor, he got another call and put me on hold. When he came back he said the other caller was a lawyer. His client, also a lawyer, had been injured in an adult, slow-pitch, softball game. He was sliding into second when he was hit at the base of the back of the neck by a ball thrown in by an outfielder. It caused brain damage. The lawyer who called wanted the Wayne State professor to testify against the ball manufacturer. The professor refused.

I have seen many a youth baseball player lose his helmet completely while running bases. They were wearing a soft baseball cap under an oversized helmet.

Neither parents nor coaches nor players understand the dangers of being hit in the head while running bases. They generally take the attitude that helmets are needed for **batting**, but not really for baserunning. They think the rule requiring helmets while baserunning is over-kill. It's not.

A better argument could be made that **all** youth baseball players on both offense and defense should wear helmets at all times. Fielders collide with each other and with base runners. Pitchers get hit in the head by line drives.

Condition

The warning label on NOCSAE helmets says,

Do not use this helmet is the shell is cracked, deformed or if the interior padding is deteriorated or modified.

I do not recall ever getting a cracked or deformed helmet from our baseball league equipment guy, but I surely was issued many league helmets with deteriorated padding. I turned them back in for new ones and recommended that they throw the ones I was turning in away. I got the impression that no one paid much attention to the condition of the helmets and that the league relied totally on the managers to spot any problems. But no one ever said we should inspect the helmets.

Annual certification

Contrast the youth **baseball** attitude with that of youth football. At all youth **football** programs, all helmets are sent out annually to certified helmet companies for recertification. The helmets are inspected, repaired when possible, and discarded when necessary. They come back looking almost like new and each has a new label signifying it passed inspection and explaining proper fit. You rarely get back as many as you send them. The others were defective and unrepairable.

What is a continuing source of amazement to me is that the youth football coaches and players are generally the **same** as the youth baseball coaches and players. The heads we are trying to protect are the same. The adults in charge of the protecting are the same. Yet the standard adhered to is **admirable** in the **fall** and a **disgrace** in the **spring**.

Facial protection

In the summer of 1991, a fast ball caved in the right cheek of Chicago Little Leaguer Jay Eubanks, shattering all the bones around his right eye. The 14-year old had plastic surgery and now has titanium plates where those bones were. A year later, he was still waiting for sensation to return to the skin around the eye.

On his ninth birthday, Steve Korey of Highland Prak, IL had a party at a local batting cage. While batting, he got hit in the eye by a machine-thrown pitch. He suffered extensive damage to his retina and may never regain full sensation around his eye. After the injury, he had been rushed to the office of his **ophthalmologist** father who was present when the injury occurred.

Tony C

On August 18, 1967, Red Sox outfielder Tony Conigliaro, the youngest player to ever hit 100 home runs, had his career cut short when he was hit in the face by a Jack Hamilton pitch which fractured his cheek bone, dislocated his jaw, and damaged his retina. Conigliaro was out of baseball for a year and a half and was never the same after he came back.

Many Major Leaguers are exempt from wearing a batting helmet with an ear flap, but you would think none would take advantage of that exemption after seeing "Goose" Gossage bean Ron Cey in his ear flap in the 1981 World Series.

Those were not freak injuries. They are common baseball injuries. A 1980 Consumer Product Safety Commission study found there were 170,000 baseball-related head and facial injuries per year among children aged 5-14—an injury rate of 75 per 1,000 participants per season. Baseball is the single greatest cause of eye injuries—35,000 per year, including over 6,000 which

are classified as severe. A 1985 CPSC study said 6,000 baseball players suffered eye injuries serious enough to require hospital treatment that year.

Mickey Cochrane's Hall of Fame career came to an end after a 1937 Bump Hadley bean ball and Hall of Famer Joe Medwick's career was never the same after he was hit by Bob Bowman in 1940. Helmets were first worn in the Major Leagues by the Brooklyn Dodgers in 1941 after their star rookies Pete Reiser and Pee Wee Reese were hospitalized for lengthy periods the previous seasons. These easily-preventable injuries have not only a human cost, they also robbed the game of some of its best players.

Shortstop Dickie Thon was leading the league in assists and game-winning RBIs in 1983 and had twenty home runs. Then he got hit in the temple by a Mike Torrez pitch. That ended his season, and, as it turned out, his career. He tried to make a come-back during the next four years, but could not.

Easily preventable

Dr. Ellen Strahlman of the National Institutes for Health did a study which found that **none** of the children who suffered eye injuries had any form of eye protection, leading to the conclusion that the vast majority of eye injuries were preventable.

M. Goldsmith, Reporting for the National Safety Council in a 1986 edition of *Family Safety and Health* said, "Baseball and other sports that involve high-speed contact and objects require total head protection—a helmet with a face mask…"

Broken faces

Facial bones are not like arm or leg bones. There is no cast or healing. When they shatter, you just vacuum them out and install titanium plates.

Here's a more graphic description of another baseball facial injury from the book *You Gotta Have Wa.*

"…[Charlie] Manuel stood in the batter's box at Fujidera Stadium as shadows gripped the field and took a fast ball to the face that dropped him to his knees and sent blood spurting from his mouth. He was rushed to the hospital where it was found that his jaw was broken clean through in six places.

"Doctors performed an operation lasting several hours to repair his mangled face. Because Manuel wore an upper bridge (playing Class A ball in Albuquerque in 1967, pitcher Jerry Reuss had hit him in the mouth with a fast ball that fractured his upper jaw, broke his nose, cut his mouth, and knocked ten teeth out) there was nothing to wire together. To keep his jaw in one piece, doctors put three steel plates in his head, removing the nerves from the affected area."

A 'breaking' ball

One day when I was playing adult hardball in the

Men's Senior Baseball League, a pitch was coming at my face at about 70 to 75 mph. I was wearing a normal batting helmet with no face guard.

At first, I did not get out of the way because I thought it might be a breaking ball. But at the last instant I saw it was not and brought my hands up to deflect it. It hit me in the heel of the left hand and hurt so much I asked for ice on the way to first base.

I actually had a great day at the plate thereafter, hitting a single and a double, but I had a heck of a time getting my **fielder's glove** on. When it did not improve the next day, I figured I ought to have a doctor look at it. Turns out it **was** a "breaking" ball. It broke my hand.

Later that year, in the off-season, I visited a batting cage and noticed that some of the helmets they provided to customers had face guards. In light of pitch that had recently broken my hand, and almost broken my face, I thought, "That's a good idea."

I asked the owner of the batting cage to order me one, which he did. I always wore batting helmets with face guards the rest of my playing career, and got them for my sons and my youth teams thereafter as well.

Medical recommendations

Some may think this is just my personal overreaction to one close call. Nope. It was common sense on my part.

But you need not rely on common sense. **All** interested medical authorities also say that baseball should require helmets with face guards. These are the guys who try to repair the damage done to their patients when they are rushed to the hospital after being hit in the face with a baseball.

American Academy of Pediatric Dentistry

In a 10/95 press release, AAPD said, "The AAPD recommends that all children participating in baseball or softball wear a helmet with a face shield.

"During the 70's, injury rates in football, hockey, and lacrosse decreased impressively because all players were required to wear a helmet, a face guard, and a mouth guard."

Dr. John B. Jeffers, head of Emergency Services at the Wills Eye Hospital, said that since 1983, when face masks were mandated for organized youth hockey, eye injuries in that sport were reduced by 95%. The only eye injuries that continue to occur in youth hockey are suffered by players who are sitting on the bench with their helmets off.

A May, 1991 position statement of the AAPD said,

The American Academy of Pediatric Dentistry expresses concern about the prevalence of sports-related injuries in our nation's youth. The increased competitiveness in youth sports during the last de-

cade has resulted in an alarming number of dental and facial injuries which, combined represent a high percentage of the total injury experience in youth sports.

And while the administrators of youth and high school football, lacrosse, and ice hockey have demonstrated responsibility by introducing mandatory protective equipment rules which have resulted in significant reductions in dental and facial injuries, such popular sports as baseball and basketball lag far behind in injury protection.

The American Academy of Pediatric Dentistry, therefore, recommends the following as critical for reducing the prevalence of oral and facial injuries as well as other bodily injuries in youth sports.

Baseball and softball
Oral and facial injuries:
• A certified face protector be required for all children age 12 and under participating in organized baseball activities.

I do not understand why the AAPD limits their recommendation to age 12 and under. Seems to me that teenagers need the protection as much, if not more.

The American Academy of Ophthalmology

In a 10/8/92 news release, the American Academy of Ophthalmology announced a yearlong study of Major League professional baseball player eye injuries:

"In the study, ninety-five percent of the Major League players injured were not wearing protective eye gear," according to ophthalmologist Bruce Zagelbaum, MD of New York. "If it can happen to professional athletes—with the best reflexes—it can happen to amateur players."

In fact, nearly 7,000 amateur baseball players suffer eye injuries each year…[1991 figures].

Fifty-five percent of the [Major League eye] injuries were caused by a batted ball. Thirty percent were sustained while at bat, 25% while fielding, and 35% where while on the sidelines.

Consumer Product Safety Commission

In a 6/4/96 news release (http://www.cpsc.gov/cpscpub/prerel/prhtml96/96140.html), the CPSC said,

Based on its analyses, CPSC found that …Face guards that attach to batting helmets and protect the face can reduce injuries to batters…will help reduce injuries.

In a Web page designed for kids, CPSC says,

So play ball with…batting helmets with face guards…

Physician and Sports Medicine Journal

Physician and Sports Medicine Journal said,

In the United States, baseball accounts for the most eye injuries. Most injuries were caused by the ball (92%) and most injured players (99%) wore no protector…We believe that the use of eye protectors in baseball must be encouraged.

How about "required?"

Prevent Blindness America

Prevent Blindness America, formerly known as the National Society to Prevent Blindness, said in 1984,

The National Society to Prevent Blindness recommends the use of a baseball helmet and face guard for all age groups. The helmet and face guard effectively protects not only the eyes but also the nose, mouth, and facial bones from pitched or hit balls. The helmet and face guard should be required equipment for all batters and base runners.

That's more like it.

American Academy of Pediatrics

The American Academy of Pediatrics has a detailed Policy Statement on the "Risk of Injury From Baseball and Softball in Children 5 to 15 years of age (RE9409)" It's on the Internet at http://www.aap.org/policy/00161.html.

They echo a position of Sports Eye Safety Committee of the Prevent Blindness America, that is, they recommend the use of batting helmets with face guards that meet Standard F910 of the American Society for Testing and Materials.

The AAP's own recommendation regarding facial protection is:

4. Baseball and softball players should be encouraged to reduce the risk of eye injury by wearing polycarbonate eye protectors on their batting helmets. These should be required for functionally one-eyed athlete or for athletes with previous eye surgery or severe eye injuries, if their ophthalmologists judge them to be at increased risk of eye injury.

AAP also has a table of sports and recommended eye protection (http://www.aap.org/policy/01497t2.htm). Here's what it says about baseball:

Baseball——Polycarbonate face guard or other certified safe protection attached to the helmet for batting and base running

The AAP Position Statement is dated 4/94. It seems to treat the Face Guards, Inc. style Lexan® face guard as the only acceptable kind. In fact, I believe that is due to ignorance of the competing **wire** versions which also meet the ASTM standard.

Sports Illustrated for Kids

Sports Illustrated for Kids said,

There is a simple way to protect your face while at bat: Use a face guard.

Functionally one-eyed kids

Medical authorities are unanimous and adamant that a child who is **functionally one-eyed** should **always** wear a face-mask batting helmet and protective goggles when playing in the field.

According to Dr. Jack B. Jeffers of the Wills Eye Hospital, the definition of a "functionally one-eyed athlete" is anyone whose worst eye is no better than 20-40 when they are wearing their glasses. If such young people lose sight in their good eye, they will be excluded from all sorts of activities like military service or getting a pilot's license.

They may even have trouble getting a drivers license. They might be limited to driving in daylight under clear weather conditions or some such. I suspect that most functionally one-eyed people were told to wear eye protection forevermore at the time their injury was first diagnosed, but it won't hurt to ask at your parent meeting if any of your players have less that two healthy eyes.

Two kinds of face mask

There are two general kinds of face masks:

• Face Guards, Inc.'s Lexan® one-piece shield
• Schutt's wire cages

Baseball batting helmet face masks are tested and certified by the American Society for Testing and Materials. They shoot baseballs at the mask at 67.1 mph (plus or minus 4.9 mph).

Initially, I wore the Face Guards Lexan® shield. Most Lexan® masks that I have seen are made of transparent polycarbonate. Polycarbonate looks like plastic, but it is the material that safety lenses are made out of.

Face Guards was founded by Lorine Caveness. She was a sixth-grade teacher in North Carolina. One of her students was injured in a baseball game and spent the next year in and out of hospitals as doctors tried to save his eye.

Her husband noticed that one of their sons seemed afraid of the ball when he was practicing with him. In 1970, Mrs. Caveness tried to find a batting helmet with a face mask. Finding none, she designed the Homesafe Lexan® face mask with the help of Dr. Creighton Hale, then Safety Director, and now past President, of Little League Baseball, Inc.

Little League Baseball authorized "**optional**" use of face-mask batting helmets in 1973. In 1978, face mask helmets were "**recommended**" for use by Little League Baseball, Dixie Youth Baseball, Pony Baseball and Babe Ruth Baseball.

"Optional!?" "Recommended!?" I absolutely do not understand that. The rules ought to be changed to **mandatory** immediately. To their credit, Dixie Baseball **did** make face-mask batting helmets mandatory. In 1993, before full implementation of the face-mask rule, the rate of eye injuries in Dixie Youth Baseball was 8%. After full implementation of the face-mask rule in 1994, the rate of eye injuries in Dixie Youth Baseball dropped to less than one percent.

Little League Baseball has a pretty good list of "recommended" stuff at the safety pages of its Web site (www.littleleague.org/manuals/asap/index.htm). But the fact is thousands of Little Leaguers are getting injured because, until the recommended protective equipment is **required**, a reduction in injuries will not happen.

Little League should also make more effort to enforce their required stuff. For example, they **require** injury reports. But when I had injuries on my team, I asked for an injury-report form and was told there was no such thing.

Little League's Web pages on safety are partly impressive and partly lame, but the discrepancy between the number of injuries and their much protested commitment to safety cause me to think that Little League's safety propaganda is more designed to protect their own butts from legal liability than to protect the safety of the children.

The same is true of the other youth leagues. They give us much **talk** about safety while simultaneously refusing to adopt the recommendations of medical and safety groups. The proof is in the pudding, that is, are the number of injuries coming down?

Except for the predictable reduction in injuries when Dixie Youth Baseball started required face-mask helmets, I am not aware of any reduction in Little League Baseball or other league injury rates.

Why transparent?

I told Face Guard I thought they made a big mistake using **transparent** polycarbonate. They said they also make opaque masks. Transparent has four problems.

One is that players and parents think you are supposed to look **through** the mask at the ball. That's impossible. It's like looking through a Coke bottle bottom.

Problem Number Two is that the polycarbonate gets **scratched** up, turning its transparency into translucency which causes parents and players to conclude that the product is no longer usable. I have heard Little League equipment managers dismiss the Face Guard mask as worthless "because it gets scratched."

Well, so does the **helmet**. But the **helmet** manufacturers were not dumb enough to make them transparent. If you have the Face Guard product, don't worry about it being scratched. You're not supposed to see through it.

Problem Number Three with the transparent Face Guard face mask is that it has a **prismatic effect on light**. The sun would hit the front of the mask and send the color spectrum into my eye. I assume the same thing happens with stadium night lights.

We fixed this by putting adhesive tape over the top edge of my mask. That was not a great solution because it got filthy and sticky and peeled off.

Problem Number Four is that transparent Lexan® **deteriorates somewhat when exposed to sunlight**.

So if you use the Face Guard mask, get **opaque** colors. That still leaves another problem I had with that mask. It is **front heavy**. My players and I had to wear football helmet chin straps to keep it in place when we ran.

All of which is why I switched to the cage-style helmet which has caused no problems for me or my players. A later model of the Face Guards mask has ribs instead of one solid piece to make it lighter—a sort of polycarbonate cage. I never tried the ribbed version.

Wire cage face mask

Cages, like Schutt's Model 2688 Pro-Guard™ Batter's Guard, are similar to football face masks only lighter in weight. There is no light problem and no need for a chin strap, although a chin strap should probably be required for everyone for the simple reason that, without it, the face mask will be driven back into your face when it is hit by a ball or the player collides with another player.

You should be aware that some cages do not fit some helmets. Schutt's warning label says to stop using the mask if there is ever more than a 1 7/8 inch gap between the bill of the helmet and the top horizontal wire of the cage. That is one potential problem with cages, the wire can get bent and may leave a big enough hole to let in a baseball. Face Guards instructions for the Lexan® mask call for no more than a two-inch gap.

My oldest son went through three football face masks his senior year of high school. One got bent so far on a pass block that Dan's entire face was suddenly exposed. And those are made of far sturdier wire than baseball-batting-helmet cages.

Do face masks hurt performance?

Many coaches have told me they will not allow face masks because they interfere with the players' vision. Many of my players have initially told me they can't hit wearing a face-mask helmet. That's bull.

I wore both types for years. The only vision problem with the Face Guard Lexan® mask was the aforementioned light prism, which we easily fixed with adhesive tape. With the wire mask, I had to learn to look with **both** eyes through one side of the vertical bar while batting. That was a bit of a distraction, but it only lasted a few minutes.

Worn in the Major Leagues

At least three pro players, Art Howe (Astros), Alan Ashby (Astros), and Don Slaught (Rangers), have worn the Face Guard Lexan® mask in Major League games. They were recovering from facial injuries at the time. I call your attention to the fact that had they worn the mask all along, they would not have **had** any facial injuries. Nevertheless, in their closing-the-barn-door-after-the-horse-had-left use of the helmets, they reported no vision or hitting problems. Art Howe is now the manager of the Oakland Athletics.

1983 Little League World Champs

Richard Hilton was a Little League coach in East Marietta, GA. One of his players was hit by a pitch and lost the sight in one eye as a result. Thereafter, Hilton made all his players wear the Face Guard mask. It apparently did not hurt their performance. They won the 1983 Little League World Series wearing the face-mask helmets all the way.

1991 National runners up

In 1991, my local San Ramon Valley Little League team won the Little League U.S. championship (before losing to Taiwan in the World Series game). The team San Ramon Valley beat to win the national championship game was from Staten Island—and they wore the Face Guard mask. If you can get to the national championship game, wearing the batting-helmet mask is apparently is not adversely affecting your performance.

Face Guards, Inc. says Chad Turner, a member of the 1990 Ohio state high school champs wore the Lexan face mask after his nose was broken by a pitch. He batted .441 after he started wearing the Face Guards Lexan® helmet.

20/20

In a *7/12/92 20/20* story on baseball safety called "Playing Hardball," Major Leaguers Don Mattingly and George Brett tried the Lexan® face mask batting helmet and said it did not interfere with good hitting.

From what I understand, face-mask batting helmets are mandatory in many eastern youth baseball pro-grams. They have also been mandatory in Dixie Youth Baseball since 1995. But I know of no youth league in California in which they are mandatory.

The 1998 Dixie Youth Baseball world champion manager, Ted Dieter, said, "In the World Series, we hit 16 home runs wearing this face mask. Our leading hitter set a new World Series record wearing this face mask. The entire team hit .375 as a team in the seven games of the World Series wearing this face mask. So I can't see where the face mask is going to alter or hurt a batting average at all."

Bean balls

When you wear the only face mask in the league, as I and my sons sometimes do, opposing pitchers often figure you must be the biggest chicken in the league. They further conclude that a pitch thrown at your head will rattle you more than it will rattle anyone else in the league.

I often got a pitch or two thrown at my head in my first at bat against a new opponent when I was wearing a face mask. It happened far less often to my oldest son because he was tall for his age and almost always one of the stars in the league. Plus he played with the same kids year after year. My adult and semi-pro games were generally against strangers.

I welcomed the balls being thrown at my head to an extent. It usually meant a 2-0 count to start with. Normally, I was probably a little bit **less** worried about getting hit than the average batter, because of the face-mask helmet. I called it my "No Fear" helmet.

'Fastball'

Another thing that happened to me was that people assumed that if I wore a face-mask helmet I must be really lousy. In one semi-pro game at Castro Valley High School, the opposing team loudly ridiculed me the first time I came to the plate. They were from Richmond, CA, a tough town that has been featured in national news stories about inner-city crime.

The outfield moved way in. The pitcher said "Fastball" before he threw each pitch, which was, indeed, a fastball right down the pipe. It got so bad that the home-plate umpire stopped the game and had a conference with the opposing manager. He then huddled with his team and the next pitch was thrown in silence, although the outfield was still playing me way in.

I gave no response, either verbally or through body language. I had been through it before, although not to that extent. I generally felt such treatment made me a better hitter because I got angry and more focused.

0-2 pitch

Unfortunately, in this case, the sun was right behind the pitcher and I simply could not see the first two pitches at all. The count was 0-2 when they stopped the game. Castro Valley High's field faces southwest and this was an afternoon winter game when the sun hangs low in the sky.

However, during the timeout , the sun moved a little bit toward the right field line. So I did catch a glimpse of the third pitch. I hit it in play, although again I could not see where I hit it because of the sun. By my second step, however, the "crowd" was going nuts. The "crowd" was just my teammates and some of their family members, but that was enough for me to conclude that I must have hit it pretty well.

My teammates told me afterward that it was a humpbacked line drive. Had my legs not been 46 years old, it would have been an inside-the-park home run. The third-base coach was waving me home as I rounded second, but he changed his mind and stopped me with a stand-up triple.

When we got home after the game, I drew a quick sketch of a baseball field to scale on a graph paper and asked my son where the ball hit the ground. The spot he picked was 350 feet from home plate. The center fielder, who was playing deep second base on the play, picked it up after it bounced off the fence at the 425 mark.

Because of the ridicule from the Richmond team, that was the most rewarding hit I ever got in my baseball career. Perhaps the parents or coaches of other only-person-in-the-league-who-wears-a-face-mask players can use that story to encourage their child.

In the post-game handshake line, the Richmond pitcher told me, "Nice hit." Later, the manager of that team, Jimmy James, and I ended up as teammates on the Pleasanton Orioles and we became good friends.

Funny with grown-ups, not with kids

Balls being thrown at the head of the only face-mask wearing player in a **youth** league are another matter. Adults do not die from being hit in the neck or upper body by a thrown ball, but children do. So anything that increases the chances of a youth player being hit by a ball should be eliminated immediately.

If I ever suspected a youth pitcher of throwing at my players because they were wearing a face-mask helmet, I would have a serious talk about the matter with the umpire and opposing coach.

→ Mouth guards

During the 1992 season, one of my players was hit in the mouth by a thrown ball. It loosened his two front teeth, which was bad enough, but at the time it happened, it was horrible. There was blood all over. It was so bad that instead of people gathering around like they usually do when someone is hurt, they turned away unable to watch.

Had he been wearing a mouth guard, he probably would have suffered little or no injury. Pediatric dentist

David C. Adams of San Diego said, "As a team dentist for children's sports, I see children walking away with small bruises instead of serious injuries because they wore mouth protection. And for my own children, I insist on mouth guards before they hit the playing field."

At that time, I had not been aware that the various medical authorities had recommended that baseball players should wear mouth guards—the same mouth guards worn by football and hockey players. After I learned that baseball players should wear mouth guards, I made my sons wear them and encouraged members of my teams to wear them. You should, too.

'Critical'

In the position Statement on the Prevention of Sports Related injuries of 5/91, the American Academy of Pediatric Dentistry (www.aapd.org) said it was

"critical" that a "…sports mouth guard be recommended for all children and youth participating in…baseball or softball.

"Baseball and basketball get a 'thumbs down' for lagging behind in injury protection. Although nearly half of all sports-related mouth injuries occur in basketball and baseball, mouth guards are not required.

"A child should wear a mouth protector whenever he or she is in an activity with a risk of falls or of head contact with other players or equipment. This includes football, **baseball**, basketball, soccer, hockey, martial arts, skateboarding, and even gymnastics. [emphasis added]"

American Dental Association

In a 7/30/99 news release, the ADA said,

Protect Your Smile with a Mouth guard -- If you like to…play softball, baseball…, the ADA recommends you wear a mouth guard. A properly fitted mouth guard is an important piece of athletic gear that can help protect your smile. Mouth guards can help cushion blows that might otherwise cause broken teeth; injuries to the lips, tongue, face or jaw and may even help reduce the severity and incidence of concussions.

Three kinds of mouth guard

There are three kinds of mouth guards: stock (Type I), mouth-formed (Type II), and custom-fitted (Type III). (One dentist on the Web says there are **four** kinds. http://www.qualitydentistry.com/dental/sdentistry/mouth.html) Your players should have the custom-fitted type. It provides more protection from dental injury and concussion and it is more comfortable.

The most common type, mouth-formed, is put in boiling water then bitten into. They do not stay in place very well, make it hard to talk, and often cause gagging.

Custom-fitted mouth guards are available from dentists. The pertinent standard is ASTM F697-80(1992) Standard Practice for Care and Use of Mouth guards (http://www.astm.org/cgi-bin/SoftCart.exe/DATABASE.CART/PAGES/F697.htm?L+mystore+uqjn3440).

Here are two position statements from the Academy of Sports Dentistry:

"For optimal safety and well-being of athletes competing in the 21th Century, the Academy for Sports Dentistry has adopted the position that the single word "mouthguard" must be placed by the term "a properly fitted mouthguard.

"The criteria for the fabrication or adaptation of a "properly fitted mouthguard" must include the following considerations:

    1. Pertinent Medical History
    2. Dental Status
        1. Dental caries
        2. Periodontal Status
        3. Developmental Occlusion
        4. Orthodontic or Prosthodontic Appliances
        5. Congenital/Pathological Conditions
        6. Jaw Relationships
    3. Demographic Factors

"With these considerations, knowledgeable persons in the field of sports dentistry should advise the athlete and/or parents of the special design for the "properly fitted mouth guard" and the individual. A fitting of a mouth guard is best accomplished under the supervision or direction of a dentist. The end product should have the properties that include:

1. Adequate thickness in all areas to provide for the reduction of impact forces.
2. A fit that is retentive and not dislodged on impact.
3. Speech considerations equal to the demands of the playing status of the athlete.
4. A material that meets FDA approval.?
5. Preferably a wearing length of time equal to one season of play.

"Approved by the Academy for Sports Dentistry Board of Directors 12/6/98 "

Position Statement on Athletic Mouth guard Mandates

The Academy for Sports Dentistry recommends the use of a properly fitted mouth guard; encourages the use of a custom fabricated mouth guard made over a dental cast and delivered under the supervision of a dentist; and supports a mandate for use of a properly fitted mouth guard in all collision and contact sports. [The American Academy of Pediatrics defines baseball as a "limited contact" sport.]

(Please see ASD Newsletter Vol 14, #3, Pg. 7-8, Jan 1999)

Approved by the Academy for Sports Dentistry Board of Directors 2/6/99

Trauma card

The Academy for Sports Dentistry offers a free Laminated "Trauma Card" which shows emergency treatment for sports dental injuries. All leagues and coaches should get one for each coach. Call 800-273-1788. There are a number of dental injuries which can be made less serious by proper first aid at the scene and prompt treatment by a dentist.

The Academy of Sports Dentistry (www.acadsportsdent.org) says,

Mouth guards SHOULD NOT BE OPTIONAL EQUIPMENT [emphasis in original]

Mouthguards should be worn when the player is batting even though he is wearing the face-mask batting helmet, just as football players wear mouthguards behind their face-masks. But the main time for baseball players to wear mouthguards is when **fielding** or **running bases**.

My oldest son once had a pitch smashed right back at him when he was pitching at the teenage level. He caught it inches from his mouth then took out and kissed the mouth guard which I had made him wear.

Orthodontia

The typical American kid today has had orthodontia to straighten their teeth. It costs about $5,000 on average and it requires the kid to wear funny looking wires and such for years. The typical set of parents who pays that $5,000 will not take no for an answer from the kid regarding whether he or she is going to have the orthodontics done.

Yet those same parents let their kid go out on a baseball field, without either the face mask or the mouth guard recommended unanimously by all interested medical and safety organizations. All those expensively straightened teeth can wind up laying in the dirt after a split-second impact on their teeth.

Then they will pay additional thousands of dollars to get their kid false teeth which will never be as functional as the teeth that could easily have been saved by the use of a $2 mouth guard or a $15 dollar face mask.

Protective goggles

The American Academy of Pediatrics recommends that youth baseball players where protective polycarbonate goggles when fielding if: 1. they are functionally one-eyed, which they define has having 20/50 vision in your worst eye when wearing glasses or 2. they have previous eye surgery or severe eye injuries, if their ophthalmologists judge them to be at increased risk of eye injury.

'Moderate- to high-risk sport'

I think that recommendation does not go far enough. Prevent Blindness America characterizes baseball as a "moderate-to-high-risk sport" for eye injuries. That category is for sports that "…involve use of a bat or stick, high-speed ball, close aggressive play (body contact), or a combination of these factors." Other sports they put in that same category include hockey, racquet ball, and squash. They further state,

> There is a direct relationship between these activities and serious eye injuries, but adequate eye protective devices are available.
> Other Risk Factors—Additional factors that can increase the risk(s) involved in sports include:
> Developmental Skills
> Coordination, balance, reaction time, speed, strength, etc. are physical characteristics that are not well developed in the young athlete, making them more vulnerable to injuries. For example, the batter in little league baseball may actually lean into, rather than away from, an inside pitch in an attempt to avoid being hit.

No parent would play racquet ball or squash without protective goggles. Squash and racquetball courts generally prohibit playing without protective eye wear. Yet those same parents will put their kids on a baseball field without protective goggles.

Frames

Prevent Blindness America recommends "Sports frames with 3 mm polycarbonate lenses for spectacle wearers in moderate to high-risk non-contact sports (i.e., racquet sports, basketball, baseball)"

The parents of players who wear glasses often say they do not need sports goggles because their child's lenses are "safety glass." Actually, they are not glass at all. They are polycarbonate, which is exactly what you need.

However, the **frames** are also an issue. Only sports frames like Rec Specs should be worn on a playing field. That's because when you get hit in the glasses, the frame will likely break and pieces of it can be driven into your eye.

Sports frames have no hinge. They are made **entirely** of polycarbonate, not just the lenses. They wrap around the head and have an elastic band around the back. No league or coach should ever allow a player wearing street frames to set foot on a baseball field. In the 1999 Little League World Series, the Toms River team had a kid who was wearing wire-rimmed glasses to bat and run without a face mask on his batting helmet. I assume he wore them to field as well. Not good.

Prevent Blindness says, "Molded polycarbonate frame and lenses (Plano/non-prescription eye wear) are suggested for…athletes who ordinarily do not wear glasses but participate in…baseball. Contact lenses should only be worn in combination with other recommended sports eye protectors."

Wearing prescription glasses inside a face mask batter's helmet or catcher's mask is problematic. On the one hand, wraparound-frame sports goggles do not fit inside face mask helmets or most catcher's masks. On the other hand, although the batter's helmet face mask and the catcher's mask offer some protection against the frame being driven into the eye, they are not total protection. They sometimes get knocked off or driven back into the face of the wearer or twisted so that the side of the mask or helmet is pushing against the face of the wearer. The players in question ought to have sports goggles that will fit inside helmets or catcher's masks. The most famous athlete to wear such goggles was Hall of Fame NFL running back Eric Dickerson.

Sunglasses

The seven-year-old batter whose photograph appears on the cover of *Time* magazine's 7/12/99 issue about "Sports crazed kids" is wearing sunglasses with his no-face-mask batting helmet. (He has no mouth guard either.) Are sunglasses safe? No way. I have never seen sports goggles with dark lenses. I suppose you could have them made special by an optometrist. But they strike me as unnecessary and probably would make it harder to see the ball.

Dr. Jack Jeffers of the Wills Eye Hospital says he is distressed to see Major League baseball players wearing Oakley-style sunglasses in games. He says they are quite unsafe for that purpose with their sharp edges and their readily bending when hit from the side.

Flip-downs?

What about the flip-down sunglasses now sold for kids in every sporting goods store? I thought they were probably the most dangerous thing a child could wear. A player who tripped and fell while running could easily drive a piece of the frame into his eye. The sunglasses portion of those are sort of pointed at the eye ball when they are in the up position. But Dr. Paul Vinger said the only problems he has seen with them is nonpolycarbonate lenses shattering and cutting open eyeballs in two cases. He agreed with me that we might not have a large enough sample to draw conclusions on the saftey of flip-down sunglasses because only a small number of players wear them.

The only frames that are acceptable are wraparound polycarbonate sports goggles. I do not believe it would be possible to make a safe flip-down sunglasses version of the approved sports goggles. They have hinges and hinges are *prima facie* unsafe.

ASTM F803

You can get non-prescription sports goggles in any

sporting goods store. You generally have to ask for **racquetball** goggles because the idea of wearing them in baseball is almost totally unknown. The correct standard for the protective goggles to be worn by baseball fielders is ASTM F803, which was the racquet sports standard. ASTM has now expanded the application of F803 to baseball, lacrosse, and field hockey.

Do NOT wear **workplace** goggles that meet the ANSI standard Z87. They are labeled "not to be worn in sports activities." In October of 1999, a new Protective Eyewear Council will start issuing certifications that should be looked for by anyone buying protective goggles.

They cost about $10 to $20 if you just buy one pair at a time. I got discounts when I bought for the whole team.

'Mandatory'

In a 4/1/99 news release, the American Academy of Ophthalmology (www.eyenet.org) says "…eye protection should be made mandatory for *all* children participating in organized athletics." [Emphasis in original]

AAO has a table showing what protective eye wear should be worn in various sports. For baseball, it says,

Polycarbonate face guard or other certified safe protection attached to helmet for batting and base running; sports goggles with polycarbonate lenses for fielding.

1993 tee-ball incident

In 1993, I coached a tee-ball team. I persuaded the parents to chip in and buy goggles for each kid. I believe they cost us $8 a pair. One father made a board that we hung on the back stop. It had a hook for each kid's goggles with his name above the hook. That kept them off the ground and thereby kept them from getting scratched. We did not wear them while batting because we had face-mask helmets. They do not fit inside the helmets, plus they are redundant.

In a game late in the season, the son of one of my neighbors, took a line drive right in the left eye. He was playing second base at the time. His goggles were knocked askew. He was bleeding slightly from where they gouged into his face. But his eye was unhurt. It is reasonable to conclude that if I had not been his coach, he might now be one-eyed.

Hit in the eye and back for more

Another year, my youngest son was playing on a AA team (9-10-year olds). My son was the only member of that team who wore goggles when fielding and a face-mask helmet when batting and base running. In one game, the manager's son was playing second base. He got hit in the eye by a bad-hop grounder. He had to be taken to the hospital and his eye was indeed injured in

some way. He missed several games as a result.

Was he wearing goggles when he came back? Remember, even the medical groups who do not say goggles should be mandatory for everyone, **do** say they should be worn by players who have previous severe eye injuries. Nope. He wore no goggles when he came back. Maybe his father figured eye patches were cheaper.

Pitchers' arms

In the 1960's, doctors started writing articles about "Little League Elbow," an injury technically described as "radiologic evidence of fragmentation of the epiconylar apophysis and osteochondrosis of the head of the radius and capitellum." Little League Elbow is more common among teenagers than subteens. It is caused by overuse (too many pitches in one day and/or too little rest between pitching performances) and poor mechanics.

Regardless of the number of pitches thrown or rest obtained, if a child's arm hurts, he should stop pitching immediately.

Curveballs

The chances that a youth pitcher will use poor mechanics increase if he is trying to throw movement pitches like curveballs. Sliders and screwballs are so dangerous to the arm that some **professional** minor league teams prohibit them. Yet sporting-goods stores now sell balls that show where the fingers go to throw curves and sliders.

Little League rules limit the number of **innings** a pitcher can pitch per day and per week and specify the number of days off he must get between pitching appearances. Those rules are inadequate. There are innings and there are innings. The arm is not affected by innings. It is affected by **pitches**.

A normal inning is about 25 pitches. You should adopt the Little League rules as your team standard, only substitute 25 pitches for the word "innings."

That makes the Little League rule read as follows:

If a player pitches less than 100 pitches one calendar day of rest in mandatory. If a player pitches 100 or more pitches, three calendar days of rest must be observed. A player may pitch a maximum of 150 pitches in a calendar week, Sunday through Saturday.

Coaches and fathers

There are two main dangers to youth pitchers' arms: coaches and fathers. Coaches often overwork a good pitcher because the coach is more concerned about his own win-loss record than he is concerned about the safety and health of his players. When I coached at the 9-10 year old level, I only allowed my pitchers to throw 50 pitches a day. The kid who threw a complete game victory against my team in 1992 probably exceeded 150 pitches that day.

Fathers sometimes teach their kid that the key to success is a powerful work ethic. There is much truth to that in baseball.

Ted Williams used to hit until his hands bled. Ozzie Smith used to throw balls over his house and run around and catch them for hours. Japanese players routinely field 1,000 ground balls per practice session.

No pain, no gain, no arm

But the ultra-long-practice session, no-pain-no-gain approach most definitely must NOT be applied to the skill of **pitching**. I saw a TV news story about a youth pitcher whose father told him to throw 100 pitches a day every day. The kids suffered permanent damage to his arm. Growing children have something adults do not have: growth plates at the end of each bone. Overuse damages those growth plates and the injury is permanent and incurable.

In the nineteenth century, children often worked in factories. Workers could tell which machine a particular child worked on by the way in which he was deformed. Repeating the same motion over and over every day maims children.

We no longer have such child-labor maiming in the U.S. since we enacted child-labor laws. But in recent years, the old child-labor deformities have crept back into our society. Only now they are occurring in **children who pursue a single sport year round**. Some sport skills, like factory machines, require that certain motions be repeated over and over. Baseball pitching is such a sport skill.

Parents and coaches must be very careful to make sure that pitchers do not overuse their arms. Informal at-home practice or sandlot pitches count the same as games or team practices.

Breakaway bases

The American Academy of Pediatrics and the Consumer Product Safety Commission both recommend that only breakaway bases be used in baseball. That's a league rather than a coach decision, but you ought to weigh in with your opinion on the subject.

Head-first sliding

The American Academy of Pediatrics recommends that head-first sliding be avoided for children less than ten years of age.

I think they are wrong to limit their head-first sliding rule to players under ten. One of my **adult** baseball teammates suffered serious permanent damage from a head-first slide. It ended his athletic career. When I talked to him a year or so afterward, he had had several surgeries as a result and was in constant pain. The prognosis was that he would be in constant pain for the rest of his life.

While writing this book on July 29, 1999, a story appeared in my local paper that said Little League recently outlawed head-first slides for players 12 and under. That's great, it more than complies with the AAP recommendation, but there is no reason to allow the slides at the teenage level.

Safe catcher's equipment

The player who gets hit the most is the catcher. He wears lots of equipment, but that equipment, like a batter's helmet, must be in good condition and fit the catcher in question properly.

Start with the helmet. Unlike the batter's helmet, the catcher's helmet protects the catcher from being hit in the head by **both** the ball and the bat. Like any helmet, it must fit properly to provide the desired protection. The typical team has seven helmets for the batter, base runners, and kid base coach. But they only have one catcher's helmet. Obviously, it will therefore be even less likely to fit than the batter's helmets.

Helmet must fit

As a coach, you must make sure each of your catchers has a catcher's helmet that fits. The typical team will have two or three players who play catcher at times. If the helmet you have does not fit all of your catchers, or **any** of them, tell the league equipment manager that you need additional catcher's helmets. Don't take no for an answer.

At the teenage levels, long-term catchers generally own their own equipment. But they are not required to.

As with batter's helmets, the catcher's helmets must not have deteriorated padding. In my experience, the batters helmets are not in too bad a shape, but the catcher's helmets are often much worse. Do not accept a deteriorated catcher's helmet.

The face mask must also be in good **condition**. It must fit the helmet. Nowadays, the helmet and the mask are strapped together and some catcher's helmets do not connect properly to some catcher's masks. There is often a huge gap between the mask and the helmet. They must be compatible.

Throat protector

The mask is required to have a "dangling type **throat protector**." (Little League Rule 1.17) Often, one side of the throat protector is not connected. Both sides must be connected. Remember ball impact on the throat is one of the killers of youth baseball players.

Snug against neck

The chest protector must have a "neck collar" according to Little League rules. The worst thing about youth catcher's equipment is the fit of the chest protector in relation to the throat and upper chest. The chest protector is supposed to be snug against the Adam's apple.

Virtually every youth catcher I have ever seen has a chest protector that has a much-too-long strap at the neck. Consequently, the top of the chest protector hangs way down to their sternum no matter how short you adjust the neck strap. If you want to see how a chest protector should fit, just turn on a TV baseball game or look at a baseball card of a catcher wearing his equipment. The recent *Complete Idiot's Guide to Baseball* by Johnny Bench has a photo of him in catcher's gear on the cover. The top of his chest protector is against his Adam's apple and even with the top of his shoulders.

The most serious safety breach

This is probably the most serious safety breach in youth baseball. The catcher is the only player who generally has no chance to get out of the way of a ball on a path to hit him. Coaches **must** insist that this be corrected before the first pitch is thrown. If necessary, get a scissors and sewing kit and modify the neck strap so it fits snugly. Parents of catchers can help by purchasing their own set of catcher's gear and making sure it fits and is in good condition.

Waist band

The waist band is another problem. It, too, is generally too long. On many occasions, I ran it through the neck strap to try to pull the neck strap down and thereby raise the front of the chest protector, as well as to make the waist tighter. Both straps must be short enough that the protector fits snugly. In my experience, youth chest protectors are always way too big and therefore endanger the catcher.

Jock and cup

Catchers are required to wear a jock and cup. I read about a youth coach who was sued because he did not make sure his players were wearing a jock or, in the case of a catcher, a jock and cup. The child of the suing parents apparently was hit in the testicles and injured.

My first reaction was, "How are we coaches supposed to check a player's undergarments?" But upon further reflection I came up with a way.

I have done this for years in baseball and football. If the kid is just wearing a jock with no cup, I have him pull the waist band up and show it to me or another coach. The waist band of a jock is distinctive. One kid tried to fool me once by pretending his briefs waist band was a jock. I made him pull it up further and saw the fabric of the briefs. We have a daily jock check form which is just a roster with daily columns next to each name.

If a kid is wearing a cup, which is required for catchers and recommended for everyone else, I have him tap it with the handle of a bat so I can hear the noise. I do not, I repeat, I do not touch either the waist band or tap the cup myself. I always have the kids do it.

'I demand to be traded to a jockless team'

The parents one of my players once demanded he be switched to another team because he did not want to wear a jock and I was the only coach in the league who checked. To my amazement, the San Ramon Valley Little League agreed to the request.

I was amazed because Little League Rule 1.17 says all male players must wear a jock. But they treated this safety requirement as if it was personality conflict between the boy and myself. I always thought that incident would play a prominent role if I ever was called to testify in a personal-injury lawsuit against the San Ramon Valley Little League.

If a kid did not have a cup, we would not let him catch in practice or in a game. If a kid did not have a jock, we would not let him play in a game or participate in any moving-ball drill in practice.

I suspect I am the only coach on earth who enforces the jock rule. If so, it would appear that the youth baseball authorities are really instituted that rule to protect their own backsides, not the front sides of the boys entrusted to them.

Shin guards

Shin guards are almost always a problem in my experience because their straps are too long or are missing or deteriorated. We often had to cross the straps in an X pattern to make them tight. And we often had to stop games to fiddle with shin guards because the straps kept coming undone, mainly because they were too loose.

Softer baseballs

In the late 1980's, my oldest son attended the Rob Andrews Baseball Camp. Rob Andrews is a former Major Leaguer. I was surprised when he told the campers that the only baseball they would be using was an Incrediball®. At the time, that was the only brand of soft baseball.

I discussed it with Andrews privately later. He said he can see the relief in the kids faces at the beginning of every camp when he makes that announcement. He said no kid would ever publicly admit preferring soft baseballs, but most secretly do.

Andrews says many high school, college, and pro coaches use soft baseballs for many drills. He used them himself when he coached college baseball.

'When I was your age...'

I am a Baby Boomer. Nowadays, my generation spends a lot of time bragging about how when we were kids in the fifties and sixties, we played ball all day.

There is considerable truth to it, but I am now going to reveal some dirty little secrets about sandlot baseball in that era.

Yes, it's true that we had wooden bats. It's also true that we played baseball even when there were no adults around. There were only three channels on TV and they only had kids shows on Saturday morning and after school on week days. We played ball all the time because we were bored by the standards of today's kids.

One dirty little secret is that we never had nine guys, let alone 18. We played "pops and grounders" or "pickle"—little three-, four-, five-, or six-man games that would be called competitive drills by a baseball coach.

Rubber baseballs

Another dirty little secret is that although our bats were wood, our baseballs were **rubber**. Sure, we occasionally got to play with a real, leather-covered baseball. A couple of times a year one of the kids in the neighborhood would get one for his birthday or from a visiting grandfather. We would rush right out to play with it. In a few hours, it would turn green from hitting the grass. Today's kids have never seen a green baseball. They don't even go after a brand new baseball when they hit one into the bushes.

Rob Andrews told me he, too, played with soft baseballs when he was a kid.

Electricians tape

By the end of the day, the stitches would start to rip and the cover would be coming off. By the next day, we would have to cover it with electricians tape. Now it was black—either shiny or sticky depending upon the type of tape. Once it was covered with electricians tape, it became heavy and hard to see.

Then we'd lose interest and go back to our normal baseball: a sponge rubber ball that was painted white to look like a baseball and even had raised, simulated stitches that were painted red. Those rubber baseballs could be bought at the five-and-ten-cent store for 10¢ to 25¢ and they lasted forever.

When all was said and done, the vast majority of the "baseballs" we played with as kids was played with those sponge rubber fake baseballs. Did we prefer them to hard balls? Probably, although we did not know it and would not have admitted it if we had known it. Very simply, we had no choice. Regular hard balls were expensive and only lasted one day. Everybody was poor then by today's standards. Rubber baseballs were cheap and indestructible.

Hard balls hurt

Hard balls are, well, hard. When you got hit by one or caught it in the palm of your glove, it hurt. Who likes getting hurt? If the rubber ones bounce and can be thrown and hit, what's the problem?

I say all this because when I start talking about using softer baseballs instead of hard balls, guys my age start muttering about "tradition." Rather than go through the whole we-used-rubber-balls-when-we-were-kids story, I just dismiss them with an "I don't pay much attention to the word 'tradition' when it comes out of the mouth of a guy whose team uses aluminum bats."

In the 90's, a number of softer baseballs have come out. Worth, Inc. has its RIF 1, RIF 5, and RIF 10 balls. RIF stands for "reduced injury factor."

NOCSAE standards only

If it were up to me, all youth baseball would be played with balls that meet NOCSAE standards. Oddly, youth baseball organizations like Little League Baseball, Inc. require batting **helmets** that meet NOCSAE standards, but they do **not** require **baseballs** that meet NOCSAE standards. As far as I know, **only one league** requires baseballs that meet NOCSAE standards. The American Amateur Baseball Congress requires them through age 12.

Youth baseball is supposed to be about **fun**. There can be no doubt that playing baseball with a RIF-1 ball is fun. It bounces. It flies through the air. You can catch it. You can throw it. If you put a group of kids on a desert island with some bats, gloves, and RIF 1 or Kenko balls, they would start playing baseball with them. They would not whine about the ball not being hard enough.

Worth did an informal test. They put an assortment of baseballs, including both hardballs and RIF 1s out for a group of kids aged 4 to 12 to play with. They were observed over a period of weeks. After initially fiddling with all types, they invariably preferred the RIF 1.

The standard youth baseball is not hard because the **kids** want it to be hard. It is hard because the **parents** want it to be hard. Actually, it's not the parents, it's the **fathers**.

More precisely, it is hard because they did not know how to make them soft when baseball was first invented, and once they figured out how to make them soft, no man wanted to make a motion to switch to the softer ball because he was afraid someone might call him a wimp.

Dr. Hodgson told me he got some pressure to eliminate the NOCSAE standard for baseballs. Companies whose balls did **not** meet the standard were embarrassed by it and feared both legal liability and lost sales. You could do a whole series of expose´s on the scandals involving youth-baseball safety.

Not in Japan

Kids die playing baseball every year in the United States. You'll recall that earlier in this chapter, I quoted the American Academy of Pediatrics as saying, "Direct contact by the ball is the most frequent cause of death and serious injury in baseball."

Baseball is big in Japan, too, so they must kill a couple of kids a year there, right? Wrong. No youth baseball player has **ever** died in Japan. How so?

The Japanese were not dumb enough to let kids play hardball. There, 90% of kids under 14 play baseball with hollow rubber baseballs, e.g., the Kenko Ball.

These are harder rubber than the sponge balls we played with in the fifties. Like the old five-and-ten-cent-store balls, they are white with raised, painted, red, fake stitches. Unlike the fifties balls, Kenko balls are dimpled like a golf ball. That makes them fly straighter and faster, same as golf balls. Kenko also makes day-glo orange baseballs which are softer for younger kids.

They are less dangerous, at least as much fun, and the Japanese kids are no slouches at playing hardball when they grow up.

NOCSAE ball standard

What makes the fact that baseball requires batting helmets that meet NOCSAE standards, but not balls that meet NOCSAE standards even stranger is the fact that the standard is the same for both: a Head Injury Severity Index of 1200. Regular youth baseballs typically cause a Severity Index reading of 2000 when they hit the "instrumented headform." Kenko says that its Air Safety Ball causes a Severity Index of just 137 when it hits the NOCSAE instrumented headform.

So organizations like Little League Baseball say that batters and base runners must wear a helmet which keeps the severity of their head injuries below 1200, but pitchers and fielders, who face balls traveling faster than pitches, are allowed to take a hit in the head that registers 2000 on the Severity Index. Go figure.

RIF balls

Worth produces three varieties of what they call RIF balls. They advertise that their product is the only "official league ball" that meets NOCSAE standards. The Kenko ball also meets the NOCSAE standards, but it is not allowed in games under most leagues' rules.

RIF balls look like regular baseballs. You can tell the RIF 1 and RIF 5 by squeezing them. They are significantly softer than regular balls. But it's hard to tell a RIF 10 from a regular ball even by squeezing. It does give more, but not much.

Worth ad brochures say that their RIF 1 has a "1% head injury risk factor when it strikes the head at 60 mph." The head injury risk factors for the RIF 5 and RIF 10 are 5% and 10%.

I like to use RIF 1 balls for **all** purposes, namely, practice, pre-game warm-up, pre-inning warm-up, and the game itself. Other than at the tee-ball level, I have been prevented from using the RIF 1 ball in games. I did get permission to use the RIF 10 ball in 11-12-year old games one year, but permission was later revoked and we had to use regular hard balls.

RIF 1 for all but game play

We still used the RIF 1 for practice, pre-game warm-up, and pre-inning warm-up. Once, by mistake, someone tossed a pre-inning warm-up ball to our pitcher. After a couple of pitches were hit in the game, I suspected it was a RIF 1 and asked to see the ball. It was indeed a RIF 1. Our players were so used to it neither the pitcher or catcher realized it. But RIF 1's can get a wicked spin if they are hit off center and I saw a wicked spin on one foul hit by the batter. We immediately replaced the ball with a RIF 10 or regular hard ball, whatever we were allowed to use at that time.

Once, when we yelled "Balls in!" at the end of a pre-inning warm-up, the left fielder threw a ball that hit me square in the knee on one hop when I was looking another direction. Had it been a regular ball, it probably would have shattered my kneecap. But it was a RIF 1 and did not even hurt. Coaches can become casualties, too. Safety balls protect coaches as well as players.

In 1992, one of the majors players in the San Ramon Valley Little League had his kneecap shattered when a regular Little League hardball one-hopped into his knee while he was playing catch.

My team used RIF 1's in practice and for warm-ups and RIF 10's in games throughout most of the 1992 season. Then one of the opposing coaches campaigned to get the RIF ball banned from our games, even though we had all agreed that my team could use it in our games at a pre-season managers meeting.

I got outvoted two to one with two abstentions in the revisiting of the issue. One of the guys who voted against the ball later admitted to me that he had nightmares about a kid being hurt by the hardball in one of my games because of his vote.

Disadvantage when switch to hard balls?

Some people thought we would be at a disadvantage when we had to use a real hardball, having used only "wimp" balls all season. Nah. We won the first hardball game 8-7. There was not the slightest indication that our team was having any trouble with the real hardball.

Worth tested the ball extensively in its home town of Tullahoma, TN. The local Little League used the RIF 10 in their National League and regular hard balls in their American League. Close track was kept of the number of hits, errors, home runs, runs scored, doubles , triples, etc. Result: almost identical numbers for the two leagues. The all-star team from the RIF 10 league advanced farther in post-season play than any previous Tullahoma team, even though they had to switch to regular hardballs in the post-season.

Can't tell the difference except by sound

A local coach said he did not like the way the RIF 10 ball bounced. There is no difference in the way it bounces. Extensive tests were done to make sure of that.

I challenged any such complainer to a videotape test. The test would have to be on **video**, with the sound turned off, because the RIF 10 **does** make a slightly different sound when it hits the bat. I'll bet that those who claim it plays different would not be able to tell which was the RIF 10 and which was the regular hardball in any test they wanted, as long as the sound were turned off. No one took the test.

In short, there is no difference between the RIF 10 and a regular hard ball when it comes to play, except for fewer injuries and a different "ping" when it is hit.

Note that the Worth company never claimed the RIF ball would reduce deaths due to being hit in the chest, only head injuries. Remember that Andrew Cook, the Omaha boy who died in 1999, was hit by a soft-core ball.

A Tufts University study published in the June, 1998 *New England Journal of Medicine* found that RIF balls **did** reduce the risk of death from chest injury. Worth had not even been aware that the study was underway until the publication. Another study published in March 1999 in *Archives of Ophthalmology* found that softer core baseballs reduced the risk of **eye** injury.

Babe Ruth Baseball's Bambino Rookie Division (7-9 years old) uses soft baseballs "…to reduce the fear factor…" They also say that use of the pitching machine all but eliminates batters being hit by pitches.

Why these safety measures have not been adopted

Leading medical and safety organizations have recommended changes in baseball rules. When those organizations did the same with football and ice hockey, those sports immediately adopted all the recommendations. What's baseball's problem?

In my research, I came across a number of comments about why baseball has refused to adopt recommended safety measures.

Mouthguard problems

The American Academy of Pediatric Dentistry surveyed parent regarding why mouthguards were not being used.

Half the parents thought sports like football and hockey had need for mouthguards, but few thought baseball had any such need. As you have read previously, they are incorrect and your parent meeting is a perfect time to enlighten them.

Parents also said their kids found the mouthguards too uncomfortable. Trimming the back of a boil-and-bite mouth guard can eliminate the gagging. But the best thing for comfort is to get a custom-fitted mouth guard made.

Parents think that **boys** may need mouthguards, but **not girls**. I have had a number of girls on my predominantly male baseball teams. In fact, more girls than boys now suffer dental injuries in youth sports.

A 3/2/99 *New York Times* story said "peer pressure" was one of the reasons individual players did not wear protective equipment that was not being worn by everybody. I can confirm that. My sons, players, and I were all taunted about our non-standard protective equipment. But fighting peer pressure to do stupid things safetywise is one of the main jobs of parents.

'Macho'

In a 7/19/87 *New York Times* story, Texas Rangers trainer Bill Zeigler said, "…I think every player ought to wear [face-mask helmets]. But a lot of guys are still tied to the macho thing." A lot? Make it "all!" Not a single Major Leaguer wears optional safety equipment.

Richard Hilton, the head coach of the East Marietta, GA Little League world champions who wore face-mask batting helmets says he still has to defend the face guard once or twice a year to some new fathers who complain about its looks. "You get remarks. It's the macho stuff."

In another 5/12/91 Associated Press news story Hilton said, "The only trouble we have now is some of these gung-ho dads who don't want their children to wear them. I guess it's a masculine thing."

Bill Kamela of the National Safe Kids Campaign explains why face-mask helmets are not required, "There's a sort of macho thing involved."

When a man proves how macho he is by taking unnecessary risks with his **own** body, that's dumb. But when he proves how macho he is by risking children who are in his care, it's criminal.

Every accepted piece of protective equipment in sports was once derided as being only for wimps. When Harvard catcher Fred Thayer invented and began wearing the first catcher's mask in 1870, he was taunted by opposing players. The same thing happened to the first catchers who wore chest protectors in 1887.

Explanations from organizations

Little League spokesman Stephen Keener said regarding face-mask helmets, "…at this point, the people who know the game best at the grass-roots level haven't felt it is necessary." That's a **politician's spin**. When a player is injured, his parents do not go to the "people who know the game best at the grass-roots level," they go to a **doctor**. It is absurd to suggest that safety policy ought to be decided by laymen against the recommendations of medical authorities.

Keener also said in *USA Today*, "Little League could make safety equipment mandatory but nobody asks about it except the media." Once again, Mr. Keener sounds like a politician counting votes rather than someone who places a high priority on eliminating preventable injuries.

Another Little League spokesperson, Dennis Sullivan, said in a 5/5/92 *Boston Herald* story that his organization does not require face masks, safety baseballs, etc. because, "We try not be so demanding that the kids can't enjoy the game. The people who say this should be mandatory can buy it for their kids."

I am not aware of any evidence that injuries increase a child's enjoyment of the game or that wearing protective equipment decreases enjoyment of the game. Baseball catchers and football players wear plenty of protective equipment. I do not recall them quitting the sport in droves when that equipment became mandatory.

Competing on leniency

I suspect one reason most youth baseball organizations do not require more safety equipment is that they are competing with each other. If, say, Little League Baseball, Inc. requires face-mask batting helmets, disgruntled local Little League chapters may switch to Pony. So each national youth baseball organization has to be as lenient as the other organizations or risk losing local chapters to more lenient programs. If that's the case, Dixie Youth Baseball deserves all the more credit for unilaterally requiring face-mask helmets.

If these organizations truly are interested in the safety of their players, there is a simple solution. Hold a **summit meeting** of all youth baseball organizations and jointly agree to simultaneously require use of the various recommended safety devices: face-mask helmets, mouthguards, protective goggles, break-away bases, and softer baseballs.

An alternative would be for the parents of dead or maimed players to sue the offending organizations out of existence, whereupon they would be replaced by new, more responsible organizations.

I am convinced that youth baseball coaches and administrators are **incapable of reforming the sport themselves**. They must be **forced** to do so by outsiders.

Football refused to reform itself safetywise until President Theodore Roosevelt, an outsider, called a summit meeting of college coaches and ordered them to reduce the number of injuries or else he would ask Congress to outlaw football entirely. Boy, did they reform! In fact, the injury-prevention mentality imposed on football by President Roosevelt at the turn of the century has survived to this day.

Whose fault is this situation?

The blame for children being killed or injured unnecessarily in youth baseball lies mainly with the **local leagues**. They can require safety equipment above and beyond what the national organization requires. Indeed, many, like the East Marietta, GA and Staten Island Little Leagues have done just that.

I tried to do it at the **team** level, and I was successful at protecting my players for the season in question, but deviating from the league norm appears to have adversely affect my oldest son's playing career and my coaching career.

For example, in 1997, I checked the "manager" box on the part of my son's league registration form that asks what work the parent will volunteer for, listed the details of my many years of experience in the appropriate blank, and was made assistant to a guy who had never coached before.

Once when I was interviewed to be a AAA manager, the San Ramon Valley Little League officials who interviewed me and who knew my son, expressed concern that he was going to be drafted into the majors and that I would quit the AAA job as a result. In fact, my son ended up two levels **down** from majors that year, in the lowest of two minor league levels. I cannot prove that my son did not make majors because he was my son, but incidents like that one strongly suggest it.

My son was cut from his high school team as a freshman and sophomore. I insisted he wear the recommended safety equipment. Sophomore year he overheard the young head coach say before the cut, "No one on my team is wearing that stupid face-mask helmet." I do not regret requiring Dan to wear the face-mask helmet. I do regret that his high school hired a macho idiot as their J.V. baseball coach.

Coach's obligations

In short, it is best if the safety requirements come from the **league** level, not the coach or parent level. However, in the absence of responsible behavior by your league, you have a moral, ethical, and legal obligation to warn your parents of the dangers and inform them about the protective equipment that is available and the recommendations of the various medical and safety groups regarding that protective equipment.

I believe **field owners** also have a responsibility. They have the power to compel the leagues to behave responsibly. It seems to me that they should adopt rules saying, "You can use our fields, but only if you comply with the safety recommendations that have been promulgated by responsible medical and safety organizations pertaining to your sport." This would have no effect on youth football and ice hockey programs, but it would force baseball and several other sports to clean up their acts.

Major League Baseball's responsibility

Major League Baseball should require the same safety equipment (although they will never change the ball because it would break the connection to the ancient records) for most of the same reasons. (There appears to be no danger of death from chest or neck ball impact for adults, but the other risks are the same.)

Major League Baseball would get two benefits from this: 1. Elimination of Tony Conigliaro-type incidents and 2. Their example would inspire lower levels to clean up their acts. Even if there were no benefit to Major League Baseball itself, they should require recommended safety equipment just so that youth, high school, and college leagues would do the same and thereby save many lives and tens of thousands of serious injuries.

High school and college

Intermediate leagues like **high school** and **college** should require safety equipment. At least then local macho youth league coaches could take cover behind the excuse that they have to use the safety equipment so their kids will be used to it when they get to high school.

The Chris Sabo Award

Major League stars could start unilaterally using safety equipment to set an example for youth players. For example, if Mark McGwire wore a face mask helmet, you can be darned sure that thousands of kids would be clamoring to have one, too.

The only Major Leaguer who I can recall unilaterally wearing recommended safety equipment for preventive reasons was Cincinnati's Chris Sabo who wore polycarbonate prescription sports goggles as a third baseman. The highlight of his career was his team's victory over the A's in the 1990 World Series. A safety or medical organization ought to create an annual award for the Major Leaguer who sets the best preventive safety example. Call it the Chris Sabo Award.

Several pros wore face-mask helmets while **recuperating** from a face injury, but as far as I know, none ever wore one to **prevent** a facial injury, which is the main idea.

Adopt a charity

It is standard for Major League and other stars to adopt a charity. I guess it's a PR thing to make the public resent them less for being rich and famous. The stars make public appearances and sign autographs. How about if one adopts youth baseball safety as his charity and he contributes to that charity not only by making public appearances, but also by setting the example on the field?

There is precedent for this. A number of pro baseball players have publicly come out against smokeless tobacco and stopped using it. Retired player Joe Garagiola spearheaded that movement, the National Spit Tobacco Education Program, and got many current and recent pros to sign on.

We need another Joe Garagiola, perhaps some retired player whose grandson lost an eye playing youth baseball, to step forward and spearhead a movement to reduce the deaths and maiming in youth baseball. I am doing my part with this book and I did my part when I was a manager and a youth baseball parent. But I do not have the gravitas or credibility that a former Major Leaguer would have.

Stars only

A pro safety example setter would have to be a **star**, because marginal players will justly fear that they may be sent down to the minors if they deviate from the norm. Deviating from the norm is a *prima facie* rebuke of the norm.

I felt that as a deviating-from-the-norm coach. Other coaches and league officials seemed to greatly resent the implication that they were not taking proper care of their players by failing to adopt the same safety standards as I did. Sorry, guys, but I'll be damned if I'll risk a kid's life or eyes or whatever just to avoid embarrassing a bunch of jerks who are, in fact, negligent regarding the safety of their players.

Stop setting a bad example

If Major Leaguers will not unilaterally **start** wearing recommended safety equipment, they might at least **stop** wearing dangerous equipment like sunglasses or batting helmets with no ear flaps. I suspect that some kids imitating their pro heroes in the sunglasses department have been blinded or seriously injured as a result.

Government

State legislatures, county governments, or **city councils** could pass laws requiring recommended safety equipment in youth sports. They already have in football. The requirement that helmets be certified annually is not in the league rule books. It is state law.

Medical and safety groups

Medical authorities are leaders in the effort to make youth baseball safer and I commend them highly for that. But measured by **results**, their efforts have been almost entirely a waste of time. They have been almost totally ignored by Little League, Babe Ruth, Pony, and American Legion Baseball and largely ignored by Dixie Youth Baseball. Only a tiny number of youth parents have unilaterally complied with the recommendations

Part of the problem is that although the **national** headquarters of the various medical groups are raising cain about youth baseball safety, the **local** doctors and dentists are all but silent. I suspect the reason is that they fear loss of business if they speak out.

That's pretty craven and mercenary. I have talked to a number of local medical professionals about these issues. They always agree with me, but they have no interest in speaking out publicly. They should be addressing the off-season meetings of the local youth baseball leagues, and failing there, to the local media and to their patients.

As I recommended with national baseball organizations, they could convene a **local summit meeting** and simultaneously announce their disapproval of local youth baseball league practices. If every dentist, ophthalmologist, or pediatrician in the area signed the statement, none should lose any business as a result.

'My son may not pitch'

I had an orthodontist's son on one of my teams. His sole safety contribution was to prohibit his son from pitching. Of course, if **every** parent on the team followed his example, we would have had no pitchers and the orthodontist's son would not have had a baseball team at all.

Normally, I do not allow a parent to adopt such a policy. But that year I was already fighting so many other battles I let that one pass. One of my football parents once announced that his son would not return punts because he thought it was too dangerous. Had I been head coach, he and his son would have been gone. The correct policy is that everyone on the team is eligible for every position and the coach is the only one who decides who goes where. Any player who refuses to play the position assigned to him by the coach should be thrown out of the **league**, not just off the team.

Parents

As the spin doctors for Little League and other organizations point out, the parents can have their child wear whatever approved equipment the parents want. And all the recommended equipment is approved. So why are parents who normally take good care of their children not taking the same level of care when they put them on a baseball field?

Youth baseball organizations are **political** in nature. Most children and their parents hope their child will be a **starter** and be chosen for the **higher levels** and the post-season **all-star** teams. Most people work for organizations where they are reminded on a daily basis of the need to play **office politics**. They see the same situation in youth baseball. So they are terrified of doing anything that might anger the powers that be in the league.

Parents agreed—for one season

I saw this in the reverse direction on my teams. At the parent meeting, I would make a pitch for the safety equipment and the parents would agree and chip in the money to buy it. I was surprised at the lack of resistance.

But the following year, I would see the same players, now on **other** teams, and few, if any, were still wearing the safety equipment. Originally, I thought I had persuaded the parents that the protective equipment was a good idea. In fact, they were apparently just doing whatever I wanted because they thought that, as manager, I had some power to hurt their kid by benching him or some such.

People, both children and their parents, are also **terrified of being different**. The vast majority of people are craven conformists.

Conformist mothers and fathers also have slightly different motives. **Mothers** are in favor of recom-

mended protective equipment, but are held back only by fear for their child politically if they insist that he or she wear it.

Fathers are a bigger problem. I surmise that almost all men are worried about how they are perceived as far as their **manhood** is concerned. Part of manhood is toughness. I would argue that another part is mature judgment, but the men who are insecure about their manhood cannot get past the toughness issue to consider things like judgment.

Almost all men fear that if they support the use of any unusual item of protective equipment, others might raise an eyebrow, or smirk, or snicker, or make a ridiculing remark. Given a choice between having to risk that smirk on the one hand or the death or maiming of a player, **including their own child**, on the other hand, almost all men take the sort of Sophie's Choice: Risk the kid. Pretty appalling.

Youth football versus youth baseball

I have written four books about tackle football, three of which are only about youth football. Do I have a long section in those books about safety? Nope. Why not? Because youth football complies with **every** recommendation made by medical and safety groups. I am told that youth ice hockey does as well.

Youth football also has a totally different attitude about safety. I wrote a letter about improving safety to the president of my local youth **baseball** association and the president of my local youth **football** association on separate occasions.

The youth-football letter complained that the prohibition against eye shields should be changed. I did my homework and stated the reasons for my request. It was **immediately granted**. They promptly changed the California Youth Football League rule book to the wording I requested.

The youth-baseball letter listed a number of saftey steps that ought to be taken. The response was no answer. They did respond positively to the suggestions in one little way. They added mouthguards to the snack bar offerings, but the mouthguards they sold were for football (they had a long strap off the front for attaching to a football helmet) and they cost double the sporting-goods-store price. I suspect the only parents who ever bought them were from my team.

A youth-football official (referee) once told me, "Our main job is safety." I have yet to hear a youth baseball umpire tell me that.

A spokesperson for Dixie Youth Baseball once said, "We can't require everything," to a reporter who asked why they did not require face-mask helmets (Dixie **does** require them now).

They **can, too**, require "everything." Youth baseball already requires "everything" for catchers. Youth football and hockey require "everything" for their players. Baseball's "everything" is a far shorter, far less expensive list than that of football or hockey. Requiring everything the medical and safety authorities recommend for baseball would cost about $40 more per player. Youth football players wear hundreds of dollars worcth of equipment, and the typical youth football program charges about the same participation fee as youth baseball.

League safety officer

Little League Baseball requires that each local league have a safety officer. They recommend that the safety officer be a **medical professional** whenever possible. In my affluent area, almost every team has a doctor parent, but who did the San Ramon Valley Little League name as their safety officer the year I wrote the letter about safety? A **lawyer**.

It reminded me of Teddy Kennedy's approach to water safety. After he drove a car containing Mary Jo Kopechne off the Chappaquiddick Bridge, the first call he made was to his lawyer. The lawyer called emergency personnel, but Ms. Kopechne did not survive the wait.

Safety summary

The safety recommendations that you should relate at your parent meeting and try to implement at the league, or if necessary, team or individual level, are:

- Lexan® or wire cage face mask that meets NOCSAE standards
- Mouth guard, preferably Type III custom-fitted that meets ASTM standard F697-80 (1992)
- Personal custom-fitted helmet in good condition that meets NOCSAE standards at 90 mph
- Protective goggles that meet ASTM standard F803 for fielders
- No sunglasses except inside helmet with face mask
- Game baseball that meets NOCSAE standards (RIF or Kenko)
- RIF-1 baseballs for practice, pre-game, and pre-inning warm-up
- Breakaway bases
- Feet-first sliding only (except diving back to base to avoid a pickoff throw)
- No players in line of fire of foul balls (no on-deck circle)
- Properly-fitting catcher's equipment

Asthma

Youth coaches need to be aware of any asthmatic players on their team. Four million children suffer from asthma in the U.S. More than five thousand **die** a year from asthma.

The only death in the 70-year history of Pop Warner Football was a 1991 incident where an asthmatic player had an asthma attack and died. (Yes, your kid is far more likely to be killed in youth baseball than youth football.) Strenuous exercise is the main cause of asthma attacks.

In an asthma attack, the child's air passages swell, extra mucous is produced, and the breathing muscles may go into spasm (contract and stay contracted), all of which cuts off his air supply. He or she needs to use an inhaler officially called a bronchodilator to reopen the air passages.

In 1997, I asked at my parent meeting if any player had asthma and one parent raised their hand. They later gave me one of their inhalers to carry to practice in case their son did not have his with him.

Asthma experts recommend that sufferers take two puffs from an inhaler 20 minutes before exercise.

An asthma attack can kill you. Let the person sit down. Do **not** make them lie down. Call 911 immediately if the player does not respond satisfactorily to use of an inhaler or if you have no inhaler.

'Is there a doctor in the house?'

I always ask at my parent meeting if any of the parents are doctors. In 1993, after I went through all my stuff about eye and other injuries, I asked if there were any doctors. Two hands went up. I asked their specialties: ophthalmology and pediatrics.

'Doggone it!" I said, "Why didn't you tell me that before my injury speech. You are better qualified than I." The ophthalmologist said, "You did a very good job of explaining the possible injuries." After the season ended, he wrote a letter of commendation about me to the League.

My 1997 team parent group had an ear-nose-throat plastic surgeon and an Emergency Medical Technician.

It's useful to know what medical personnel you have among your parents in case of an emergency at a game.

Throwing bats

Some kids tend to throw bats. This must be stopped. I mention it at my parent meeting because the parents generally know if their kids are bat throwers. I will bench a child who does that for the safety of the players on both teams. The solution is to have him hit the ball a bunch of times in practice while concentrating on hanging onto the bat. But do whatever it takes to stop this bad habit.

No metal spikes

Metal spikes are illegal in many youth baseball programs, even if the child is old enough to play high school baseball where they can wear metal spikes. They do not make any small-size metal spiked baseball shoes. But if your child has large feet or is high school age, he may be offered a pair of metal spiked shoes at a shoe store. Be careful that you do not buy a pair that is illegal in your league.

Heel cups

Whenever you wear spiked shoes, including those with rubber spikes, you need heel cups. If you do not have heel cups, you will bruise your heel, maybe so severely that you will be unable to play for several days or more. The injury occurs when a spike lands on a hard object like a stone or concrete and thereby puts a greatly increased number of pounds per square inch on the spot on the bottom of the heel right above the spike. Heel cups prevent the injury, and they speed your recovery if you already have the injury.

They are sold in shoe stores. Every one of your players should get them.

Knee pads

When I or my players slide, we lacerate our sliding knees. Supposedly, if you slide perfectly, you do not lacerate your knee, but I have never figured out how to do that or coach it. So when I play baseball, I wear a knee pad on my sliding knee. My oldest son also wore a knee pad on his sliding knee. I recommend to my parents that they get their children a knee pad.

The knee pad must be long, at least eight inches, because they have a devilish tendency to slide off the knee when they are needed. When my kids were smaller, I found the best knee pad for them in the sporting goods stores was an **adult elbow pad**. It must fit snugly and many pads that are knee pads *per se* are too loose because young children's legs are so thin.

Some years, my team was in a league where we had to turn in our baseball pants at the end of the season. The equipment manager sometimes commented to me that all our pants were unusable because one knee was destroyed in each pair. That's because we were the best and most frequent sliders in the league by far.

I also found it necessary to recommend some sort of shorts under the baseball pants. Sporting-goods stores sell sliding pants that are supposedly for this purpose, but I find they do not work. They are too thin and too soft.

The padding in sliding pants appears to be very soft to the consumer's touch because that's what makes sense to the idiot consumer. But when you drop a 50- to 200-pound body onto the gravel of a baseball infield while running at ten to twenty miles an hour, a thin sheet of soft foam rubber is useless.

What I have found that works is a too-large pair of denim shorts. Normal-size jean shorts are too constricting.

The notion that baseball base runners need to wear padding to slide appears to be one of the best kept secrets since the location of the D-day invasion. I have read a zillion baseball books including several that are just about base running. I do not recall ever seeing a word about the need to pad your knee and hips.

This is one piece of protective equipment that I did not have so much trouble selling. Typically, a kid would think he did not need it because he never did on previous teams. Then we he saw how much sliding we did, and scraped his knee and hip in the process, he would reconsider and get the pads I recommended.

Many times, they would come back to the bench bleeding at the knee. I would point out the blood to their parent and say, "Remember at the parent meeting I said to get a knee pad. They really need it." That usually did the trick.

Most of all, the pads and denim shorts were invisible to opposing players. They did not make my kids different in a way that could be seen.

Our opponents rarely slid because they did not know how and when they tried, it hurt. The main reason my opponents' players did not slide was that they had no knee pad or hip protection.

Always wear long pants to practice

I always tell my parents that their child should never wear short pants to baseball practice, but when the weather gets warm, there are always a few who show up in the same short pants they wore to school that day.

I practice sliding at every practice. You cannot slide at short pants. The fact that girls softball teams wear short pants blows my mind. I slid in shorts during a grad-school softball game once. I had about 15 bloody lines about ten inches long on my thigh—one for each bit of gravel that was under my thigh during the slide.

Eye test

In his book, *Pete Rose on Hitting*, Rose says, "I would suggest, no matter how old you may be, that before the season begins you go to an eye doctor and have your eyes examined." Ever since I read that, I give an eye test to my players the first day of practice.

I made five lines of block letters of decreasing size in my computer and printed it out. I then put it on the wall and paced on twenty feet. With my glasses on, I have 20/20 vision. The smallest line I could read with my glasses on from twenty feet was 3/8 inches high.

You can get standard eye charts off the Internet. For example, there is one at www.njeyes.com/info/chart1.htm.

The first player I tested was my oldest son. Guess what? He needed glasses and that test was the first indication we had of that. An eye doctor confirmed what my test indicated. On another occasion, my eye test revealed that one of my players needed to update his prescription. Another revealed that I had a player who needed glasses, but did not want to wear them.

At one parent meeting, when I said I was going to test eyes, a mother snarled, "Are you a licensed optometrist." "No. And that would explain why I'm not going to write a prescription for your son if he flunks the test."

For some reason, many people hate to be tested in anything. If you announce that you are timing players for speed, in advance, some will be "sick" the day of the test. I have had players tell me all season long that they were too injured or sick to be tested for running speed, but that they were OK to play in the games.

You should give your players an impromptu eye test the first day of practice and tell the child's parents the results. Just print out a chart from the Internet and post it twenty feet away from the player and ask him to read it.

If a child appears to need glasses and refuses to wear them, urge them to reconsider. If they still refuse, it may be a safety issue that would require the player to leave the league. He cannot get out of the way of something he cannot see coming. Child safety trumps child vanity.

Batters obviously need good eyesight to pick up the ball as soon as it leaves the pitcher's hand. Infielders need good eyesight to see balls coming at them at high speed from a relatively short distance away.

Probably the greatest need for good eyesight is among **outfielders**. They must see a less-than-three-inch diameter ball come off the bat from hundreds of feet away. The older the players, the more important good eyesight is for outfielders because the ball doesn't get any bigger, but the distance from outfield to home plate does.

Dominant eye

It is interesting to know which eye is dominant for each player. The standard test for this is to line up two objects in your line of sight with both eyes open. Then close each eye separately. When you close your **dominant** eye, the near object will appear to jump sideways in relation to the far object.

I test a simpler way. I just hand each kid a cardboard towel core (the tube that is left when you use up a roll of paper towels) and ask him to look through it at something. He will unconsciously put it up to his dominant eye. The test only takes a second.

The ramifications of eye dominance for hitting are explained in the batting chapter.

I make note of the player's eye dominance then tell his parents if it indicates that he might do better from the other side of the plate.

Optimum bat weight

Parents typically buy their kid a bat for each season. I try to steer them the right direction by telling the correct weight. I discussed bat weight in detail in the batting chapter.

At the parent-meeting stage I am only trying to minimize the incidence of eleven-year olds who show up with 24-ounce bats which are like fence posts in their hands. The parent meeting is a good time to rub the bat weights and level or gender designations off the bats of the kids on the team. I do not specify bat weights for teenagers because they do not listen to coaches on such matters. If I were coaching a high school team, I would probably insist that players not use a too-heavy bat.

Buying a bat that is too heavy is the most common parent mistake. With twelve-and-under players I choose their bat weight in practice and games. In most cases, that means I have to tell a kid who has a brand new bat that he has to save that bat for a future year when he is bigger. The kids, and sometimes their fathers, protest, but I insist.

Batting gloves

Batting gloves are not necessary to play baseball, but they look cool to many and they do enable players to engage in prolonged batting practice if they wish. I do not do team batting practice at all, but some players want to go to batting cages outside of practice on their own.

Batting gloves are more useful for **baserunning**. The player should take them off and hold one in each hand. That discourages them from putting a hand down when they slide, which is a cardinal sin and causes injured hands. When they reach base, Major Leaguers usually take off their batting gloves and carry one in each hand for the reason I just stated. So here is one rare instance where imitating the Major Leaguers is actually the **safe** thing to do.

Batting mechanics

I do not teach much batting mechanics. I discussed that in the batting chapter. At my parent meeting, I urge the fathers **not** to coach their kid as to batting mechanics. I am not sure how successful I am because coaching batting mechanics seems to be a core activity of fatherhood.

Correct batting mechanics requires an effort similar to getting a black belt in karate. Hardly any kids have that kind of dedication. Heck, hardly any **fathers** have that kind of dedication as far as working with their kid is concerned.

Consequently, teaching batting mechanics is opening a Pandora's Box of problems—problems that you do not have time to fix. If you teach batting mechanics, all you will accomplish is to make the child self-conscious, less confident (because you told him his swing is "wrong"), and trying to think about mechanics in the batter's box, which interferes with hitting.

I tell parents I will be glad to teach batting mechanics **when the season ends**. I urge them to send their children to Christmas vacation hitting camps where all they do is batting mechanics for a week. But I tell them if you mess with your child's mechanics **during** the season or pre-season, your child will hit less well than if you had left them alone.

The basic idea is to get the bat on the ball and most kids can do that in spite of all the things they are doing "wrong." Leave them alone.

Left-handed hitting is better

All baseball players should bat left-handed. If you have a beginner, start him out in the left-handed side. If the kid already bats right-handed, ask whether he hopse to play in high school or higher levels. If so, he should switch to left-handed batting. If not, he'd be best off staying with what he knows.

Switch hitting

Waste of time at all levels. See the batting chapter.

Batting order

Some parents, especially fathers, are sensitive to what place their child bats in the batting order. So I discuss how to create my batting order at the parent meeting.

I believe all youth baseball leagues should have **full-team** batting orders. That is, if there are thirteen kids on the team, you have to get thirteen batters to the plate to "bat around." Another way to put it is that there may be some players on the bench when the team is in the **field**, but **no one** is on the bench when the team is **at bat**.

That was the rule in the Orinda Mustang League in which I coached in 1997. I explained my approach to batting order in the batting chapter. Whatever approach you use, you should explain it to the parents at the meeting.

Position assignments

Early in my coaching career, I let every player play every position. It seemed like the nice-guy, touchy-feely thing to do. I have since concluded that it is an idiotic way to run a baseball team.

The practice of having every player rotate through all the positions shows disrespect for the game. It implies that baseball positions are easy to master. The opposite is true. Baseball positions are very difficult to learn.

Do youth-baseball players rotate through all the roles in their **school play**? Nope. Somebody gets the lead and somebody gets "Boy #2."

Do youth-baseball players rotate through all the instruments in the **school band**? Nope. Somebody gets the drums and somebody gets the tuba.

How come elementary school drama and music teachers have the guts to assign positions, but many middle-aged, male, youth-baseball coaches do not?

Teamwork

Furthermore, although baseball is not the most team-oriented of team sports, it is still a team sport and the teamwork generally relates to players who play in adjacent positions. The pitcher and catcher need to learn to work together. So do the pitcher and first baseman. The right fielder and center fielder need to learn to work together. And so forth.

So not only does a player need to learn his position, he needs to learn to work with his neighbor.

The more positions, the more failure

There is a tremendous amount of failure in youth baseball. Much of that failure comes from catching and throwing errors. By moving a kid around to each position, you **increase** the amount of failure he will have to endure.

Also, you **increase the frustration level for his teammates**. For example, suppose your rotation has put a weak fielder at first base. The batter hits a grounder to the shortstop who makes a great diving catch, then throws from one knee perfectly to the first baseman, who drops the ball.

This is not fun. It's not fun for the shortstop. It's not fun for the members of the team who were not involved in the play. And it sure as heck is not fun for the first baseman who feels terrible for lousing up the play.

Specializing maximizes success

By specializing the players by position, you maximize each child's success. You also maximize the number of successful cooperations between two, or sometimes three players.

There is only one purpose for rotating defensive positions. It enables a cowardly manager to avoid facing the father of the right fielder.

Managers who do this claim it's so each player can experience each position. Bull. It's so no set of parents is embarrassed about their son having to play right field.

Indeed, I have never seen a rotating coach actually stick to that policy 100%. They quickly learn that rotating a non-pitcher through the pitcher's mound is a great way to walk in a dozen runs. They also learn that rotating every player through the catcher position is a great way to have a passed-ball fest. Also, most players do not **want** to play catcher.

So the players who ought to be in the outfield are really only rotated through second base and third base in the typical case.

Cut the crap. Assign everyone to a position and leave him there so he can master it and learn to work with his position neighbors. That way, with each passing game, each of your players will become more comfortable at his position, he will work better with his neighbors, and his performance will get better and better as the season progresses. Also, he will have increasing confidence in his teammates as he sees them getting better and better at their positions.

Their career is almost over

The notion that you have to let everyone try every position, year after year, so they can find out what's best for them at the higher levels is bogus. For one thing, as

I explained earlier, there will **be** no higher level for the vast majority of your players. They will stop playing at age 12.

The top players will play in the correct positions generally. It is only the weakest, and therefore most likely to drop out of baseball, who will play the less prestigious positions.

I tell the parents at my parent meeting that I will audition all the players for every position and assign them according to my best judgment as to what's best for the team.

'Out of position'

I warn them that occasionally, I will have to play a player "out of position." That means that although the best position for him may be X, he will play Y because the team needs him there more. That could happen because someone else is better at X or because, although no one else is better at X, the second-best X ain't so bad, but the second-best Y is awful and Y is a more important position.

Baseball is a team sport and that means the interest of the individual must be subordinated to the interest of the team when there is a conflict.

'I'll expect to see my son playing infield'

One season, one father, who did not come to the parent meeting, complained about his son playing right field all the time. I explained that was the best place for him. The father ordered me to let him play infield also, ending the phone call with the words, "I'll expect to see my son playing infield at the next game."

I said, "I think you're going to be disappointed. I'll take another look at him in practice, but I doubt I'll change the position assignments. It wasn't that close when I decided to put him in right field previously."

And the kid stayed in right field. His father watched games silently with a sour expression and no one from that family attended the post-season party.

The child in that case, apparently stirred up by his dad, initially seemed unhappy about playing right field. But as the season wore on, he seemed to accept it and grow comfortable there. He knew his job and was getting better at it. At second base, he was uncomfortable and frequently made mental errors like not covering the bag or forgetting to go out to relay a throw.

Play catch with your kid

Another aspect of the position decision is the fault of the player's father. Some fathers play catch regularly with their child. Others play catch rarely or not at all. Guess which kids turn out to be the better fielders? Outfield takes the least time to learn how to play. If the father is going to stick me **entirely** with the job of teaching his kid to catch and throw, I am forced to make the kid an outfielder where I have the best chance of getting him to a satisfactory level.

If I put him in the infield, I also have to teach him to cover bases, put the tag on the ground, cut a ball off, etc. If the father has practiced with him so he can catch and throw decently, I can then put him in the infield and teach him the additional skills needed there. But if the father delivers an "entry-level" player to me, I will be forced to put him at the "entry-level" position: outfield.

I urge the folks at my parent meeting to play catch with their sons and daughters. I assure them that I can tell if their kid never plays catch outside of team practice and, although I will not punish them for not playing catch *per se*, the kid will have fewer options when it comes to assigning positions if he or she is a poor fielder.

Pitcher position

My pitching rotation is based on performance with one caution: I try not to draw conclusions on a particular pitcher until I have lots of data. What I do is try to arrange as many **practice games** as possible and put as many pitchers on the mound as possible. I try to see each pitcher against three or four teams on three or four different days before I draw conclusions. Then I use the numbers to rank the best pitchers.

'The human changeup'

It's actually a bit more complicated than that. Our best pitcher is 1991 was Michael Ramos. Michael did not have much velocity, but he had great control. However he did it, he got batters out better than any of our other pitchers.

Because he was our best pitcher, we started him as the first pitcher in a game. He did not do so well. We discovered that we had to **start** the game with Jason Blatter, who threw smoke, **then** bring in Michael, whom I started calling "the Human Changeup." Opposing batters would adjust their timing to Blatter's speed, then they would face the slower Ramos and their timing would be off.

I adhered to a 50-pitch limit that season, so Blatter would typically pitch two innings, then Ramos would pitch two innings, then a third, relatively fast pitcher would finish. We had to sandwich Ramos between two faster pitchers to get maximum success for him and our team. When we did that, he resumed his position as our most successful pitcher.

I do **not** choose pitchers based on bull-pen performance. I put them games in keep a score book and judge only by results. I give no style points. So, as with the batting order, **I** do not make the pitching rotation, the **players** do by their performance.

Catcher position

The catcher is the most important player on a subteen

team. A strong pitcher can have a bigger effect on a game, but pitchers are only part-time help at the 12 and under level. Catchers are full-time.

As with pitchers, I keep book on the catchers. We have a catcher score I created. It is simply a combination of passed balls, steals, assists. We try to have two or three catchers and stick with the one who has the best score. The killer in youth baseball is passed balls. You also need a catcher who can throw people out at second and third. That takes a strong, accurate arm.

Least competition for the position

Usually, there are not a lot of kids who want to play catcher. I tell parents that catcher is the best position to play if you want the least competition for your kid throughout his playing career. Although at the high-school level, you either are a catcher or you're not. No amount of trying to be one if you're not will work unless your team has no real catcher.

So as with batting order and pitching rotation, my catcher depth chart is determined by the players' performance, not by my opinion.

Left-handed infielders

Generally, baseball coaches will not put left-handed fielders anywhere but pitcher, first base and outfield. I will play left-handed fielders at all nine positions and not give it the slightest thought.

Position clinics

I hold special clinics for each position after practice each night. So another answer I have for the disgruntled right fielder father is, "You know I held a clinic for second-basemen after the April 2 practice. It was mandatory for the assigned second baseman and his backup and optional for everyone else. Your son did not attend. So now I would have to give that clinic all over again just for him. That's not fair to the players who **did** attend, or to me."

Playing time

My policy on playing time is to give everyone equal playing time unless doing so is very likely to reduce the number of games we play. Virtually every season I have coached, the league policy was that **all** teams make the playoffs. In that situation, I treat the whole season like a pre-season. That means I give everyone equal playing time.

The way I do it is I keep track of cumulative total innings played by each player. Missed games count as complete games or six innings played to discourage absenteeism. The four players with the most cumulative playing time share playing time for the next game. That means they'll each get three innings instead of six.

Only on the bench when I was his coach

My oldest son commented when he was twelve that the only times he ever sat the bench in Little League were the seasons when I was his coach. When other men were his coaches and I just helped out, he always started and played every game.

Once the playoffs begin, I switch to the format followed by my opposing coaches every game: I play the best the whole game, two relatively weak players play four innings, and the two weakest players play two innings (the minimum number permitted).

That's because the playoffs are generally single-elimination tournaments so by maximizing our chances of winning, I maximize our chances of getting to play another game. In a single-elimination tournament, **nobody** gets any more playing time if you **lose**.

Single-elimination for us, double- for Al

We got burned by my equal-playing-time policy in 1992. There were five teams in our league. Because of the odd number of teams, it was agreed at our pre-season coaches meeting that the tournament would be a single-elimination for everyone except the first-place team which would have double-elimination.

Equal playing time

I then gave all my players equal playing time during the season and we lost twice to Al Cuthbert's team. He was playing his best players full-time all season. Then, when we met them in the playoffs, we played our first-string the whole game and had our weakest four share playing time. That was the game where we destroyed Cuthbert's team 25-4 in four innings.

League champs?

But who won the league championship? Cuthbert. His team had to be beaten **twice** because they finished in first during the regular season. We beat him once in the playoffs and never got to face them again. We fell to the weakest team in the league the game after we beat Cuthbert's team, and Cuthbert's team beat them in the championship.

However, if I had the 1992 season to do over I still would have given all my players equal playing time during the regular season. Little League is for the kids, not guys like me and Cuthbert. On the other hand, I would not have been so quick to agree to the double-elimination deal for the first-place team if I had it to do over.

If standings determine playoff berths, play it by ear

In a league where standings determine who is in the playoffs, my policy would be to **try** to give equal playing time during the regular season, but I would not risk losing our playoff berth to achieve equal playing time. Whenever we were dropped out of the playoff rankings in the standings, I would go to a first-string-plays-the-most lineup card.

Another thing I like about the all-teams-make-the-playoffs policy is that it enables me to cheer up my assistants and parents when we lose a regular season game. "Hey! What's the problem? We're in the play-offs."

Baseball glove

When I was a kid, I thought there were just three types of gloves: fielder, catcher, and first baseman. Now, it appears there are six kinds: pitcher, catcher, first baseman, middle infielder, third baseman, and outfield.

A **pitcher's** glove has a solid web so the batter cannot see the way the pitcher is gripping the ball before he throws it. **Outfield** and **infield** gloves have a lattice web so the fielder can see through it to catch fly balls. **Middle infielders** have tiny gloves so they can get the ball out fast to turn the double play. Also a middle infielder's glove will retain a bowl shape when you set it down.

In contrast, an outfielder's glove will close up and lie flat like a manila folder. A **third baseman's** glove is kind of a cross between a middle-infielder's glove and a outfielder's glove.

For youth baseball however, I think there are only **four** types of gloves: pitcher, catcher, first base, and everyone else. Middle infielders cannot turn double plays at the subteen level and darned few teens can do it. One of my semi-pro teams turned exactly one two-throw, double-play all season. I then recruited a much better team and we used to turn one or two a game. But that is a very advanced play for youth players. So forget the Major-League-style tiny glove for middle infielders. Better they should have a big glove so they can catch the darned ball easier.

Used glove

All baseball gloves should be purchased at **used** sporting-goods stores. They sell them cheaper. But that's not my reason. They should actually charge **extra** for used gloves because most have already been broken in.

There are few things as worthless as a brand new catcher's mitt. You might as well use a ping-pong paddle to catch with. I suspect the same is true of a new first-baseman's mitt. New **fielder**'s gloves are generally usable. Some even have an already-broken-in texture and pliability. The outfielder's glove that I use is one I bought new. But I bought it at a special store for baseball players only. It was owned and run by a former pro player and his wife and tucked away in an industrial park. It had everything, excellent quality stuff, and knowledgeable help.

The gloves for sale at the garden-variety store look and smell great, but they generally are too stiff.

Breaking in a glove

Everybody says all you have to do to break in a glove is rub neatsfoot oil on it, stick a ball in the pocket and put a rubber band around it. Bull!

I bought a new, $50 catcher's mitt for my son at that special baseball-only store. I put oil on it. I put a ball in the pocket. We opened and closed it thousands of times while watching TV and riding in the car. I pounded it with a pocket maker. We drove over it with the car. We asked everybody what to do, including a number of guys who had been in baseball so long their **faces** looked like well-broken-in gloves. We tried everything we were told. Nothing worked.

We finally sold it to a used-sporting-goods store and bought one at another used sporting goods store. We were absolutely thrilled with the catcher's mitt we got at the used-sporting-goods store. Other catchers used to borrow it. Coaches and players who saw it would comment about what a great-looking catcher's mitt it was. They were referring to its performance potential, not its appearance.

You wanna know how to break in a glove? Ask someone other than me. I don't **know** how to break in a glove. But I **do** know that the correct answer is **not** neatsfoot oil, ball in the pocket, drive over, open and close, etc. I suspect the best answer is to start with a very supple new glove, then use it for an extended period.

For youth-baseball players, you don't have time for all that nonsense. Just buy a used, already-broken-in glove. You're crazy to do otherwise if you need a catcher's mitt. The youth league-supplied catcher's mitts are generally nicely broken in. The same may be true for first-basemen's mitts.

Hyper-stiff gloves

Some gloves are made of plastic. That is survivable if the **pocket** is leather. But I do not believe a totally plastic glove is acceptable. And I suspect few partially plastic ones are acceptable because they probably are a low-quality product in general.

As I mentioned earlier in the book, I have every year noticed that at least one of my players could almost never catch a ball now matter how good his technique was. Then I tried playing catch with his glove and **I** couldn't catch anything with it either.

Some gloves are so poorly designed or constructed that they simply do not function for the intended purpose, which is to catch a moving ball. You should warn your parents that such gloves are common in sporting-goods stores and that they must **not** buy one for their kid. If they have a doubt, tell them to show you the glove before they use it.

You should try to catch with any glove that looks suspect. If you cannot, you should tell the parents their kid needs another glove.

First-baseman's mitt

I have long been amazed at the lack of first-baseman's mitts in youth baseball. The league provides **catcher's** mitts, which are required by rule. Actually, because they are used and about as beat up as the batting helmets, league-provided catcher's mitts are quite broken in and serviceable.

First-baseman's mitts are permitted, but not required, so they are not provided by the league. But they seem to be very helpful so I wonder why leagues that are interested in performing well do not provide them.

Parents are reluctant to buy them because they do not know which position their child will play.

Short hops

The hardest part of the first baseman's job is catching a ball that **short hops** toward them. A short hop means the ball is traveling **upward** when it reaches the fielder. A long hop is typically what an outfielder gets when he catches a base hit on the first or second bounce. A long hop is traveling **level** or **downward** when it reaches the fielder.

Long hops are easy to catch because their trajectory is easy to see. Short hops are hard to catch because their trajectory is unknown. Under perfect conditions, the laws of physics say that the angle of reflection equals the angle of incidence.

That means a ball that comes **in** at a 35-degree angle bounces **back up** at a 35-degree angle. But conditions in a baseball game are not perfect. The angle of reflection (after the bounce) may be different from the angle of incidence (before the bounce) because the surface was uneven or soft or damp or the ball had a strong spin on it. Furthermore, the fielder at whom the ball is going does not have a good vantage point from which to **see** the angle of incidence even if the conditions were perfect.

The bigger the better

All of which makes it good to have a **large** glove that will catch the ball no matter what angle it leaves the ground at. The first baseman's mitt is the largest glove allowed plus its design is like a large funnel. So youth first basemen ought to take advantage of the right to use this unusual glove. That means their parents ought to buy them a first-baseman's mitt.

Again, a used-sporting-goods store is the best place to go. I also warn the parents that even if they do buy a first-baseman's mitt for their child I may switch him to another position. In that case, they can sell the mitt back to the used-sporting-goods store and thereby only suffer as small net cost.

Pitch from the stretch only

I have my pitchers pitch from the stretch or set position only. Ostensibly, that makes no sense at the subteen level because the runners cannot take a pre-pitch lead. At the parent meeting, I explain that I do this and why.

If you plan to have your pitchers throw only from the stretch as I do, you need to tell the fathers at the parents meeting because the fathers will otherwise not understand. Please tell the moms to go home and tell the fathers. If the fathers do not hear the explanation, they tend to think you're some kind of idiot when your pitchers throw from the stretch all the time.

Safety tips for pitchers working on their own or with family members

- Do not overuse your arm
- Never throw as hard as you can
- Always warm up before throwing hard
- Do not pitch the day after pitching in a game
- Throw only lightly 30 to 40 pitches the second and third day after pitching in a game
- Never pitch or continue pitching if your arm is sore
- Do not throw breaking balls if you are not yet a teenager
- If you are a teenager, make sure you get good instruction on **how** to throw a breaking ball before you do so
- Do not throw sliders or screwballs
- Do not practice with balls that weigh less than official weight

Sportsmanship

No one on our team—not players, coaches, or parents—may direct any remarks at or publicly refer to any member of the opposing team—player, coach, or parent. Only the manager may speak to the umpire and then only about non-judgment issues. Players may not throw equipment.

The umps will make bad calls. We will not react to bad calls. Bad calls are part of the game. If **you** were the ump, **you** would make bad calls. If you cannot quietly accept the fact that we will be the victim of bad calls, do not come to the games.

In general, everyone will behave in a way that we will be proud of.

Player-parent behavior reflects manager

I have found that the behavior of the players and parents reflects the manager. My players and parents have always been well-behaved. There have only been two occasions when my guys acted up—both in response to incessant taunting from the opposing parents and players.

In a game against Dublin when I had a 13-year old

team and no assistant coach in the dugout, I was coaching third base. The Dublin parents and players spewed out a steady barrage of taunts and harassment. I quietly asked the ump, who was from Dublin, to do something about it. He declined.

My unsupervised players in the dugout began to respond in kind. I told them gently twice to knock it off. When they continued, I yelled in a loud, angry voice, "Hey Blue Jays! Shut Up!"

That accomplished my mission. When the half inning was over, I called the team around me and apologized for my language, but I added that I had told them at the first practice that we were not going to act that way and that the fact that the Dublin parents and players were acting like jerks did not change my policy about that kind of behavior. I had no more trouble from my players that season. The Dublin parents and players continued to act like jerks.

Parent problem

On another occasion, I had an assistant in the dugout so my players were no problem. But the opposing parents, Blackhawk people, were waging their usual incessant psychological warfare against the kids on my team. I was coaching first and our parents were in stands behind me. One of our mothers couldn't take it any more and made a responding comment to the Blackhawk parents.

She was moderate in her wording and tone, but I immediately turned around and made a calm-down motion with my hand indicating that we were not going to respond to the opposing parents in any way. The parent in question said no more and my other parents behaved.

Handshake-line fights

In some teenage games, I have sensed great hostility. At the end of those games, I have all the parents join my players in the hand shake line. We intersperse them player-parent-player-parent to prevent fights. There has never been a fight at one of my games—where I was **present**.

Ejected

In 1994, I was ejected from a 13-year old game. That is the only time in 27 seasons that I have been ejected. The assigned base umpire did not show up so a parent from the opposing team became the base umpire.

Early in the game, my pitcher faked a pickoff throw from the rubber and was called by the opposing father for a balk, which was correct. I said nothing except to explain to the pitcher what he did wrong. (He had been trained about that but...)

Later in the game, when we were down by one run and had a runner at third, the opposing pitcher came set with his hands together, then adjusted his cap. I said,

"That's a balk."

No reaction from either ump. Two pitches later, he did it again. I said. "That's a balk. How come you call balks against my guys, but not against theirs?"

The teenage home plate umpire instantly ejected me. There had been no previous disputes or warning during the game. The call, or non-call, that I protested was not a judgment call so it was proper for me to question it. Furthermore, I was right about the balk.

Fight

I went to the snack bar, which was out of sight of my game, and watched another game. When my game ended and my players approached, I asked if we won, they said, "Yes," but they all had funny grins.

"What?" "There was a big fight." In the post-game handshake line, a brawl had started. They tell me one of the moms from my team slammed one of the instigators from the opposing team up against the back stop and cursed at him like a sailor. See what happens when I am **not** around.

Actually, we cannot be sure that it would not have happened had I not been ejected. But, as I said, I have never had a fight in 27 seasons, including semi-pro baseball and football. I suspect that if I had stayed at the fight game, I would have sensed extremely high tension and eliminated the handshake line altogether.

I probably would have been criticized for that, but handshake lines have been eliminated after games in some states because of fights. The only fight death ever in Little League occurred at a teenage game in Castro Valley, California, one of the places where I have played. It was a handshake line brawl. The dead spectator was hit in the head by a bat.

At the teenage level, you must take extraordinary measures to prevent fights. The post-game handshake is a sportsmanlike tradition. But it is also often a fight starter. Preventing fights is more important than upholding tradition.

Sliding cardboard

To practice sliding, I need several large sheets of heavy cardboard. During the typical season, most teams have several parents who have buy appliances or computer that come in large cardboard boxes. I ask that if they have any such box, they give it to me so I can use it for sliding practice.

Quiet during games, please

I ask my parents to try to be quiet during games except to applaud good play after the play is over. Parents, especially fathers, are powerfully tempted to yell out instructions as to where to throw the ball and how to swing.

In recent years, I try to sit in the stands with the parents during games to help me keep my own mouth shut and to try to get the parents to do so as well.

I had one father in 1997 who was a problem. He did not come to the parent meeting, so he did not hear my spiel on that subject. At the games, he was constantly coaching his son. I quietly explained to him that I had asked parents not to do that at the parent meeting and that I would appreciate it if he would refrain from doing that because I thought it probably hurt more than it helped and because it adversely affected players other than his son.

He complied somewhat, but mostly he looked at me like I was some kind of nut. Like most fathers, his feeling was, "Hey, my kid is screwing up out there. I have to tell him what he's doing wrong so he can correct it."

Screwing up is part of baseball. Correcting it during the game is distracting and embarrassing to the players. Almost all of the corrections involve mechanics, which can only be corrected in a long-term, off-season program.

Players must act on their own initiative. If fathers yell instructions, the players start to wait for instructions instead of doing what needs to be done during a play. There rarely is enough time for that. Plus the fathers had their chance to play in past years. Now it's the kid's chance and playing includes making decisions on what to do.

Coach's background

My approach to coaching youth baseball is unusual in many ways. But I also have an extensive background in coaching, which causes many parents to give me the benefit of the doubt.

If you have an unusual approach, which I hope you will after reading this book, and your background is strong, I recommend that you tell your parents about your background. That might include:

- playing experience
- coaching experience
- clinics attended
- books and articles written (in my case)

Roster corrections

I create a Web site for each team I coach. One page at that site is the team roster. It has the names and jersey numbers of the players, their parents' names, addresses, home and work phone numbers, fax numbers, pager numbers, and email addresses. For the parent meeting, I convert the Web site roster page into an overhead-projector slide and ask if there are any roster corrections or additions. There always are mistakes and the registration forms are always missing some information.

Stats page of Web site

I put team stats on the Web page and update them after every game. I also put any tryout stats like running speed on the team Web site stats page.

Stats, as I said above, determine much of how I run my team, namely batting order, pitching rotation, and catcher depth chart.

I also audition all players for the various other defensive positions and keep the stats of that audition on the team Web site. So at any time, any disgruntled parent can check the stats and see why their kid is not starting or pitching or playing shortstop or whatever.

Objective and fair

I find that because of the stats, my parents complain far less than other coaches tell me their parents complain. I am not surprised. If you run your team in a subjective, secretive manner, players and parents will suspect you of making decisions on an improper basis like nepotism or favoritism or racism. I am not afraid to face such accusations, but I find that I make most decisions using stats so why not share those stats with the players and parents.

Some people think it's embarrassing to publish stats because inevitably some people don't do so well. Welcome to baseball. Welcome to life.

It all happened in public

For one thing, everything the stats reflect was taken from a public performance called a game. So we are not releasing videotape of a kid in his family room at home. We are just preserving a record of what they did outdoors in front of 15 to 40 witnesses.

'Unlisted' Web site

Secondly, my team Web site is "unlisted." I give the members of the team the Web address, but no one else. I do not register it with any search engines and it is not linked to any registered page.

'Know thyself'

Third, sports teaches great lesson for life. One of the most important life lesson is that we each have strengths and weaknesses. In any group endeavor, we each need to play a role, hopefully one that fits our mix of strengths and weaknesses. Kids should learn from being on my team, and I emphasize this at the post-season party, that no one is good or bad at everything, but that some of us are better at some things than others.

A season on one of my teams should teach you that baseball is not your sport, if indeed it is not. If it **is** your sport, a season on one of my teams should help you figure out what position you should play on defense and how you can best contribute on offense.

Imposters hate stats

Stats will mollify most parents and players, but they will enrage a few others. Those are the ones who have been "BS"ing their way through the sport in the past. They do not like being found out.

When I coached high school volleyball, I had a kid who thought he was God's gift, or at least thought he could trick the rest of us into thinking that. I did my stats. He had some big holes in his game.

Accordingly, I substituted for him when he was in the spot in the rotation where he was weak. He went nuts. I ended up having to throw him off the team.

Conclusion

I end my parent meeting with a reminder about the first practice and a request for their cooperation in helping me make each player's experience as safe and rewarding as possible.

Bibliography

I have read a lot more baseball books than these. Only the useful ones are listed below.

Art and Science of Aggressive Baserunning by Cliff Petrak.

Art and Science of Hitting by Rod Carew. Viking Penguin, Inc. 1986

The Art of Hitting .300 by Charley Lau. E.P. Dutton. 1980

The Art of Pitching by Tom Seaver. Hearst Books. 1984

The Baseball Encyclopedia. Simon & Schuster. 1997.

Baseball for Brain Surgeons and Other Fans by Tim McCarver. Villard Books. 1998.

Baseball for Dummies by Joe Morgan. IDG Books. 1998

Baseball: Pitching by the rules (video), National Federation of State High School Associations.

Baseball Playbook by Ron Polk. (no publisher, copyright notice, or date is printed in the book)

Baseball Players Guide to Sports Medicine by Pat Croce. Leisure Press. 1987.

Baseball, Play the Winning Way by Jerry Kindall. Winners Circle Books. 1988.

Baseball Scoreboard. Stats, Inc. 1998.

Baseball's Knotty Problems. The Sporting News. 1990.

Batting Basics by John W. White and Charles T. Prevo. Quali-Type, Inc., 1986.

Billy Ball by Billy Martin. Doubleday & Co., 1987.

Bunts by George Will. Scribner. 1998.

Coaching Baseball Skills & Drills by Bragg A. Stockton, Human Kinetics. 1984.

Complete Baseball Handbook by Walter Alston. Championship Books. 1984.

The Complete Baseball Player by Dave Winfield. Avon Books. 1990.

The Complete Guide to Outfield Play by Cliff Petrak. Harding Press. 1998.

Complete Idiot's Guide to Baseball by Johnny Bench. Alpha Books, 1999.

Defensive Baseball by Rod Delmonico, Masters Press, 1996.

The Diamond Appraised by Craig R. Wright and Tom House. Simon & Schuster. 1989.

The First Pitching Book by IBI. Individual Baseball Instruction. 1985.

The Game According to Syd by Syd Thrift. Simon & Schuster. 1990.

Steve Garvey's Hitting System by Steve Garvey. Contemporary Books, Inc. 1986.

Tony Gwynn's Total Baseball Player. St. Martin's Press. 1992.

The Hidden Game of Baseball by Thorn and Palmer. Doubleday. 1985.

High Percentage Baserunning by Howard Southworth. Leisure Press. 1989.

Hit and Run Baseball by Rod Delmonico. Leisure Press. 1992.

Hitting by Bob Cluck. Contemporary Books, Inc., 1987

Hitting by Jay Feldman. Little Simon. 1991.

A Hitting Clinic the Walt Hriniak Way. Harper Perennial. 1988.

The Inner Game of Tennis by W. Timothy Gallwey. Bantam Books. 1974.

Bill James Historical Abstract. Villard Books. 1988.

Keep Your Eye on the Ball by Watts and Bahill. W.H. Freeman and Company. 1990.

Leadership Training for Little League Managers and Coaches by Ted Kerley. Little League Baseball, Inc.

Little League Drills and Strategies by Ned McIntosh. Contemporary Books. 1987.

Little League's Official How-to-Play Baseball Book by Kreutzer and Kerley. Doubleday. 1990.

Little Team that Could by Jeff Burroughs. Bonus Books, Inc. 1994.

The Major League Way to Play Baseball by Bob Carroll. Little Simon. 1991.

Managing Little League Baseball by Ned McIntosh. Contemporary Books, Inc. 1985.

Maximizing Baseball Practice by John Winkin, Human Kinetics, 1995.

Men at Work by George Will. Macmillan. 1990.

The Mental Game of Baseball by H.A. Dorfman and Karl Kuehl. Diamond Communications, Inc. 1989.

Nine Sides of the Diamond by David Falkner. Random House, Inc. 1990.

Off Base Confessions of a Thief by Rickey Henderson.Harper Collins. 1992.

Peak Condition by James G. Garrick, M.D. and Peter Radetsky. Harper Perennial. 1986.

Parent's Guide to Coaching Baseball by John P. McCarthy, Jr., Betterway Publications. 1989.

Pete Rose on Hitting, by Pete Rose, Putnam Publishing, 1985.

The Physics of Baseball by Robert K. Adair. Harper Perennial. 1994.

Pitching by Dan Schlossberg. Simon & Schuster. 1991.

The Pitching Book. Individual Baseball Instruction. 1985.

Pitching From the Ground Up by Bob Bennett. Coaches Choice. 1997.

Playing the Field by Jim Kaplan. Algonquin Books. 1987.

Play it Safe. Little League Baseball, Inc. 1989.

The Right Call: Knotty Problems in Little League Baseball. Little League Baseball, Inc., 1988.

Nolan Ryan's Pitcher's Bible. Simon & Schuster. 1991. This book has a neat little device. At the upper right corner of each page is a sequence of Ryan throwing from a full windup. By flipping the pages, it becomes a "motion picture" of an excellent pitching motion.

The Science of Hitting by Ted Williams. Simon & Schuster. 1986.

Sports Illustarted Pitching by Pat Jordan. Winner's Circle Books. 1988.

Stump the Ump by Richard Kent. Funsport Publication, Inc. 1988.

The Swing's the Thing by Ben Hines. McBee Sports enterprises, Inc. 1985.

The Techniques of Modern Hitting by Wade Boggs. Putnam Publishing Group. 1990.

Throwing Heat by Nolan Ryan. Doubleday.1988.

Total Baseball by John Thorn, Pete Palmer, Michael Gershman, and David Pietrusza. Total Sports. 1999.

The Winning Hitter by Charley Lau. Hearst Books. 1984.

You can teach hitting by Dusty Baker, Jeff Mercer, and Marv Bittinger. Bittinger Books, Inc. 1993.

You Gotta Have Wa by Robert Whiting. Vintage Books. 1989.

Youth League Baseball by Skip Bertman. Athletic institute. 1989.

Youth League Hitting Like a Champ by Tony Oliva. The Athletic Institute. 1989.

Youth Sports Injuries by John F. Duff, M.D. Macmillan Books. 1992.

Catalogs

Baseball Express, 12018 Warfield, San Antonio, TX 78216, 800-WE-PITCH, www.baseball.xp.com, fax 800-460-9986

Championship Books & Video Productions, Inc., 2730 Graham Street , Ames, IA 50010, 515-232-3687, 800-873-2730, 515-232-3739 (fax), www.ChampOnline.com

Coaches Choice, 11971 Saddle Road, Monterey, CA 93940, 800-327-5557

Cybertown.net, 1072, Casitas Pass Road, #121, Carpinteria, CA 93013, 800-585-8567, www.cbyertown.net

The Scholar's Bookshelf, 110 Melrich road, Cranbury, NJ 08512, 609-395-0755, www.scholarbookshelf.com/baseball

Sysko's Sports Books, 30 West Main Street, P.O. Box 6, Benton, WI 53803, 800-932-2534, fax 800-932-2511, www.syskos.com

Manufacturers

Face Guards, Inc. P.O. Box 901, 21 West Main Street, Salem, Va. 24153, 800-336-9683 FAX 540-389-4013, fguard@bellatlantic.net

Hillerich & Bradsby Co., Louisville Slugger, P.O. Box 35700, Louisville, KY 40232, 502-585-5226, fax 502-585-1179, www.slugger.com

Schutt Sports, 1200 E. Union, Litchfield, IL 62056, 800-426-9784, http://www.schuttsports.com/baseball.html

Worth, Inc., www.worthsports.com, 2100 North Jackson St., P.O. Box 88104, Tullahoma, Tennessee 37388-8104, (931) 455-0691, FAX:

(931) 454-9164

Organizations

Academy for Sports Dentistry, www.acadsportsdent.org, 875 N. Michigan Ave., Suite 4040, Chicago, Illinois 60611-1901, 800-273-1788 inside of U.S.A.

American Academy of Opthalmology, www.aao.org, P.O. Box 7424, San Francisco, CA 94120-7424, (415) 561-8500

American Academy of Pediatrics, www.aap.org,141 Northwest Point Boulevard, Elk Grove Village, IL 60007-1098, 847-228-5005, 847-228-5097 (Fax)

American Academy of Pediatric Dentistry, www.aapd.org, 211 East Chicago Avenue, #700, Chicago, IL 60611-2663, 312-337-2169, FAX 312-337-6329

American Baseball Coaches Association, 108 South University Avenue, Suite 3, Mt. Pleasant, MI 48858, www.abca.org

American Dental Association, www.ada.org, 211 E. Chicago Ave., Chicago, IL 60611, 312-440-2500, Fax: 312-440-2800

American Legion Baseball, www.legion.org/baseball/home.htm, 700 North Pennsylvania Street, P.O. Box 1055, Indianapolis, IN 46206, 317-630-1200, Fax: 317-630-1223

American Society for Testing and Materials, www.astm.org, 100 Barr Harbor Drive, West Conshohocken, Pennsylvania, USA 19428-2959, 610-832-9585, Fax: 610-832-9555

Babe Ruth Baseball, www.baberuthbaseball.org,1770 Brunswick Pike, P.O. Box 5000, Trenton, NJ 08638, 609-695-1434 Fax: 609-695-2505

Consumer Product Safety Commission, www.cpsc.gov, Western Regional Center, 600 Harrison Street, Room 245, San Francisco, CA 94107-1370, 415-744-2966

Dixie Youth Baseball, www.dixie.org, P.O. Box 877, Marshall, TX 75671, 903-927-2255, FAX: 903-927-1846

Little League Baseball, Inc., www.littleleague.org, P.O. Box 3485, Williamsport, PA 17701

National Federation of State High School Associations, 11724 NW Plaza Circle, P.O. Box 20626, Kansas City, MO 64195, 816-464-5400, fax 816-464-5104

National Institutes of Health, www.nih.gov, National Institutes of Health (NIH), Bethesda, MD 20892

National Operating Committee on Standards for Athletic Equipment, www.nocsae.org, P.O. Box 12290, Overland, Kansas 66282-2290, 913-888-1340, Fax: 913-888-1065

National Safe Kids Campaign, www.safekids.org, 1301 Pennsylvania Ave, NW, Suite 1000, Washington, DC 20004-1707 202-662-0600, 202-393-2072 Fax

National Safety Council, 1121 Spring Lake Drive, Itasca, IL 60143-3201, 630-285-1121; Fax: 630-285-1315, www.nsc.org

National Youth Sports Safety Foundation, Inc., formerly **National Youth Sports Foundation for the Prevention of Athletic Injuries**, 333 Longwood Avenue, Suite 202, Boston, MA 02115, 617-277-1171, Fax: 617-277-2278, www.nyssf.org

National Spit Tobacco Education Program, Oral Health America, 410 N. Michigan Avenue, Suite 352, Chicago, IL 60611, 312-836-9900

Pony Baseball, www.pony.org, P.O. Box 225, Washington, Pennsylvania 15301, 724-225-1060, Fax: 724-225-9852

Prevent Blindness America, www.preventblindness.org, 500 East Remington Road, Schaumburg, IL 60173, 800-331-2020

Protective Eyewear Council, unknown

Society for American Baseball Research, 812 Huron Road, Suite 719, Cleveland, OH 44115, (216) 575-0500, Fax: (216) 575-0502, www.SABR.org

Periodicals

Baseball Parent, 4437 Kingston Pike, Knoxville, TN 37919, 800-714-5768, http://members.aol.com/baseparent

Coaching Digest, American Baseball Coaches Association

Collegiate Baseball Newspaper, PO Box 50566,

Tucson, AZ 85703 (520) 623-4530, FAX: (520) 624-5501, www.collegiatebaseball.com

Publishers

Algonquin Books, P.O. Box 2225, Chapel Hill, NC 27515

Athletic Institute, 200 Castlewood Drive, North Palm Beach, FL 33408

Avon Books, 105 Madison Avenue, New York, NY 10016

Bantam Books, 201 East 50th Street, New York, NY 10022

Betterway Publications, P.O. Box 219, Crozet, VA 22932, 804-823-5661

Bittinger Books, Inc., 3011 Whispering Trail, Carmel, IN 46033

Bonus Books, Inc., 160 East Illinois Street, Chicago, IL 60611

Championship Books, 2460 Kerper Boulevard, Dubuque, IA 52001

Contemporary Books, Inc., 180 North Michigan Avenue, Chicago, IL 60601

Diamond Communications, Inc., P.O. Box 88, South Bend, In 46624, 219-287-5008

Doubleday, 666 Fifth Avenue, New York, NY 10103

E.P. Dutton, 2 Park Avenue, New York New York 10016

W.H. Freeman and Company, 41 Madison Avenue, New York, NY 10010

Funsport Publication, Inc., 2032 Weston Road, Box 114, Weston, Ontario, Canada M9N 1X4

Harding Press, P.O. Box 141, Haworth, NJ 07641, (toll-free) 877-767-7114, hardingpress@earthlink.net

Harper Perennial, 10 East 53rd Street, New York, NY 10022

Hearst Books, 105 Madison Avenue, New York, NY 10016

Human Kinetics, P.O. Box 5076, Champaign, IL 61825, 800-747-4457

Individual Baseball Instruction, 1527 San Carlos, Orange, CA 92665

Leisure Press, P.O. Box 5076, Champaign, IL 61820, 800-342-5457

Little Simon, Simon & Schuster Building, Rockefeller Center, 1230 Avenue of the Americas, New York, NY 10020

Macmillan Publishing Company, 866 Third Avenue, New York, NY 10022

Masters Press, 2647 Waterfront Parkway, East Drive, Suite 300, Indianapolis, IN 46214

McBee Enterprises, Inc., P.O. Box 834, Burlington, NC 27215

Ron Polk, P.O. Drawer 5327, Missippi State University, Missippi 39762

Putnam Publishing, 200 Madison Avenue, New York , NY 10016

Quali-Type, Inc., 4047 First Street, Suite 201, Livermore, CA 94550

Random House, Inc., New York, NY 10022

Scribner, 1230 Avenue of the Americas, New York, NY

Simon & Schuster, Rockefeller Center, 1230 Avenue of the Americas, New York, NY 10020

The Sporting News, 1212 North Lindbergh Boulevard, St. Louis, MO 63166

Sports Illustrated's Winner's Circle Books, Rockefeller Center, 1271 Avenue of the Americas, New York, NY 10020

Stats Publishing, 8131 Monticello Avenue, Skokie, IL 60076, 800-63-STATS, fax 847-676-0821, www.stats.com

Total Sports, 445 Park Avenue, New York, NY 10022

Viking Penguin, Inc., 40 West 23rd Street, New York, NY 10010

Villard Books, www.randomhouse.com

Vintage Books, New York

Winners Circle Books, Time and Life Building, New York NY 10020

Index

Order form

_____ Coaching Youth Flag Football $ 21.95 $_____

_____ Coaching Youth Football,—2nd edition $ 21.95 $_____

_____ Coaching Youth Football Defense, —2nd edition $ 19.95 $_____

_____ Football Clock Management $ 19.95 $_____

_____ Youth Baseball Coaching $ 23.95 $_____

                      Subtotal $_____

Discount 5% for order totaling over $100 $_____

California residents: add your area's **sales tax** $_____

Shipping: $4.00 for first item $___4.00

$2.00 for **EACH** additional item $_____

                      Total $_____

For more information, visit my Web site at
www.johntreed.com/coaching.html

Method of Payment: _____ Check enclosed payable to John T. Reed

_____ Visa   _____ MasterCard

Card # _____ Exp. Date _____

Signature _____

Ship to: Name _____

Telephone_____

OR PHONE ☎

Street Address _____

925-820-7262

City _____ State _____ Zip _____

Fax _____

Please mail your order to: John T. Reed, 342 Bryan Drive, Alamo, CA 94507

These prices are effective 3/00 and are subject to change.

You can also **fax** your order to 925-820-1259 or **E-mail** it to johnreed@johntreed.com or use the order form at the Web site

Your Opinion of this Book is Important to Me

Please send me your comments on this book. I'm interested in both compliments and constructive criticism. Your compliments provide guidance on what you want. And, with your permission, I'd like to use your favorable comments to sell future editions of the book. Constructive criticism also helps make the book's next edition better.

Evaluation of *Youth Baseball Coaching*

Circle one: Excellent   Good   Satisfactory   Unsatisfactory

Circle one: Too Advanced About Right   Too Basic

What part did you like best? _____

_____

What part did you like least? _____

_____

How can I improve the book? _____

_____

My promotional material includes brief comments by people who have read the book and their name, city, state, and occupation. I would appreciate any remarks you could give me for that purpose:

_____

_____

_____

Name _____ Age of players coached _____

Address _____

City _____ State _____ Zip _____

Feel free to leave blanks if you prefer not to answer all of these questions. I would appreciate receiving your evaluation even if you only fill out one line.

If your comments will not fit on this sheet, feel free to write them on additional sheets. Please send your evaluation to:

John T. Reed
342 Bryan Drive
Alamo, CA 94507